GW00763527

The Complete Aquarium Guide

FISH, PLANTS AND ACCESSORIES FOR YOUR AQUARIUM

The Complete Aquarium Guide

FISH, PLANTS AND ACCESSORIES FOR YOUR AQUARIUM

KÖNEMANN

Original title: Le Grand Guide de l'Aquarium

Könemann Verlagsgesellschaft mbH
Bonner Strasse 126, D – 50968 Cologne

Translation from French: Matthew Clarke and Ian West in association with First Edition Translations Ltd.
Editing: Kay Hyman in association with First Edition Translations Ltd.
Typesetting: The Write Idea in association with First Edition Translations Ltd.
Project Management: Beatrice Hunt for First Edition Translations Ltd., Cambridge, England
Project Coordination: Nadja Bremse-Koob
Production: Ursula Schümer

Printed in Italy by STIGE - Turin

ISBN 3-8290-1736-7

10 9 8 7 6 5 4 3 2 1

CONTENTS

INTRODUCTION

There was a time when the keeping and study of exotic fish was the preserve of serious researchers closeted in their laboratories; today, it is an established and popular hobby. Dealerships and specialized sales areas in large stores are springing up everywhere, paralleling an explosion in the number of public aquariums and books or magazines devoted to the subject. More and more people of all ages are falling under the spell, enjoying permanent access to a part of the natural world that was formerly beyond their reach. There are almost as many kinds of hobbyists as there are types of fish: the semiprofessional, the "small" and the "modest" collector, the specialist. There are the fanatics, who spend every minute of their time and energy on their aquariums, while for others fishkeeping is just a passing fad. Enthusiasts include the young – and the not so young; those with scientific knowledge or mere novices; those actively working and the retired. Such an immensely varied following guarantees that the world of the aquarist is full of interest and color.

A WINDOW ONTO ANOTHER WORLD

We have all become familiar with how our television screens offer us, from the comfort of our living rooms, a small window onto the wide world outside. An aquarium also provides a glimpse into a different universe – but this time inhabited by real, live creatures.

A lot of thought and work goes into a top-class aquarium. We select the best site, we want fish and decor which satisfy our sense of beauty. Before long, our new purchase has relegated to the background our photos, pictures and even the TV.

The last ten or so years have seen the aquarium come into its own in institutions and public buildings. In educational establishments it represents an important teaching aid, enabling students to observe creatures in conditions resembling their natural habitats. The medical profession has likewise realized its benefits. The fish gliding through their silent, predominantly green world in a kind of underwater ballet are the perfect sedative for nervous patients; it is by no means unusual to come across tanks in the waiting-rooms of doctors and dentists, in physiotherapy rooms, hospitals, and indeed in psychiatric clinics. More recently, aquariums have been introduced into prisons.

In a dentist's surgery, a tank of Amazonian fish faces the patient's chair. ▼

FISHKEEPING, SCIENCE, AND AQUACULTURE

Keeping fish contributes to the development of scientific research into aquatic environments, and is relevant to the study of animal and plant biology, ecology, reproduction, feeding, and behavior. Researchers use some species to test the toxicity of pollutants or suspected pollutants.

Aquaculture or fish farming – the production of living creatures with the principal aim of selling them as food – has features in common with fishkeeping. In both cases, it is a matter of maintaining fish in captivity and encouraging them to reproduce, always under the best possible conditions. The use of aquariums has allowed us to improve our knowledge of, for

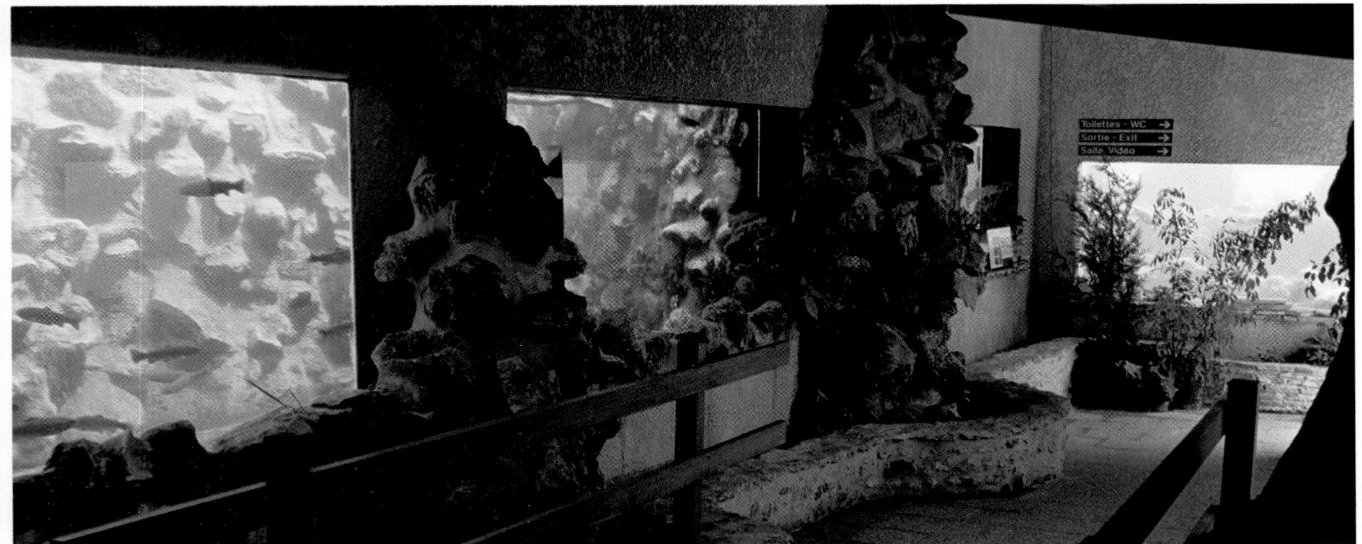

▲ Salmonidae *in Le Bugue Aquarium. Public aquariums have an important role to play, offering unrestricted access to the beauty of this miniature world.*

example, the breeding of marine larvae destined eventually for human consumption. It can also aid the preservation of species threatened with extinction for various reasons; we can study their behavior and reproductive methods with the aim of rearing young which can be released into their natural habitats.

On the other hand, aquarists are regularly accused of being party to the destruction of certain environments.

The fact is that though the vast majority of freshwater fish kept in aquariums are the result of captive breeding, the same is not true of marine fish, which are caught mainly in their natural habitats. The numbers taken are out of all proportion to the needs of aquarists owing to unsatisfactory conditions of capture and transport. For every marine fish which arrives alive in an aquarium, how many have died as they were being caught – often in a highly questionable manner – or during shipment or in the course of acclimatization? In this sense, the accusation is justified. The only solution is to impose stricter controls and improve techniques so that the number of fish caught to supply aquarists remains within a safe limit.

A SYSTEM IN EQUIPOISE

The days of goldfish swimming in endless circles in a glass bowl are long past. Today, an aquarium is something much more sophisticated: we are able to reconstruct Nature in microcosm, which requires the maintenance of a constant equilibrium. Nature, if not disturbed by some cataclysmic imbalance, obeys a finite set of laws. As aquarists, we need to understand these laws and reproduce them on a smaller scale, where the density of animals and plants is considerably higher. Everything that takes place within this mini-universe is under our control – up to a point. The final, inviolable law is that conditions in the aquarium must always approach those found in Nature. If not, the ecosystem will break down, spelling disaster.

THE AQUARIUM: AN ALTERNATIVE APPROACH TO ECOLOGY

A closed system like this lends itself particularly to the understanding of ecology, providing an excellent introduction to a branch of science which emerged in the 19th century but has acquired a high profile only in the last twenty or so years. It is not concerned simply with Man and his world, as many believe, but covers all the mechanisms regulating relationships between living creatures and their environments, so that all can live in harmony.

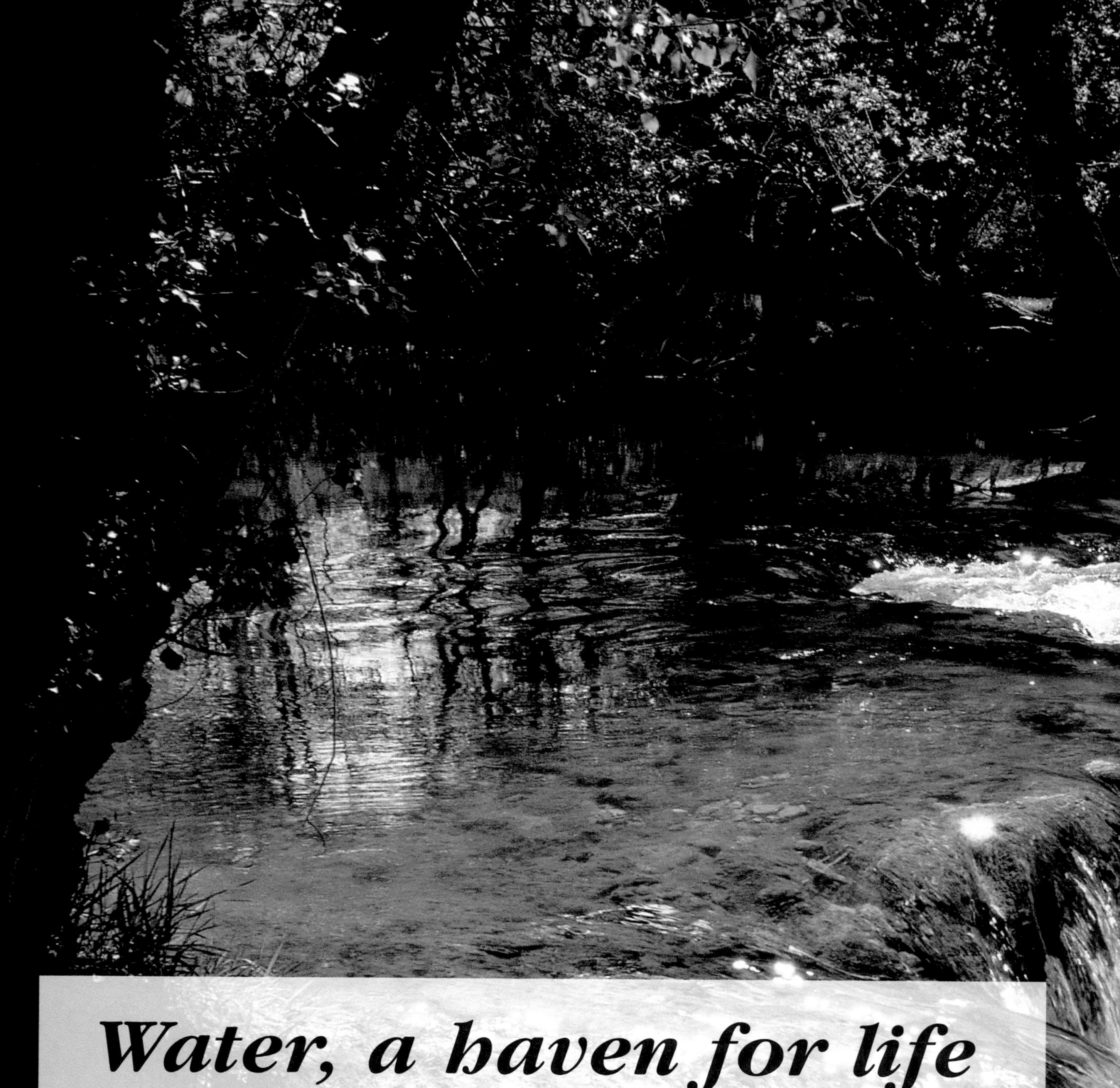

Water, a haven for life

Without water, there would be no life on our planet. Excessively pure water, however, does not enhance the development of living organisms, as it is the elements contained within water that make this possible. Getting fish and plants to live and reproduce in an aquarium therefore requires some basic knowledge of the characteristics of water, which, although a constant presence in our daily existence, is often little understood as an environment that supports living organisms.

FRESH WATER

This type of water is also known as Continental water, a more accurate term from the scientific point of view. Continental water accounts for only 2.6% of the Earth's water, the rest being made up of seas and oceans. Of this volume, 98% consists of sterile water, in the form of glaciers and underground water, leaving only the water of rivers, lakes, and ponds as shelter for living organisms – barely 2% of the total volume of Continental water.

TEMPERATURE

An important parameter for aquatic life, the temperature regulates the growth of animals and plants and exerts an influence not only on oxygen levels but also on many other factors.

Whereas mammals have a regulated and practically stable internal temperature, that of fish and other aquarium creatures varies according to the temperature of the water around them. They can survive only at certain temperatures and some species are more sensitive than others to variations in this parameter.

▲ *The use of a heating kit allows the water in an aquarium to be maintained at an almost constant temperature.*

The temperatures of fresh tropical waters, ranging from 20 to 30°C, are characterized by less significant variations than those found in temperate regions. In some places the shade provided by the tropical forest cools the water, while in calm water the temperature goes up under the direct influence of the sunlight.

The mean temperature most often recommended for aquariums is 25°C, and variations of 1 or 2° are of little consequence. Fish are even capable of withstanding even more significant variations for brief periods (under 24 hours). On the other hand, their metabolism (i.e. their general bodily functioning) is in danger of serious disturbance over any longer periods, and sooner or later they may die. It must also be noted that excessively low temperatures sometimes favor the development of certain diseases.

OXYGEN AND CARBON DIOXIDE

Since air contains around 20% oxygen, even the most oxygenated water rarely contains more than 1% dissolved oxygen. Fish have special organs – branchiae – which allow them to extract most of this (see Anatomy and Biology, page 42).

Oxygen contributes, in addition, to the respiration not only of plants but also of organisms which are invisible to the naked eye and often forgot-

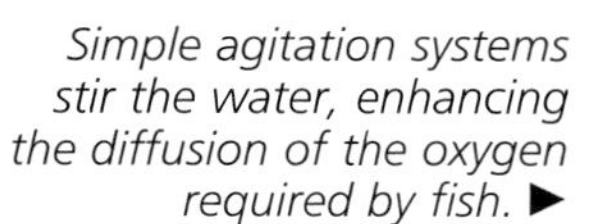

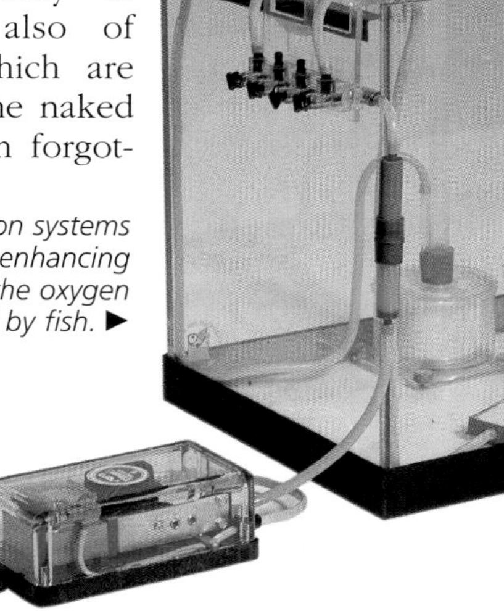

Simple agitation systems stir the water, enhancing the diffusion of the oxygen required by fish. ▶

EXAMPLES OF WATER TEMPERATURES IN AQUATIC SETTINGS (IN°C)				
TEMPERATE ZONES		TROPICAL ZONES		
Mountain rivers	Sea-level rivers	South American, Amazonian rivers	South-East Asia, marshy zones	Africa, the Great Lakes
4–14/15	6–18/20	23–28	26–28	25–27

PRODUCTION AND CONSUMPTION OF OXYGEN

Production
Consumption
Agitation of water
Only by day
Night and day
Bacteria and chemical changes

PRODUCTION AND CONSUMPTION OF CARBON DIOXIDE

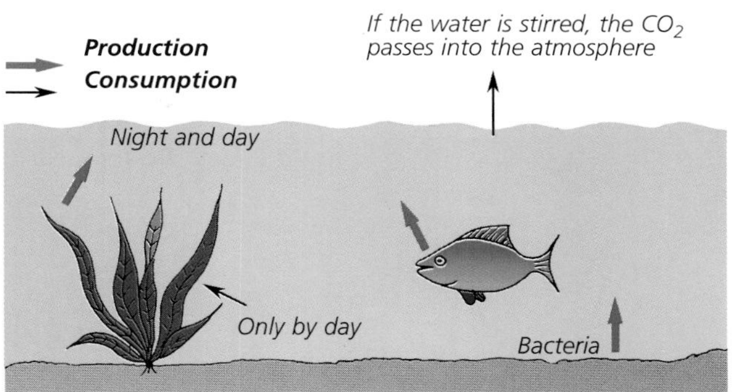

By day and by night, all living beings absorb oxygen and discharge carbon dioxide. By day only, plants produce oxygen, through photosynthesis, having previously absorbed carbon dioxide.

ten: the bacteria. The latter transform the organic matter emitted from living beings (excreta and various other residues), and these chemical reactions similarly require oxygen.

The oxygen in water comes from the dissolution of the oxygen in the air, a process enhanced by movements in the water produced by wind, currents, or downward flow. The more water is stirred, the more it is oxygenated. Plants also provide oxygen, which they produce through photosynthesis, although this process occurs only by day. The maximum amount of oxygen that water can contain is determined by its temperature: the higher this is, the less oxygen the water can contain (at 25°C there is 18% less oxygen than at 15°C).

Oxygen is measured in mg/liter, and its control is quite a complicated matter. The most turbulent, and therefore the most oxygenated, water contains 8–10 mg/liter, while the most deficient water sometimes has less than 2 mg/liter.

The oxygen content in an aquarium is usually at its maximum, providing the recommendations for stirring the water are followed. The rare problems which do occur are the result of negligence as regards the overall balance of the aquarium (overpopulation of fish, small number of plants), or non-functioning of equipment due to forgetfulness, breakdown, or a power cut.

Carbon dioxide derives from the respiration of fish, plants, and bacteria. Stirring the water enhances its oxygenation, thereby reducing the levels of carbon dioxide in the water, and passing it into the atmosphere. Carbon dioxide is quite rare in an aquarium, and this can, to some extent, prove prejudicial to plants, as they absorb it by day through photosynthesis to extract the carbon they need to grow.

It is therefore vital to establish a permanent equilibrium between oxygen, carbon dioxide, plants, and fish, although this balance changes at night, when plants stop producing oxygen.

Carbon dioxide is also one of the main factors affecting the pH.

pH VALUES

The pH measures the acidity or alkalinity of water, with the value 7 representing neutrality. Below this level the water is acid, and above it the water is alkaline (or basic). Categorizing water as acid does not mean that it contains dangerous acids. In forest streams and rivers the water accumulates with acid organic fluid (humic acid) derived from the decomposition of plants (humus), producing an amber yellow color.

Generally speaking, aquatic life can exist only between pH 5 and 9. These extreme values are rarely found in an aquarium, where the pH ranges from 6 to 8 according to the type of water, and usually lies between 6.5 and 7.5. In aquariums, the term acid water corresponds to a pH between 6 and 6.8, while alkaline water

Maximum oxygen content of water as a function of temperature ▼

T °C	O_2 mg/liter
15	10.1
16	9.9
17	9.7
18	9.5
19	9.3
20	9.1
21	8.9
22	8.7
23	8.6
24	8.4
25	8.3
26	8.1
27	7.9
28	7.8

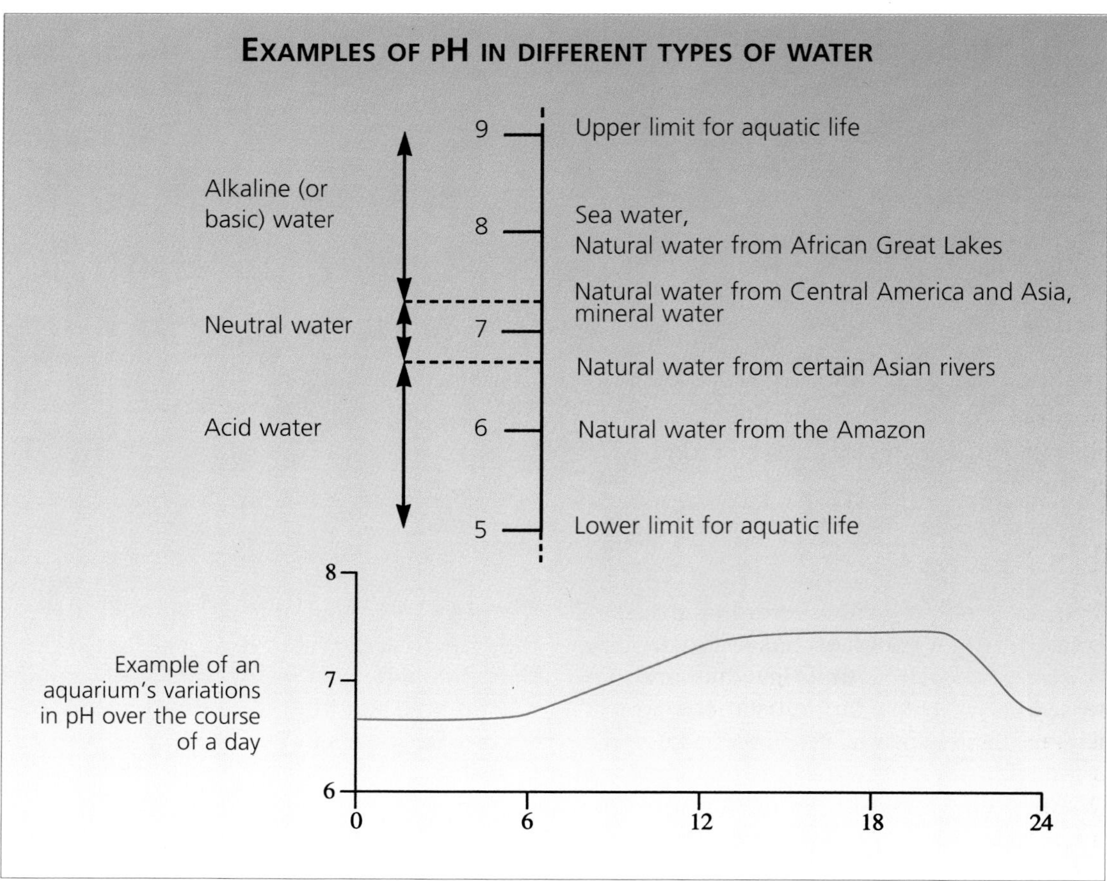

refers to one between 7.2 and 8, and a pH between 6.8 and 7.2 is considered neutral. Variations in pH are mainly the result of biological activity: the carbon dioxide produced by living beings acidifies the water at night and the pH goes down slightly. Once the carbon dioxide has been absorbed by the plants during the day the pH goes up again.

Although slight variations are therefore normal, more extreme changes can be a warning signal. The pH is a good indicator of an aquarium's equilibrium, and it should therefore be measured regularly. A colored marker dipped into a sample of water is used to compare the color obtained with the scale provided. Electronic meters are also now available for testing pH values.

pH is measured by using a color test: water from the aquarium containing a few drops of the test is compared to a color scale that provides a reasonably precise determination of the pH value. ▼

pH 5,0 5,5 6,0 6,5 7,0

pH 7,0 7,5 8,0 8,5 9,0

Adjusting the pH

The pH of domestic water may not always be particularly suited to the fish you have chosen. Furthermore, when an aquarium is in use the pH can rise and fall, slowly but very regularly. There are some aquarium products on the market that enable adjustments to be made to the pH, but there are other ways of modifying it.

• *If the pH is too high*

– the water can be diluted with another more acid water;

– the stirring of the water can be reduced. Carbon dioxide is eliminated less quickly and remains in the water to acidify it. Be careful, because decreasing the stirring also lowers the oxygenation;

– the water from the aquarium can be filtered over peat, which will release certain acids. The amount of peat needed to maintain a specific pH value must be found through trial and error, with regular measurements of the pH.

• *If the pH is too low*

– the water can be diluted with another more alkaline, and generally harder water (see Hardness, below);

– the agitation of the water can be increased, enhancing the elimination of the carbon dioxide dissolved in the water and therefore lifting the pH;

– the water can be filtered over calcareous material, rock, or oyster shells broken into little pieces. In this case, the hardness also increases (see below).

Hardness

The hardness of water refers to the combination of substances based on calcium (Ca) and magnesium (Mg) that are contained in it. The main substances, known as salts, are carbonates, bicarbonates and sulfates.

Water with zero hardness does not contain any of these salts; this is the case with distilled water.

The water in some areas can be particularly hard, mainly due to the presence of limestone (or calcium carbonate).

The hardness of water really depends on the land through which it has passed: the more calcium and magnesium the rocks contain, the harder the water. The effects of this can be seen in domestic use: a washing machine, for example, will require more detergent. Above certain limits of hardness (see the table on page 17), water is unfit for human consumption or any other use. Water with a low degree of hardness, i.e. containing few calcium and magnesium salts, is considered soft. Water with a high degree of hardness is classified as hard.

There are kits on the market that offer even the novice aquarist the panoply of tests required to control the majority of the main parameters for water. ▼

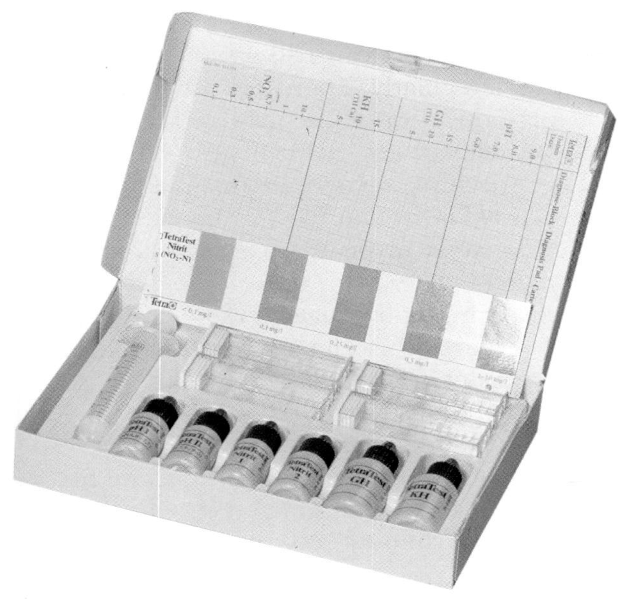

Food chains

In nature

Life in water, as on land, is not possible without light. Vegetation (microscopic plankton or plants) absorbs it with carbon dioxide (CO_2) and uses the mineral salts, which act as nutrients. This vegetation serves as food for herbivorous or omnivorous fish, which in their turn provide nutrition for carnivorous fish. From this point, the next link in the chain can be aquatic (dolphin, shark), terrestrial (man), or aerial (bird). When aquatic organisms die, they fall to the bed. Their bodies are degraded by the action of bacteria, the material is recycled into mineral salts, and so the chain comes full circle. (While they are alive, it is their excreta that are recycled.)

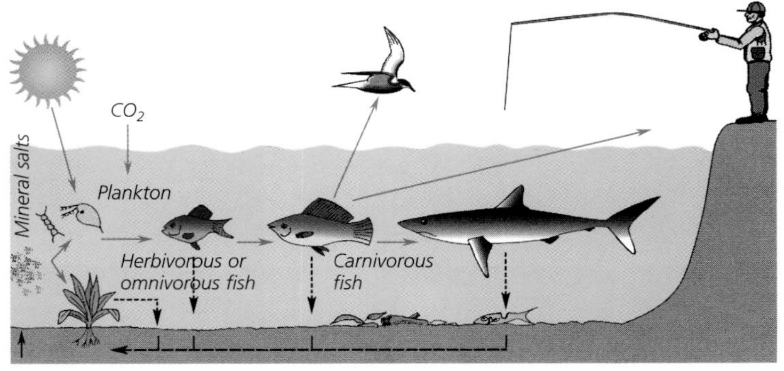

In the aquarium

In an aquarium, the chain is simple: it is obviously out of the question to have carnivorous fish cohabit with their prey! The fish are fed by the aquarist, although in some cases they can feed on the vegetable matter growing in the aquarium.

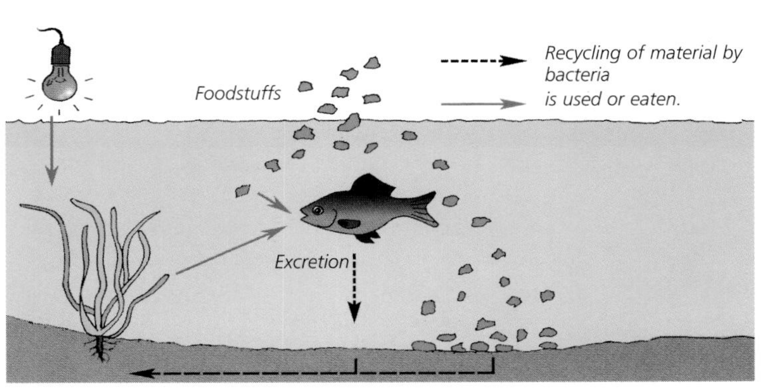

Peat

Peat derives from the decomposition of vegetation in an acid environment lacking in oxygen. This process, which lasts several centuries, gives rise to a peat bog from which compact, fibrous peat can be extracted.
It endows water with both a yellow amber color and acidity, which gives it slightly antiseptic properties. This means that some diseases are less common in acid water. The use of horticultural peat, which often has been enriched with various products, must be avoided in favor of the peat for aquarium use that is commercially available. Boil it for around 15 minutes before use.

Hemigrammus erythrozonus. ▲

In the Amazon region of South America, the color of the water ranges from amber yellow to brown, due to the leaves and branches floating in it. In an aquarium, peat can be used in the filtering equipment to reproduce the characteristics of this type of water (low hardness, pH under 7, coloring).

Pterophyllum scalare. ▼

Calcium (Ca)

Calcium is a very important element in aquatic life. Vegetation contains only a little of it, but animals have a great deal more: calcium plays a role in the composition of the skeletons of fish, the carapaces of crustaceans, and the shells of mollusks (in the latter two cases, in the form of calcium carbonate, $CaCO_3$). Calcium and magnesium are more abundant in hard water.

The hardness of water is expressed in German degrees (°GH or °DH), not to be confused with Celsius degrees (°C) for temperature: 1°GH is equivalent to 17.9 mgCa/liter, or 17.9 parts per million (ppm). The term most often used to classify hardness is general hardness (GH), although total hardness (TH) can also be used.
There are three main categories of water in fishkeeping:
– soft water, which is generally acid, at 3°GH or 50 ppm;
– medium water, which is neutral or slightly alkaline, at 6°GH or 100 ppm;
– hard water, which is highly alkaline, at 12°GH or 200 ppm.
We will go on to discover that some fish families can adapt only to certain types of water.

Measuring GH

A colored indicator is used: the number of drops needed to obtain a change in color indicates the degree of hardness.
It should be noted that the degrees of hardness used in analysis kits may vary according to the country in which it was manufactured; in some cases French degrees are used. These can be converted as follows:

1°Fr = 0.56°GH

• *How can the degree used by a manufacturer in a product be identified?*
To confuse matters further, you may also come across °Clark in older books on fishkeeping. The old-fashioned Clark system for hardness was somewhat laborious, being based on measurement of the foam created by a soap solution, and has now become obsolete. If you have any doubts about the units used by the manufacturer of an analysis kit, just measure a GH you already know, such as that of bottled water (see page 23).

The relationship between GH and CH

We have already seen that significant changes in the pH are prejudicial to aquatic life, especially if they occur too abruptly. To

The hardness of water

Softened water and osmosed water

Domestic softeners produce water in which the calcareous salts are trapped by a special resin but, on the other hand, they are loaded with other substances, such as sodium. Their use is not recommended for aquariums.
Osmosed water, very slightly mineralized, is obtained by using an osmoser connected to a supply of drinking water. A special membrane allows this machine to retain several substances, including calcium-based salts.
The water obtained in this way is of great use to the aquarist. However, it is important to calculate your individual requirements, as an osmoser represents a substantial investment which is not really essential for a hobbyist with only a few aquariums.

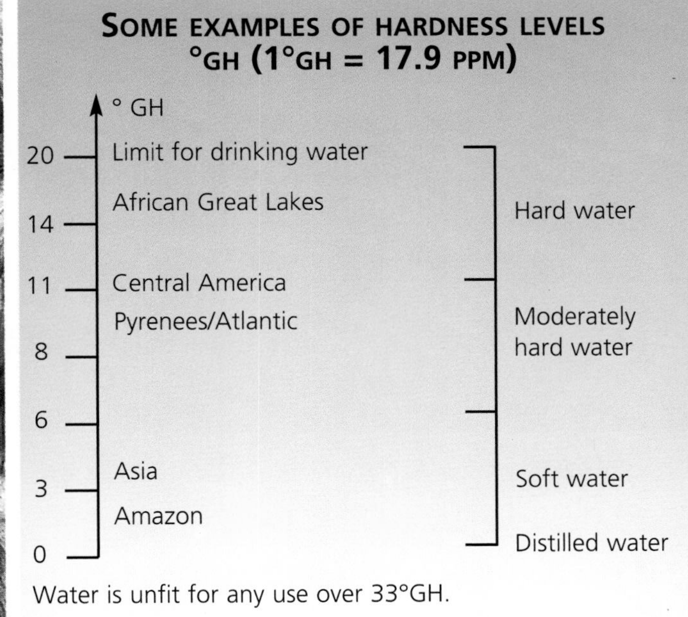

How can hard water be quickly identified?

Hard water produces a great deal of foam with soap, and this is not the case with fresh or distilled water.

Hardness: avoiding confusion

The use of different terms and abbreviations sometimes makes hardness a somewhat confusing concept. The table below presents the expressions most often found in recent aquarium books.

Term	Abbreviation	Degree value	Metric value	Characteristics
General hardness (total hardness)	GH (TH)	°GH (°DH) 1°GH = 17.9 ppm	mg/liter; ppm	Measures all the calcium and magnesium salts
Carbonate hardness	CH	°KH 1°KH = 17.9 ppm	mg/liter; ppm	Measures only the calcium and magnesium carbonates and the bicarbonates.

The general hardness is one of the main parameters to be taken into account when monitoring the water in an aquarium. The carbonate hardness only measures carbonates and bicarbonates, the latter being in the majority in soft water with a pH less than 8.

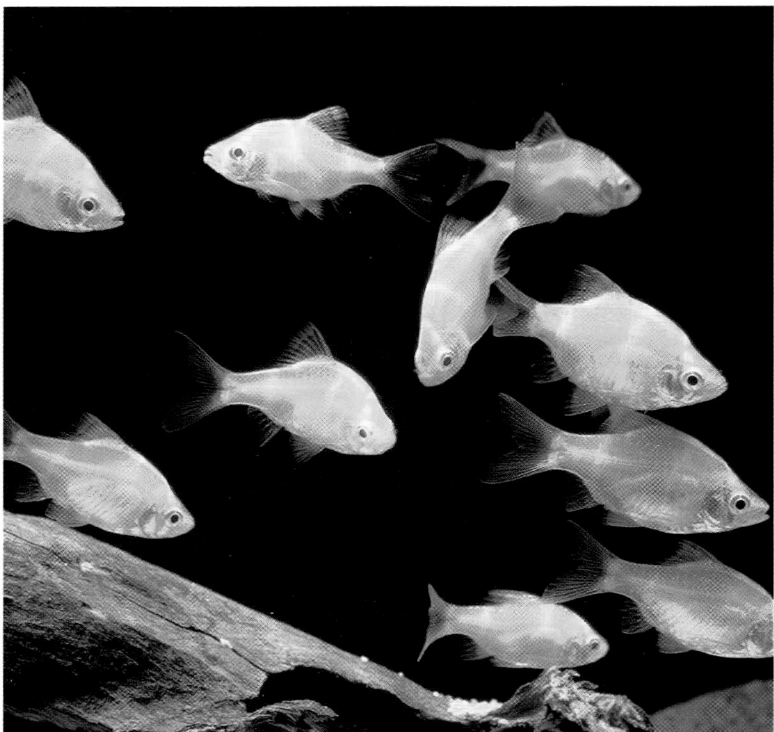

▲ *Capeta tetrazona (here the golden variety) prefers soft to medium-hard water, especially for reproduction.*

compensate for this, nature has provided a screening device, the CH (carbonate hardness, i.e. the hardness due to calcium and magnesium carbonates and bicarbonates). The higher this is, the less the risk of any major variations in the pH, and vice versa. This phenomenon, known as buffering, can therefore only occur in acid fresh water. There is a relationship between the CH and the general hardness: the closer the CH value comes to the GH value, the more balanced the water. If the CH is less than 75% of the GH, you are likely to encounter a problem, and it is therefore not advisable to use water with these characteristics in an aquarium.

Modifying the hardness of water

Sometimes the water available presents a hardness value inappropriate for its intended use in an aquarium. In most cases, the water will be a little too hard, and so the GH must be brought down for use in a mixed aquarium or a rearing tank. In other, less common cases, the water can be slightly too soft, and so the GH needs to be raised.

• *Reducing the GH*

Water with a low hardness value can be mixed with water that is too hard. There are several alternative sources of water (see pages 21–23):

- rain water;
- spring and well water;
- defrosting water from a refrigerator;
- water from melted snow;
- distilled water, available in bottles;
- some brands of mineral water;
- natural flowing fresh water.

The volume of water that can be obtained, and its price, obviously depend on which of these sources is used. Filling a tank with a capacity of several hundred liters with water of a precise hardness can sometimes be a laborious process. A final piece of advice: avoid using water from a domestic softener, as the calcium salts are replaced by other salts. Osmosed water (see page 17) is an attractive option, but the equipment represents a substantial investment.

• *Increasing the GH*

The water in question can be diluted with harder natural water, generally easier to find than soft water, or put some calcareous rocks in the aquarium, regularly monitoring the GH, or filter the water over oyster shells crushed into tiny pieces.

Any modification in the hardness of water is matched by a modification in the pH: increasing the hardness of the water also increases its pH, and vice versa.

Obtaining water with a precise hardness

Let us suppose we have two types of water, one hard and one soft, with which to "manufacture" an intermediate water:

- water A, with a GH of 9°GH;
- water B, with a GH of 3°GH;
- target water, with a GH of 5°GH.

Calculations:

GH water A – GH target water = 9 – 5 = 4.
GH target water – GH water B = 5 – 3 = 2.

The combination of 4 liters of water B and 2 liters of water A results in 6 liters at 5°GH. Filling a 180 liter tank will require 180 (6 × 30 times this mixture, i.e. 60 liters of water A and 120 liters of water B).

Another example with the same water: filling the same tank with water at 7°GH will require 120 liters of water A and 60 liters of water B.

TURBIDITY

The turbidity of water refers to the presence of suspended matter – either living organisms forming plankton (rare in an aquarium) or inert matter, such as animal or vegetable remains or particles of sediment, particularly mud.
The size of this suspended matter ranges from a few thousandths of a millimeter to several millimeters. In calm, unstirred water it forms sediment at a speed in proportion to its weight. In running or turbulent water, some of the matter remains permanently suspended, giving rise to more pronounced turbidity.
In aquariums, where the water is always in motion, systems of varying degrees of sophistication (see Filtration, page 237) allow fishkeepers keep their water clear. The effects of this are entirely positive:
– the visual appearance is improved;
– the light required by the plants penetrates the water and reaches them more easily;
– there is less risk of disease, particularly in the fishes' branchiae;
– there is little sedimentation on the base of the tank, reducing both the possibility of any warping due to excessive weight and the decomposition of organic matter.

NITROGENOUS PRODUCTS AND THE NITROGEN CYCLE

Nitrogen (N) is one of the components of certain substances, largely derived from the excretion of fish, that are dissolved in water. These substances, of varying structural complexity, are quickly converted into ammonia (NH_3 or NH_4+), which is highly toxic for animals. At this point oxygen and bacteria intervene to convert the ammonia into nitrites (NO_2-), which are also very toxic. Other bacteria, still accompanied by oxygen, transform them in their turn into nitrates (NO_3-), slightly toxic for fish but which can be used by plants as nutrients. These transformations, taken as a whole, are referred to as the nitrogen cycle. In nature, land-based elements can also participate (see diagram). As plants are at the base of the food chain, they also take part in the nitrogen cycle.

In an aquarium, the situation is different. Some fish partly feed on plants, but most of them are fed by the aquarist; sometimes there is a surplus of foodstuffs and the nitrogen cycle is altered as a result. It is very important to respect the equilibrium of this cycle. That is why you should not keep too many fish and you should not overfeed them. It is also a good idea to provide the aquarium with a sufficient amount of vegetation, and to enhance the development of bacteria, while ensuring that the water is well aerated. Partial and regular water changes make it possible to eliminate surplus foodstuffs, various types of organic matter, and any nitrates that have not been used by the plants. A biological filter enhances the development of the nitrogen cycle.

THE NITROGEN CYCLE

In the natural setting

Terrestrial contributions (NO_3- from farm land)
NO_3^-
Oxygen + bacteria nr. 3
Nutrients
Excretion
Plant debris
Oxygen + bacteria nr. 1
NH_4^+ NH_3
Oxygen + bacteria nr. 2
NO_2^-
Cadavers

Eventual consumption of vegetable matter
Transformation of nitrogen compounds

The nitrogen molecules derived from animals or vegetable matter are transferred into ammonia, which is highly toxic, and then into nitrites, which are similarly very toxic. These go on to produce nitrates, which are much less dangerous and can be used by plants as mineral salts. This process requires the presence of various bacteria to consume the oxygen left over from the transformation of the nitrogenous molecules – which is why the tank must be well oxygenated.

In the aquarium

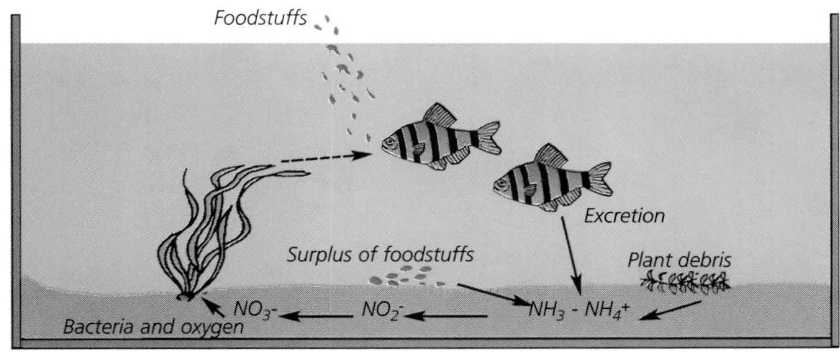

NITROGENOUS COMPOUNDS				
Nitrogenous compounds	**Symbol**	**Concentration in natural setting**	**Limits for content in aquarium**	**Observations**
Ammonia	NH_3, NH_4^+	0.005–0.05 mg/liter	0.4 mg/liter	1 mg/liter can be tolerated for a few hours.
Nitrites	NO_2^-	0.001–0.05 mg/liter	0.1 mg/liter	0.5 mg/liter can be tolerated for 24 hours
Nitrates	NO_3^-	0.01 mg/liter to several tenths, depending on the region	100 mg/liter	It is wise not to exceed 50 mg/liter.

Bacteria in the nitrogen cycle

Rarely found in open water (around 1% of the total count), bacteria colonize essentially the floor and the decor. They feed on nitrogenous compounds in the water, extracting the oxygen from them.When an aquarium is brought into use, bacterial colonization of the environment is a slow process, and so it is advisable not to introduce the selected fish until 2 or 3 weeks have elapsed.

The toxicity of nitrogenous compounds

The concentration of nitrogenous compounds in an aquarium is higher than in a balanced natural setting, and there are some limits which must not be exceeded (see table above).

Ammonia is found in two different forms in water, and the sum of the two must not be more than 0.4 mg/liter. Dissolved NH_3 ammonia gas is the most dangerous, although it only appears above a pH of 7 and rarely exceeds 10% of the total ammo-

Nitrates, the final products in the nitrogen cycle, are used as mineral salts by the plants. ▶

LEVEL OF NITRITES (NO_2^-)

No nitrogenous substance should pass the threshold limit in a well-balanced aquarium. As ammonia and nitrates are more difficult to assess, it is the nitrites that must be analyzed regularly. There is a colored marker commercially available, which gives a stronger color according to the amount of nitrites present. If the latter are too abundant:

– either there is a general imbalance (too many fish, too much food in the water) which entails a high production of ammonia and, therefore, nitrites;

– or there is a problem connected with the transformation of nitrites into nitrates, often a lack of the oxygen required by bacteria.

The level of nitrites, like the pH level discussed above, is a good indicator of the equilibrium of an aquarium, and it is therefore important to measure it regularly.

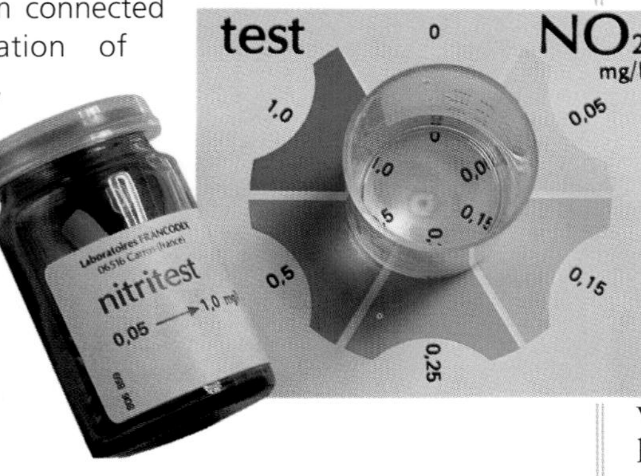

▲ *The darker the pink color, the more nitrites there are in the tested sample.*

nia. The more common ionized NH_4^+ form is slightly less dangerous.

OTHER DISSOLVED SOLIDS

A great many other substances are to be found dissolved in water. Their content is generally low and does not pose any problems, and some of them, such as micronutrients, are even very beneficial. This term covers a variety of elements including vitamins and metals, which in tiny quantities are indispensable to life.

Iron, for example, plays a role in the composition of hemoglobin, the red blood cells which transport the oxygen taken in by the branchiae. It also participates in the photosynthesis of plants, which have a tendency to turn yellow if there is an iron deficiency. Manganese is equally important, as it is one of the components of chlorophyll, the green pigment in plants that allows them to absorb light and develop.

There are, of course, other metals that are also naturally present in water, but their concentration hardly ever exceeds a few thousandths of a mg/liter, and some, such as copper, become toxic if it goes beyond this limit.

Origin and quality of fresh water used in aquariums

The simplest and cheapest means of obtaining water is turning on a faucet, but there are other possibilities, especially when it comes to obtaining natural water.

• *Domestic water*

As long as water is drinkable, there is no reason why it is not suitable for fish. In some regions the water is sometimes too hard (general hardness above 11°GH), and so the option of mixing it with softer water must be considered.

Domestic water must never be introduced in large quantities into an aquarium which already contains fish. It is also advisable to let it settle for 24 hours to eliminate any excess of gas (caused by the pressure). When filling a tank before putting it into operation, this step is not compulsory, as it will not be housing fish immediately.

• *Natural water*

Natural water close to home usually shares many of the characteristics of domestic water, as it makes up a large part of the public water supply.

However, it should be possible to find water with different characteristics not too far away.

• *Spring water*

This is the most desirable water, as it is the purest, with no suspended material, little or no organic matter and a high bacteriological quality.

• *Well water*

This is of a similarly good quality, although it sometimes contains an excess of gas. It can occasionally be slightly ferruginous (containing iron), which favors the growth of plants.

Optimum characteristics of fresh water suitable for aquariums		
Parameters	**Optimum characteristics**	**Observations**
Color	Colorless	Yellow-colored water contains organic matter.
Turbidity	None	The water must be limpid and crystal-clear.
Smell	None	Sometimes water containing organic matter has a characteristic smell of humus.
Temperature	Under 25°C	It is advisable to collect water with a temperature between 5 and 15°C.
pH	6–9	It should preferably be between 6.5 and 7.5.
Oxygen	The maximum	This is the case with springs and streams. Stagnant and still water is not suitable.
Hardness	Under 16.8°GH	Beyond 11.2°GH, it must be mixed with fresh water (except in rare cases, for certain fish).
Ammonia	Under 0.4 mg/liter	This value is rarely attained in balanced water.
Nitrites	Under 0.1 mg/liter	This is the drinking water threshold.
Nitrates	Under 50 mg/liter	This is the threshold for drinking water, often exceeded in farming areas.

Water usable in aquariums		
Type of water	**Characteristics**	**Use in aquariums**
Domestic water	Variable according to region, often a little hard and alkaline in major urban areas.	Untreated, or first mixed. Total or partial filling of an aquarium.
Defrosting water from refrigerator	Zero or very low hardness, pH close to neutral.	Dilution of hard and alkaline water.
Distilled/demineralized water	Neutral, fresh.	Dilution of hard and alkaline water.
Bottled water	Variable. Volvic is one of the softest.	Dilution of hard and alkaline water. There are several brands of mineral water soft enough for this purpose.
Natural water		
Rainwater	Fresh and acid (or neutral), often containing pollutants.	Dilution of hard water. Its use to be avoided in an urban or industrialized area.
Water from melted snow	Barely mineralized and close to neutrality.	Dilution of hard water. Only to be collected if it is very clean.
Spring or stream water	Variable according to region, generally with little turbidity.	Total or partial filling of an aquarium, mixture with other water.
Well water	Variable according to land bored, with little turbidity.	Total or partial filling of an aquarium, mixture with other water.
Ponds, down-river water	Variable, but often turbid.	Not to be used, microbiological risk.

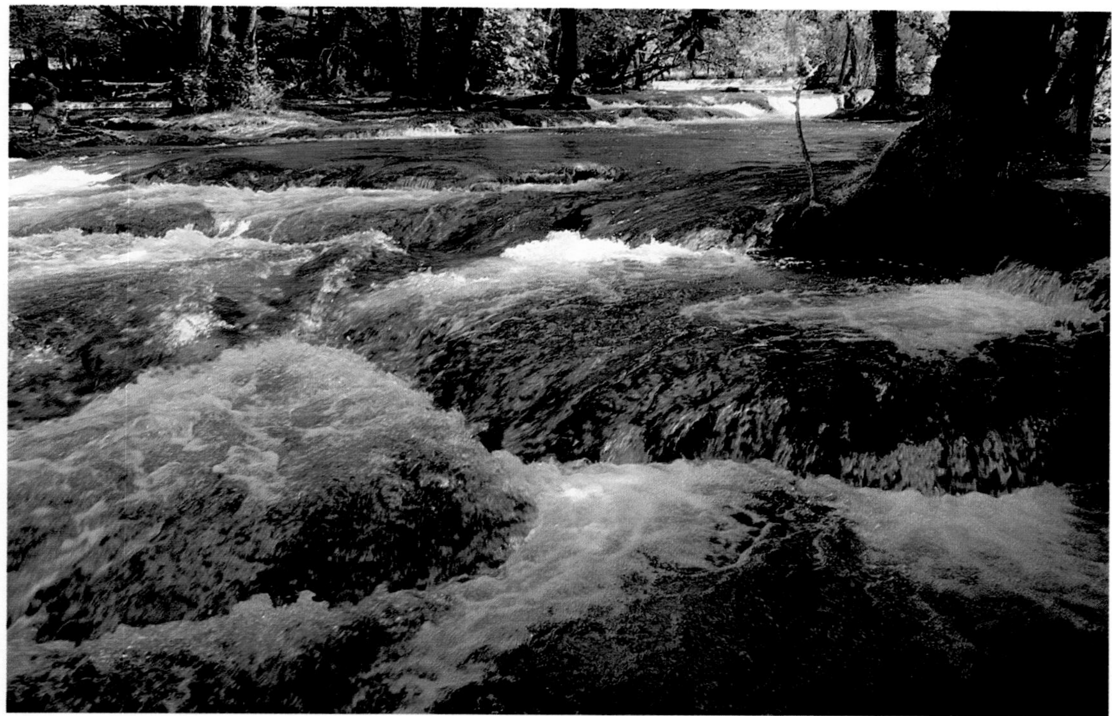

◀ *Movement in water, whether in a natural setting or in an aquarium, is the best means of enhancing its oxygenization.*

• *Rainwater*

Rainwater is soft and acid, so is useful for diluting water that is too hard. It should be collected in plastic containers; if these are put under a gutter, take care not to collect the first water, as this will have cleaned the roof. In urban and industrial areas, rainwater is liable to contain pollutants, and it is therefore not advisable to use it.

• *Stagnant water (ponds) and still water (down-river)*

Such water can pose a microbiological risk, and it is not advisable to use it.

• *Demineralized and distilled water*

Their pH is neutral or very slightly acid, with little or no hardness. Their high price means that they are only used for mixing with hard water, or for filling a small rearing aquarium. Do not forget that softened water cannot be used.

• *Bottled water*

This is often referred to as mineral water – erroneously so, as some brands contain hardly any minerals and are quite soft. These are certainly not used to fill up huge tanks, bottle by bottle, as this would be too expensive and time-consuming, and therefore serve a similar function to that of distilled water.

◀ *Some mineral water can be used in aquariums.*

CHARACTERISTICS OF SOME BOTTLED WATERS

Brand	pH	GH (°GH)	CH (°CH)
Volvic	7	3	3
Valvert	7.2–7.4	8–9	7.5–8.5
Evian	7.2–7.4	16–17	16–17

Volvic is well known among aquarists who need soft water to encourage reproduction in certain species of fish. Valvert is an example of a water with medium hardness, and Evian reaches Rift Valley hardness levels.

SEA WATER

The main difference between fresh water and sea water is that the latter contains a great many salts which give it certain specific characteristics, and these must be understood by any aquarist who wishes to keep marine fish.

▲ *Very high quality sea water is required in marine aquariums, especially if they contain invertebrates, particularly anemones and corals.*

Temperature

The temperature of tropical sea water varies little over the course of a day, or even a year. Furthermore, marine fish are generally more sensitive to abrupt changes than freshwater fish. The temperature in an aquarium must, therefore, be fairly stable, remaining at around 25–26°C.

Salinity

The most important salt found in sea water is sodium chloride (NaCl), widely used for domestic and culinary purposes, but there are plenty more.

The salinity of water, i.e. the quantity of salts in the water, is expressed in ‰ or in g/liter. The mean salinity of the Earth's oceans is around 35‰, or approximately 35 g salts/liter.

Whatever its salinity, sea water boasts one remarkable property: the proportion of each element is constant.

Desalinated water does not therefore contain less of one or more salts, but the combination of salts is present in a lower concentration.

The salinity of sea water varies according to longitude. It is at its highest in open seas in the tropics, it is lower near coasts and after heavy rain, and it is at its lowest near the poles (due to the influence of melting snow).

Density

In marine aquariums, it is not the salinity of water which is measured, but the density (often expressed as specific gravity, S.G.), which can be calculated according to the following formula:

$$\text{density} = \frac{\text{weight of 1 liter of sea water}}{\text{weight of 1 liter of pure water}} \times 1\,000$$

There are no units of measurements. The saltier the water, the higher its density. The density also varies according to temperature (it goes down as the temperature goes up). The table overleaf shows the relationship between salinity and density with respect to temperature, which is relatively constant (25–26°C) in aquariums. The density, expressed as specific gravity, a value which is easy to use, is all that is required to calculate salinity: it must range between 1.022 and 1.024.

The CH

Unlike the general hardness (GH) which is used to describe fresh

The hydrometer, an indispensable tool in marine aquariums. ►

Measuring density

Density is measured with a hydrometer, whose buoyancy increases as the water gets saltier. In the aquarium trade, most hydrometers also include a thermometer. The specific gravity at water level must be read with care; in fact, it is preferable to use the hydrometer outside the aquarium, as the movement of the water makes it difficult to read. In this case, decant the water into a test tube or a transparent container (a PVC bottle, for example) and float the hydrometer in it. When it stops moving, read the value corresponding to the level of the water (1.023 in the diagram below, and not 1.022). To check whether your hydrometer is working properly, just measure the density of a distilled or very soft water: it must equal 1.000.

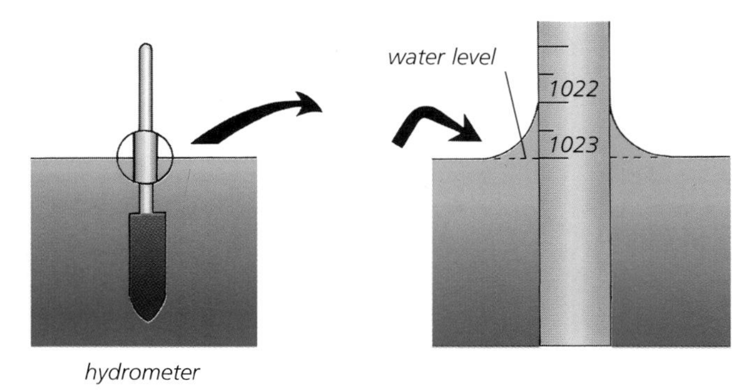

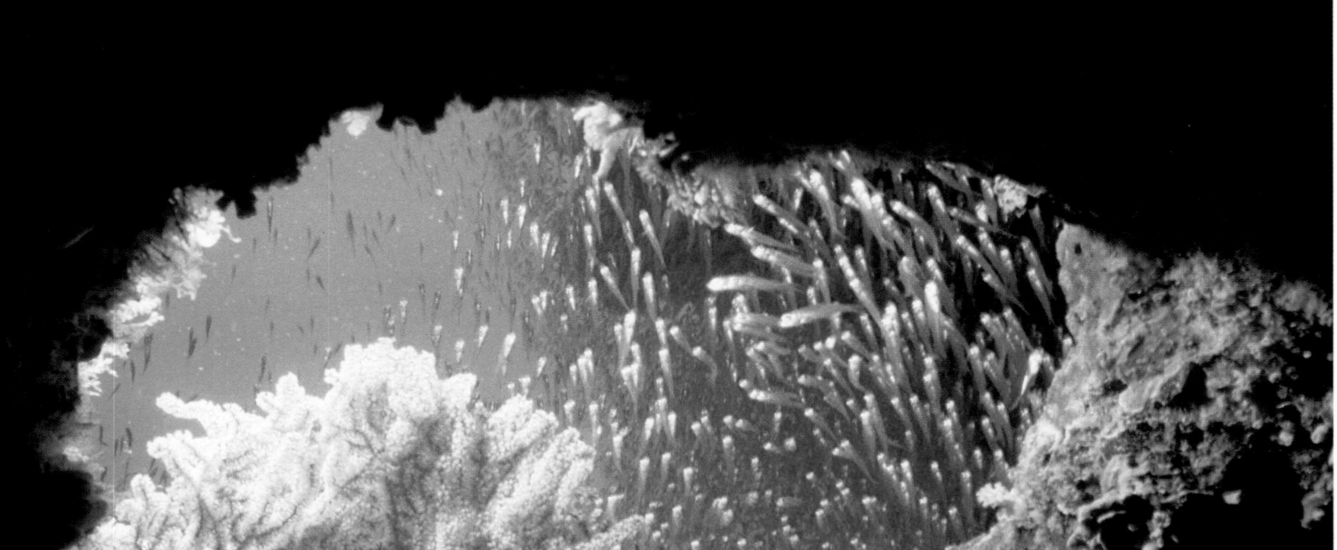

Some examples of the salinity and density of sea water

Geographical areas	Cornish Atlantic coast	Western Mediterranean	Atlantic Ocean	Tropical reef zones	Red Sea
Salinity in %	25–35	33–37	34–35	32–35	35–38
Density	1.015–1.025	1.022–1.027	1.022–1.023	1.021–1.024	1.023–1.026

water, carbonate hardness (CH) is used in sea water, where it serves to measure the quantity of calcium and magnesium carbonates and bicarbonates present.
This is crucial for maintaining the pH, and for growing corals, which have skeletons made of calcium carbonate.

The main components of sea water

Sea water contains more than 60 elements. The main one is chloride, which accounts for more than 54% of the total mass of salts, followed by sodium, with around 30%.
When these two elements bond, sodium chloride is formed. This is the main salt in sea water, comprising around 85% of the total; the other salts therefore represent only 15% in all, but they all play an equally important role. Magnesium, sulfur, calcium, potassium, and bromide are the most abundant elements, after sodium.

pH values

As sea water is salty, its pH is therefore higher than that of fresh water. Pure sea water in the middle of the ocean has a pH of 8.3. Near the coasts, this drops to about 8 or a little less, as its dilution with fresh water lowers the salt content. The pH of sea water in an aquarium must vary between 8 and 8.5; beyond these values, animals will experience certain physiological problems.

Variations in pH in a marine aquarium
Sea water contains a great deal of calcium carbonate and bicarbonate, and there are only slight variations in pH in a natural setting.
It is a different matter in an aquarium, a restricted habitat operating as a closed cycle. The pH must not fall below 8, but a slow and regular decrease in this parameter may be seen. Why? The water in an aquarium sometimes contains too much carbon dioxide, which has a tendency to lower the pH.
What can you do? The first step is to measure the CH:
– if it is under 7.2°CH, add calcium or replace some of the water. This situation is, however, fairly rare in an aquarium without corals, solely occupied by fish;
– if it is over 7.2°CH, there is an excess of carbon dioxide. Stirring of the water must therefore be increased by using diffusers or an electric pump.

The nitrogen cycle

This occurs in the same way in sea water and fresh water. In a marine aquarium the vegetation is often less abundant than in fresh water, and so the nitrates, the end products of the nitrogen cycle, will have a tendency to accumulate.
At high doses these pose little danger to fish but are toxic for invertebrates, especially corals. It is therefore important to eliminate them by partial, but regular, water changes.

Salinity (in ‰) as a function of temperature and density

T °C	Density							
	1.012	1.019	1.020	1.021	1.022	1.023	1.024	1.025
22	26.7	28.1	29.4	30.7	32.0	33.4	34.7	36.0
23	27.1	28.4	29.8	31.1	32.4	33.7	35.1	36.4
24	27.5	28.8	30.1	31.5	32.8	34.1	35.4	36.8
25	27.9	29.2	30.5	31.9	33.2	34.5	35.8	37.2
26	28.3	29.6	30.9	32.3	33.6	34.9	36.2	37.6
27	28.7	30.0	31.3	32.7	34.0	35.3	36.7	37.8
28	29.1	30.9	31.8	33.1	34.4	35.8	37.1	38.4

In aquariums, the density (S.G.) must be between 1.022 to 1.024 for a temperature of 25–26°C

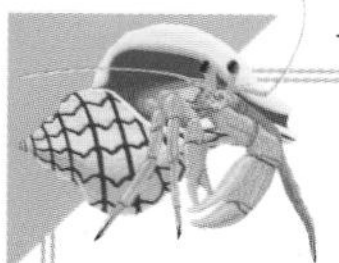

Finding out the characteristics of natural water

The European Union has set compulsory standards for drinking and environmental quality, but the strict legislation in the UK goes well beyond these. In England and Wales, for example, domestic water is monitored by the Drinking Water Inspectorate, which regularly checks up on the practices of the water companies and investigates any possible infringement of the law.
The Environment Agency, on the other hand, is responsible for the quality of water in rivers, estuaries, and coastal areas. It issues licenses to discharge waste into these waters and takes chemical and biological samples to monitor the effect on the environment. The results of these controls are available to the public.

Once a marine tank has been put into operation, the nitrogen cycle is slower to take effect than in a freshwater tank: around 3–4 weeks (although this is a generalization, as every aquarium is unique).
Fish or other animals must not therefore be put into the water during this period, although the length of time can be reduced by various means (see Assembling your Tank, page 218), based on the principle of introducing bacteria. In any event, measuring the nitrite levels is an excellent indicator of the progress of the nitrogen cycle.
Once the water has been put into the tank, this parameter must be measured regularly; when the quantity of nitrites goes down close to zero, the nitrates appear and you only need to wait a few days before inserting the fish. Nevertheless, measuring the nitrites at regular intervals is still highly recommended, as long as the aquarium is in use.

Other dissolved substances

Sea water contains more than 60 elements, some of them in microscopic amounts: for example, there is 1 g/m^3 of gold in sea water.
All the solids dissolved in sea water serve a purpose, and that is why the salts that are used to reconstitute water must be of excellent quality.
Some substances can accumulate in sea water and in high concentrations give rise to concern. This is especially true in the case of organic matter, but it is possible to eliminate them by partially changing the water or using certain devices, such as an aerator (page 250).

Development of the nitrogen cycle once a marine tank is in operation

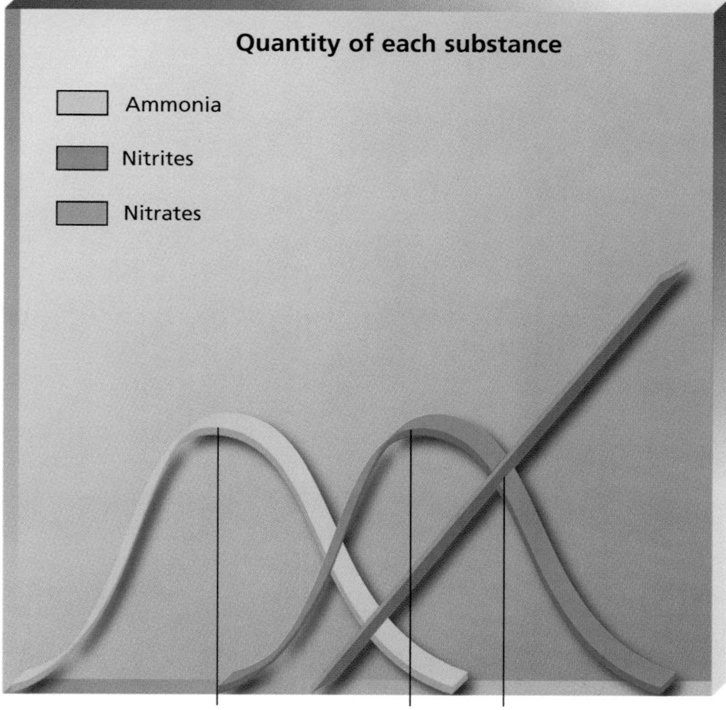

As soon as the water is put in the tank, the ammonia content rises until, as shown in the graph, it reaches its maximum level after 8 to 10 days.
Simultaneously, the bacteria wich transform this ammonia are developing and nitrites are formed, reaching their peak around the 15th day. Other forms of bacteria also develop, converting, in turn, these nitrites into nitrates. While the nitrites disappear between the 20th and 25th days, the nitrates must be eliminated by partial water change.
The establishement of this cycle requires at least 3-4 weeks. During this period the ammonia and nitrites reach levels that are sometimes ten times that of toxic doses (identical to those of fresh water, see page 20).

CALCIUM IN SEA WATER

Reef waters contain between 400 and 500 mg/liter of calcium, which is up to 20 times more than fresh water. Calcium participates in the composition of calcium carbonate ($CaCO_3$), necessary for the formation of coral skeletons, the carapace of crustaceans, and the shells of mollusks. If you are raising these animals, the CH must be between 6.7 and 14°GH; if it is below this level, part of the water must be changed or calcium must be added. This is not necessary if there are already fish in the tank.

TURBIDITY

Clarity is more important in sea water than in fresh water. Tropical environments in particular contain very few dissolved solids and they are the most transparent waters on the planet. A marine aquarium must therefore be filtered more efficiently and to a greater extent than a freshwater tank (see Filtration, page 237).

THE ORIGIN OF SALT WATER IN MARINE AQUARIUMS

The first idea which springs to mind is that of collecting natural sea water, but this is difficult for somebody who lives a long way from a coast or requires large quantities. Moreover, although sea water does present advantages, it also has its inconveniences. While some aquarists filter it before using it to totally or partially fill up their tanks, the majority use reconstituted sea water. In theory, the recipe is a simple one: dissolve the salts in the water. In practice, however, not just any water or any salts can be used, and it is out of the question to use table salt or that derived from salt marshes. Furthermore, good sea water cannot be reconstituted using poor quality fresh water.

The collection of water from a coastal area is to be avoided, especially when the locality is used for dumping urban or industrial waste. ▶

Where and when to collect natural sea water?

The ideal solution would be to go to the open sea, where the water is likely to be less polluted and to have more constant characteristics. Near the coasts, the following must be avoided: urbanized or industrialized areas and ports, which are susceptible to pollution; anywhere near river mouths, estuaries, or bays, where the water is desalted; and areas of stagnant sea water (pools at low tide) and salt marshes.

Coasts with sand dunes are suitable in principle, but the water is often laden with suspended sediment. Rocky coasts are preferable regions from where water can be collected.

The best periods for collection are autumn and winter, because plankton develop in spring and tourism increases the risk of pollution in summer. Calm weather is preferable, in order to avoid suspended material, although a heavy swell reoxygenates the water. In this case, the water can be collected 1–3 days later, the time in which the suspended material turns into sediment. However, the water must be filtered in all cases, first roughly and then more finely.

◄ *Salt collected in salt marshes is not suitable for reconstituting sea water intended for an aquarium.*

Advantages and disadvantages of natural sea water and reconstituted sea water

	Natural sea water	Reconstituted sea water
Advantages	• It is economical and contains all the elements necessary for life, as well as "good" bacteria.	• It does not contain suspended sediment, organic matter, pathogenic bacteria, or pollutants. • It is manufactured with the desired salinity and can be stored in a concentrated form (3–4 times the desired salinity).
Disadvantages	• It must be collected (traveling and containers). • According to where it is collected, it may contain suspended sediment, organic matter, pollutants, and pathogenic bacteria. • The salinity varies according to when and where it is collected. • It may contain plankton, with the risk that this may develop in the aquarium – hardly desirable.	• More expensive than natural sea water, it sometimes lacks certain micronutrients. • It does not contain "good" bacteria. • It cannot house animals for several weeks, the time taken for the nitrogen cycle to be established.

Generally speaking, the advantages of one correspond to the disadvantages of the other, which is why some aquarists mix both types of water.

The reconstitution of artificial sea water
The quality of the fresh water used is important: it must be as pure as possible. It is best to use water with a hardness of less than 8.4, although reconstitution is still possible with higher levels, providing the CH is equal to at least 75–80% of the general hardness value. Take care to avoid water containing nitrates (often found in farming areas), to which invertebrates are very sensitive, or metals, toxic for some animals where present above certain limits.

Making sea water in an aquarium, before putting it into operation
Fill the aquarium with fresh water and aerate it for 24 hours. Calculate and weigh the quantity of salts to be dissolved, then introduce them into the aquarium. Then just aerate for another 24–48 hours and check the density, adjusting it as required.

ARTIFICIAL SALTS

Several companies have special aquarium salts on the market, and it is even possible to find concentrated sea water. Some salts are intended for marine tanks for fishes, others for aquariums with invertebrates. Their quality is satisfactory, although there are likely to be improvements in the future, and, as they are enriched with calcium, micronutrients, and vitamins, they are obviously relatively expensive. There have been no adverse reports to date about the use of these salts in aquariums: in those areas where accidents do occur, they are usually due to miscalculations on the part of the aquarist.

▲ *Artificial sea water can be reconstituted with the help of special salts available in aquarium stores.*

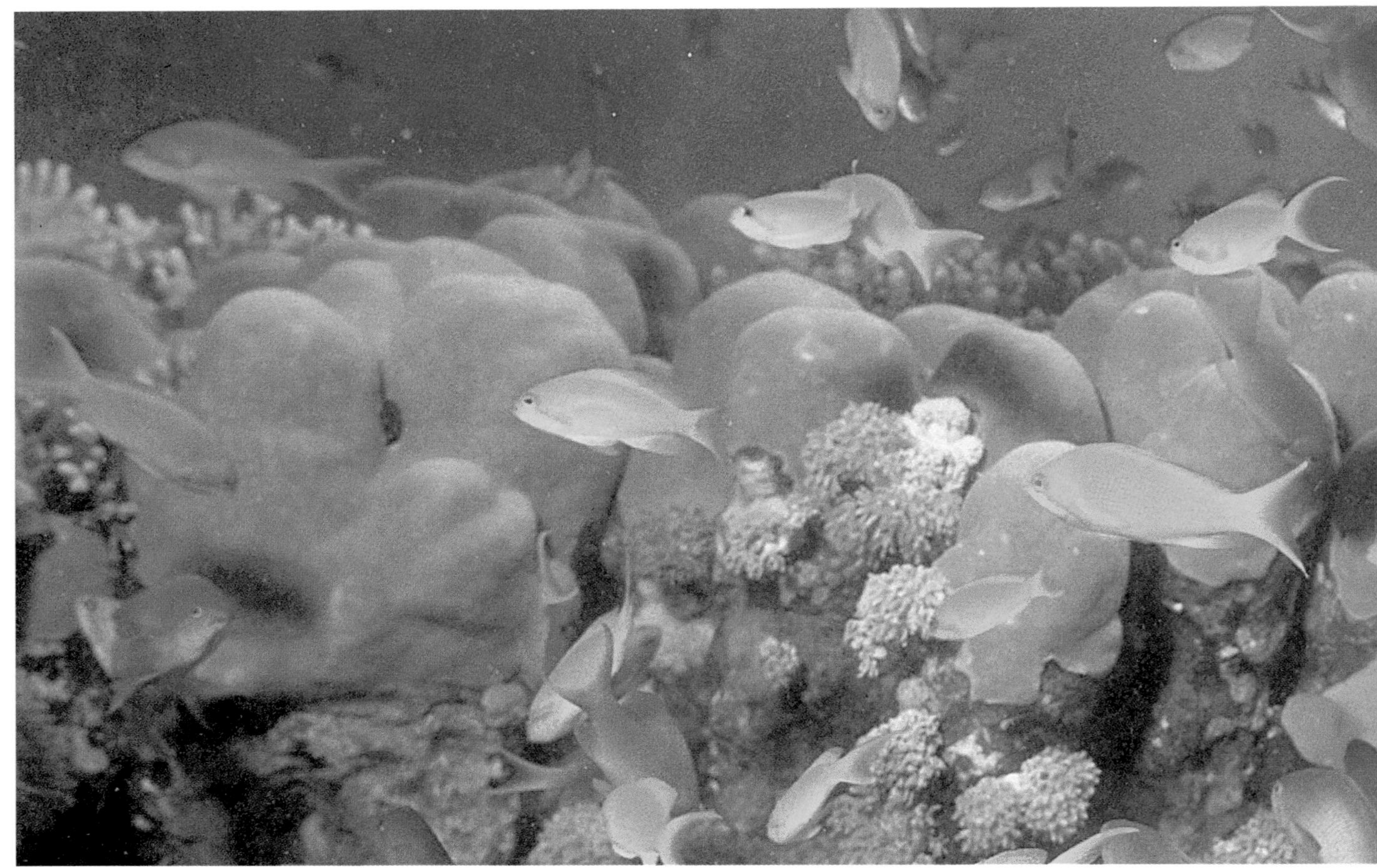

Making sea water for storage and back-up

The method is the same, except that plastic food containers are generally used. The quantity of salt can be multiplied by three or four to manufacture concentrated water that will therefore occupy less storage space.

Transportation and Storage of Natural Water

Water collected in a natural setting is transported in plastic containers, such as jerry cans. As these generally have a limited volume (under 30 liters), quite a few are required to fill an aquarium of several hundred liters. The water can be stored in these containers, protected from heat and sunlight (cellar, garage, storeroom, attic).
Some aquarists with several tanks store their water in cisterns covered with polyethylene; these are available commercially.

Adjusting the density

• *The density is too high*

Part of the water is siphoned off – this can be stored for later use – and the softest water available is added, taking care to measure the density. When the water level of a marine aquarium goes down because of evaporation, it is not the sea water which is evaporating but the fresh water, and it is therefore the latter which must be added to make up the level. The addition of sea water would entail an increase in density.

• *The density is too low*

In this case, salts must be added. These must be dissolved beforehand in a container which is then gradually emptied into the aquarium, with constant checks on the density. Both these operations must be performed with care if the aquarium already contains fish, in order to avoid causing any excessively abrupt changes that could be detrimental to the fish.

Artificial sea water, reconstituted with commercially produced salts, creates an environment that is perfectly suited to fish. ▼

DIFFERENT TYPES OF AQUARIUM

An aquarium is not just a motley collection of plants and fish. Some aquarists aim to reconstruct the biotope of a specific geographical region (Central America, the Amazon, Asia, Africa), while others concentrate on a single group of fish (for example, livebearers, Cichlids, or marine fish). Whatever the option, an aquarium must be attractive and well-balanced for its occupants to thrive, and this entails some understanding of the various habitats, as well as their inhabitants.

▲ Community tank.

An aquarium is a collection of elements – fish, plants, soil, rocks, water – which are compatible with each other. However, there are several types of aquarium, all sharing the same general principles and techniques but differing with respect to the environment created. Aquariums are divided into two main groups:

– temperate aquariums, often mistakenly called cold water aquariums, where the water temperature can range from 5 to 25°C;

– tropical aquariums, with either fresh or sea water. These cover the areas lying roughly between the tropic of Cancer, to the north of the equator, and the tropic of Capricorn, to the south, where the water temperature varies by only a few degrees throughout the whole year.

TEMPERATE WATER AQUARIUMS

These are not heated, and ideally the water temperature should vary to the same extent that it does in nature (from 5 to 25°C, approximately). This is difficult, as room temperature barely falls below 15°C and is often over 18°C. Apart from this difference, the underlying principle is the same as in any aquarium: to recreate an environment. This demands just as

much time and care as with tropical aquariums. It must be stressed that we are not talking about goldfish bowls!
Temperate aquariums house robust species, among them the fish found in our rivers and ponds, which fall beyond the scope of this book. On the other hand, we will cover goldfish (*Carassius auratus*), all too often neglected in favor of tropical species, but which, in their innumerable variety, give great pleasure to many hobbyists.
Still within this temperature range, mention must be made of garden ponds, where goldfish and koi carps (colored varieties of the common carp) can be kept and bred. If they are well designed, such ponds can recreate a natural biotope, with aquatic and terrestrial plants, invertebrates, and amphibians. Sometimes they can also play host to tropical fish for a brief summer stay, if the temperature permits. After all, fish can take vacations too, especially if they coincide with yours! It is a practical solution when there is nobody to look after an aquarium during a long absence, and when you come back you may be amazed by the weight the fish have put on, or by some unexpected new arrivals.
On the other hand, do not be too surprised if some fish have disappeared, unable to tolerate the change of setting – or the predatory instincts of the local cat.

▲ *Garden pond.*

Tropical aquariums

The community aquarium

Here fish and plants not native to the same region are found side by side, creating an environment that does not exist in nature. The results may be charming and ingenious, but this type of aquarium is often disparaged by purists.
A community aquarium is often a popular choice with beginners creating – or "mounting", in aquarists' jargon – their first tank, although this is not a general rule.

The specialist aquarium

In this case, the hobbyist concentrates on a particular species, type, family, or group of fish with common characteristics. The choice of this kind of aquarium can be dictated by several factors: interest in reproduction, the attainment of varieties not found in nature (sometimes for competition), or quite simply a fascination which is difficult to explain. As in the previous section, the fish and plants do not have to come from the same region, and the latter are sometimes merely secondary elements.

The Dutch aquarium

In this type of aquarium fish serve as a foil to the plants, which play the leading role, although the former do also contribute to the equilibrium of the setting, which is not easy to maintain. The plants and fish can come from different geographical areas. The results can be ravishing, sometimes amounting to a veritable aquatic garden, with the aquarist becoming a horticulturist in order to maintain it.

◄ *Dutch aquarium.*

As its name suggests, this type of aquarium is highly prized in the Netherlands, and in Germany too, although it is little (too little?) seen in the rest of the world.

Regional aquariums

Here the trick is to reconstruct as faithfully as possible a natural biotope in which everything harmonizes: the water, the soil, the rocks, the plants, and the fish. The density of living beings is higher than that of a natural setting, however. Mounting an aquarium of this type requires a certain knowledge of the geographical area concerned, to ensure the compatibility of the various elements.

• *Central American aquariums*

There are two possible options. The first is the recreation of a habitat suitable for livebearers from the Poeciliid family: hard water with a temperature of 26°C or more, and plants playing an important role. The second is the assembly of a tank for Cichlids: rocky decor, a few hardy plants, with the water fairly soft, well-filtered, and oxygenated.

• *South American aquariums*

Mainly devoted to the Amazon, these can be divided into two main categories. The tanks with limpid colorless water, neutral or slightly acid, are inhabited by small Characins that are somewhat difficult for

The elements of a South American tank. ►

THE AMAZON

The second longest river in the world (6,280 km), the Amazon transports 15% of all the Earth's running water, with a flow of up to 190 million liters per second. Along with its tributaries, it drains an area (known as the basin) covering 7 million km^2 (three-quarters the size of the United States or 30 times that of the United Kingdom).
In the Amazon basin, the temperature of the water is always higher than 20°C and the climate is characterized by alternating dry and rainy seasons. The latter brings with it suspended substances and makes the water rise substantially (up to 10 m in the Amazon itself!). The water then spreads over vast expanses, which it floods; when the waters retreat, they often leave behind pools and marshes. This region is the richest in the world for fishes.

Central America

The combined influence of the sun and the temperature produces abundant vegetation. The waters close to the sea are hard or very hard (sometimes very slightly salty) and warm (over 26°C). The inland streams have clear, well-oxygenated water.

◀ Lake Tanganyika.

amateurs to keep. The aquariums with brown, but still transparent water, recreate an Amazon-style river under the forest roof. Its acidity and its color (sometimes even black) are the result of acids derived from humus. These tanks house other species of Characins, or Cichlids, particularly the famous angelfish and discus. The water is very soft in both these types of aquarium.

• *African aquariums*

A biotope of a West African river can be reconstructed in an aquarium.

The water, which must be well-filtered, is neutral and quite soft. The fish will include the Congolese tetra, one of the rare Characins found on this continent, and certain Cichlids. The typical plants in this environment are *Anubias*.

Tanganyika-type aquariums are characterized by their calcareous and decidedly alkaline water. They have few plants, as these are often treated roughly by the fish, but they have a rocky setting, with hiding places and swimming areas to the liking of several species of Cichlids.

The general characteristics of aquariums for Mbunas from Lake Malawi are roughly similar.

• *Asiatic aquariums*

Running water Cyprinids can be kept in a tank with clear water which is well-filtered, slightly acid, and soft, at a temperature of 25–26°C. Barbs and danios are the usual occupants of this type of aquarium, some species being particularly recommended for beginners to fish keeping. Marshes can be reconstructed with profusely planted aquariums (or aquaterrariums). It is advisable to use genuinely aquatic plants. The water is slightly acid and barely mineralized, to suit barbs, labeos, or fish from the Anabantoid family. Always avoid a mixture of active and placid fishes.

▲ Lake Malawi.

Africa

▲ *Aquarium with a collection of several species from Lake Malawi.*

West Africa is lined with rivers and streams with an acid pH, and temperatures of up to 27°C. The swampy areas disappear in the dry season, but the fish which frequent them have devised various strategies to overcome this difficulty: some species, such as the killies, lay eggs which are able to resist drought.

East Africa is characterized by the presence of large lakes, veritable inland seas, only with unsalted water. The most important of these are, from north to south, Lake Victoria, Lake Tanganyika, and Lake Malawi. They are mainly inhabited by fish from the Cichlid family, three quarters of which are only found in this region.

Lake Victoria, which stretches over nearly 7,000 km², with a maximum depth of 80 m, contains very hard water which can reach a temperature of 26–27°C. Its fish represent a substantial source of nutrition locally, although they have been in decline since the deliberate introduction of a carnivorous predator, the Nile perch.

The lake most familiar to aquarists, Lake Tanganyika, is one of the biggest (31,900 km², the second largest in the world) and the deepest (a maximum of 1,400 m!). Only the first couple of hundred meters contain fish, which are accustomed to its extremely hard water, a pH between 7.5 and 9.2, and temperatures of up to 27°C. The clear, well-oxygenated surface waters house few plants, the main vegetation being the carpet of algae covering the rocky areas. The species living there sometimes form different population groups, quite close to each other, which can mainly be distinguished by their color. Some fishes take refuge in the empty shells of Gastropods on the sandy shores. This lake is also exploited by the locals as a source of food, but the Cichlids are actively bred and exported all over the world.

This is also the case with Lake Malawi, at 26,000 km² almost as large as Tanganyika, but not as deep (700 m). Its water is slightly less calcareous and its temperatures range from 24 to 26°C. Some species of Cichlids found there are nowadays known as Mbunas.

South-east Asia

The water in the rivers and streams is acid, sometimes colored, with temperatures often exceeding 25°C. The swamp and marsh areas are shallow, allowing the sun to exert a greater influence, and their water temperature can be higher than 28°C. Natural sites collect rain and floodwater, while the artificial sites consist of rice fields. The exuberant plant life is either completely aquatic (totally submerged) or paludal (partially underwater; in very wet environments, the base of the plants is often submerged).

Aquatic zone in Asia, colonized by sea lentils. ▶

▲ *Asiatic tank.*

The brackish water aquarium

This is characterized by water with less salt than the sea, pH values of between 7.7 and 8, and fairly high temperatures, 26–27°C. The decor consists of branches and roots, but never rocks. Few plants survive in this type of water, and only a few species of fish can tolerate it (see the box on Brackish water species, pages 124–125).

Tropical seawater aquariums

The water must be of a very high quality: clear, therefore well-filtered and oxygenated. It can be natural or reconstituted,

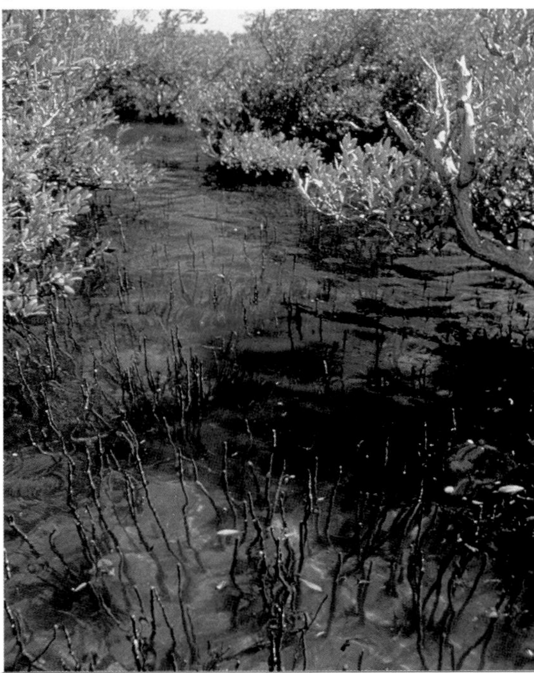

◀ *Roots tangled underwater provide shelter for fish.*

Mangroves

The borders between the sea and the land provide muddy, swampy areas (often estuaries), in which certain trees – mangroves – plunge their roots. Mangroves is also the collective name for these tropical regions in Africa, Asia, and Australia. The water reaches very high temperatures, of 30°C or more, and the sea water exerts a very strong influence. The salinity is therefore variable, leading to the presence of fauna specific to these areas. The best-known occupant of mangroves is the periophthalmus, an amphibious fish which can develop out of water on account of the form of its pectoral fins.

or a combination of the two. Marine plants are not common, but algae can appear spontaneously and cover the decor of rocks or dead corals – although their growth is imperceptible to the naked eye, it is fairly rapid. They are introduced to the aquarium in various ways. The soil is very grainy, as the sand is made up of shells and corals.

Under bright light, a marine aquarium often forms a colorful environment in which fish develop among inert or living decorative elements, which they can share with invertebrates, including certain shrimps. Novice aquarists are often advised not to plunge into keeping a marine aquarium without first finding their water wings in a freshwater tank, which is easier to tackle. The same ecological rules govern the two types of setting, however, the main difference obviously being the salinity of the water. Let us just say that it is more sensible to start with fresh water, as the plants and fish are more robust and their price is often more accessible. To be realistic, problems with sea water, involving the accidental loss of expensive fish, would discourage many beginners. Nevertheless, apart from the price of marine fish – and there are some cheaper species – it should be pointed out that marine aquariums are not much more expensive to run.

Tropical marine habitats

Tropical sea water is renowned for its clarity. Its transparency allows light to penetrate deeply enough to illuminate firstly the shallow reef areas (up to 10 m) and then the lower slopes (up to 40 m). The fish in these regions, renowned for their vivid colors, thrive in the turbulent and well-oxygenated waters. They share this environment with a wide variety of invertebrates, such as the famous corals – this generic term covers both true corals and similar species – and anemones. The tentacles of some of the latter contain micro-algae (*Zooxanthellae*) which, like all algae, need light, explaining why these anemones are found in well-lit waters.

The tropical freshwater aquaterrarium

These days aquarists are not just concerned with water but often incorporate an adjoining piece of land. Though aquaterrariums are quite tricky to design, the results can often prove spectacular. The aquatic element requires skills similar to traditional aquarium maintenance, while the cultivation of its terrestrial neighbor is not that different from looking after houseplants, except in a very humid setting. The former usually houses fish, but the latter can play host to amphibians, and even reptiles such as sea turtles.

The generous dimensions of this aquaterrarium can house water turtles as a complement to several species of fish. ▶

Special purpose aquariums

This category includes:

– breeding aquariums, often a simple glued glass tank with no soil, for temporary use;

– hospital-aquariums;

– large aquariums. These are large by virtue of their length, as their depth and breadth cannot exceed certain limits for technical and practical reasons. They sometimes present installation problems, due to the weight on the base and the special materials required for their construction.

Large tanks are often given over to large species which require ample living space on account of their size. They can also be used for the other purposes mentioned above, because it is generally considered that the bigger the aquarium, the easier it is to maintain its equilibrium. Contrary to what is often thought, their maintenance does not imply more problems if an equilibrium is really achieved.

PUBLIC AQUARIUMS

In public aquariums, fishkeeping takes on a new dimension. The general trend is to offer the public extremely large tanks, in which the behavior of the animals reflects as closely as possible what actually goes on in their natural habitat, usually beyond the reach of most people. These "living museums" serve not only to present aquatic animals but also to study them, as much still remains to be discovered about some biological phenomena (for example, the reproduction of marine fish). This new generation of "real conditions" aquariums includes among its ranks the Deep-Sea World in Fife, Scotland, the Fenit Sea World in County Kerry, Ireland, and the Clearwater Marine Aquarium in Florida, not forgetting illustrious precursors such as the National Aquarium in Washington and the Belle Isle Aquarium, Detroit, which opened in 1873 and 1904, respectively.

There are now literally hundreds of public aquariums in both Europe and North America, some of which specialize in the fauna of their local region, such as the recently opened aquarium in Touraine, France, the largest in Europe.

Space does not permit an exhaustive list, but readers can obtain information about public aquariums from the Fish Information Service (FINS) (www.actwin.com/fish/public.cgi).

Freshwater room in the tropical aquarium in Tours. ▶

Tropical lagoon tank in La Rochelle aquarium. ▼

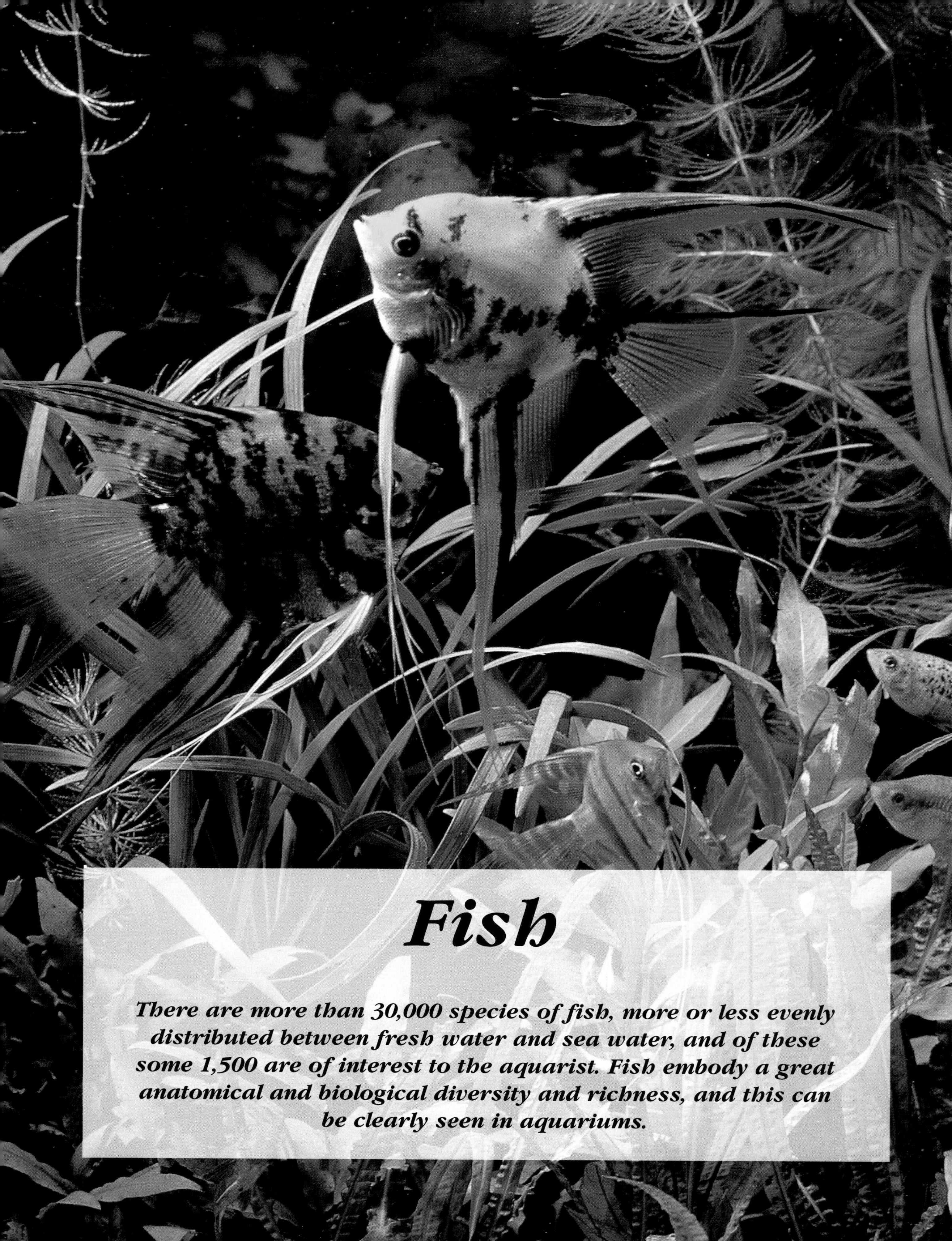

Fish

There are more than 30,000 species of fish, more or less evenly distributed between fresh water and sea water, and of these some 1,500 are of interest to the aquarist. Fish embody a great anatomical and biological diversity and richness, and this can be clearly seen in aquariums.

ANATOMY AND BIOLOGY

Whatever type of aquarium you choose, a minimal knowledge of the anatomy and biology of the species you are raising is an essential prerequisite. The information below, presented in layman's language, allows you to keep your fish in good health, in the best possible conditions, to feed them appropriately so that they can grow, and to facilitate their reproduction – in short, to understand them better in order to take better care of them.

EXTERNAL ANATOMY

The body

Hippocampus kuda. ▼

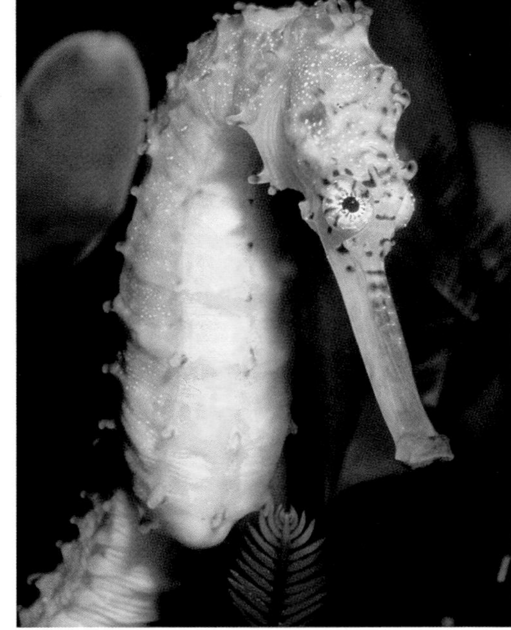

A fish is typically drawn as an elongated spindle, and in fact this is the most common form, as it makes it easier to swim in open water. These hydrodynamic characteristics permit rapid acceleration and not inconsiderable speeds (sometimes up to 20 km per hour) in a medium (water) that offers a certain degree of resistance.

However, there are other forms, that are also all connected with the lifestyle of the fish in question: bottom-dwellers have a flat stomach, while those that live in water obstructed by plants and branches have compact, thin bodies that enable them to squeeze through the obstacles. This is equally the case with the countless fish in the coral reefs, which thread their way through the blocks of coral. Finally, there are certain fish that are unclassifiable, so varied and strange are the forms they flaunt, although they always correspond to a particular lifestyle.

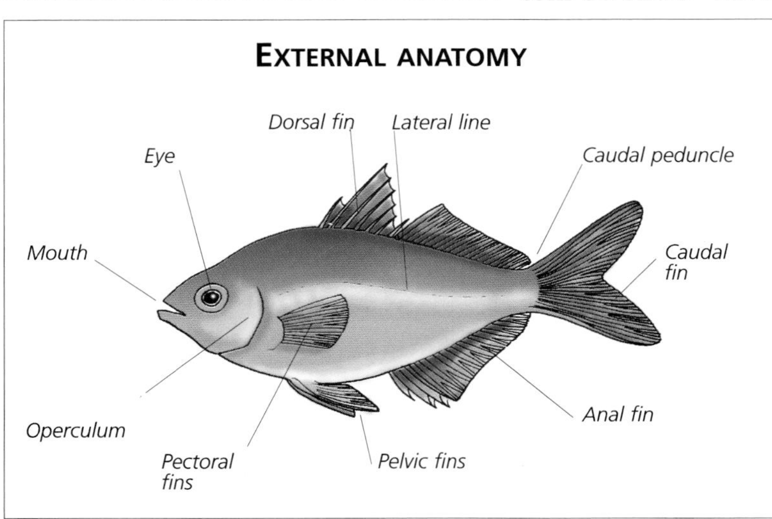

▲ Pterois volitans.

The fins

Fish have several types of fins, each one playing a precise role. Their forms and names are often used to classify them into different families.

Of the unpaired fins (i.e. consisting of a single fin), the most noteworthy are the dorsal and the anal fins. These serve to stabilize the fish when it is not going very fast or is coming to a halt, and they are tucked in when the fish swims more quickly. The caudal fin (incorrectly referred to as the tail) supplies propulsion, in conjunction with the rear part of the body. In some species, particularly the Characins and the catfish, there is a small extra fin between the dorsal and the caudal fins, known as the adipose fin, although this is not really used. The paired fins, attached symmetrically to each side of the body, are called pectoral and pelvic fins. They are used for stabilizing, stopping, slowing down, or changing direction: vertically, from the water surface to the bed, and vice versa, from side to side, from left to right, from right to left. Fins consist of a membrane stretched on spokes, and they can all be tucked in along the body, with the exception of the caudal fin. The adipose fin is merely a fold of skin, without any spokes. When the spokes are longer than the fins they are known as spiny fins, and they can represent a danger to the aquarist, as in the case of the scorpion fish, for example.

The mucus, skin, and scales

Fishes' bodies are covered with a mucus that plays a double role: it reinforces the hydrodynamics by "smoothing" the skin, and it affords protection against the penetration of parasites or pathogenic elements. The latter point is extremely important, and it explains why fish must not be moved by hand: this risks damaging the mucus and facilitating the development of certain diseases.

◀ Some species of fish are protected by the bony plates covering their head and body

Contrary to a widely held belief, the scales do not stick out of the body but are an integral part of the skin, and they are visible through a fine layer of transparent epidermis. When a scale is raised, damaged, or torn off, the skin itself is equally affected and becomes vulnerable to the action of pathogens.

Coloring

Every fish has a basic coloring that can be modified. Their shiny, metallic appearance, derived from the crystals present in the cells of the skin, varies according to the direction of the light striking them. A fish's color is a result of the different pigments located in the epidermis. These can change, slowly, for reproduction and camouflage, under the control of hormones, or more quickly, for flight or aggression,

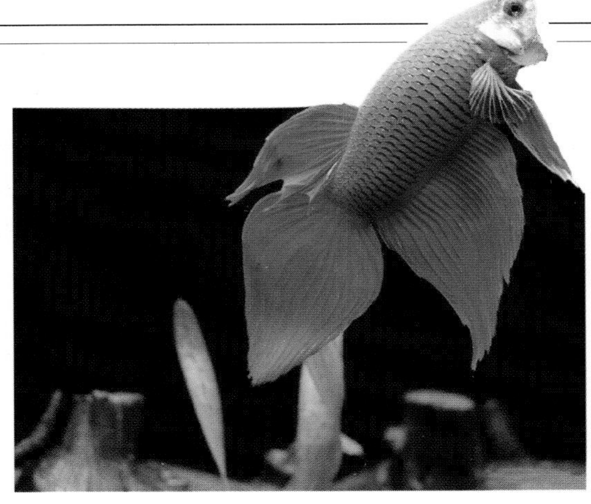

◀ *Male fighting fish* (Betta splendens).

Spectacular fins may be nurture not nature

Some aquarium fish have fins that are very different in shape or size from those that are found in nature. They are the result of patient breeding carried out by aquarists over a period of years. The visual effect is guaranteed, but the fish's behavior is sometimes altered, especially its velocity when moving around. Fish with large fins in the form of sails have little more than a remote relationship with their wild cousins, which have gone out of fashion and are no longer to be seen in tanks. The purpose of these selections can sometimes be in doubt: they undeniably result in highly attractive fish, but what advantage do they have over other stunning natural specimens?

Xipho (Xiphophorus helleri), *bred with overdeveloped fins.* ▶

◀ Euxiphipops navarchus.

Coloring: protection, warning, and seduction

The black bands of the scalare enable it to hide.

The coloring of a fish varies according to its age and mood. Some fish living in coral reefs reject individuals of their own species or a related species with a coloring similar to their own (Pomacanthids, also known as angelfishes, for example) because they consider newcomers as enemies wishing to appropriate their territory and their food supply. This is why their offspring have a very different coloring from that of adults, so as not to be considered intruders. In their desire to protect themselves, some fish adopt a camouflage to merge in with their surroundings, or, in contrast, reduce the intensity of their color to pass unnoticed. Thus, the vertical black stripes on the scalare allow it to hide among submerged branches and plants (see drawing above).
In some species, the male and female sport very different colorings, enabling them to be distinguished – a gift of nature much appreciated by aquarists! This is true of a large number of the Cichlids in the African lakes. At mating time, the male can flaunt vivid colors, not only to seduce the female in the courting ritual but also to impress his rivals and scare them off. This occurs with the meeki, a Central American Cichlid – the underside of its head turns red at mating time.

The coloring of fish exists not merely to satisfy the eye; it plays an equally important social role. ▶

▲ *Certain fish, such as this murena, have very sharp teeth, indicating that they are predators.*

controlled by nerves. The coloring of a fish can also vary when it is suffering from disease or nutrient deficiency.

The head

Whatever its form – conical, elongated, or stocky – the head houses some important organs:
– first of all, there are *the eyes*, which have no eyelids and are highly mobile. This mobility, coupled with their position on the side of the head, allows a fish to command a broad field of vision – around 270°. In contrast, the clarity of its vision is unexceptional: beyond a certain distance, it distinguishes masses and forms rather than details. Fish are very sensitive to variations in light – detecting low intensities of light, such as that of the moon – and they can recognize colors.

▲ *Fish have a particularly wide field of vision.*

– next comes *the mouth*, with a size and shape related to its feeding habits. Carnivorous fish generally have a large mouth that can open wide and is endowed with an array of pointed teeth, which are sometimes curved towards the back to keep hold of their prey. Omnivorous and herbivorous fish have a smaller mouth, with flat teeth ideally suited to grinding food.

The premonition of danger in fish

There are times when it seems that fish have a sixth sense, especially when a net is put into the aquarium! In fact, they analyze the situation with their lateral line and their sense of smell and in this way they deduce whether there is a possibility of danger. This premonition of a danger or a particular event seems to be heightened in those fish that are normally the most friendly. It is therefore perhaps better to talk of hypersensitivity in these species.

▲ *The mouth of this marine fish* (Forcipiger flavissimus, *the yellow longnose butterfly) allows it to capture its prey in the crevices of the coral.*

The position of the mouth can similarly reveal eating habits:

- a mouth in the upper position indicates a top-feeder;
- a mouth in the terminal position is the sign of a fish that hunts underwater;
- a mouth in the lower position indicates a bottom-feeder.

Upper position

Terminal position

Lower position

Breathing

Water is aspirated through the fish's mouth, passes through the branchiae and is expelled due to the movements of the operculum, which covers them. There is always some water washing the branchiae of the fish.

Oxygen requirements are not directly proportional to the size of the fish, with the smallest species being the greatest consumers of oxygen: ten fish weighing 1 g each consume more oxygen per gram of body weight than one fish of 10 g.

The barbels

Fish that live on the bed or in dark environments (colored or turbid water) have barbels around the mouth (*Corfdoras*, *Botia*, for example).

These appendages have a tactile and sensory role. By complementing or replacing the eyes, they enable the fish to detect possible sources of nutrition.

The nostrils

Two or four in number, these are located in front of the eyes. They play no part in respiration but, extended inside the head by an olfactory sac, they perceive and analyze smells.

The operculum

This protects the branchiae and guarantees the circulation of water through the regular movements of the valve, ensuring that the branchiae are always in contact with the water from which they extract oxygen. The term "gills",

The glass silurid detects its food partly as a result of its barbels. ▼

▲ *The blind tetra* (Anoptichthys jordani) *does not have any eyes but detects its prey and enemies with its lateral line.*

sometimes incorrectly used, refers to the opening produced by the movements of the operculum, which serves as an exit for the water that has irrigated the branchiae.

The lateral line

Running symmetrically along each side of the fish's body, the lateral line is more or less visible, according to the species. It consists of a succession of pores that communicate with a canal situated under the skin. This important organ does not exist in any other vertebrates.

While the senses of taste and smell, highly developed in fish, allow them to recognize a greater number of smells than humans, at very low concentrations, the lateral line, with its special cells, detects and analyzes the vibrations of the water and sends this information to the brain. In this way a fish can be aware of the proximity of an enemy, of a prey... or of the approach of the aquarist (see box, p. 47). The importance of the lateral line is apparent in the blind tetra *(Anoptichthys jordani)*, which never bumps into an obstacle even though it has no eyes.

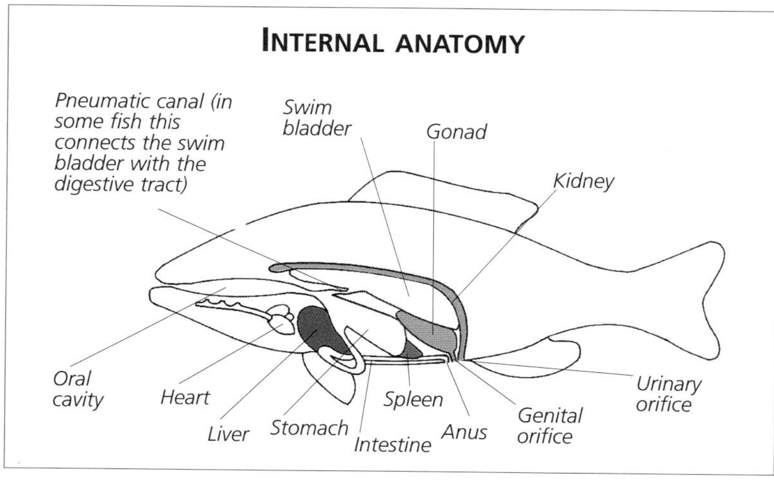

Internal anatomy

The sum of the internal organs accounts for roughly 50 to 60% of the body weight in a classically shaped fish.

The brain

This is fairly simple in fish, when compared to other more evolved animals. The parts corresponding to sight and smell are particularly well developed, demonstrating the importance of these two senses.

The skeleton

Obviously, this supports the fish's body, but it is less sturdy than that of a land animal, as a fish, partially freed from gravity, is "carried" by the water. Nevertheless, the relative fragility of the skeleton is a handicap and it is not uncommon to find fry that emerge from their egg "twisted".

The respiratory and circulatory system

This system is highly distinctive. The blood loaded with carbon dioxide is pumped by the heart to the branchiae, where it is oxygenated. Nature has provided fish with

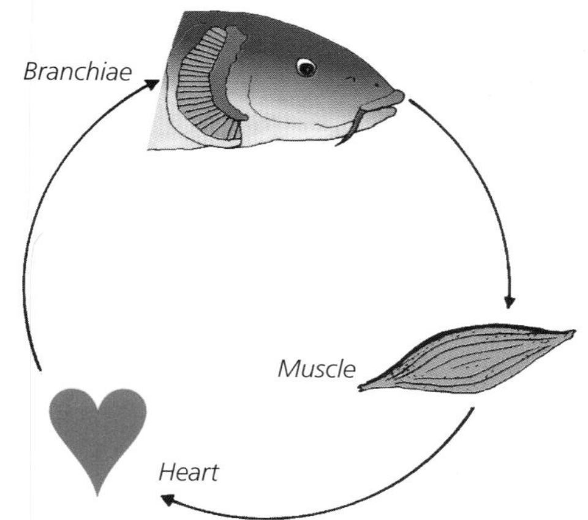

eight branchiae (four on each side), each made up of two leaves. The total surface area of these essential organs, when spread out, would be nearly equal to that of the fish's body. The vivid red color of the branchiae is due to their abundant irrigation of blood; a darker color is a symptom of a respiratory problem. The branchiae are fragile organs, susceptible to damage from suspended sediment or parasites, resulting in a reduced intake of oxygen, with all its unfortunate consequences. After traveling through the branchiae, the

vivid red blood, rich in oxygen, irrigates the body, and the oxygen goes on to break down the foodstuffs in the organs.
The fish in the Belontiid family, which live in water in which the oxygen is sometimes rarefied, have a special organ for trapping atmospheric oxygen.

▲ *In Poeciliids (livebearers), the anal fin in the male (below) is transformed into a coupling organ.*

The digestive system

This has no special characteristics, apart from the fact that the stomach can stretch to hold large prey, especially in carnivorous fish. This is where digestion starts, and it then continues in the intestine. With large prey the process can last several days, but in an aquarium, with artificial food, it will not take more than a few hours.

The excretory system

This allows undigested matter to be evacuated through the anus in the form of excrement, or feces. The urine is formed in the kidneys, situated under the spinal column; it is evacuated through the urinary pore. It is worth mentioning that fish also excrete nitrogenous substances via the branchiae. All excreted substances contain nitrogen and are toxic for animals, but in a well-balanced aquarium they are eventually converted into nitrates and thus cause no harm.

The swim bladder

Fish have a swim bladder, also known as an air bladder. This is an organ connected to the digestive system, which fills up with gas and helps fish to regulate their flotation when moving between two different types of water. They empty it to dive and fill it up when they need to come nearer the surface. Bottom-dwelling fish generally have a smaller swim bladder, or none at all, as they rarely swim in open water.

The reproductive organs

Males have two testicles that are linked to the vas deferens, while females have ovaries extended by the oviducts. In both cases the sexual products – the spermatozoa and ova – are expelled via the genital orifice. As the fertilization of the eggs is external and takes place in the water, there are no organs for coupling and fertilization, except in the case of livebearers.

Do fish recognize their owner?

Countless aquarists have noticed that some of their fishes react more enthusiastically to their presence than to that of strangers. If they do "recognize" the person who looks after them, how do they do it? They are capable of distinguishing the special characteristics of the vibrations caused by the footsteps of such and such person, which are transmitted to the water of the aquarium. Not only that, their sense of sight, although not perfect, helps them in this task of "recognition."

Which of the two recognizes the other first? ▶

Do fish sleep?

When an aquarium is abruptly switched on in the morning, it is noticeable that its occupants do not immediately resume their normal activity. Some of them are on the bottom of the tank, some in the plants, and others remain almost immobile in the water. It is difficult to speak of sleep in the generally accepted sense of the word, but it is certain that fish have periods of restfulness, of varying degrees. This can be verified at night, with the aid of a small flashlight: the fish are practically stationary (apart from nocturnal species), but their eyes are not closed as they have no eyelids.

Do they feel physical pain?

The sensation of pain is sent to the brain via the sensory nerves. As fish are endowed with the latter, it can be assumed that they feel pain when they are hit or wounded, and perhaps even when they are sick.

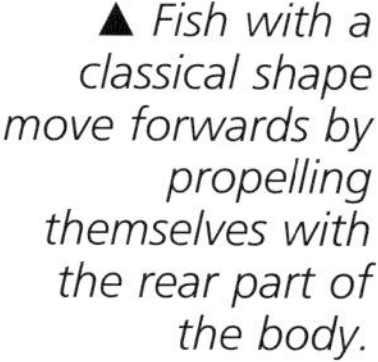

▲ Fish with a classical shape move forwards by propelling themselves with the rear part of the body.

Biology

Swimming

It is essentially the rear part of the body, particularly the caudal fin, which serves to propel the fish, while the other fins play a stabilizing and steering role. Of course, the more hydrodynamic a fish's form, the more it is capable of setting off abruptly and swimming quickly, indispensable for catching prey or fleeing an enemy.

Aquarists are sometimes advised not to let quick and lively fish (like Barbs) cohabit with slower and more placid species (like loaches), as the latter may be frustrated in their attempts to eat the food provided by their owner.

Behavior

Fishes' behavior in an aquarium reflects their lifestyle in a natural habitat, albeit modified by the fact that they are living in a more cramped environment, coming into contact with other species more quickly and easily. Fish from the same species can behave differently from one aquarium to another, according to the capacity and the other occupants.

- *Territorial behavior*

When fish are in their original biotope, their territorial behavior is reproduced in captivity, and is sometimes even intensified. A territory is a living space – either permanent or temporary (as in the reproduction period) – with an extension proportional to the size of the fish. Its occupant rebuffs individuals from the same species, from related species, or even from totally different ones. The surface area must be sufficient for the fish to find refuge, foodstuffs, and fish of the opposite sex with which to reproduce. With some fish, particularly marine species, it is important to plan a territory in the aquarium that will provide shelters and hideaways.

- *Group behavior*

Strength is to be found in unity, and living in a group permits a better defense against enemies. Indeed, from a distance a group or school of fish takes on the appearance of a mass that is capable of

Some fish live in groups, which makes it easier not only to defend themselves but also to reproduce. ▶

surprising and intimidating an enemy. Group life also facilitates reproduction, as an individual has a greater chance of finding a fish of the opposite sex. A group's unity and organization are governed by a series of signals which are invisible to human eyes: the use of the lateral line, for example, prevents fish from colliding with each other.

• *Dominance behavior*

The biggest members of a species dominate the smallest ones: when the latter get bigger they are ejected from the territory. Dominance behavior has practical and social implications, as the dominator will have priority in food and the choice of a fish of the opposite sex. At the bottom of the social ladder, the most dominated fish is permanently subject to aggression and harassment and has to hide most of the time, with its growth being prejudiced as a result. This is the case with some species of African Cichlids.

• *Prey-predator relationships*

Some fish feed on other smaller ones in a natural habitat, giving rise to incompatibilities in an aquarium: take care, for example, not to let South American Cichlids cohabit with Characins.

• *Aggression*

Sometimes an aquarium is a stage for aggression between different species. This aggression is always justified, as it is related to the defense of territory or offspring. It is a problem of space – these phenomena are rarely seen in big aquariums. However, a new fish introduced into a tank will often be considered as an intruder, or prey, and will be harassed.

Growth and longevity

Unlike human beings, fish continue to grow throughout their life, quickly at first, and then more slowly with age.

The size of fish in aquariums is mostly smaller than that found in the wild, undoubtedly as a result of the restricted living space at their disposal. This can easily be put to the test: an individual whose size has seemingly stabilized starts to grow if it is put into a bigger tank.

As regards longevity, this varies according to the species: a year, more or less, for the small species, and two to five years for the majority of fish. Some patriarchs live to the ripe old age of ten or more – these are large fish, particularly marine species. It is very difficult to postulate an optimal life span for a given species in captivity, as environmental conditions introduce too many variable factors.

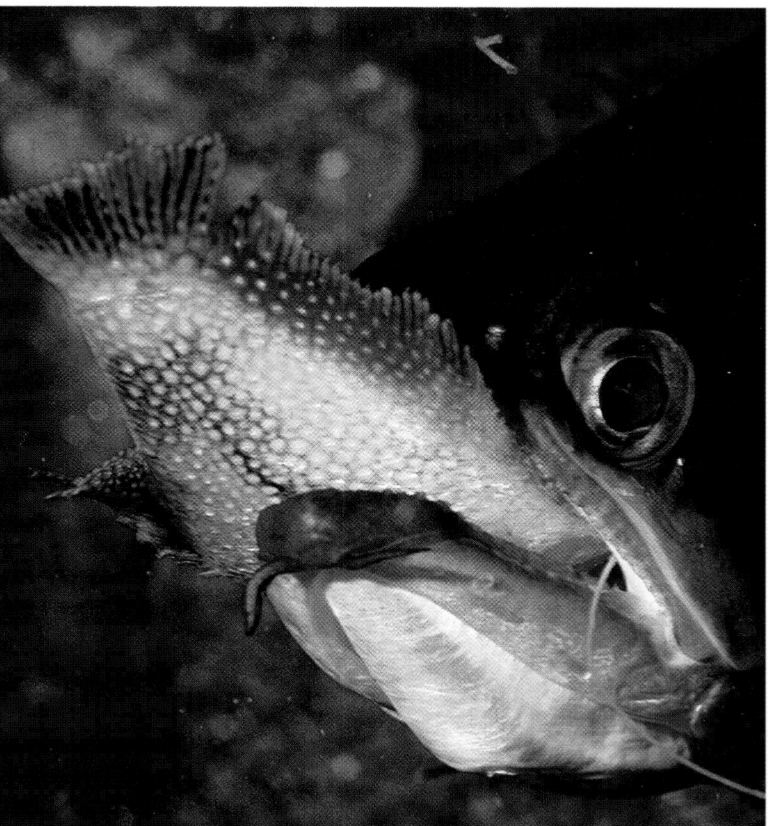

▲ *In nature, the biggest fish often feed on smaller ones – obviously something to avoid in an aquarium.*

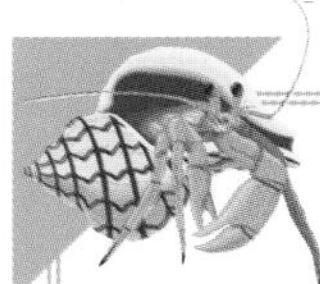

How to reduce acts of aggression in an aquarium?

Only put together those fish which are known to be compatible, particularly in the case of marine fish, and give them as much space as possible. Be sure to provide a number of nooks and crannies, appropriate for the dimensions of the residents. Another solution is to mix species with different lifestyles – for example, free swimmers (like Barbs and Danios) and bottom-dwellers (like loaches) – that will not compete with each other.

FEEDING

Food must provide fish with the elements needed to "build" their body (proteins) and the energy (from proteins, carbohydrates, and lipids) required for its smooth functioning. Feeding a fish properly ensures that it will grow satisfactorily, as well as facilitating its reproduction and helping it to combat disease. Quality and quantity are two important concepts in feeding: an aquarist must learn to avoid over-feeding and to diversify the food supply.

DIETS AND NUTRITIONAL REQUIREMENTS

With regard to fishes' feeding habits and dietary requirements, there are three main groups:
– carnivores, which feed on worms, crustaceans, insects, or other fish;
– herbivores, with a diet mainly comprising vegetable matter (plants, algae) which they graze or grind;
– omnivores, which have a very varied diet as they eat both animal prey and vegetable matter.

In practice, diets are not always so easy to define. In a natural setting fish eat what they find, and so sometimes a herbivore will eat a small animal taking shelter in the plants that it normally eats.

Carnivorous fish mainly require proteins and lipids, while herbivores have a special need for carbohydrates, and omnivores demand a mixture of proteins, carbohydrates, and lipids.

Bearing in mind the limitations of these definitions, all three diets can be found among those given to aquarium fish, although there are some exceptions.

The aquarist should also take care that vitamins and mineral salts form part of a varied and balanced diet, especially through the addition of fresh or live food.

A wide palette of foodstuffs stimulates the growth and reproduction of the aquarium's inhabitants and strengthens their resistance against disease. As such, it is the best precaution that can be taken against disappointing results and lack of success.

FOOD PORTIONS

There is a tendency to overfeed aquarium fish and produce some rather flabby specimens. Moreover, there is an increased risk of pollution in a confined space: the more a fish eats, the more it excretes nitrogenous substances, and that is without counting the foodstuffs that quickly decompose in the water in the aquarium.

An adult fish only eats 1 or 2% of its own body weight per day, although a juvenile consumes twice that amount. Very light flakes involve little risk of overdosing, in contrast with other foodstuffs which can sometimes slip out of the hand. Whenever possible, it is advisable to divide the daily input into separate portions, twice a day for adults, more often for fry.

As fish in their natural habitat are unlikely to eat regularly every day, most aquarium fish will therefore cope well with a short-term fast. Some aquarists impose a one-day fast per week to compensate for the likelihood that the fish have been overfed on the other days. Fasting is however not suitable for fry as it may slow their growth considerably.

Specialist aquarium stores supply artificial fish food in a variety of forms and sizes. ▶

▲ *Flakes of vegetable matter.*

Artificial Food

This is dry food which is commercially widely available in specialist aquarium stores.

In the last twenty years the entire range has diversified considerably, and today there is a wide variety, adapted to the needs of different groups of fishes: for juvenile and adult fish, for freshwater and seawater fish, etc. These foodstuffs are characterized by a high level of proteins (generally 40–50%) and come in different forms: in flakes (the most common), granulated, or compressed.

The flakes float for a while before they sink, which makes them easier to grasp for surface and open-water fish. There are obviously also different sizes of foodstuffs, according to the size of the fish's mouth. This artificial food is fragile and deteriorates if it is not kept in the correct conditions. It must therefore be stored in a dry place protected from the light. Its composition is only guaranteed for a certain period, so it is advisable to buy a small box if you have only one aquarium and a few fish.

Some aquarists do not hesitate to give their residents trout food, which they buy at fish farms. This food is very rich in proteins and lipids, thus ensuring the rapid growth of trout bred for eating, but this is not vital in aquariums. Although such food contains pigments intended to change the flesh color of salmon fish, aquarists who have used it have not reported any modifications in the external color of their fish. In any case, this food can prove very economical for large-scale breeding or garden ponds.

Marine fish sometimes refuse artificial food, either for a short period after their introduction to the aquarium, or on a permanent basis. One trick is to progressively incorporate increasing amounts of commercial food along with fresh food or live prey. This gradually accustoms the fish to its smell and taste until they finally accept it on its own.

▲ *Flakes for guppies.*

◄ *Flakes for adult herbivores.*

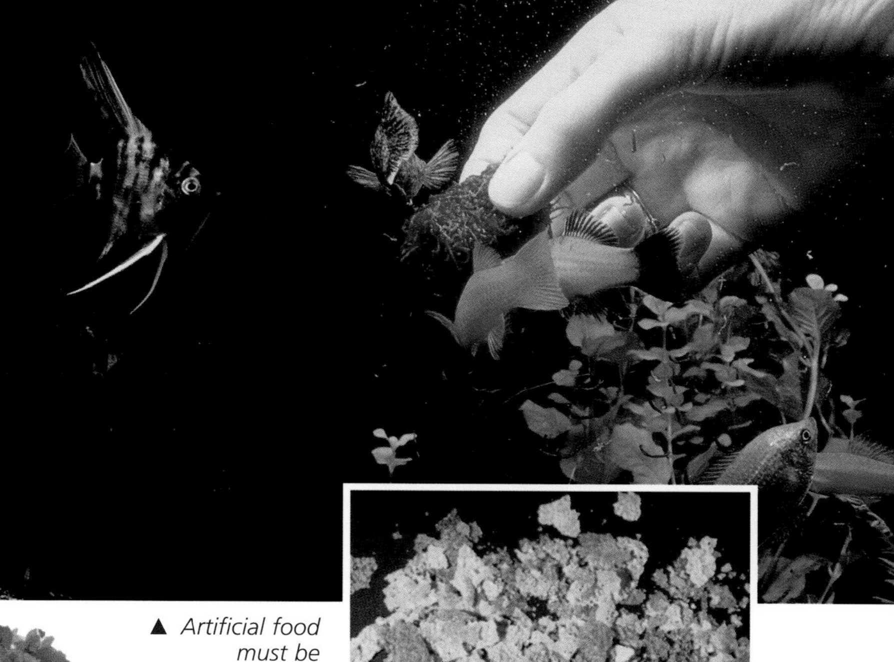

▲ *Artificial food must be complemented with live prey or fresh food.*

◄ ▲ *Typical artificial food for adults.*

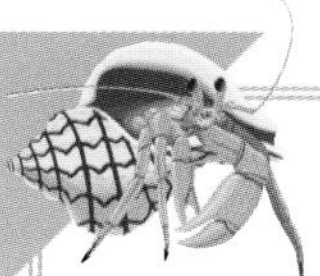

Different Types of Food for Aquarium Fish

The artificial foodstuffs currently on the market are very effective for aquarium fish. In order to cover their needs as fully as possible, fish can also be served small, live prey, which are similarly available commercially and are an important source of vitamins and mineral salts. There are other possible options: white meat and mussels, for example.

◀ *Artificial food in the form of tablets.*

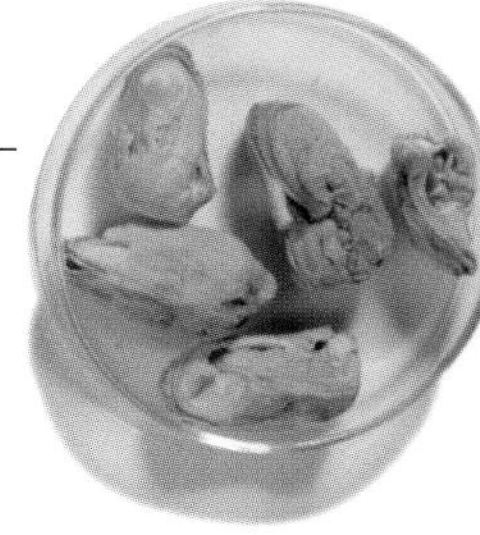

Freeze-dried mussels. ▲

◀ *Beef heart, similarly freeze-dried.*

FOODSTUFFS OF NATURAL ORIGIN

Freeze-dried food

It is possible to buy freeze-dried food items – small animals, shrimps, worms, or plankton – in which the water content has been greatly reduced so that they can be preserved more effectively. This treatment does clearly make them expensive, but they are at least as nourishing as flakes and very popular with fish. They must be stored in a dry place. Feed them to the fish according to the manufacturer's directions and do not exceed the quantities recommended.

▲ *Frozen food: crab and phytoplankton.*

Frozen food

Frozen products – shrimps, fish, worms, and plankton – can also be used, once they have been separated and rinsed. They have a very high nutritional value, as freezing does not modify their composition. They are obviously stored in the freezer and must not be refrozen after thawing, in order to reduce the risk of microbial contamination. They are more expensive than freeze-dried foodstuffs.

◀ *Cubes of freeze-dried tubifex worms.*

Domestic food items

Finally, domestic food can be provided fresh or after freezing and thawing. It is best to avoid red meats as they have too much fat. Beef heart, rich in both blood and lipids, can only be given only to large fish. White meats are preferable: chicken, turkey, or ham. As for seafood, white fish can be used – although it must be handled with care, as it can break up in the water – as well as mussels, cockles, and shrimps, which can be bought preserved naturally. Vegetables are sometimes needed for herbivorous fish: lettuce or spinach that has been blanched, i.e. put into boiling water for a few minutes.

▲ *Freeze-dried shrimps.*

VITAMINS

Vitamins are just as important in a fish's diet as in that of a human being. They play a role in the formation of the skeleton, enhance growth, and strengthen resistance to disease. A fish which suffers from vitamin deficiency becomes weak, although this is not visible at first.

Vitamins do not keep well as they deteriorate under the influence of heat, oxygen, and light. This is why aquarium fishes' vitamin supply mainly comes in the form of fresh food, live prey, or frozen products.

Live prey

These are ideal food items for carnivorous fish: they retain all their nutritional value and move around to attract the fish. They are a problem to keep as they only last a few days, but they can be frozen.

► *Frozen smelts.*

Dried daphnias

These were once very popular – so many aquarists have started with them! Nowadays they are out of fashion; in fact they are not the ideal food for fish and it is best not to use them. More complete and suitable products, particularly those in the form of flakes, are now available, even for goldfish.

Live prey and home preparations

The artificial food on the market these days is very effective for aquarium fish. To diversify and balance their requirements, they can also be served some of the small, live prey that are commercially available – an important supply of vitamins and mineral salts – or fresh food or homemade mixtures.

One of the best fresh foods: mussels

This mollusk, prized by humans, is equally appreciated by fish, especially those marine species that refuse artificial food. Widely available, inexpensive, easy to freeze, mussels are a top-class dish: they are rich in proteins and carbohydrates, with few lipids. Furthermore, they contain many minerals (such as calcium, phosphorus, magnesium, iron) and even vitamin C, which plays an important role in the fight against disease. Mussels must be well cooked before using and their shells and connective filaments removed. Cut them into pieces before distributing or freezing them.

Homemade food

An aquarist can easily make his or her own fish food – the possibilities are enormous. The following recipe is just one of many.

Take some cooked white meat (chicken, turkey, ham) and some seafood (mussels, cockles), also cooked, and mince them with a little water to make a homogenous paste. A vitamin supplement, available from aquarium stores, can be added during this process.

This mixture can then be mixed with gelatin (from a sachet of powder, for example) so that the paste does not break up in the water, as this may become a source of pollution. One portion can be distributed immediately, while the rest can easily be frozen in ice trays. The models designed for small ice cubes are particularly recommended for making a large number of small portions. Once frozen, they can be slipped out of the ice trays and bagged up in freezer bags for use as required.

▲ *Cooked mussels, frozen or otherwise, provide both practical and nourishing fare.*

Bloodworms

In fact, these are not worms but the aquatic larvae of various species of non-biting mosquitoes. They are also commonly used as bait in fishing. Although it is sometimes thought that they live in mud, they are actually found in the water of areas that are well endowed with organic matter. It is useless trying to collect them yourself, but they are sold in the aquarium trade. They keep for a few days in the refrigerator, wrapped in moist newspaper. They are a good source of nutrition, as they are rich in protein.

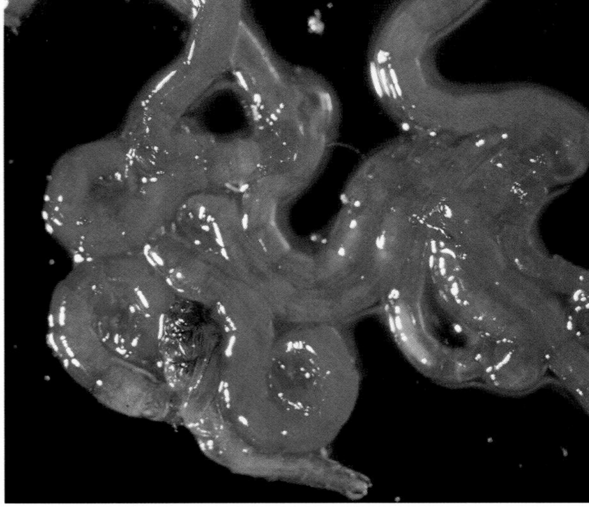

▲ *Rich in proteins, bloodworms are a prey much appreciated by carnivorous fish.*

Tubifex worms

These are worms that are gathered from the mud in environments rich in organic matter. Some people think that they represent a risk when they are introduced into an aquarium, as they may carry undesirable bacteria.
This risk is very slight, however, and there have been no reports of any serious incidents. The specimens which are commercially available can be kept for a few days in the refrigerator, in domestic water, but it is essential that this water is changed every day.

Tubifex in a natural setting. ►

Shrimps

Flowing and well-oxygenated fresh water are home to small river shrimps of up 2 cm that swim along the banks. These are rarely sold live, but they can be found in a freeze-dried form. You will find that your fish will definitely enjoy them.
The small marine shrimps found on some coasts are also highly prized, especially by marine fish. These are often sold in fishing stores along the coast. If you are lucky enough to live in such an area, you can also collect them yourself and keep them in an well oxygenated seawater aquarium. Both types of shrimps can be frozen after being cooked and rinsed under the faucet, or they can also be ground and turned into a homemade dish (see box, page 53).

Tubifex worms can be distributed to fish by means of a special accessory. ▼

◄ *Coastal shrimps, live or cooked, are recommended fare for big fish.*

Small fish

Either fry or small fish can be used to feed marine fish doubtful about artificial food, or large freshwater fish. With this in mind, some aquarists breed prolific species that reproduce easily (Poeciliids, for example).

Other live prey (larger than 1 cm)

Keeping and breeding worms or insect larvae is also possible, though it sometimes proves time-consuming. The range of live prey listed above is adequate for the needs of your fish.

Planktonic food

Freshwater or marine plankton contain a host of organisms barely visible to the naked eye (0.1–1 cm) but valuable for feeding fish, especially the fry. Collecting them in a natural setting is tiresome, and involves a risk of introducing potential microscopic hosts into the aquarium and spreading disease. Some planktonic food is available on the market in frozen form.

Brine shrimps

This is the "magic" food that every aquarist should breed. This primitive crustacean grows to 1 cm when adult and is called *Artemia salina*.

They live in the heavily saline waters of salt marshes, feeding on the micro-algae that they gather with their filtering legs. Their characteristic most relevant to the aquarist is that their eggs can be stored dry, with their development interrupted, for use later on. Once the eggs are returned to salty water, they hatch rapidly and

Artemia salina *(Brine shrimp) nauplii (below): these are indispensable for feeding the fry of most species of fish.* ◄ ▼

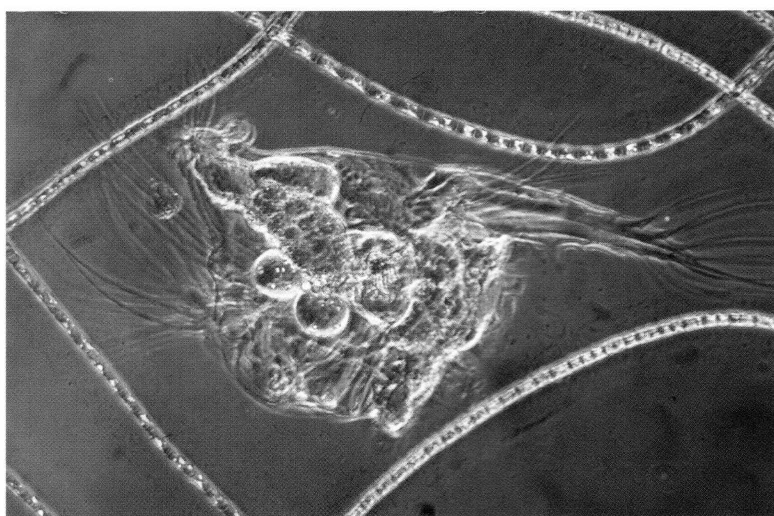

▲ *Some clubs breed rotifers, vital food for the fry of marine fish, especially clownfish.*

produce a larva called a nauplius, which measures only 0.3 mm and is particularly suitable for feeding to fry.
Feeding brine shrimps to fish is easy, even for an amateur (see box). They are still too big for the fry of some fish, however, especially marine species. In such cases, it is possible to use rotifers, animals halfway between worms and crustaceans, which have a crustacean-like shell and never grow to more than 0.2 mm.

Rotifers

These are more complicated to breed than brine shrimps, as they must be fed planktonic micro-algae which also need to be cultivated. It is therefore best to obtain them from a laboratory specializing in oceanography or marine biology, and to get advice on the essential steps required to look after them for a few days – the time within which the fry for which they are intended will be big enough and sufficiently developed to move on to a diet of brine shrimp nauplii.

Copepods, among the constituents of natural marine plankton, form the basis of the diet of certain fish. ▼

Food distribution

When they are healthy and well adjusted to captivity, fish eat at a regular time and become accustomed to the spot where the food is given out. It is advisable to divide the daily ration into two parts – one in the morning and one in the evening, for example. The end of the day – 1 or 2 hours before turning the aquarium lighting off – is usually the most practical for the aquarist. In any event, food distribution offers a special opportunity to observe the behavior of your residents and check their state of health. Allowing the fish to come and feed out of your hand is particularly enjoyable, but take care, because some large specimens have impressive teeth!
If the water is too agitated, artificial or natural food may be dispersed too quickly and washed to a corner of the aquarium where the fish will not be able to recover it, thereby creating a potential for pollution. The stirring of the water must therefore cease when food is being distributed and eaten.

Feeding the fry

When they are born, the fry of egg-laying fish feed on the reserves in their vitellin vesicle, as their mouth does not open until a few days later. They will then often accept the fine powders which are available commercially.
If this is not the case, give them brine shrimp nauplii for a few days – newly hatched nauplii are most suitable for the first two days. After that, they can be offered nauplii that are 48 hours old.
Daily production over a period of several days must therefore be planned for. If brine

Breeding brine shrimps

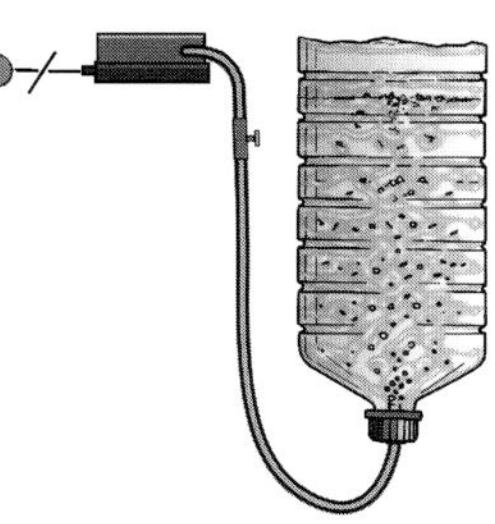

▲ *Hatching brine shrimp eggs in gently stirred water.*

The dry eggs (known as cysts) are available in aquarium supply stores. They must be kept away from light and moisture. In order to make them hatch, salt water must be prepared with the following characteristics: temperature 25°C, salinity 35%, i.e. a specific gravity of 1.023.

The salt water can be natural or reconstituted with special aquarium salts, or even with rough kitchen salt (easier for aquarists who do not keep marine fish). The water can be colder and less salty (up to 20°C and 20%, i.e. a specific gravity of 1.014), but the hatching rate will be lower (50–60% against 80–90%). Any small glass or PVC container can be used – bottles, for example – although specialist equipment is available. The eggs are placed in the still water for a quarter of an hour, the time required for their rehydration. If we estimate that 250,000 eggs weigh around 1 g, a tiny amount (the tip of a knife, for example) will produce sufficient brine shrimps. Aerate the water slightly to produce small bubbles, which will disperse the eggs, but be careful not to stir the water too vigorously, otherwise some of the eggs will crash against the sides of the container and will not hatch. The hatching occurs after 24–36 hours at 25°C, or after up to 48 hours at 20°C. Finally, switch off the aeration: the empty shells will float to the surface, the unhatched eggs will fall to the bottom, and the brine shrimp nauplii will be swimming just under the surface. It is then easy to siphon them off (with an aeration pipe, for example) and strain them through a small filter (available commercially), or, alternatively, through the thin mesh of a piece of old curtain, or even a very fine pantyhose. To make this operation easier, you can group the nauplii together using a flashlight, as they are attracted by light. You can then go on to feed them to the fry. They will only survive for a few minutes outside salted water, and they will not eat on the first day after hatching. If you want to keep them for several days to obtain larger or more mature larvae, special food is commercially available. This makes it possible to keep brine shrimps until they are adults.

▲ *Equipment available in aquarium stores for hatching brine shrimps.*

▲ *Collecting brine shrimp nauplii through siphoning.*

Adult brine shrimps

Adult brine shrimps are sold live in small sealed sachets containing salt water and air. They are passed through a sieve before being given to the fish, which enjoy hunting them down. They survive for a few minutes in unsalted water. Brine shrimps can also be bought frozen.

◄ *When feeding, it is important to avoid any overdosing, whether with artificial food or live prey, such as the adult brine shrimps pictured here.*

shrimps are unavailable, another option is the production of infusorians. Live-bearing fish (the Poeciliid family) accept artificial food from birth, and they also thrive on brine shrimp nauplii. As for marine fish, rotifers, discussed above, should be used, as they easily fit into the small mouths of the fry.

◄ ▼ *Automatic food distributor for artificial food. Each section corresponds to a daily dose.*

Infusorians

These are microscopic, unicellular animals, easy to produce in fresh water. They are usually present in small numbers in an aquarium.
Riccia, a surface plant, gives them a chance to grow, as they find food (organic matter) on its leaves. They can also be produced by leaving a piece of potato, a lettuce leaf, or some paddy rice (unhusked rice, available in grain stores) to soak in a receptacle containing aquarium water.

What if a fish does not eat?

Sometimes a fish refuses to eat, or appears to be incapable of doing so. It is therefore a question of finding the cause and eliminating it. A newcomer to a tank rarely eats on the first day. This is normal, as it feels lost in its new environment. Small species and more lethargic fish are often dominated by their bigger and faster cohabitants at feeding time. They must therefore always be fed separately, preferably with mobile, live prey, once the other fish have been distracted by other food.
A fish can also refuse to eat if it is sick, and this will be reflected in its behavior, color, and other symptoms which may eventually be seen on its body. In this situation it must be isolated in another aquarium, treated, and given rich food,

▲ *In captivity, the fry can be fed with brine shrimp nauplii and then with fine commercial powders.*

Golden rules for feeding

– Give fish a varied diet;
– give them a little, but often. Two portions a day is ideal. For fry, the feeding can be more frequent.
– do not wait until the fish are sated and stop eating. Stop feeding once the ration is complete;
– siphon off any food surplus as quickly as possible, as the leftovers are pollutants.

▲ *Paddy rice can be used to produce infusorians. It is "sown" on the bed or placed in a tubifex worm "feeder".*

comprised of live prey or fresh produce. Sometimes fish can systematically refuse to eat artificial food, although this is rare in fresh water, but less so in marine aquariums. There is no point in being stubborn: change to a varied diet based on live prey and homemade fare.

▲ *Preparing defrosted food before feeding it to large fish.*

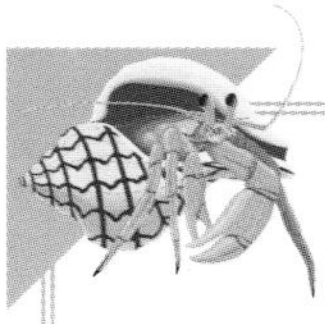

A MIRACLE FOOD FOR FRY

A hard-boiled egg yolk is added to water in a glass. This forms microparticles which are then sieved.
This nutritious liquid is then given to the fry, taking care not to put too much into the tank, as it is always important to minimize pollution. Egg yolk, rich in proteins and lipids, can be used as a complement or as a replacement for other food.

▼ *Some aquarists use oysters to nourish their fish, which seem to enjoy them.*

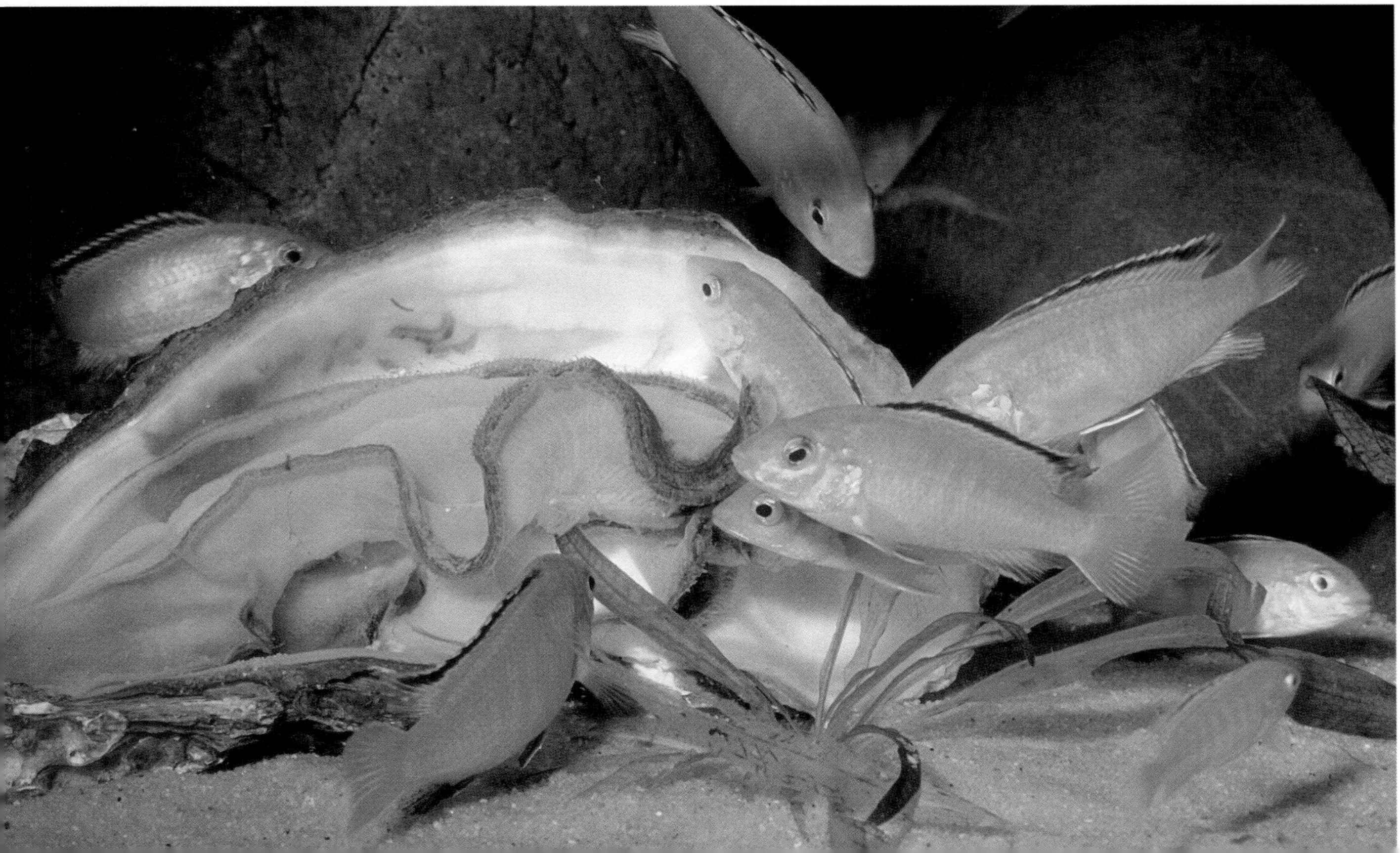

REPRODUCTION

In the world's temperate regions, the reproduction of fish generally depends on the season: in other words, it is determined by the temperature. There is only one high season, during which a species usually reproduces only once. In a tropical setting, where variations in temperature are less important, other factors influence on reproduction, especially rain. Fish can lay eggs several times a year, at intervals of sometimes less than a month.

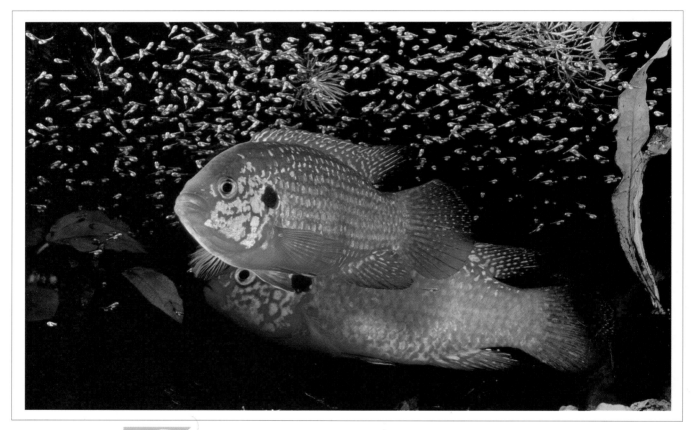

▲*Pair of* Hemichromis bimaculatus *(jewel cichlid) surrounded by their young.*

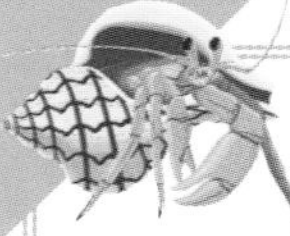

THE KEYS TO SUCCESSFUL REPRODUCTION

– Have well-fed and healthy parents.
– Provide them with the best possible environment:
  • a rearing tank;
  • high-quality water, with characteristics as close as possible to their native setting.
– Anticipate how you are going to feed the fry.

GENERAL PRINCIPLES

Most fish kept by aquarists are oviparous (egg-layers), but there are some exceptions – viviparous fish (or livebearers).
A varied and rich diet enables fish to accumulate reserves of proteins and lipids, which help them form eggs and spermatozoa. This is the maturing phase. When the female's ovary swells, she is ready to lay eggs. This only needs a stimulus to trigger it off, such as, in the natural setting, rain, sunlight, or moonlight (research is presently in progress on the influence of

the moon on reproduction). In an aquarium, egg-laying is sometimes sparked off by the early morning sunlight, which beats down on the tank with varying degrees of intensity, or by a partial change of water.
The laying of eggs can be preceded by a courting ritual, during which the male seduces the female or, in rare cases, bullies her and violently sees off any rivals. The female then expels her eggs into the water, and these are immediately fertilized by the male.
This is obviously only a general description that leaves room for the huge diversity found in aquarium fish, particularly as regards the future fate of the eggs: they can be abandoned, or even sometimes eaten, by their parents, or they can be guarded and defended in the first days of their life, and a similar variety of parental behavior is found in the treatment of the developing fry.
The incubation of the eggs, which lasts several days, sees the development of the embryo. When this is completely formed, it moves about until it breaks the egg's membrane: this is the hatching. A larva emerges, differing from an adult in its form, size, and the proportion of certain organs. The larva has highly developed eyes, for instance, allowing it to spot its prey. It also has a vitellin vesicle, which provides it with food reserves during the first days following its emergence from the egg (except in livebearers of the Poeciliid family).
The larva gradually evolves, over the course of a few days or weeks, depending on the species, and modifies its behavior to become more and more like an adult. It turns into fry.

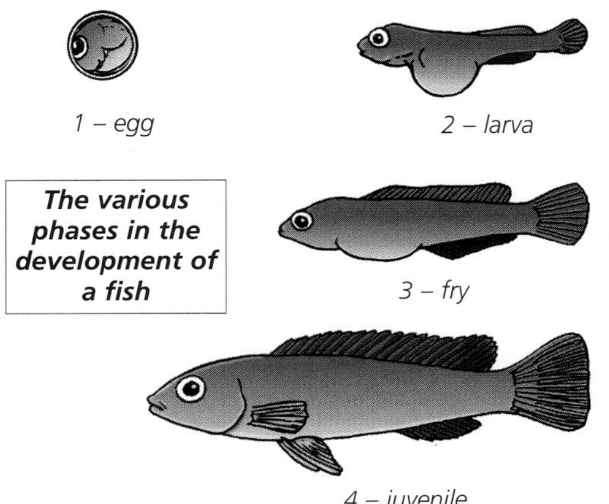

The various phases in the development of a fish

The gender of fish

In theory, this is a simple matter: there are males and females. In practice, the situation is sometimes less clear, especially in marine fish. In fact, some species can change sex: this is known as successive hermaphroditism, and can be seen in groupers, *Anthias*, rainbow wrasses, and some Labrids, which are first female and then male. Clownfish present male characteristics when they are young, but they cannot reproduce at this stage. When they mature they become either a fertile male, or a female. As these are species in which individuals live alone, changes in sex increase the probability of forming a pair. This phenomenon has a similar basis in those species which adopt the harem system, i.e. a male living with several females: if he should die, one of the females can become a male to ensure the continuing survival of the group as a whole.

◄ Some fish lay their eggs on a horizontal support, then ventilate and protect them from the rapaciousness of other species.

The vitellin sack of these 15-day-old larvae has been practically all used up. ▼

The vitellin sack

The vitellin sac, or vitellin vesicle, constitutes the fish larva's food reserves in the first days of its life. It derives from the vitellin of the egg – the equivalent of the yolk in poultry – accumulated by the female over the course of the maturing process. It is sent along the blood vessels, which distribute these reserves around the body of the larva. This allows it to survive until it is able to catch prey itself, i.e. a few days after emerging from the egg.

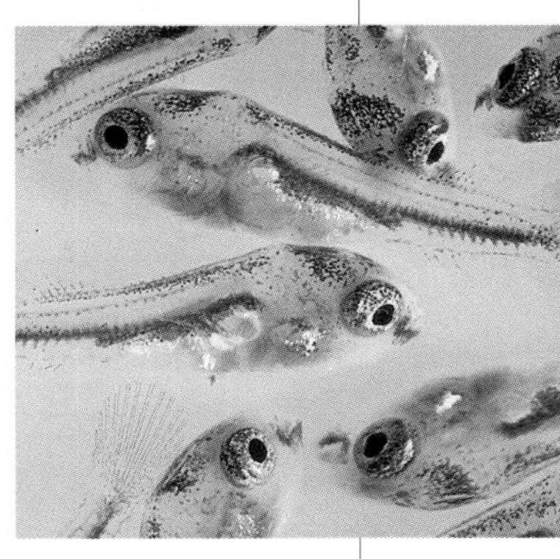

THE REARING TANK

This is normally modest in size, as it is used to isolate a pair of reproducing fish and their future offspring. There is no need for a bed, except for some species (the Cichlasomas, for example). A rearing tank must be heated but only moderately filtered. Avoid any systems which may "swallow" the eggs and the fry. Aeration is not obligatory. Fill the tank with water taken from the parents' aquarium, which can then be gradually modified to obtain the precise characteristics required by the reproducing fish (pH and hardness). A support should be provided for the egg-laying, and this can be either natural (plants, rocks) or artificial (PVC). More detailed information on this subject, family by family, can be found below.

This female Cichlid, which incubates her eggs in her mouth, finds greater peace in a rearing tank. ►

REPRODUCTION STRATEGIES

Reproduction ensures the survival of a species, and nature has planned several strategies for it. In the case of small eggs produced in large quantities, these are often transparent, in an attempt to hide them from their predators.

As for large eggs, if there are only a few their parents protect them most of the time. In both cases, the aim is to reduce the number of losses as far as possible. In an aquarium, the intervention of the fish-keeper considerably increases the chances of success, and the survival and proliferation of a species is normally guaranteed.

Sometimes reproduction takes place in a communal tank, catching the aquarist unawares. ▼

Reproduction techniques for aquariums

These vary according to the different families of fishes, and they will be discussed in greater detail in the "Catalogs of Fishes" (pages 75 and 126). However, it is possible to advance some general precepts on the subject here.

Choosing the reproduction site

Reproduction can occur spontaneously in a mixed tank, or in a specialized or "regional" aquarium. This often happens with novice aquarists, unaccustomed to spotting the approach of egg-laying in a female. In such cases the future of the fry is a matter of chance. Some of them will serve as prey for the other inhabitants of the tank, and the survivors are sure to have problems in getting enough to eat, since they have to compete with adults.

This is why it is advisable to use a tank specially intended for reproduction.

Choosing the reproducing fish

Although it is sometimes difficult, at the best of times, to distinguish between males and females, it is easy enough to spot a female's swollen stomach and the attentions bestowed on her by one or several males – signs of the approach of the mating season.

It is therefore time to transfer the fish in question into the rearing tank prepared for this purpose.

▲ *The selection and feeding of the parents are important factors in successful breeding. Here, a pair of* Colisa lalia, *the male is on the right.*

Caring for the parents

Successful reproduction depends on the good health of the reproducing fish, and to achieve this they have to remain undisturbed, and therefore isolated, in a rearing tank. Their feeding is especially important, as the quality of the eggs, and above all that of the vitellin, depends on it. Fresh food, particularly live prey, must be provided, with an emphasis on variety. Although artificial food can be used as a substitute, it must never constitute the basic diet.

Egg-laying

One encouragement for egg-laying is light, whether it is the morning sun or the aquarium's artificial lighting. Also, if you think that your fish are taking a long time to lay, you can change around 10% of the water volume, and this may provide them with the stimulus they need.

Fish with free or non-adherent eggs

When the eggs fall to the bed, they must be protected from the voracity of other fish – and this can be done in a normal aquarium. There are a couple of ruses that are useful in this situation:

– divide the aquarium into two horizontal sections by means of a grille which only lets through the eggs;

– cover the bed of the aquarium with glass marbles – the eggs will slide between them and can easily be recovered by siphoning them off.

◄ ▼ *There are several tricks for shielding the eggs from the voracity of their parents: the grille system (A) and glass marbles (B).*

Most fish that produce free eggs do not take care of them, and the parent fish must therefore be removed from the tank to ensure that they do not devour them. There are some species within the Cyprinodontid family whose eggs can survive outside water, provided they are kept within a moist environment.

Semi-natural reproduction

Semi-natural reproduction can be carried out with those fish which normally live in groups and do not form stable pairs, such as the Characins. A group of ten can be inserted into a rearing tank adjusted to their requirements and left to reproduce. There are then two possible scenarios:

– the adult fish are removed and the aquarist looks after the fry;

– the adults and the fry are left together, so hiding places must be provided for the young – plants on the water surface, rocks, etc. The fry are not moved until they measure 5–10 mm, when they are transferred to another tank to grow into adults. The remaining adults can reproduce again as soon as the maturing phase has passed. The advantage of this method is its relative ease: one or several pairs are allowed to form and they can reproduce whenever they want. Leaving them with the eggs and fry allows a type of natural selection to come into play, whereby only the strongest and most agile will be able to escape the predatory instincts of their parents.

◄ *The semi-natural reproduction method can be used for neons* (Paracheirodon innesi).

◄ *Fish which lay non-adhesive eggs deposit them on a support (above), in a natural or artificial cavity (center), or in a depression hollowed out of the sediment (below).*

Fish with adhesive eggs

Fish such as the Characins that do not look after their offspring lay them on fine-leaved plants (like *Myriophyllum* and *Cabomba*), which you should make available in the aquarium. Alternatively, it is possible to use a web made of Perlon wool, which is commercially available for use in filters. This provides a very good artificial support. The parents must be removed after the eggs are laid.

Some species not only look after their eggs, but also sometimes their fry. Some, such as the scalares, lay their eggs on a plant with hard leaves, while others, such as certain American Cichlids, do so on a vertical or horizontal rock face. An artificial laying support can also be provided, by using a PVC tube or plate, for example.

Other Cichlids – Africans from Lake Tanganyika or Americans, such as species of the *Apistogramma* genus – lay their eggs in a cavity or small cave, sometimes even on the ceiling, if this is the only suitable place. In all cases where the eggs are laid on a rigid support, this is generally cleaned by one of the parents before the female deposits the eggs that the male will go on to fertilize.

The male will then defend the site against any possible enemies, while the female ventilates the eggs with her fins. There are some occasions when the parents swap roles, and others when one of the two even separates out dead eggs, distinguishable by their opaque white color.

The fry are then supervised by their parents until they are independent.

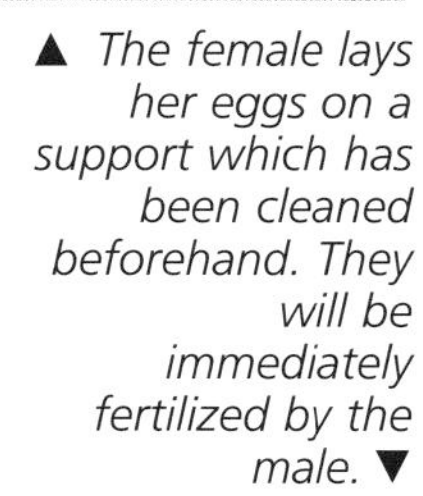

▲ *The female lays her eggs on a support which has been cleaned beforehand. They will be immediately fertilized by the male.* ▼

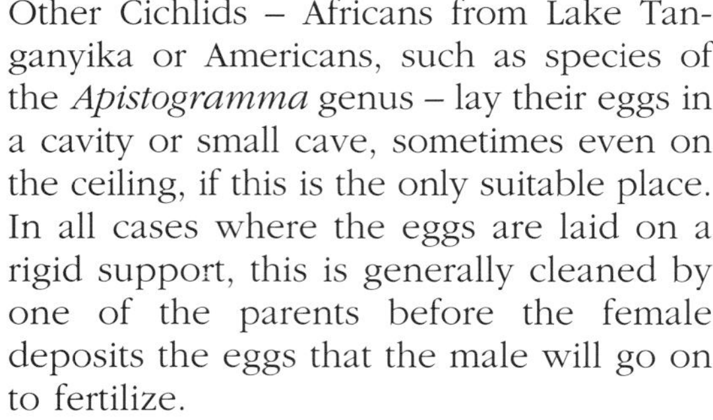

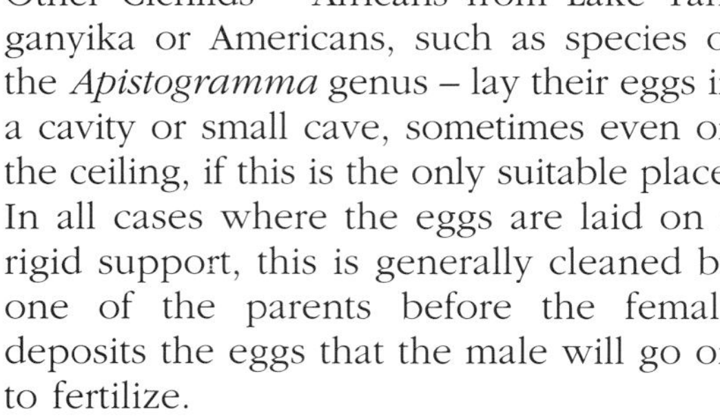

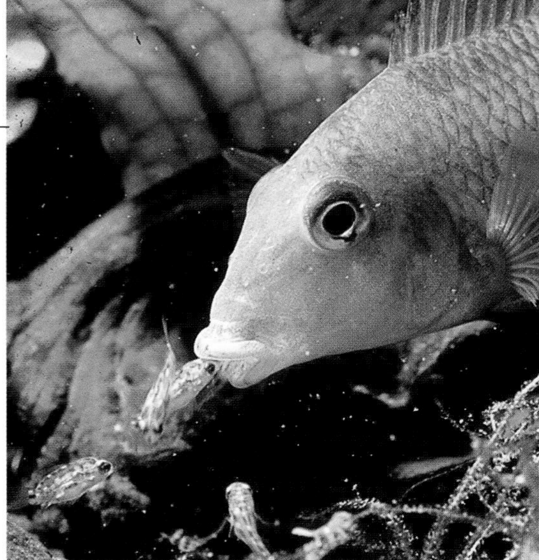

▲ *In the case of Cichlids that use oral incubation, the fry can return to the shelter of the female's mouth (here* Geophagus steindachneri*).*

Mouth brooding

This reproduction technique, used in particular by the African Cichlids in Lake Malawi, ensures a noteworthy survival rate for the eggs and fry, both in the wild and in the aquarium.

The males, generally more intensely colored than the females, have small, brightly colored patches on the anal fin. The female lays the eggs on the bed and immediately gathers them up in her mouth. Nearby, the male flaunts his anal fin and rolls around on the spot. The female then tries to grab the patches at the same time as the male ejects his sperm, which the female inhales. The fertilization therefore takes place inside her mouth.

The embryos develop for 1–3 weeks and during that time the female does not eat. The swelling formed by the eggs in her "throat" is clearly visible. She moves the eggs around in her mouth in order to help them to hatch.

The fry gradually emerge from their mother's mouth, but dart back inside at the slightest sign of danger, and the mother continues to take care of them until they can look after themselves. This technique means that these fish can reproduce in a mixed tank. However, it is

▲ *The fry can return to the shelter of the female's mouth, although this is very unusual if she is isolated in a rearing aquarium.*

possible to remove the female delicately and, with great care, make her "spit out" her fry in order to raise them in another tank separately.

The bubble nest

Fish from the Belontiid family construct a nest of bubbles under the surface of the water, where the oxygen concentration is higher, compensating for the low oxygenation in their living environment. This refuge also affords the fry a certain degree of protection.

The male builds the nest by taking in air at the surface and forming bubbles that are stuck together with his saliva. Then he sets out to seduce the female, clasping her near the nest and fertilizing the eggs she lays, before putting them into the nest with his mouth. This operation is repeated several times. The male then repulses the female, sometimes with great violence – in which case she must be removed from the aquarium to protect her from his aggression – and he watches over the nest. After hatching, the fry stay inside for a few days, and then they disperse. The male must be removed, as he is capable of eating them.

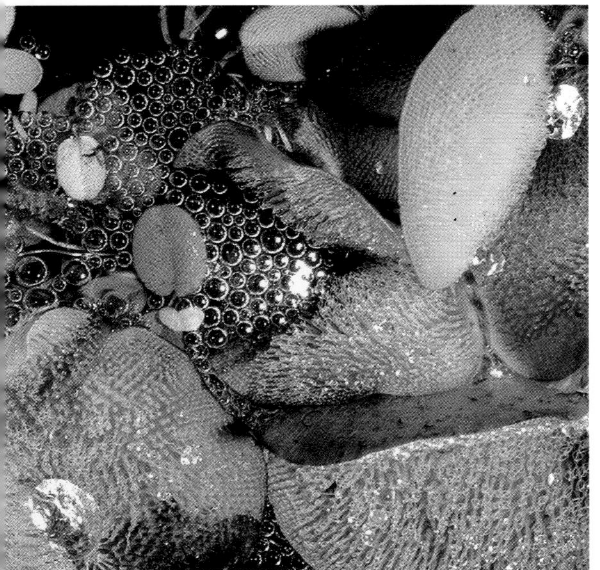

◄ *Bubble nest built by a male* Colisa lalia *(Belontiids) on the surface of the water.*

And if it doesn't work out?

You have selected one or several pairs for reproduction, carefully placed them in a rearing tank, and ... nothing happens!
There could be a number of reasons for this:
– The fish do not lay eggs. Maybe they do not find each other attractive? Put in some different couples, or several males for one female.
– The eggs have been laid, but they do not hatch. Perhaps they have not been fertilized by the male, or maybe the fertilization has indeed taken place, but it is the quality of the water which has caused the failure, its characteristics being unsuitable for the incubation of the eggs.
– You have obtained fry, but they quickly die. This is undoubtedly the result of an inadequate diet. Also, sometimes the parents may not show any interest in their eggs and neglect to ventilate them. In this case remove the fish, place a low output diffuser near the eggs to replace the parents, and take out any dead eggs.
In any event, do not despair. Closely observe the behavior of your fish, and always have a rearing tank handy – as well as food for any future fry that may be produced.

Livebearers

These do not lay eggs; instead, the latter develop and hatch in the female's abdomen. The fry are therefore born alive and completely formed, and they immediately start to search actively for their own food. This type of reproduction is found in only a few fish families, such as the Poeciliids, so these are sometimes considered to be more highly evolved than other families of fish.

Marine fish

Few marine species reproduce regularly in aquariums. Apart from the clownfish and other related species, any success is an exception. Scientific research in this field still has a great deal of ground to cover. The use of hormones, widespread in fish farming, is proving promising, but unfortunately it is not as yet an option open to amateurs.

The different phases of reproduction in Belontiids: construction of the bubble nest by the male (the female is in a separate compartment), the laying of eggs, the removal of the female. ▼

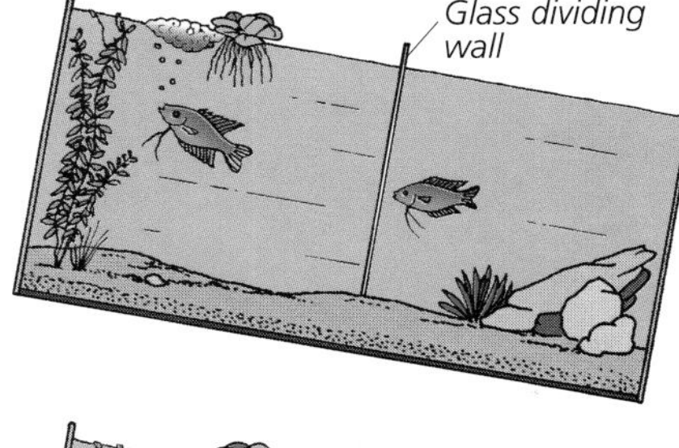

HEALTH

The aquarist must learn how to detect signs of ill health, and above all establish good habits as regards tank maintenance and food hygiene, in order to prevent disease. A fish can not only fall sick, but can also be a carrier of a disease without actually being sick itself – then it is known as a healthy carrier. The disease will appear under certain conditions or will be passed on to its companions.

The origin of diseases

The origin of a disease can be outside the aquarium

– the introduction of a fish stressed by importation, or by the living conditions at a retail store; it can fall sick and contaminate other fish;
– the introduction of a healthy carrier or diseased fish;
– the introduction of polluted water from a natural source;
– the accidental introduction of various harmful substances, such as cigarette smoke and aerosol fumes.

Obviously, every precaution must be taken to avoid such accidents on the part of the aquarist.

The origin of a disease can be inside the aquarium

This is generally due to a disruption of the general balance, leading to the development of the diseases latent in a healthy carrier:
– reduction in temperature or thermal shocks, i.e. abrupt variations – whether increases or decreases – brought about by a disorder in the heating system;
– reduction in the oxygen levels;
– excess of nitrogenous matter, due to a filter malfunction or too many fish;

The hospital aquarium

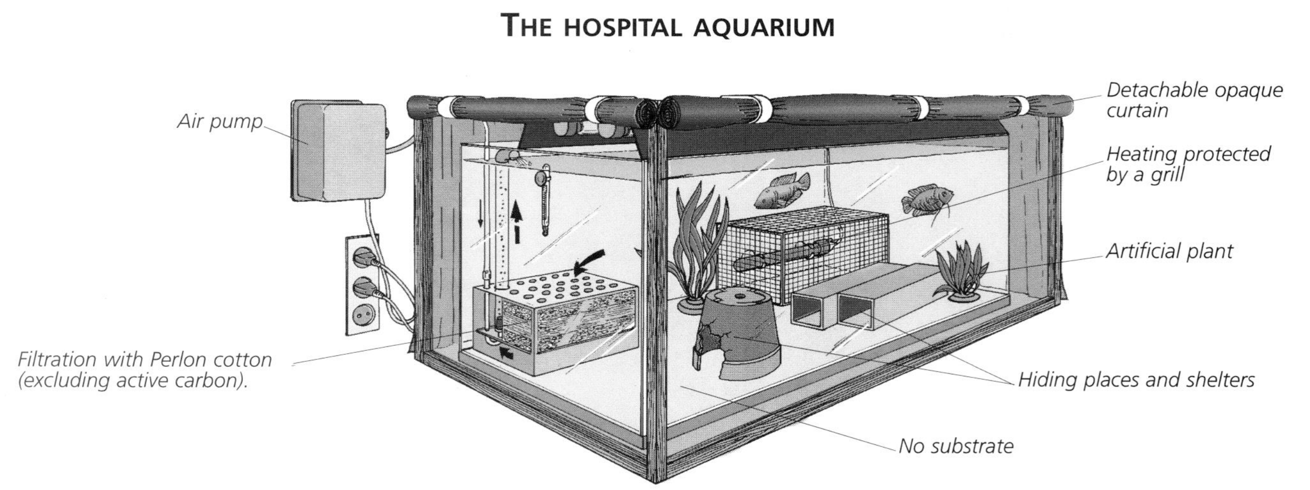

A small tank of glued glass is used, containing only the equipment necessary for treatment. Therefore, there are no plants, bed, or decor, except in the case of naturally shy fish, which can be furnished with a shelter made of an artificial material like PVC. Normal filtration is not required; the most that is needed is a small internal filter containing only Perlon cotton. On the other hand, there must be substantial aeration, as this influences the oxygen levels. The temperature should be raised to 27–28°C.
Ideally, the hospital aquarium should be in a quiet spot with little light, in order to enhance the healing process. It is also possible to cover the glass sides.
After it has been used, both the aquarium and its contents must be disinfected, using 4 ml of bleach for every 100 liters of water, followed by stirring of the water over a period of 24 hours and then several successive rinses.

▲ Scatophagus argus, *in a poor condition, with damaged fins.*

– the general quality of the water;
– an injury sustained in the course of a fight or an overexcited mating ritual, or from collisions with or scrapes against the decor;
– underfeeding or a poorly balanced diet.

Prevention

Prevention is better than cure: this wise old proverb is perfectly applicable to fish-keeping. Prevention entails daily observation of your fish and their environment, and this requires a certain degree of knowledge. In the end, the best prevention comes from maintaining a good balance in the aquarium.

Diseases and their treatment

Generally speaking, there are two types of diseases – infectious and non-infectious. The former are caused by microorganisms, such as bacteria, fungi, or viruses carried by the fish. The triggering factors are well-known: stress, bad diet, decrease in temperature. Some pathogenic organisms have a mixed life cycle: one part on the fish, one part in the water.
Non-infectious diseases are not caused by pathogenic organisms, but by the environment (low-quality water, underfeeding).
It is important to avoid any cocktails of medicines and useless or harmful overdoses. The treatment schedule must always be respected, even if the symptoms quickly disappear.
When taking care of sick fish, it is best to feed them moderately, but with natural foodstuffs. Once the illness is cured, provide a varied and well-balanced diet, in order to consolidate the healing process.

How to recognize a sick fish?

Diseases are not particularly easy to detect, especially if they do not manifest any external symptoms. However, several indications can lead an aquarist to think that a fish is sick. These phenomena can be seen in isolation or together.
– General behavior: the fish hides, is easily scared, and is stressed out.
– Swimming: uncoordinated, and the fish may scrape against the decor or the bed.
– Feeding: weight loss, refusal of food.
– Breathing: the fish comes to the surface to "stock up" on air.
– External symptoms: white spots, whitish marks, swelling of one or both eyes or the whole body, bristling scales, several wounds, etc.

▲ *The bearing of this fish* (Macropodus opercularis) *and its slightly raised scales suggest a poor state of health.*

... and a fish in good health?

There are two things to take into consideration: the fish's appearance and its behavior. This requires a good knowledge of its anatomy, biology, and ecology. A fish in good health has bright colors and sparkling eyes. Its body is not swollen and its scales and opercula do not stick out. It comes to eat in a normal way, in terms of both the feeding process itself and the amount it eats. It does not hide without a good reason.

▼ *Bright colors and fully deployed fins are signs of good health.*

The most common diseases and their treatments are listed in the table on pages 70–71.

The stages of treatment

1. Put the fish in a hospital aquarium.
2. Raise the temperature to 27–28 °C.
3. Stop the filtration, and maybe the protein skimmer in salt water, while at the same time increasing the aeration.
4. Dilute the medicine as required.
5. Pour the medicine little by little into the aquarium. It is best to spread this operation out over a period of at least one hour, or one day when administering copper sulfate.
6. Leave it to act for the recommended period.
7. Empty out half the aquarium, then top up by adding water that is identical to the original.
8. Change 10% of the volume each day for 5 days, always using an identical water.
9. Repeat the treatment if necessary, following the steps above.
10. Switch the filter on again and, where applicable, the protein skimmer.
11. Gradually reduce the temperature to its original level. This operation must be spread over 3 days.
12. Bring the aeration to its original level.

In a mixed aquarium, the process obviously begins at point 2.

THE GOLDEN RULES OF PREVENTION

– Know your aquarium; regularly analyze certain parameters – nitrites, pH; have good-quality water;
– Know your fish and their habits – behavior, feeding.
– Avoid overpopulation.
– Avoid both overfeeding and underfeeding;
– Avoid any permanent stress, particularly from mixing fish that are incompatible due to their size or behavior, or from a lack of shelters and hiding places.
– Do not introduce new fish directly into the aquarium.

Knowing your fish well – their color and behavior – constitutes one of the main rules for disease prevention in an aquarium. ▶

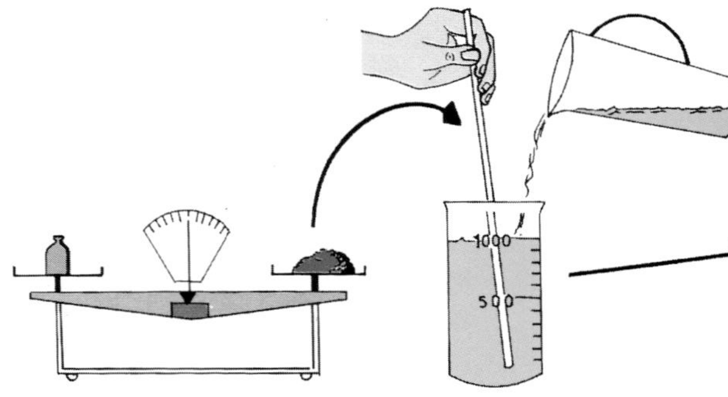

▲ *Powders such as copper sulfate and methylene blue are weighed and then diluted in water to form a mother solution.*

Medicines

There are a great many medicines on the market, specifically formulated for one or several diseases. Constant progress is being made in this field, with new medication for marine fish also being produced in the last few years. It is important to respect the instructions regarding both the dosage and the treatment schedule.

Bacterial diseases can be combated with antibiotics. However, the use of these substances, which are difficult to obtain, is not recommended, and could lead to the creation of resistant strains.

Various chemical products can be used in treatment, provided the dosages are fully adhered to.

Firstly, and only to be used in fresh water, there is *kitchen salt*, which is effective in certain cases. It must be added gradually to the water until a level of 5–10 g/liter is reached, but this dose must not be exceeded. Once the fish is cured, the water is returned to its initial unsalted state, by means of successive changes of 25% of the volume of the tank per day.

Methylene blue is efficacious against fungi. Dissolve 1 g of powder – which can still be found in some pharmacies – into 1 liter of water. Treat fish with 0.5–1 ml/liter of this solution, and eggs with 1 ml/liter.

The product is then eliminated through gradual changes of 25% of the volume of water. Methylene blue cannot be used in sea water.

Malachite green is particularly effective against fungi, but also against ichthyophthyriasis (white spot disease). A solution of 1.5 g per 10 liters is prepared just before

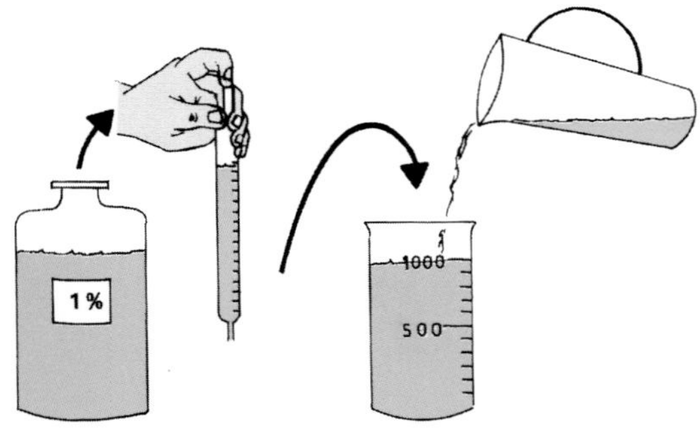
1%
1000
500

▲ *The quantity required for treatment is taken from the bottle on the left, which can then be stored.*

use, and the treatment should not last more than 2 hours.
Formol is active against external parasites. A commercially available 40% solution of formaldehyde is used, after diluting at the rate of 20 ml/100 liters of water. Generally speaking, 15–20 minutes of treatment is sufficient, but in any case it must never exceed 30 minutes. The treatment can be repeated twice, at 48 hour intervals.
Copper sulfate is often used in sea water, but it is toxic for invertebrates and some plants. The ailing fishes must therefore be treated in a hospital aquarium if they are not the sole occupants of the marine tank. Dissolve 16 g of the crystals into 1 liter of water; the treatment dose is 10 ml of this dilution per 100 liters of water. As a precaution, the product's introduction into the water can be spread out over one day. The dilutions of methylene blue, malachite green, and copper sulfate must be carried out with distilled water. All these products, apart from the salt, must be kept in a cool, dark place – ideally, in the refrigerator.
However, be aware of any possible dangers, especially to children, who might be attracted by the colored liquids formed by copper sulfate and methylene blue.

The most common diseases

There are very few aquarists who have never been faced with diseases associated with white spots or fungi.

Ichthyophthyriasis

In the former case, the infection is caused by a protozoon (unicellular animal) which alternates its existence between the fish and the water. It is extremely contagious.
This disease is particularly likely to develop when there is a drop in temperature, or after the introduction of a new fish. It is treated with commercially available products or with formol.
The same conditions also apply to the "foam" caused by fungi, including the *Saprolegnia*. Its proliferation is enhanced by skin wounds. The treatment is carried out with commercial products, or with either methylene blue or malachite green.

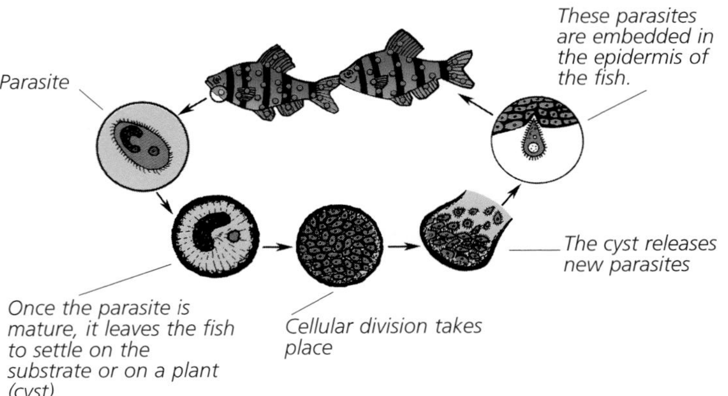
Parasite
These parasites are embedded in the epidermis of the fish.
The cyst releases new parasites
Once the parasite is mature, it leaves the fish to settle on the substrate or on a plant (cyst).
Cellular division takes place

Oodinium

This is caused by a unicellular parasite that bears a flagellate, which allows it to move about. It alternates its existence between the water and the fish. This very contagious disease appears when a fish has been weakened, as up to then it was a healthy carrier. It can be treated with copper sulfate or with a commercial medication.

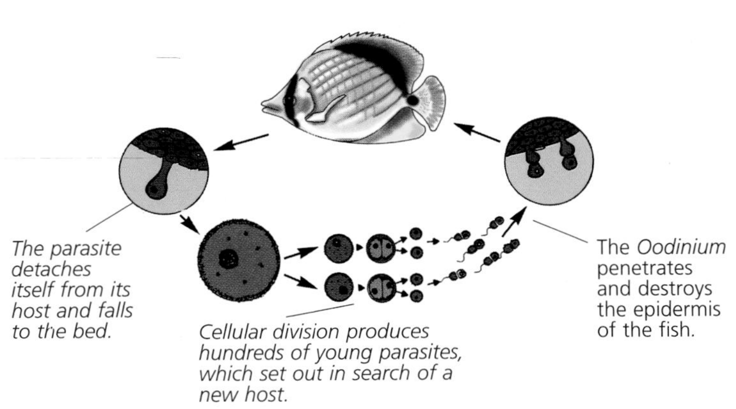
The parasite detaches itself from its host and falls to the bed.
Cellular division produces hundreds of young parasites, which set out in search of a new host.
The *Oodinium* penetrates and destroys the epidermis of the fish.

The most common diseases

Symptoms	Name of disease or problem	Cause	Type of water
White spots on the body and the fins (the size of a pinhead, 1 mm maximum).	ICHTHYOPHTHYRIASIS.	Protozoon parasite, *Ichthyophthirius.*	Fresh water.
White spots, smaller than the above, forming a fine veil, the fins often stuck, scraping against the decor.	OODINIUM.	Unicellular parasite, *Oodinium*, equipped with a flagellate to move around.	Fresh water, but above all in sea water.
Identical to the above, but with bigger spots.	CRYPTOCARYON DISEASE.	Protozoon parasite, *Cryptocarion.*	Sea water.
White clumps with a cotton-like appearance, foam.	FOAM, SAPROLEGNIA.	Fungi, including *Saprolegnia.*	Fresh water, rare in sea water.
1 or 2 eyes abnormally swollen.	EXOPHTHALMUS.	Bacteria, viruses, fungi, sometimes all together.	Fresh water and sea water.
Swollen abdomen, bristly fins.	DROPSY.	Mainly bacteria.	Fresh water and sea water.
Opercula sticking out, unsteady swimming, tiny flukes on the branchiae.	GYRODACTYLIASIS.	Parasitical fluke, *Gyrodactylus.*	Fresh water.
Gasping for air at the surface.	Lack of oxygen.	Defective aeration, general balance of the aquarium disturbed.	Fresh water and sea water.
Weight loss, poor growth.	Dietary problems.	Underfeeding, or lack of vitamins.	Fresh water and sea water.
Agitation, uncoordinated swimming, unusual behavior.	Bad maintenance conditions.	Oxygen problems, poor quality of water (especially nitrogenous substances).	Fresh water and sea water.
Fry with deformed skeletons.	Hereditary problem.	Genetic origin (the parents).	Fresh water and sea water.

This Neolamprologus multifasciatus *has foam on its wounds*

IN AN AQUARIUM

Treatment	Observations
Increase in temperature, formol, malachite green, commercial medication.	Contagious, appears if there is any significant drop in temperature.
Copper sulfate, commercial medication.	Sometimes difficult to detect at first, common in sea water, contagious.
Copper sulfate, commercial medication.	It is sometimes associated with small bloody spots; fish can experience breathing difficulties.
Salt, malachite green or methylene blue (except in sea water: copper sulfate, commercial medication).	The disease's development is favored by wounds.
Copper sulfate, commercial medication.	Sometimes difficult to treat.
Copper sulfate, commercial medication.	Contagious, sometimes difficult to treat.
Salt, copper sulfate.	Not very easy to detect.
Increase the aeration, check and adjust the parameters of the water.	Gasping for air can also be a symptom of an infectious disease.
Fresh food alternated with live prey.	Possibility of incorporating commercial vitamin solutions into the food.
Increase the quantity of oxygen, change one third of the water, check its quality (nitrites, pH).	The symptoms can also correspond to an infectious disease.
If a lot of fry are affected, there is a genetic problem in the parents, and they must therefore be separated.	It is not unusual for a few of the fry in a batch to be affected.

▲ *Fish afflicted by white spot disease (ichthyophthyriasis). Easy to detect – the body is covered with white spots – this disease is very contagious.*

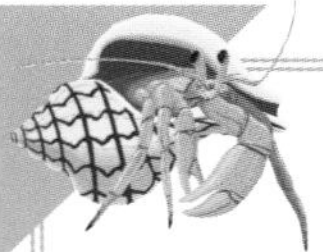

What you must do for a sick fish

– Act immediately.
– Administer the appropriate treatment.
– Take care of the fish in a hospital/quarantine aquarium.

Treatment must be given as soon as the disease appears, i.e. when you see the first symptoms, and you must act quickly.

Treating a sick fish in a mixed aquarium is not without its risks: some substances can have undesirable side-effects on other species or on the plants. It is therefore preferable to use a hospital aquarium, or a quarantine aquarium.

▲ *A fish's swollen abdomen is often the sign of dropsy, a bacterial disease.*

NOMENCLATURE AND DISTRIBUTION OF AQUARIUM FISH

The inhabitants of our aquariums – fish, plants, or small invertebrates – all have individual names. These, however, are often the subject of unresolved disputes: a single species can, in fact, have several different names! Let's try and shed some light on this...

NAMING FISHES: THE CORRECT TERMINOLOGY

Xiphophorus helleri exists in a considerable number of varieties: hifin, lyretail, wagtail, etc. ►

Scientific and common names

• *Scientific names*

The scientific name is the only one which is recognized internationally: it ensures a universal means of communication between workers in the field. It is given in Latin, following a tradition dating back to the 18th century, and consists of two parts:

– the *genus name*, with an initial capital or uppercase letter.

–the *species name*, without a capital.

The scientific name is chosen by whoever discovers the fish, but new scientific advances may cause the name to be changed. The old name, now of secondary importance, continues as a synonym. These changes mostly affect the name of the genus. When the species name is not known for certain, we use the abbreviation *sp.*, an abbreviation of the Latin word *species.*

• *Common names*

Often the origin of the common name is obscure. It may be translated from Latin, from another language, borrow a scientist's name, or simply be invented as circumstances dictate, often somewhat controversially. The absence of any strict rule gives rise to confusion; while some fish have no common name, others have several. Such is the case with *Gymnocorymbus ternetzi*, which has been variously called the black tetra, the black widow, the blackamoor, and the petticoat fish, but all referring to the same fish.

PRINCIPLES OF THE CLASSIFICATION OF LIVING CREATURES

A genus can comprise several species sharing common characteristics. A group of genera related biologically and anatomically is called a family. Related families make up an order. This gives us the following general scheme:

Order	Families	Genera	Species
Cypriniformes	Cyprinidae	*Barbus*	*oligolepis* *schwanenfeldi*
		Capoeta	*schuberti* *titteya*
	Cobitidae	*Botia*	*macracantha*
		Acanthophthalmus	*kuhli*

► Barbus oligolepis.

Where problems arise

Problems of nomenclature – commoner with fish and plants than with invertebrates – can involve confusions between one species and another. Sometimes the Latin name continues to be used in the literature, among commercial dealers, and in contacts between aquarists, until the new scientific name asserts itself. Some newly discovered species are initially designated by a numerical code or a provisional name. On the other hand, sometimes the "new" species turns out to be one already known: the result is that one species now has two names. In this case it is the confusion between species which gives rise to the problem. The multiplication of breeds, varieties, and hybrids hardly helps matters; scientists themselves sometimes have trouble finding their way through the maze, so what hope for the ordinary hobbyist?

In this book, we employ the scientific names in common use today and have deliberately omitted those too recently coined to win general acceptance. You will also find Latin synonyms, and names of breeds and varieties.

Breeds, strains, and varieties

In the natural world, local breeds and strains exist, often differentiated by color. In addition, breeders try to evolve new colors and shapes by crossing. In both instances these varieties are denoted by adding epithets to the original scientific or common name. So we speak of the marble angelfish, the smokey angelfish, and the veiltail angelfish; or the veiltail swordtail, lyretail swordtail, or Berlin swordtail.

Crosses and hybrids

Different species – usually, but not necessarily, belonging to the same genus – can be crossed; this rarely happens in the wild, but is a technique in common use among aquarists. Crossbreeding, if successful, produces a hybrid combining the characteristics of both parents. This hybrid will not receive a special name, but will be known by the joint names of the two parents, separated by the sign "x," which simply indicates crossbreeding: *Fish 1* x *Fish 2*. If the hybrid does not prove sterile, it can interbreed in its turn, either with another hybrid or with a purebred. After several generations, it is hard to tell exactly what you are dealing with! This is true of certain species of plants and fish found in the aquarium trade: the Latin name is frequently unreliable, and the plant or fish will have moved on a long way from the original, recognized species and exhibit different characteristics.

Where do aquarium fish come from?

Feral and captive-bred fish

Today's hobbyist is unlikely to come across more than 300–500 of the 1,500 so-called aquarium species. Formerly, these went under the name of tropical fish, as they were caught in their natural habitats in tropical areas all over the world (see map on following page). Nowadays, 80–85% of freshwater species are bred in captivity, and by no means always in their native regions, so the term "tropical" is no longer appropriate.

The dominant output is from South-East Asia, shared between Hong Kong, the Philippines and Singapore, accounting for over three-quarters of species. The neon tetra, for instance, originally from South America, is bred at the rate of thousands per month.

Other areas of the world produce a limited range of species; some, like the former Czechoslo-

◄ *Parrot cichlid: a cross between* Cichlasoma labiatum *and* Heros labiatus.

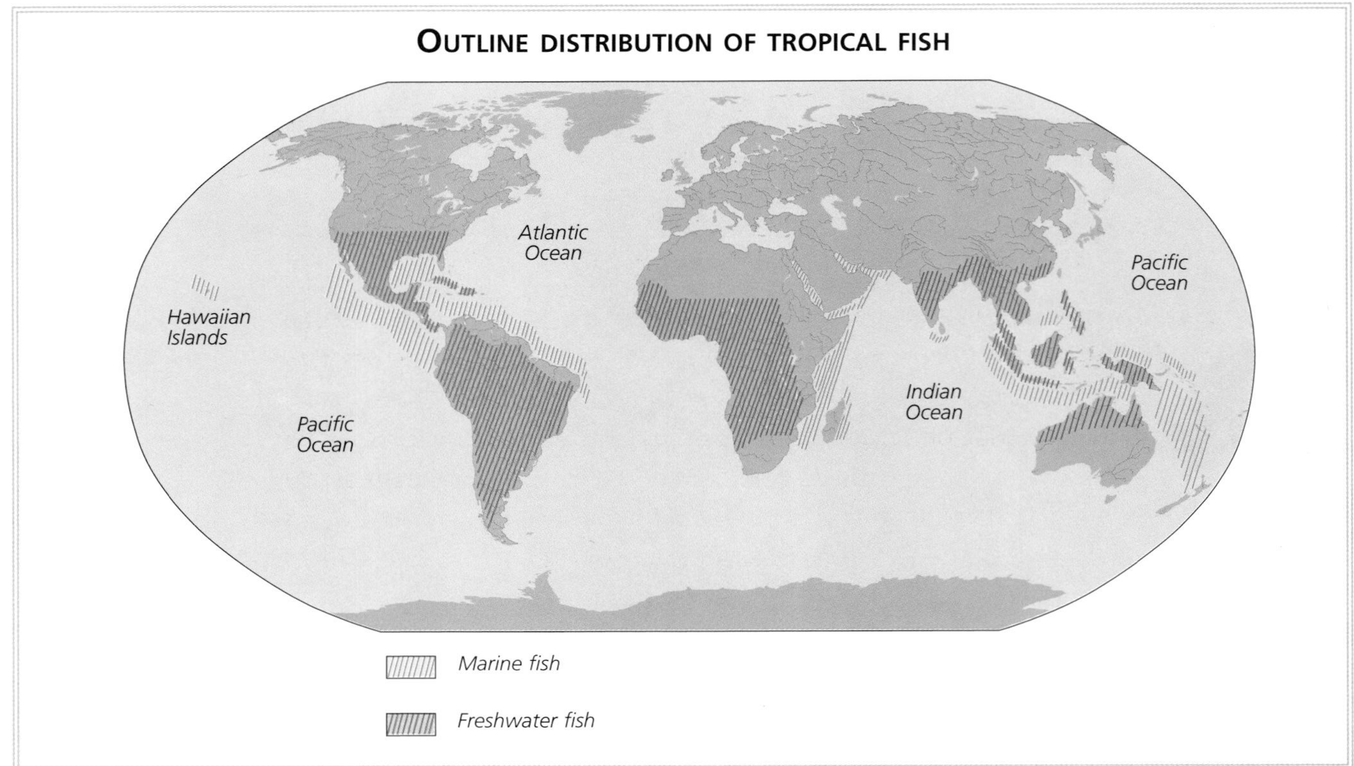

vakia, are beginning to breed on a large scale. Breeders either use imported juveniles or raise their own stock, thus reducing the number of catches made from the wild and helping to preserve the natural fauna. All the same, some species no longer exist in their former abundance – for example in the Amazon basin – and proposals are afoot to declare certain areas protected zones to safeguard local populations.

As for marine fish, almost all species are caught in the wild. Aquarists are frequently accused of abetting the plundering of coral reefs; the argument is that, for every fish arriving in our aquariums, nine die at the time of capture, during transport, or at various stages of handling. Without precise studies, it is extremely difficult to know the real effects on the natural environment of catches that are made to supply aquariums.

Catching tropical fish with a net. ▶

Harvesting of tropical marine fish

There was a time when any method of catching fish was considered legitimate; explosives or cyanide were used to stun them, for example, inflicting severe losses on their populations. At the present moment, the genuinely professional firms employ more sophisticated and humane methods: a team of several divers works around a section of reef after sealing it off with a net. After selecting fish according to various criteria (especially size) and catching them in hand nets, they carefully bring them to the surface and house them in holding tanks to await export.

Protected species

Hobbyists do not keep protected species; it is therefore unfair to blame them for the reduction in numbers or disappearance of these fish from the wild. Most aquarium species exist in large numbers in Nature; some even provide a food source for the local human population.

Freshwater fish

These inhabit various biotopes in tropical and equatorial regions. Basically they may be divided into two groups. The first comprises those for which soft, acidic conditions are essential. Some require a very low level of hardness, with a typical pH of around 6. The second group prefers hard, alkaline conditions. For some species the level of hardness must be extremely high, with a pH of up to 8. A few species can survive in brackish water. There are some fish which are not dependent on water quality. These are consequently ideal for the beginner, who can, in principle, fill the aquarium from the household supply. Though there are over 10,000 species native to inland waters, only a few hundred need concern the aquarist.

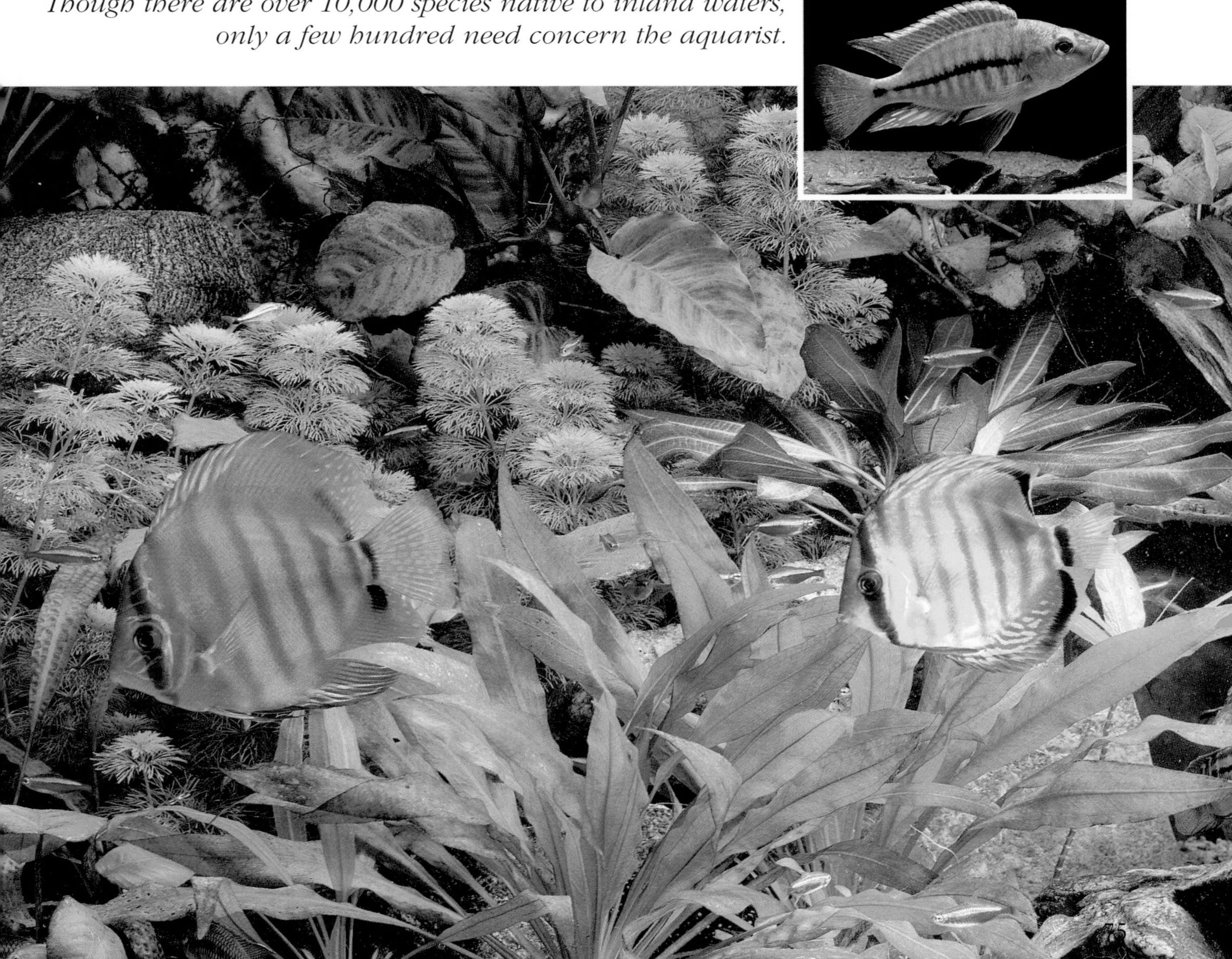

CHARACIDAE (CHARACINS)

The majority of characidae commonly known as Characins (over 1,000 species in all) live in South America, especially in the Amazon basin, but not all are aquarium fish. You can usually identify them by a small adipose fin situated between the dorsal and caudal fins; however, this is not always present, and is also found in certain catfish species. Their solid teeth indicate that they are carnivores: their diet consists, among other things, of insects and insect larvae.

Characins live in groups or shoals in running water and pools where there is plentiful shade and vegetation, factors which guarantee the protection of their eggs. Gregarious and peaceful, they can be kept in community tanks of no great size, provided the water is soft and acidic; this requirement applies particularly to the black water Amazonian species, such as neon tetra, cardinal tetra, glowlight tetra, and black tetra.

There must be abundant plant life in the tank in order to diffuse the light. The Characins will accept manufactured food, but they are voraciously fond of small, live prey. Getting them to spawn, once considered a problem, is within the scope of the hobbyist with some experience: most species reproduce indeed in the same manner. The aquarium should be small – 50 liters or less – and you need to use marbles, peat, or fine-leafed plants to protect the eggs. The water must be soft and acidic, and the light levels low: the aquarium can even be placed in total darkness. Remove the breeding pair (or all adults if you have used two males to one female) after mating, or they will devour their own eggs. The fry – which grow rapidly – will take small, live prey just a few days after hatching; you can then restore the normal lighting.

◄ Anoptichthys jordani

As a result of geological upheavals, the *blind cave tetra* found itself trapped in a number of subterranean rivers in Mexico. Over the course of time it lost the use of its eyes, but it can still find its food on the riverbed, thanks to its sense of smell. The sensory organs of its lateral line allow it to avoid obstacles, even unanticipated ones, such as the human hand. Size: 8–10 cm.

***Cheirodon axelrodi* ▲**

The **cardinal tetra** needs peat-filtered, acidic water to bring out the best in its coloration. For breeding, water hardness must be practically zero; pH can be as low as 6. The development of the eggs (300–500 approximately) must take place in darkness. Size: 4–5 cm.

Aphyocharax anisitsi

The **bloodfin** is a free swimmer living in shoals and requiring uncrowded conditions. It will eat dried food, but prefers small, live prey. Size: 4–5 cm. ►

Gymnocorymbus ternetzi

The **black tetra** or **black widow** breeds best in low light levels and can lay up to 1,000 eggs in soft, acidic conditions. A veil variety, with noticeably larger fins, has been evolved through artificial selection. Size: 5–6 cm. ▼

THE EXCEPTION

Phenacogrammus interruptus (the **Congo** or **Zaire tetra**) does not share the same origins as other Characins. It lives in shoals in soft, mildly acidic conditions, and needs plenty of swimming space. The male is recognizable by the tubercle on the middle of the anal fin. Size: 10–13 cm.

▲ ***Hemigrammus bleheri***
The **rummy-nose tetra** prefers brown water. Often confused with related species *H. rhodostomus* (**red-nose tetra**) and *Petitella georgiae* (**false rummy-nose**), but distinguished from them by the extension of the red coloration to the beginning of the lateral line. Size: 5 cm.

▲ ***Hemigrammus caudovittatus***
Somewhat shy at first, the **Buenos Aires tetra** nonetheless acclimatizes easily, especially within a shoal of ten or so individuals. The female can lay up to 1,000 eggs. Size: 8–10 cm.

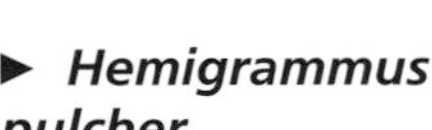

► ***Hemigrammus pulcher***
The **garnet tetra** delights in small, live prey. Breeding is considered problematic: pH 6.5, hardness 0–1.12%GH (0–20 ppm), low lighting. Size: 4–5 cm.

Hemigrammus hyanuary
The **January tetra** is still fairly rare in commercial outlets. It thrives on regular water changes and moderate light levels. Size: 4–5 cm. ▼

Hemigrammus erythrozonus
The **glowlight tetra** will spawn under dim lighting, in soft, acidic water (pH: 6.5). Use peat filtration. A shoal of ten or so of these very tranquil fish produces a stunning effect in a South American-type tank. Size: 4–5 cm. ▼

Hasemania nana
The **silver-tipped tetra** can be distinguished from other Characins by the absence of an adipose fin. It lives in shoals in acidic, densely planted conditions. Size: 4–5 cm. ▼

▲ ***Hyphessobrycon peruvianus***
The **Loreto tetra**, little commercialized, remains relatively unknown. It thrives and breeds best in shady, peat-filtered water. Size: 4–5 cm.

▲ ***Hyphessobrycon callistus***
The **callistus** or **jewel tetra** is frequently confused with *H. serpae* (**serpae tetra**) and *H. bentosi* (**rosy tetra**). It likes clear, well-planted water. Spawns prolifically under moderate lighting in soft, acidic conditions. Size: 4–5 cm.

◄ ***Hyphessobrycon bentosi***
The absence of a black spot behind the head distinguishes the **rosy tetra** from *H. callistus*: the **callistus** or **jewel tetra**. The male's dorsal fin is taller than the female's. After spawning, the eggs sink to the bottom, and the parent fish must be prevented from eating them. Size: 4–5 cm.

▲ ***Hyphessobrycon herbertaxelrodi***
The **black neon tetra** likes clear, acidic water, and sometimes seeks out shaded areas. It will breed at 26°C in very soft water; the eggs need very dim light to hatch. Size: 4–5 cm.

Characins for the Beginner

Breeding from this family is not always something for the beginner, though day-to-day care is not particularly difficult. We suggest the novice try two species:

Hemigrammus ocellifer
The **head- and tail-light fish** is one of the commonest characins, and also one of the least fussy about water quality for breeding. In general, males have a small, elongated white spot on the anal fin. Size: 4–5 cm.

▼ ***Hyphessobrycon pulchripinnis***
The **lemon tetra** lives in a shoal among vegetation. The eggs are laid in the foliage of particular plants. Size: 4–5 cm.

Hyphessobrycon erythrostigma
The dorsal fin of the **bleeding heart tetra** is more elongated than the female's. Breeding is difficult and requires peat filtration, with fine-leafed plants for a "spawning substrate." Incubation must take place in darkness. Size: 4–5 cm. ►

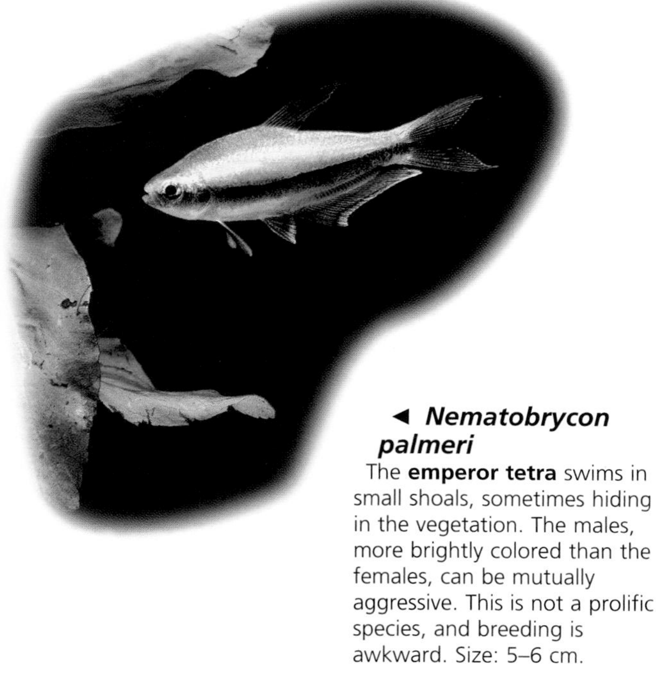

◀ ***Nematobrycon palmeri***
The **emperor tetra** swims in small shoals, sometimes hiding in the vegetation. The males, more brightly colored than the females, can be mutually aggressive. This is not a prolific species, and breeding is awkward. Size: 5–6 cm.

▲ ***Paracheirodon innesi***
The coloration of the **neon tetra**, set off to perfection by dark water, has earned it both its name and tremendous popularity. Breeding requires good water quality with peat filtration: pH close to 6, hardness level approaching 0. Size: 4–5 cm.

▲ ***Prionobrama filigera***
The **glass bloodfin** is a top-feeder which hangs around the filter outlet. It can also leap out of the water. Does not require such soft or acidic conditions as other Characins. Size: 5–6 cm.

Moenkhausia sanctaefilomenae ▲
The **yellow-banded Moenkhausia** prefers still water, swimming in shoals among the vegetation. Breeding is awkward, and demands diffused light and very soft water. Size: 5 cm.

Megalamphodus megalopterus
The **black phantom tetra** lives in shoals, in acidic, clear water, and needs plenty of swimming space. Breeding is difficult: use diffused lighting, and peat filtration giving a pH of 6. Under these conditions, the female, recognized by her shorter dorsal fin, can lay up to 300 eggs. Size: 4–5 cm. ▶

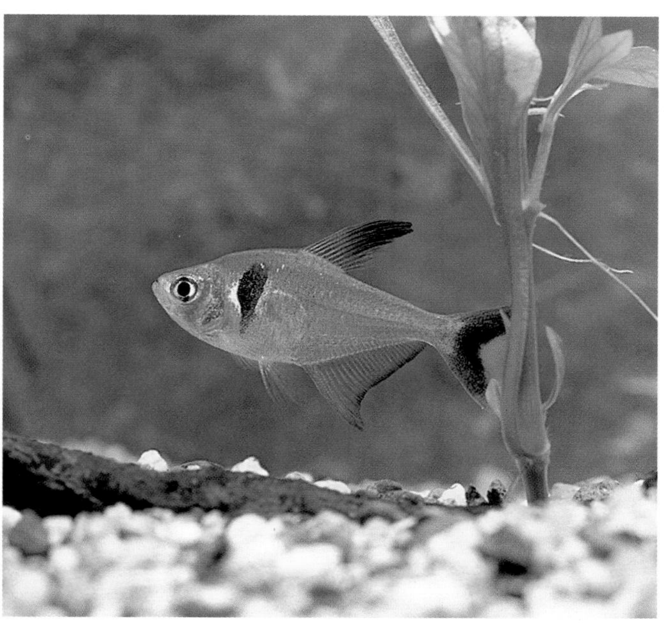

▲ ***Pristella maxillaris***
The **X-ray fish** is robust, quite tolerant of water quality, but hard to breed. Size: 7 cm.

Thayeria boehlkei
Boehlke's penguin swims obliquely, head uppermost. It prefers dark water and diffused light. Breeding is uncomplicated; the female lays around 1,000 eggs. Size: 4–5 cm.▼

FAMILIES RELATED TO THE CHARACIDAE
Lebiasinidae – Gasteropelecidae – Serrasalmidae – Anostomidae

A few fish with certain anatomical resemblances to *Characidae* are found in hobbyists' tanks. In the wild they are native to South America, living in soft, acidic waters.

The ***Lebiasinidae*** (**pencilfish**) are top-dwellers and can leap out of the water. The high position of the mouth indicates that they catch small prey near the surface.

The ***Gasteropelecidae*** (**hatchetfish**) owe their name to the shape of their bodies. Their rectilinear backs and slightly upturned mouths denote that they too are surface-feeders; they also share the pencilfish's acrobatic ability. They flourish in calm, shady conditions.

The family ***Serrasalmidae*** includes piranhas, whose behavior and aggressiveness are well known, but also exaggerated; they are only dangerous in the presence of blood, the scent of which drives them into a frenzy. They are voracious carnivores favoring a meat-based diet.

Metynnis belong to the same family as the piranhas and resemble them. However, they are inoffensive, and their diet is predominantly herbivorous.

Anostomidae are somewhat aggressive. In their natural habitat, their streamlined bodies and transverse or longitudinal stripes serves a camouflage, blending them in with the vegetation.

Leporinus striatus
(Anostomidae)
The **striped leporinus** is an omnivorous species, but requires extra vegetable material. Its size and aggressiveness require it to be kept in a large, covered tank, as it is capable of leaping out of the water. Size: 20–25 cm. ▶

◄ ***Metynnis argenteus* (Serrasalmidae)**
The **silver dollar** closely resembles the piranha, but it is herbivorous, needing large supplements of vegetable material; without these, it will nibble away the vegetation. Size: 10–15 cm.

▲ ***Carnegiella strigata* (Gasteropelecidae)**
The **marbled hatchetfish** lives in small shoals and is a surface-feeder. It shows a preference for live prey, but will not refuse commercial foods. Size: 5 cm.

***Nannostomus trifasciatus* (Lebiasinidae)**
The **three-lined pencilfish** requires shady vegetation but also swimming space. Though the female lays prolifically (around 1,000 eggs), hatching and rearing are traditionally considered difficult. Size: 5–6 cm. ▼

▲ ***Serrasalmus nattereri* (Serrasalmidae)**
This is the **red-bellied piranha**. In captivity, **piranhas** must be isolated from other species in a spacious, well-planted tank. They are by preference carnivorous: feed meat, mussels, or small, live fish. Reproduction is difficult in captivity. Size: 20–30 cm.

***Gasteropelecus sternicla* (Gasteropelecidae)**
The **silver hatchetfish** is somewhat larger and more timid than *C. strigata*, but shares its reluctance to breed in captivity. Size: 5–6 cm. ►

◄ ***Nannobrycon eques* (Lebiasinidae)**
The **hockey-stick pencilfish** or **brown-tailed pencilfish** swims at an angle of 45°, head upwards. Fairly timid, it lives in shoals, and is often somewhat awkward to breed. Size: 5 cm.

CYPRINIDAE

Widely distributed over the planet the *Cyprinidae* (barbs, danios, rasboras, labeos, carp, etc.) form one of the largest freshwater families, with more than 2,000 species. The smallest species – only a few centimeters in length – are very well known and extremely popular with hobbyists. The largest, which can grow up to 1 m in length, constitute an important human food source: the annual captive production of various types of carp – the most familiar member of this family – exceeds 6 million tonnes, and if we lump together all species (including freshwater and marine aquaculture) we end up with a figure of around 17 million tonnes.

The Cyprinidae are characterized by a frequently thick-set body and rather broad scales; most surprisingly, the teeth do not grow from the jaw but are relegated to the throat. These fish originate from quite diversified biotopes, but acclimatize to the domestic aquarium without difficulty. They are omnivores, and some species detect their food by means of their barbels.

▲ ***Barbus oligolepis***
The **checker barb** is a gregarious species. Spawning (relatively uncomplicated) demands slightly acidic conditions and fine-leafed plants. It is easy to cross with other barbs. Size: 5 cm.

Barbus schwanenfeldi
The **tinfoil barb** or **Schwanenfeld's barb** can exceed 25 cm in the aquarium. More or less peaceful, it does however require plenty of space, with abundant food, including supplements of vegetable material. Size: 25–30 cm.

Barbs

Barbs are native to Asia and Africa, living in shallow, moderately fast-flowing waters rich in vegetation; among the hundred-odd known species in Nature, only a dozen or so are currently available commercially under this collective name. The different species can be distinguished by the number of barbels, which varies from none to four. They are active fish, living in groups or small shoals, and the liveliest ones may even tease other species with quite large fins. They are best kept in aquariums with plenty of plants and where the water is soft, slightly acidic, and well-filtered and oxygenated. Barbs are omnivorous (taking small, live prey or vegetable material) and adapt well in captivity to artificial foods. Spawning (reasonably straightforward) requires soft, mature water; the optimal temperature is usually around 28°C. After hatching, the fry measure just over 3 mm; food when they are at this stage should be *Artemia nauplii.*

Barbs for the Beginner

The ***rosy barb*** (*Puntius conchonius*) is very gregarious. It breeds easily (the male taking on a pink coloration) in soft, seasoned water. The eggs – sometimes over 100 in number – adhere to plants and other supports; the parent fish must be removed after laying. Hatching takes place after 36 hours. For the first 2 days after they are free-swimming, feed the fry on infusoria. Enthusiasts have evolved a veil variety by selective breeding. Size: 8 cm.

Crossbreeding

Some species of barbs can be crossed to produce viable fry, as with *Puntius nigrofasciatus* (**black ruby barb**) and *Capoeta tetrazona* (**tiger barb**), a hybrid of which is shown here. Size: 5–6 cm.

Capoeta semifasciolatus
The **green barb** or **half-striped barb** is perhaps the species responsible for the production, by mutation or hybridization, of the golden barb – see ***C. schuberti***. The male is more elongate and brightly colored than the female. Size: 8–10 cm. ▶

▲ ***Capoeta titteya***
The **cherry barb** is one of the smallest members of this family. It owes its common name to its color, which, in the male, deepens noticeably at mating time. It is quite timid, preferring shaded areas. The female can produce several hundred eggs. Size: 5 cm.

▲ ***Capoeta schuberti***
The **golden barb** is a curiosity: unknown in the wild, it is most likely a mutation or a hybrid of related species. It is gregarious, swimming actively in groups. Breeding is quite easy; the eggs hatch in 36 hours in water at 26°C. The fry grow quickly and mature within 10–12 months. Size: 5–6 cm.

▲ ***Capoeta tetrazona***
Golden tiger variety.
Size: 5–6 cm.

◀ ***Capoeta tetrazona***
The **tiger barb** is one of the most common species. During mating, the males become markedly aggressive towards the females. The stripes appear on the fry within 2 weeks or so. There are several varieties of this species: the green tiger, the albino tiger, and the golden tiger (without the black pigmentation).
Size: 5–6 cm.

▼ ***Banded barbs*** Certain species have "stripes", mainly in the form of transverse bands; their size and number serve as a means of identification. Size: 5–7 cm.

Capoeta tetrazona (tiger barb)

Barbodes pentazona (five-banded barb)

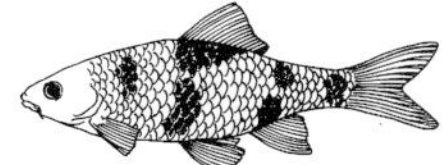

Barbodes everetti (clown barb)

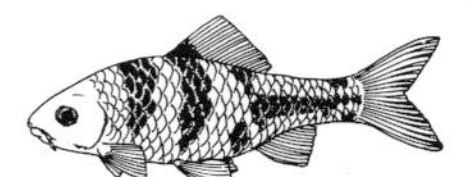

Puntius lateristrigata (T-barb or spanner barb)

Puntius nigrofasciatus (black ruby barb)

Danios

Hardy, continuously active, easy breeders, unfussy eaters, danios have the ideal qualities for a starter fish. Like barbs, they are extremely gregarious.

Spawning the Zebra Danio

You can breed the zebra danio in a tank without substrate using a mixture of new water with some taken from the parents' aquarium. The hardness level must be low, pH neutral, and the optimum temperature is around 26–27°C. To prevent the parent fish devouring the eggs, which they will do with gusto, keep the depth of water between 10 and 15 cm. The eggs will then sink quickly: a layer of marbles prepositioned on the bed will provide safe lodging places. Alternatively, suspend a layer of fine netting halfway down, allowing the eggs through but not the parent fish. For a set-up like this, use two males to one female, choosing a female with a plump belly, indicating that she is ripe. After laying – which seems to be stimulated by the first rays of the morning sun – remove the parent fish. Incubation of the eggs (up to 200 or 300) lasts 2–3 days, with the fry swimming between the 6th and 7th days. It is vital to feed them small, live prey – infusoria or rotifers if you can get them.

▼ *Danio aequipinnatus*
Larger than its cousins, the **giant danio** is just as hardy and easy to spawn. Size: 8 cm.

▲ *Brachydanio frankei*
This species, which resembles a tiny trout, appears not to exist in the wild, possibly deriving from isolated laboratory stock. The fish currently sold commercially originate from localized breeding centers in South-East Asia. The **leopard danio**, as it is commonly known, lives in shoals near the surface and acclimatizes easily. A veil form exists, with markedly elongated fins. Size: 5–6 cm.

A Danio for the Beginner

Known, raised and bred in Europe since the early 1800s, the **striped** or **zebra danio** *(Brachydanio rerio)* has given countless hobbyists their first real thrill of excitement. Twenty years or so ago, a veil form appeared, though, curiously, this fish has not given rise to other selective forms. Its hardiness and its readiness to spawn have been put to use by scientists to test the toxicity of certain substances. Recently they managed to produce a line of clones: genetically identical fish, and therefore with the same reactions to a given phenomenon, thus eradicating the influence of genetic variability on experiments. Size: 5–6 cm.

Brachydanio albolineatus
The **pearl danio** is a shoal-swimming, voracious feeder. It can survive temperatures below 20°C. Size: 6 cm. ►

Rasboras

These small, lively fish live in groups or shoals in fast-flowing, shallow water, their forked fins clear indicators of their swimming ability. A robust species; they are easy to care for in soft, slightly acidic conditions, but breeding is a less straightforward proposition.

▲ ***Rasbora heteromorpha***
The **harlequin rasbora** is one of the most popular species of this group. It spawns in acidic conditions (pH 6, with peat filtration), ideally in a darkened tank, sticking its eggs on or underneath large leaves. Size: 5 cm.

Rasbora borapetensis
The **magnificent rasbora** or **red-tailed rasbora** will spawn (up to 500 eggs) in a small, darkened tank containing fine-leafed plants. The fry must be fed with small, live prey for 2 weeks. Size: 5 cm. ▼

◀ ***Rasbora elegans***
The **elegant rasbora** lives near the surface of open water, and requires plenty of swimming space in captivity. To set off its coloration to perfection, use a dark bed. Keep the water acidic and slightly hard. Size: 5 cm.

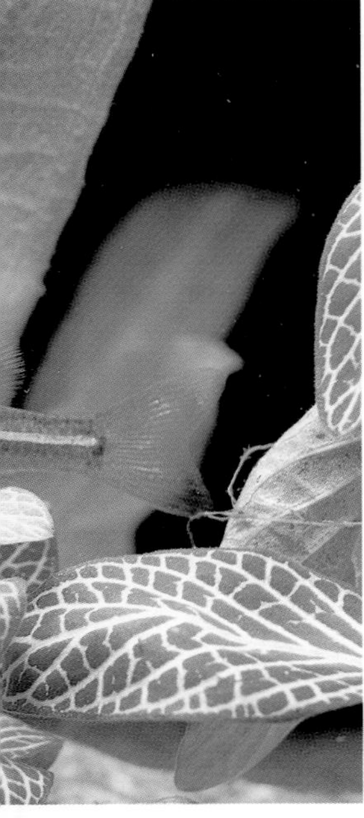

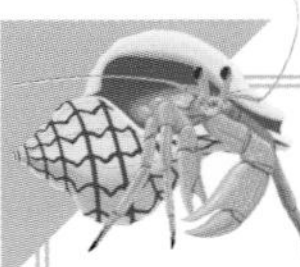

THE BEGINNER'S RASBORA

The **scissortail** (*Rasbora trilineata*) owes its name to its tail movements and needs plenty of room.
The eggs, only slightly adhesive, are laid in the fine foliage of certain plants, hatching in 24 hours.
It accepts both artificial foods and live prey. Size: 10 cm.

Labeos

One look at the labeos' shape reveals that they are bottom-dwellers in fast- flowing water: quite streamlined to minimize current drag, with a flat belly for resting on the bed and barbels for sensing prey on or in the substrate. These fish are primarily "twilight" (nocturnal) species; they are also aggressive toward conspecifics in defense of their territory, though coexisting peacefully with other species.

As is the case with other aquarium fish, it has become possible to breed the labeo borrowing techniques recently developed by scientists for propagating marine species. This involves the use of hormones, and is a method unavailable to the amateur breeder.

What happens is that the hypophysis – a small gland located at the base of the brain – is removed from carps or related species and crushed in a slightly saline solution. A minute quantity of this solution – containing the diluted hormone – is injected into the chosen fish; if she is "ripe," she will start to lay within 24 hours, producing hundreds of eggs.

Labeo frenatus ►
Albino variety.
Size: 10–15 cm.

◄ ***Labeo frenatus***
The **red-finned shark** or **rainbow shark** is distinguished from *Labeo bicolor* by a less intense body coloration and by its red fins. Sometimes a commercial albino variety is found, which can be mated with the normal variety; the fry will then display the coloration of one or other of the parents.
Size: 10–15 cm.

▲ ***Labeo bicolor***
The **red-tailed black shark**, rather nocturnal in its habits, obtains its food by sifting the bed of its natural habitat. In captivity, it needs extra vegetable material. By day it lurks in various hiding places (rocks, roots, etc.) which form an essential part of the aquarium furnishings. Size: 10–15 cm.

The goldfish: theme and variations

The goldfish is the oldest "domesticated" fish; its story began long before hobbyists started keeping it in aquariums. The feral form, less brightly colored than the present fancy varieties, can reach 40–50 cm. Originating from Asia, it has now spread throughout all the temperate waters (5–25°C) of the globe. The classic red variety was selectively bred from feral stock, probably before the time of Christ, though breeding has made enormous advances since the Middle Ages. The earliest importations to Europe date from the 17th century, in the form of gifts made to the French royal family. There are many varieties, all of which have been isolated, after a long and painstaking series of selections, using the familiar red strain as a starting-point.

▼ Goldfish varieties (Carp family)

◄ Shubukin
The dorsal and caudal fins are markedly elongate. Coloration: variegated, with no fixed pattern. Size: 10–15 cm.

Koi

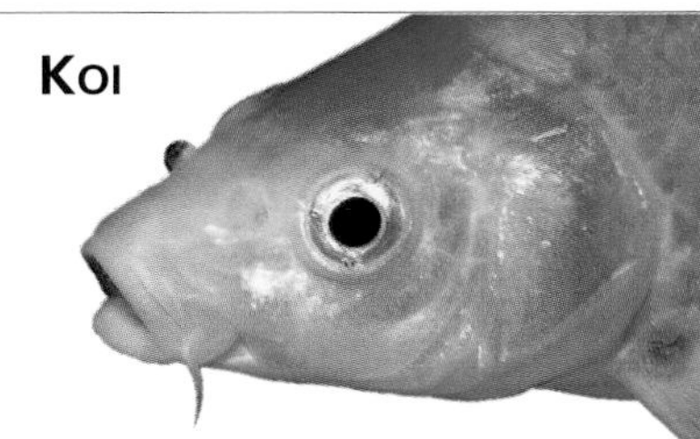

Though people often confuse koi with goldfish, these are in fact different varieties of carp selected (starting from the feral variety) over more than 1,000 years. They can reach 1 m in length, and the presence of barbels clearly distinguishes them from the smaller goldfish. Size: 20–50 cm.

Japanese veiltail
The **veiltail** has a caudal fin composed of two or three lobes. Size: 10 cm. ►

◄ Telescope-eyed goldfish
The eyes of this variety are globular and protruding; sometimes the dorsal fin is absent. The commonest varieties are entirely black. A close relative is the **celestial** goldfish. Size: 10 cm.

Caring for goldfish

Goldfish must be kept in conditions corresponding to their natural habitat; the aquarium must be big enough to let them swim freely among the plants, while the substrate can be fairly coarse. Filter the water, but do not use heating: goldfish are considered hardy, but the maximum temperature should be 20–22°C, while below 5°C the fish become noticeably sluggish. Hardness and pH are not so critical as with other species of aquarium fish.

◄ The bubble-eye
You can spot this variety at once by the bubble-like pocket under the eyes. The caudal fin may be normal, or divided into several lobes. Other varieties of goldfish exist; in addition, there is much crossbreeding between those mentioned here. In every case, color may be uniform or appear as red, yellow, gold, white or black splashes. Size: 10 cm.

◄ Lionhead
The **lionhead** has protuberances in the form of swellings on top of the head. Sometimes there is no dorsal fin. Size: 10 cm.

The goldfish (*Carassius auratus*): a roaring commercial success

Breeding goldfish, which are unlikely to go out of fashion, is an important commercial activity. Besides its popularity with hobbyists, it is used as live bait – under stringent legal conditions – for the capture of carnivores. The modern varieties are raised in Italy, though the most sophisticated forms (often called "Chinese") are produced in Asia.

A goldfish Hilton

If you want to offer your goldfish the very best conditions, keep them in a garden pool where they will grow much larger; they will overwinter safely, even if the water partially freezes. Breeding is by no means impossible outdoors, provided the minimum pool temperature is 19–20°C. However, the parents will try to gobble the eggs. The fry acquire the characteristic coloration only after several weeks.

Other Cyprinidae: *Balantiocheilus – Epalzeorhynchus – Tanichthys*

As well as the groups already mentioned, which are those most commonly obtainable from commercial outlets, there are a few other species of interest to the amateur aquarist.

Epalzeorhynchus kallopterus

Tranquil enough – even timid – except with its own species, the **flying fox** is a bottom-feeder. It has not yet been successfully bred in the aquarium. A closely related species, *E. siamensis* or **Siamese flying fox**, has the reputation of keeping down green algae which can sometimes proliferate; it is distinguishable from *E. kallopterus* by the longitudinal black band running along the middle of the body only as far as the caudal fin. Size: 10–15 cm. ▼

▲ *Tanichthys albonubes*

The common name of this small fish is the **white cloud mountain minnow**. Beginners will find it worth trying for its sturdy constitution: it can withstand temperatures as low as 18°C. It is also simple to breed from, as the parents do not eat the eggs. Size: 5 cm.

Balantiocheilus melanopterus

You will need a large tank for the **bala** or **tricolor shark**, which revels in swimming and can leap out of the water. There is no evidence that it has been successfully bred in the aquarium. Size: 20–30 cm. ▶

COBITIDAE

The *Cobitidae* are close relatives of the *Cyprinidae* and are found in both Europe and Asia. They possess a small number of barbels which they use to detect prey as they search the substrate. Given this feeding procedure, it is preferable to use a fairly fine, smooth sand. You can recognize these fish by the presence of a spine under the eye; this is designed for defense, but can also entangle the fish in the hand net. Loaches, as they are commonly known, are bottom-dwellers, and basically twilight species; they hide away during the day, so you will need to provide lurking places. They are happy with artificial food, but will not spawn in the aquarium.

Acanthophthalmus kuhli

The **coolie loach**. A number of species are available commercially under this name; they differ only in the pattern of their coloration. Shy and non-aggressive, they can leap through any tiny gap in the aquarium lid. They have been successfully bred with the aid of hormones, like the labeos; otherwise they rarely reproduce in captivity. Size: 12cm ▶

Botia macracantha

The **clown loach** is the most well-known and commercially successful species of the genus *Botia*. All species are bottom-sifters, i.e., they search the substrate for food. None will breed in captivity. A twilight fish, mainly hiding away during the daytime, the clown loach can be aggressive when cramped for space or defending territory. Size: 15 cm. ▼

▲ *Botia lohachata*

The **Pakistani loach** is less nocturnal than its relatives, and will not hide away when the aquarium is illuminated. Size: 10 cm.

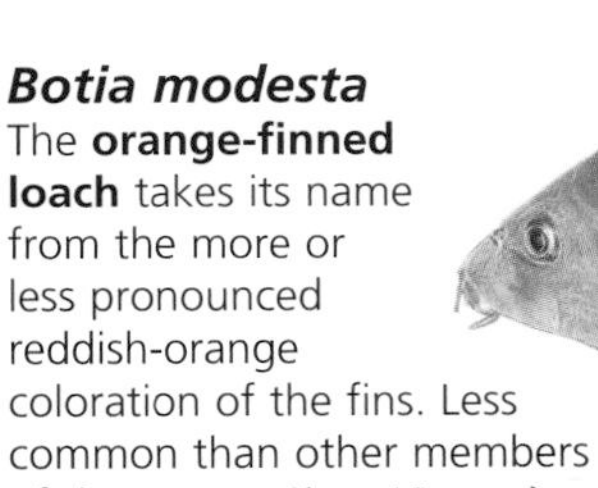

Botia modesta

The **orange-finned loach** takes its name from the more or less pronounced reddish-orange coloration of the fins. Less common than other members of the genus. Size: 15 cm. ►

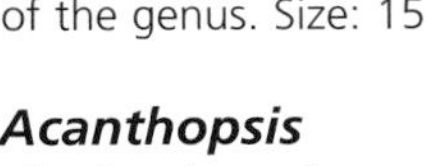

► *Botia horae*

Hora's loach changes color according to its moods, sometimes displaying pale banding. Rather more active than related species. Size: 10–12 cm.

Acanthopsis choirorhynchus

The **horse-faced loach** or **long-nosed loach** is another twilight species, burying itself in the sand during daylight, with only its head showing. Size: 15 cm. ▼

Botia striata

One of the prettiest of the loaches, the **zebra loach** has thin transverse bands along its body. Size: 10 cm. ▼

▼ The four main species of *Acanthophthalmus*

A. kuhli kuhli

A. kuhli sumatranus

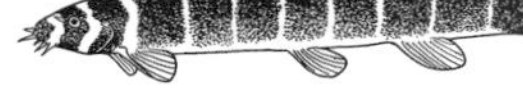

A. myersi (slimy myersi)

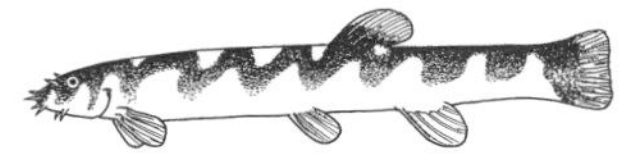

A. semincintus (half-banded loach)

CATFISH

Catfish belong to different families, but are all members of the order *Siluriformes*. They possess barbels, live a solitary life on the bottom, and are mainly twilight species. Not very fussy about water quality, they play a major part in maintaining the balance of the aquarium as they scavenge algae or particles which have sunk to the bottom.

Two families are of particular importance: the *Callichthyidae* and the *Loricariidae*. The ***Callichthyidae*** include the genus *Corydoras*; these fish do not have scales, but their flanks are covered in layers of overlapping "shingles" (bony plates) They can also be recognized by the barbels round their mouths and the spines on their dorsal and pectoral fins. Their flat bellies indicate that they live and search for food (artificial, or small live prey) on the bottom; they are active mostly at dusk and during the night. Originally native to South America, *Corydoras* species are ideal subjects for keeping in a regional aquarium along with Characins, angelfish or discus. Ten or so species are currently available in the trade; others appear on the market intermittently.

The ***Loricariidae*** live on the beds of streams and rivers in South America. Their mouths resemble suckers, their bodies are "armor-plated," and they often have spines on their fins. All are either partially or completely herbivorous. It is very rare to hear of them breeding in captivity.

***Corydoras arcuatus* (Callichthyidae)**
The **skunk catfish**. The Latin *arcuatus* (banded) refers to the broad black band running along the back from the eye to the caudal peduncle. Generally considered a difficult subject; this includes breeding. Size: 5 cm. ►

***Corydoras trinileatus* (Callichthyidae)**
The arrangement of spots on the three-line **corydoras** varies according to its origins. Prefers diffused illumination. Harder to breed than the peppered cory. Size: 5 cm. ►

***Corydoras melanistus* (Callichthyidae)**
The **black-sail corydoras** or **black-spotted corydoras** has a distinctive black smudge near the dorsal fin. The female lays 100–200 eggs which hatch in a week or so. Size: 5 cm. ▼

***Corydoras punctatus* (Callichthyidae)**
In color, the **spotted catfish** resembles the skunk clownfish, with which it is often confused, but the black markings on the back are absent. Size: 5 cm. ►

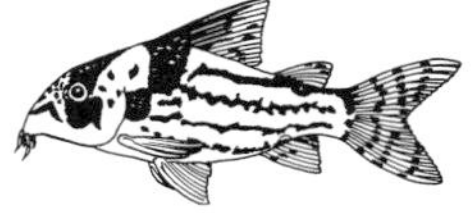

C. schwartzi

C. schwartzi (Surinam sub-species)

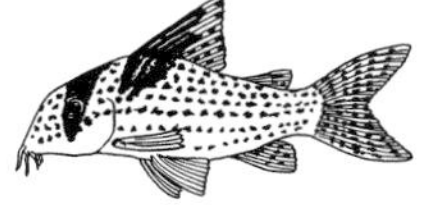

C. melanistus

C. melanistus (sub-species)

Corydoras species for the beginner

Two robust and sturdy species are particularly recommended to the beginner.

The **aeneus catfish** or **bronze catfish** (*Corydoras aeneus*) is rather drab: there is also an albino variety created through artificial selection. As with many *Corydoras* species, the male's dorsal and pectoral fins are more pointed than the female's.

The **peppered corydoras** (*C. paleatus*) has long been familiar to aquarists, and is raised in South-East Asia. The female lays 50 eggs a day, sticking them to a suitable surface, even the walls of the aquarium; she may continue laying like this for several weeks. Size: 5 cm.

◄ ***Corydoras aeneus***

◄ ***Corydoras paleatus***

Corydoras aeneus
Albino variety. ►

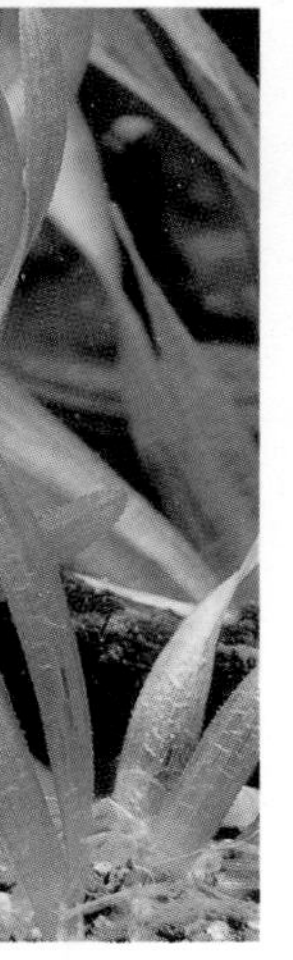

▲ *Corydoras julii* (Callichthyidae)

One of the most attractive *Corydoras* species is the **leopard catfish**, so known because of its distinctive spot pattern. Rather shy, and difficult to breed, it is easily confused with species having similar markings. Size: 5 cm.

Corydoras metae (Callichthyidae)

The female of the **bandit catfish** fastidiously cleans plants or the glass of the tank before sticking her eggs to them. Size: 5 cm. ▼

▼ *Corydoras schwartzi* (Callichthyidae)

Schwartz's corydoras is often confused with other species: its coloration varies according to region. Given that there are over 150 feral species of *Corydoras*, it is not hard to see how confusions arise in distinguishing between fish species. Size: 5 cm.

Breeding *Corydoras*

Once considered extremely difficult, this is now within the scope of the experienced and meticulous hobbyist. There is a boisterous mating display, with the male chasing the female for perhaps several days. Spawning may be triggered by a variation in atmospheric pressure, a water change, or a rise in temperature. The male stations himself near the female, sometimes hanging perpendicularly in the water, to ensure his milt thoroughly fertilizes the tiny eggs. The female takes the eggs between her ventral fins and deposits them on a suitable surface which she has previously meticulously cleaned. The pair may repeat this ritual several times and hatching takes place a few days later. Note that the fry are very sensitive to any changes in their environment.

Hypostomus plecostomus (Loricariidae)

The **pleco** feeds on algae, spending the night on the bottom. Once it has reached a certain size, it can become invasive and disturb the decor, so it needs a roomy tank. Size: 20 cm. ▼

► *Ancistrus sp.* (Loricariidae)

Several species of the **bristlenose** are sold in commercial outlets under a confusing variety of names. Mature males can be distinguished by the presence of long barbels on the head. *Ancistrus* browses encrustant algae. The female deposits her eggs on carefully selected sites, though captive breeding is rare. Size: 13 cm.

◄ *Farlowella sp.* (Loricariidae)

The mouth of the **twig catfish** is positioned well back underneath the head. This is a nocturnal bottom-dweller, not known to spawn in captivity. Size: 15 cm.

▲ *Acanthodoras spinossimus* (Doradidae)

The **talking catfish** has spines along its pectoral fins. It prefers darkness and soft, acidic conditions. It is omnivorous and quite shy. Size: 12 cm.

A little scavenger for the beginner: *Otocinclus vittatus* (Loricariidae)

This is a small, peaceable fish that lives on a diet of algae. It very rarely spawns in captivity. Size: 5 cm.

Gyrinocheilus aymonieri (Gyrinocheilidae)

The **Chinese algae-eater** has a sucker-like mouth for grazing algae. As this fish grows, it can become aggressive. It clings to rocks, foliage or the glass. Size: 15–20 cm. ▲

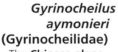

Sorubim lima (Pimelodidae)

The peaceable **shovel-nose catfish** can reach 60 cm in length; a spacious aquarium is therefore essential. Mainly nocturnal; it is a greedy feeder, taking live prey or fresh food. There is a serrated spine on each pectoral fin. ►

◄ ***Synodontis nigriventris* (Mochokidae)**
The adult of the **black-bellied upside-down catfish** swims, as the name suggests, belly upwards, while juveniles behave quite normally. A nocturnal, peaceable species, it is omnivorous, but will require a small amount of extra vegetable material. Rarely breeds in captivity. Size: 10cm.

▲ ***Kryptopterus bicirrhis* (Siluridae)**
The **glass catfish** or **ghost catfish**, one of the few aquarium species with a transparent body, has two long barbels acting as organs of touch. In the wild it lives – and breeds – in shoals in open water. It is not suitable for mixing with boisterous species, and will not spawn in the aquarium. Size: 10–12 cm.

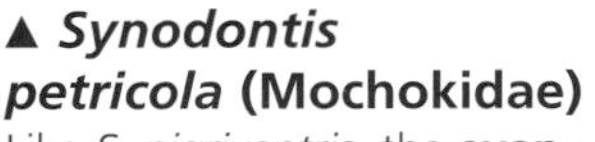

▲ ***Synodontis petricola* (Mochokidae)**
Like *S. nigriventris,* the **even-spotted synodontis** is a native of Africa. It swims in a normal position and often remains hidden during the day. A few other species of ***Synodontis*** are available commercially. Size: 10 cm.

▲ ***Eutropiellus debauwi* (Schilbidae)**
A good swimmer, the **three-striped glass catfish** lives in shoals, frequently hanging in an oblique position, and is likely to die if kept in isolation for long. Omnivorous, it prefers soft, acidic conditions, seldom spawning in captivity. Size: 8 cm.

▲ ***Pimelodus pictus* (Pimelodidae)**
A twilight species, somewhat solitary, the **angelicus pimelodus** lives on the bottom and requires plenty of swimming space. As yet it has not been successfully bred in captivity. Size: 15 cm.

◄ ***Pangasius sutchi* (Pangasiidae)**
An omnivorous species, the **Siamese shark** swims restlessly in shoals, and will need a capacious tank. There is no evidence of successful captive breeding. Size: 20–30 cm.

ATHERINIDAE

The Atherinidae are characterized by long, streamlined bodies which immediately suggest their speed and agility in the water. They are preponderantly marine species, with very few inhabiting inland waters.

▼ *Telmatherina ladigesi*
Some experts consider that the **Celebes rainbowfish** belongs to another family: the *Telmatherinidae*. *T. ladigesi* lives in shoals, preferring hard water and uncrowded conditions. The rays on the dorsal fin are more developed in the male. Size: 6–8 cmcm.

▲ *Bedotia geayi*
The **Madagascar rainbow** appears more or less indifferent to water quality and is a restless swimmer. It is reasonably straightforward to breed, as the parent fish will not devour the eggs, which sink to the bottom and hatch in 5 days. Feed the fry on live prey until they are ready for fine dried food. Size: 10 cm.

MELANOTAENIIDAE (RAINBOWFISH)

Commonly called rainbowfish, they come form the rivers and swamps of Australia and New Guinea. They thrive best in hard water with a pH above 7. Coloration varies according to mood, breeding condition, and hierarchical position. Water quality is not too important.

◄ *Melanotaenia maccullochi*
Several closely-related species are marketed under the name of **McCulloch's rainbowfish** or **dwarf Australian rainbowfish**. All are robust, demanding a large, uncluttered tank where they can swim in peace – but make sure there is a planted area. The eggs – quite large and hatching in 7–10 days – are fixed to plants by fine filaments: an unusual feature in aquarium fish. The fry remain clinging to a surface (the aquarium wall or a plant) until free-swimming; their initial growth is quite slow. Size: 10–12 cm.

Melanotaenia boesemani
Boeseman's rainbowfish is one of the most colorful of this family, and another which prefers hard water. Breeding is straightforward, though the fry accept only tiny prey. Another gorgeously colored species, *M. herbertaxelrodi* **(Lake Tebera rainbowfish)**, is sometimes available commercially. Size: 10–12 cm. ►

CYPRINODONTIDAE (KILLIES, ETC.)

The Cyprinodonts (meaning "toothcarps") flourish in virtually all the world's tropical inland waters (Australia excepted), with over 500 species in all. They have teeth, and their mouths are oriented upwards to seize prey on or near the surface; some species can even leap out of the water. They dwell in calm, stagnant, and shallow waters, sometimes mere puddles, which are liable to dry up. In this case, the adults perish, but their eggs survive: see *Reproduction*, page 60. They are small in size, rarely exceeding 8 cm, vividly colored, and are prized by some enthusiasts for their remarkable breeding habits.
There is much confusion between species, especially since coloration varies between geographically diverse populations. Only a few are regularly handled by dealers; most are exchanged between killie-fanciers, killies or killifish being the popular name for these species.

How killies reproduce

Those killies whose habitat never dries out deposit sticky eggs which take several weeks to incubate. Those dwelling in areas prone to periodic drought have developed a special method to ensure the survival of their species. The eggs spawned in the mud undergo a period of dormancy in their development (the diapause) for as long as the drought lasts. At the first rains, development resumes and the eggs hatch. Thus their incubation period may last from 3–6 months, and they have no need to be adhesive. You can tell that hatching is imminent when you can see the eyes of the embryos through the eggs.

Caring for killies in the aquarium

Ideally, you should provide a special small tank (10–15 liters) for each species. It is also possible to put males of different species in one tank; this will provide a colorful spectacle, but do not put females together, as many of them are so much alike that you will have trouble telling which species is which.
Conditions must be soft and acidic, so you will need to use peat filtration; sometimes, if you put a layer of peat on the bottom of the tank, the fish will use it to lay their eggs on. The maximum temperature should be 24°C. Killifish are very fond of small, live prey, but will also take dried foods.

Floating plants

Remove parent fish after spawning

Eggs in peat layer

◀ Seasonal killies

◀ Continuous-breeding killies

Preserving and transporting eggs

Hobbyists who live a long way from one another can exchange killie eggs through the mail. The incubation period is sufficiently long to enable them to be transported, as long as they are kept in damp, cool conditions. The seasonal species can withstand much drier conditions than continuous breeders: lower temperatures serve to prolong the diapause.
Make sure that the boxes or plastic bags used for transport are completely airtight. To start the eggs hatching, return them to water.

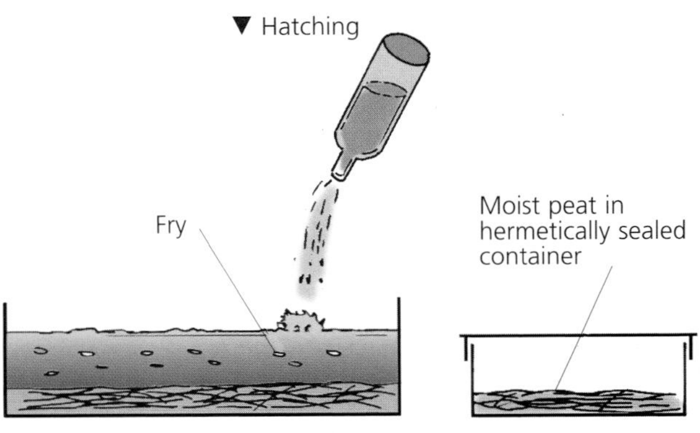

▼ Hatching

Aphyosemion

Species of this genus inhabit most areas of Africa east of Benin (formerly Dahomey), and particularly from the Niger to the Congo. Seasonal species are less common than the continuous breeders of drought-free areas; some species exhibit breeding patterns intermediate between both types.

▲ ***Aphyosemion bivittatum***
The **two-striped aphyosemion** reaches 6 cm in length, but its growth is slow. The sticky eggs incubate in less than 2 weeks. It is a continuous breeder. Size: 6 cm.

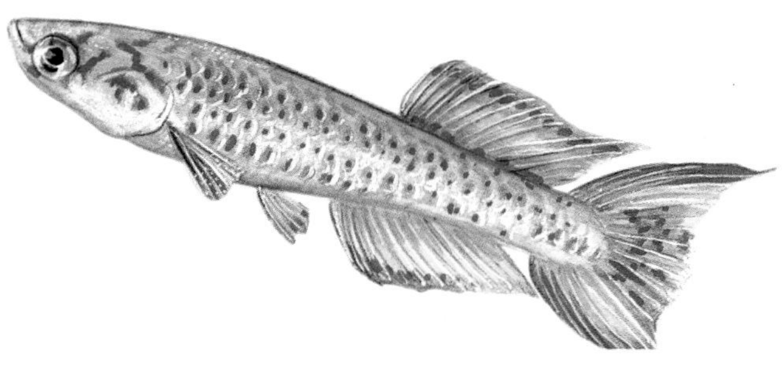

◄ ***Aphyosemion walkeri***
Walker's aphyosemion or **Walker's killifish** is a seasonal breeder. Kept in continually moist peat at 18–20°C, the eggs hatch in under 15 days. Size: 6 cm.

Aphyosemion sjoestedti
The eggs of the **blue gularis**, a seasonal killifish, incubate in 5 weeks at 22°C. Size: 12 cm. ►

▲ ***Aphyosemion gardneri***
The exact coloration of the **steel-blue killie** varies according to its geographical origin. It is a continuous breeder. The eggs hatch in 2–3 weeks. Size: 6 cm.

Aphyosemion marmoratum
The **marbled killifish** employs an intermediate form of reproduction. If you leave the eggs in the aquarium, incubation lasts 15–20 days, and hatching will be correspondingly staggered. Kept in peat, they will take longer to hatch, but all the fry will emerge simultaneously. Size: 6 cm. ▼

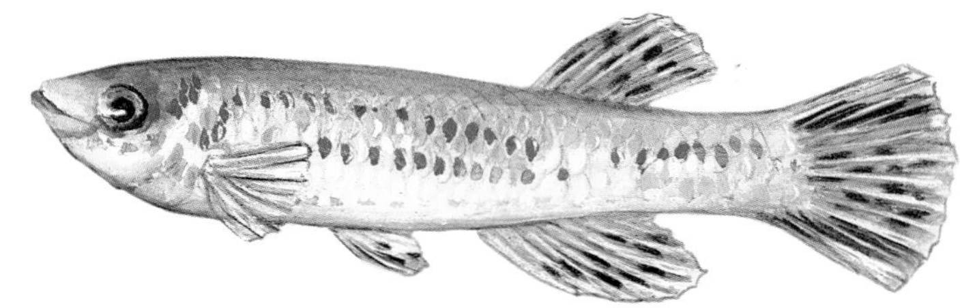

Aphyosemion australe ►
The **Cape Lopez lyretail** or the **lyretail panchax** is obtainable from most commercial outlets and is the species of aphyosemion most frequently recommended to hobbyists wishing to familiarize themselves with the genus. It is hardy, and spawns continuously without particular problems. Prepare a bed of peat in a small tank, introduce fine-leafed plants and keep the temperature below 23°C. The pH should be between 6 and 7, with almost zero hardness. The female lays 50–100 eggs, each only 1 mm in size, which hatch after 2 weeks. Remove any infertile eggs (cloudy instead of transparent). Hatching can be accelerated by raising the level of dissolved CO_2 (carbon dioxide) – a technique also valid for other species. One way to do this is by blowing gently down a tube into the water. Size: 6 cm.

Other Cyprinodontidae: *Roloffia – Epiplatys – Aplocheilus – Fundulus – Rivulus – Nothobranchius – Cynolebias*

Besides *Aphyosemion*, there are several other genera popular with hobbyists. They are not normally available from commercial outlets, but you can obtain them through clubs and aquarists' associations.

Roloffia species are native to the African coastal countries west of Benin, unlike their close relatives *Aphyosemion*. They prefer soft water (23–24°C maximum) and moderate levels of light.

Epiplatys is a genus of killifish found from Senegal to Chad and even as far south as the Congo, in the watercourses of tropical forests. They are continuous breeders, usually sticking their eggs to plants.

The genus ***Aplocheilus*** consists of a small number of species native to Asia. Their breeding habits resemble those of *Aphyosemion*.

Fundulus is a genus originating from the United States – some species are found in Canada – and Central America. Specimens are rarely found on the commercial market. The eggs adhere to plants, hatching in around 2 weeks.

Rivulus, from Central America or the northern zones of South America, is a genus preferring calm waters, with a moderately warm temperature of around 24°C. Note that these fish can jump out of the aquarium. They are continuous breeding, laying eggs on plants or on the bottom.

Nothobranchius species live in the waters of East and South-East Africa, in those areas with alternating rains and droughts. Fish of this genus have more slender bodies than those belonging to ***Rivulus***, but are just as colorful.

Cynolebias comprises seasonal killies from South America. Some species will even bury themselves in the peat to lay their eggs. There are several species, closely related to the two illustrated below.

Cynolebias nigripinnis
The **black-finned pearl fish** is a seasonal species; the eggs must be kept in peat for 4 months. Size: 5 cm. ▼

Cynolebias bellottii
The males of the **Argentinian pearl fish** will sometimes fight one another or harry the females. The breeding of this seasonal species is difficult. The eggs must be kept for 3–6 months in moist peat; after replacement in water, they hatch within a week. Size: 5–6 cm. ▼

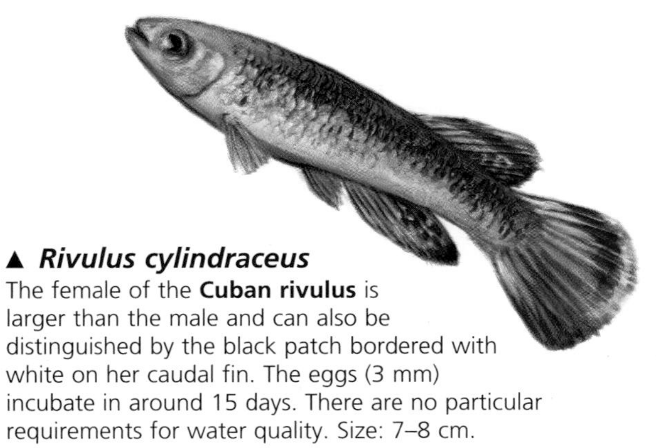

▲ ***Rivulus cylindraceus***
The female of the **Cuban rivulus** is larger than the male and can also be distinguished by the black patch bordered with white on her caudal fin. The eggs (3 mm) incubate in around 15 days. There are no particular requirements for water quality. Size: 7–8 cm.

◄ *Aplocheilus lineatus*

The **striped panchax** requires a large tank, as it can reach 10 cm in length, with plenty of vegetation. The eggs are laid in the plants; the fry are tiny, and they require live prey small enough to swallow. Size: 8–10 cm.

Epiplatys annulatus

The **clown killie** is only 3–4 cm long and is a top-dweller. It lays its eggs in fine-leafed vegetation; they hatch after 8–10 days. ▼

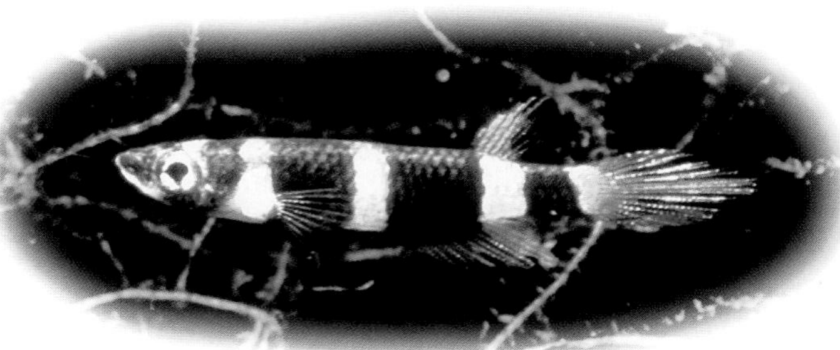

► *Notobranchius guentheri*

A seasonal, difficult breeder, **Gunther's notho** is small but very handsome. You need to preserve the eggs in peat for 6–12 weeks; return them to water, and they will hatch over a period of 2 weeks. Size: 3–4 cm.

▲ *Roloffia occidentalis*

The **golden pheasant** is a seasonal species spawning in soft, acidic conditions. The diapause can last 4–5 months, sometimes longer. The male is brightly colored, the female duller. Size: 8–9 cm.

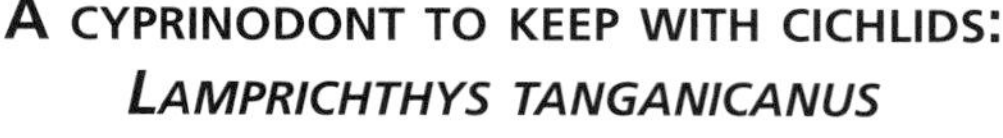

A CYPRINODONT TO KEEP WITH CICHLIDS: *LAMPRICHTHYS TANGANICANUS*

This is a species of interest to anyone seeking tankmates for Cichlids (see page 104). Both originate from the same habitat: Lake Tanganyika. *L. tanganicanus*, the **Tanganyika pearl killie** can reach 12 cm and its lively, shoal-swimming behavior makes it an ideal companion for Cichlids, though a fascinating subject in itself. Unfortunately, you are unlikely to obtain this species from your dealer.

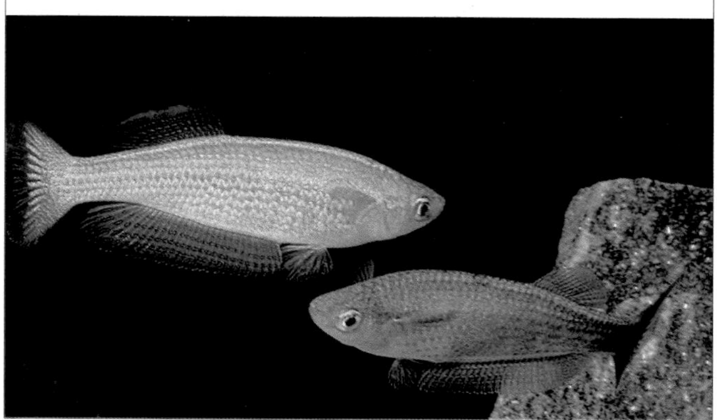

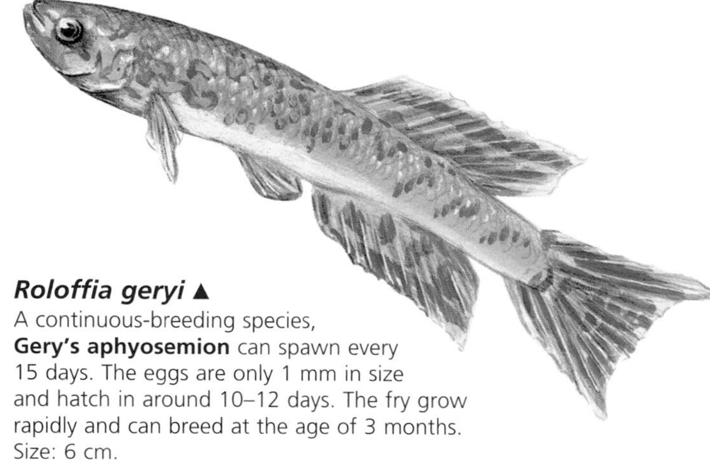

Roloffia geryi ▲

A continuous-breeding species, **Gery's aphyosemion** can spawn every 15 days. The eggs are only 1 mm in size and hatch in around 10–12 days. The fry grow rapidly and can breed at the age of 3 months. Size: 6 cm.

POECILIIDAE

The *Poeciliidae* inhabit considerable areas of the American continent, favoring hard, alkaline, and sometimes even slightly brackish conditions where the water is rich in plant life and normally calm. This is a family of active, energetic fish, ideal for the beginner. They will accept any form of food, including small, live prey, but appreciate extra vegetable material.

The male is normally smaller than the female, though often more vividly colored. His anal fin, by a modification of the third, fourth and fifth rays, has developed into a gonopodium (see illustration), a tubiform copulatory organ, through which he deposits his milt (sperm) into the female's genital pore during a fairly brief pseudo-coupling. The female can then produce several successive broods separated by a few weeks without intervention by other males, a feature which distinguishes this family from the *Goodeidae*. A darkish patch on her belly – the gravid spot, near the genital pore – signals imminent spawning in a ripe female. The eggs hatch inside her ovary; she then immediately expels the fry, often still in a curled, foetal position. These are much bigger than the fry of oviparous (egg-laying) fish: they are able to swim and eat fine artificial food on birth. To encourage reproduction, raise the temperature by a few degrees; the female will then spawn every 3–4 weeks.

Poecilia latipinna
This is known as the **sailfin molly** and should be kept in identical conditions to *P. sphenops*. (Both are popularly referred to as simply the **molly** or **black molly**.) The dorsal fin is both higher and longer then that of *P. sphenops*. The **black lyretail** variety is probably a hybrid of the two species, rather than a variety of one or the other. Size: 8 cm. ►

▲ *Gambusia affinis*
A native of the southern United States, the **spotted gambusia** or **mosquito fish** has been widely introduced to tropical and temperate areas of the world. It is met in southern France, for instance, close to the Mediterranean coasts and even as far north as Bordeaux! These deliberate importations were designed to reduce plagues of mosquitoes, since the fry are voraciously fond of the aquatic larvae. In a sense, then, it is not a "true" aquarium fish, but it is very sturdy and spawns prolifically. You can raise it as live food for voracious predators like the Cichlids; or for those fish with a tendency to refuse artificial foods, like certain marine species, as it can survive a few minutes' immersion in salt water. Size: 5 cm.

▼ ► *Poecilia sphenops* (molly)
The common variety of **short-finned molly** or **pointed-mouth molly** has a silvery-gray body, with varying degrees of black spotting. The **black** variety is more popular with some enthusiasts. The molly prefers hard water, to which you can add 1% seawater – or 1 teaspoonful of table salt to 10 liters of water. It is also a good idea to feed supplements of vegetable material. Size: 8 cm.

◄ ► *Poecilia velifera*

The **Yucatan sailfin molly** has an overdeveloped dorsal fin. A black variety exists, but it is less common than the "gold"; the latter is rather incongruously named, since it is practically an albino, as its red eyes imply. Breeding is straightforward, and even easier if you raise the temperature a few degrees. The females can produce up to 100 fry. Size: 15 cm.

TRUE OR FALSE LIVEBEARERS?

The term "livebearer" or "viviparous" is applied to fish of the following families: *Poeciliidae*, *Hemirhamphidae*, and *Goodeidae*. Their fry are born live (already hatched), a phenomenon rare among fish. In actual fact, the descriptions are scientifically inexact in the case of the first two families: there is no anatomical connection between the egg and the mother fish as there is in certain sharks and in mammals. Only the *Goodeidae* can be classed as true livebearers, but aquarists commonly lump all three families together under this heading.

Poecilia reticulata
Half-black red.
Size : 5 cm. ►

◄ *Poecilia reticulata*

Even those who have never kept an aquarium will have heard of the **guppy**! Discovered in the middle of the 19th century, it is one of the most popular species owing to its uncomplicated breeding habits and the large number of available varieties, which are classified according to overall coloration and the shape of the caudal fin. The guppy prefers hard, alkaline conditions, but it is extremely tolerant. A female can produce up to 100 fry every 4 weeks if the temperature is raised to 27–28°C. Feral guppies are unspectacular in color, with sometimes one or two black patches, and the fins are of normal size. Size: 5 cm.

Poecilia reticulata
Size: 5 cm. ►

Poecilia reticulata
Feral guppy
Size: 5 cm. ►

▼ Varieties of guppy, classified by dorsal fins

basic variety

pointed-tail

spadetail

lyretail

top sword

A LIVEBEARER FOR THE BEGINNER: THE PLATY

XIPHOPHORUS MACULATUS

In addition to the guppy, the platy or *Xiphophorus maculatus* is an ideal starter fish. There are many varieties available commercially. They produce about 50 fry, and you can cross the platy with the swordtail and *Xiphophorus variatus* (variegated platy or "variatus"). Common varieties of platy are:

- **red:** one of the most popular;
- **lemon:** cream-yellow body;
- **wagtail:** red or orange-yellow, with black fins;
- **tuxedo:** red and black;
- **black:** blue- or greenish-black metallic sheen;
- **Simpson hi-fin:** overdeveloped dorsal fin.

▲ ***Xiphophorus helleri***
Gold variety. Size: 15 cm.

▲ ***Xiphophorus helleri***
Wagtail variety. Size: 15 cm.

◄ *Xiphophorus helleri*

The photo opposite clearly shows why *X. helleri* is known as the swordtail. A very lively fish, it can leap out of the aquarium, and the male is sometimes truculent. Females do not have the "sword."
The female can produce up to 200 fry and exhibits behavior very rare among fish and indeed all other animals: after one or two spawnings, she can undergo a spontaneous sex reversal, and function in all respects like a male!
Size: 15 cm.

lower swordtail

double swordtail

flagtail

delta

fantail

▼ *Xiphophorus variatus*

The **variegated platy** has fewer varieties than *X. maculatus*, with which it can be crossed. The female can produce up to 100 fry. Size: 5 cm.

▲ *Xiphophorus montezumae*

This is the **Montezuma swordtail**. Most swordtails – the specimen illustrated here is a feral variety – have shorter "swords" than *X. helleri*. They are rarely sold commercially. Size: 5 cm.

Varieties of swordtail

Swordtails are distinguished by their color and/or the shape of the finnage:

- **green:** more or less bright green, with a broken red line on each flank; probably closely related to the feral form;
- **red:** entirely red body, the commonest variety;
- **tuxedo:** red background, large black streak from back of head to caudal peduncle;
- **Berlin:** red, spotted with black;
- **wagtail:** red body, black fins;
- **black:** in reality blue or green, with dark metallic sheen;
- **Simpson (hi-fin):** highly-developed dorsal fin;
- **veiltail:** all fins are larger than normal;
- **lyretail:** upper and lower sections of caudal fin prolonged by filaments.

▲ ***Xipho helleri***
Red veiltail variety. Size: 15 cm.

Xipho helleri
Veiltail variety. Size: 15 cm. ►

Xipho helleri
Green variety. Size: 15 cm. ▼

Xipho helleri
Simpson hi-fin variety. Size: 15 cm.▼

THE *POECILIIDAE*: CROSSES AND VARIETIES

There are very few aquarists who have seen, let alone owned, the wild stock from which captive varieties are descended. These varieties do not exist in Nature, but they are readily obtainable commercially. Some aquarists enter their prize specimens for shows, where they are judged on color, shape, and the development of the finnage.
How many varieties are there? At the present time, there are five different color varieties of swordtail, plus another three for fin shape. Given that similar figures would also hold good for the platies, and that all species of *Xiphophorus* (swordtails, platies, variegated platies, etc.) can interbreed, the number of varieties becomes enormous; there's no way you'll remember them all!
You sometimes hear aquarists remark that the present varieties, which have been patiently evolved through selection, are less hardy than earlier ones. Though the truth is somewhat more complex, beginners, who are encouraged to try these fish – mainly because they breed easily – may be slightly disappointed.

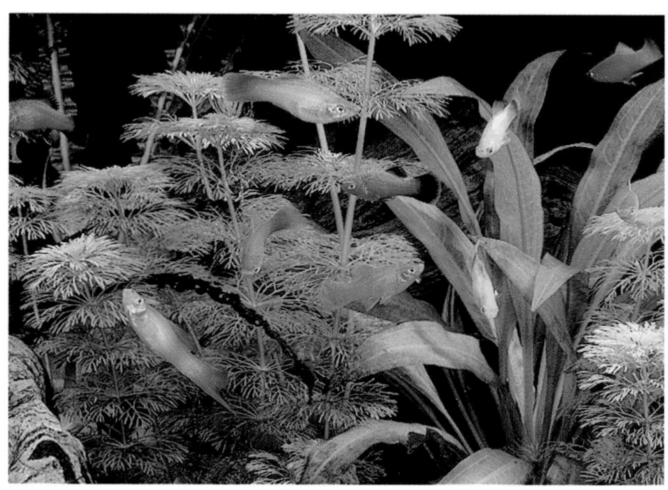

HEMIRHAMPHIDAE – GOODEIDAE

The *Hemirhamphidae* (which are false livebearers) originate from Asia, where they live in hard, sometimes brackish waters. They are characterized by a lower jaw which projects distinctly further than the upper. The *Goodeidae*, natives of Mexico, are true livebearers. Contrary to what happens with the *Poeciliidae*, the females produce only one brood after mating.

▲ ***Xenotoca eiseni*** **(Goodeidae)**
The **red-tailed goodeid**. The males, recognizable by their orange hindparts, are sometimes slightly aggressive. Gestation in the female lasts up to 2 months, with the fry (40–60) growing rapidly. Size: 7 cm.

▲ ***Ameca splendens*** **(Goodeidae)**
The male **butterfly goodeid** is more brightly colored than the female, and his anal fin less clearly modified than in males of the *Poeciliidae*. Breeding requires hard water, with the addition of salt: 1 teaspoonful per 10 liters. Size: 8–10 cm.

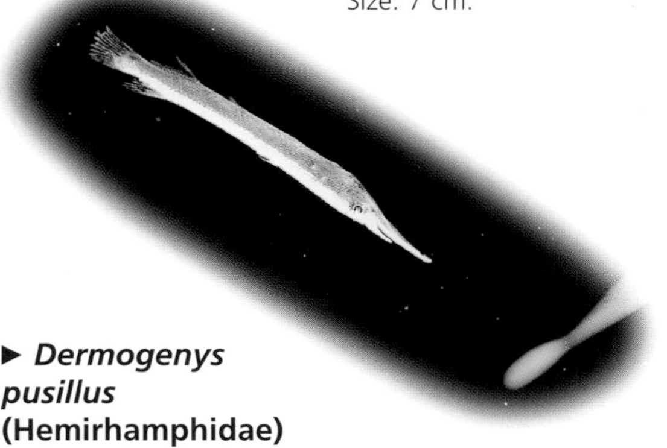

► ***Dermogenys pusillus*** **(Hemirhamphidae)**
Dealers offer several species under this name. The **Malayan halfbeak** proper lives and feeds just below the surface. Breeding is less prolific than with the *Poeciliidae*. The fry acquire the characteristic "beak" only after several weeks. Size: 7 cm.

CICHLIDAE

Cichlids have acquired a none-too-flattering reputation for trouble – persistently quarreling with other (and their own) species and wrecking the decor. But this is not always the case. There are more than 1,500 species (related to the European perch), which throng the freshwater areas of America, Africa, and, to a lesser extent, Asia. Often quite large and powerful-looking, these toothed carnivores are voracious feeders. Their anatomical characteristic is the single, elongate dorsal fin. Some species possess a distinct personality and are decidedly temperamental; basically lively and boisterous, they can become quite belligerent, at least under certain circumstances, such as during spawning or in defense of territory.
The breeding habits of Cichlids vary. One particularly interesting technique is mouthbrooding: the female shelters the eggs and fry in her buccal cavity, affording them a greater chance of survival.

CICHLIDS: FACT AND FICTION

BELIEF	TRUE	FALSE
Cichlids are always big.	Some African and American varieties can reach 20–30 cm in captivity.	Some species, notably South American, do not exceed 10 cm or so.
They are miniature bulldozers, overturning the decor and uprooting plants.	Some species will disturb rocks or uproot plants, especially during breeding. Others are merely lively and "bump into" things, often accidentally.	Small Cichlids, and some larger species, respect their environment, even during breeding, and ignore the vegetation.
They are vicious, intolerant of other fish. See also "Cichlids: behavioral characteristics"; table, page 105.	A few species are permanently aggressive; others only when defending territory or breeding.	Some species, not necessarily the smallest, are sociable, even timid and shy, except sometimes during breeding.
They must be isolated in a large species aquarium.	This is best with the largest and least sociable Cichlids. (Minimum volume: 300 liters.) They will tolerate other species of their own size, regarding smaller ones as potential prey.	The more peaceful varieties can be kept in a regional aquarium alongside tranquil species, provided the tank is suitably large in relation to the size of the Cichlids: 100–200 liters minimum.
Cichlids are often impossible to obtain from dealers.	The less well-known Cichlids, rare varieties, or recently discovered species as yet without a scientific name and only designated by a code number, can be acquired through aquarists' clubs – notably those specializing in this family.	The commonest varieties, raised in their native regions or in Asia as opposed to having been caught in the wild, are available through the trade. Some stores, particularly in the larger cities, specialize in Cichlids.

CICHLIDS: REPRODUCTIVE METHODS BY SPECIES			
	Eggs laid on vertical/horiz. surfaces: natural (stone, plant leaf, etc.) or **artificial** (e.g. PVC pipe cut lengthways).	**Eggs hidden in natural shelter** (cavity, crevice, cave) or in **artificial "burrow"** (plant container, coconut shell, wide-bore pipe).	**Incubation in mouth of female and/or male** (usually after eggs laid on suitable surface).
The Americas	*Aequidens,* *Papiliochromis ramirezi,* *Geophagus brasiliensis,* *Cichlasoma species,* *Uaru amphiacanthoides,* *Pterophyllum, Symphysodon.*	*Nannacara anomala,* *Apistogramma.*	*Geophagus steindachneri.*
Africa	*Hemichromis bimaculatus,* *Tilapia buttikoferi,* ▼ *T. mariae.*	*Pelvicachromis pulcher,* *Julidochromis,* *Neolamprologus,* *Telmatochromis.*	*Astatotilapia burtoni,* *Haplochromis,* *Oreochromis,* *Aulonocara nyassae,* *Labeotropheus,* *Melanochromis,* *Pseudotropheus,* *Cyphotilapia frontosa,* *Tropheus.*
Asia	*Etroplus* ►		

CICHLIDS: BEHAVIORAL CHARACTERISTICS BY SPECIES			
	Peaceful species sometimes timid; keep apart from other large or boisterous fish.	**Species temporarily aggressive** with conspecifics (during mating, territorial disputes), otherwise coexisting peacefully with their tankmates.	**Belligerent species**, The "bad guys": almost permanently aggressive, even vicious.
The Americas	*Aequidens maroni,* *Cichlasoma bimaculatum,* *C. crassa,* *Geophagus steindachneri,* *Nannacara anomala,* *Pterophyllum,* *Symphysodon.*	*Apistogramma, Papiliochromis,* *Aequidens curviceps,* *A. pulcher,* *Thorichthys meeki,* *Heros severum,* *Geophagus brasiliensis,* *Uaru amphiacanthoides.*	Other *Cichlasoma,* *Astronotus ocellatus.* ▼
Africa	*Pelvicachromis pulcher,* ▼ Les *"Haplochromis" ahli,* *annectens, boadzulu,* *moori.*	*Steatocranus, Astatotilapia,* *"Haplochromis" compressiceps,* *electra, linni,* *Aulonocara nyassae,* ▼ *Labeotropheus trewavasae,* *Julidochromis,* *Neolamprologus leleupi,* *N. sexfasciatus,* *Cyphotilapia frontosa.*	*Hemichromis, Tilapia,* *Oreochromis,* Other species of *"Haplochromis,"* *Melanochromis,* ▼ *Labeotropheus fuelleborni,* *Pseudotropheus,* *Neolamprologus tetracanthus,* *N. tretocephalus,* *Tropheus.*
Asia	*Etroplus.*		

CICHLIDAE: AMERICAN SPECIES

In general these prefer slightly acidic, soft conditions, and sometimes appear sensitive to any change in water quality. The aquarium (300–400 liters minimum for the largest species) must be equipped with hiding places and an efficient filtration system. Feeding is no problem: these fish particularly appreciate live prey and fresh foods. They deposit their eggs on a suitable surface: existing sites are usually sufficient. The exceptions to the rule are the mouthbrooders.

The genus *Cichlasoma*

The genus *Cichlasoma* originates from Central and South America. These fish are considered as potentially aggressive, especially during spawning, though some species remain reasonably peacable. Because of their temperament and their size, it is important to keep them in large tanks: 200 liters for the smaller species and at least 400 liters for the largest. The decor should consist of rockwork and sturdy plants. These fish are omnivorous; there is no problem keeping them in captivity, but be aware that they are quite voracious.
In general, the female is smaller than the male. She lays her eggs on a rigid surface which she has previously mouthed clean; the male then fertilizes them. After some 2 days' incubation, they are carried to nursery pits hollowed out of the sand to encourage them to hatch. The hatchlings remain there for a few days, while the male defends the territory.

▲ *Cichlasoma citrinellum*
The **Midas cichlid** is rather aggressive, requiring a sizable tank: at least 500 liters. The golden yellow coloration is less common in the wild, where most specimens are more or less gray. Size: 30–35 cm.

***Cichlasoma (or Parapetenia) salvini* ▲**
The adults of **Salvin's cichlid** are belligerent, but they take good care of their fry (several hundred per brood) which become free-swimming 5–6 days after hatching. A 250-liter tank containing hard, alkaline water, is perfect for these fish, with some sturdy water plants as a finishing touch. Size: 15 cm.

Cichlasoma crassum
Quite timid and tranquil, despite reaching up to 30 cm in length, the **Chocolate cichlid** can be recognized by its bulbous forehead. A native of the Amazon basin, requiring soft, acidic conditions and a large tank. ►

Cichlasoma maculicauda
The **blackbelt cichlid** is equally intolerant, especially of conspecifics. The female is capable of producing up to 1,000 eggs and the parent fish nurse the young for 3 weeks. The species prefers alkaline and moderately hard water similar to that found in their home waters of Central America.
Size: 15–20 cm. ▼

◄ *Mesonauta festivus* (Old genus name *Cichlasoma)*

Unlike other Cichlids, the **flag cichlid** – sometimes called the festive cichlid, and not to be confused with the other flag cichlid, *Aequidens curviceps* – lays its eggs on vertical surfaces, while the larvae are subsequently attached to another support by the parents. A temperamental fish: keep it separate from smaller species. Size: 20 cm.

▲ *Cichlasoma labiatum*

Easily distinguishable from related species by its large, blubbery lips, this species is commonly known as the **red devil**, and is aggressively territorial. It is best to separate the parent fish from the young after hatching. It is easy to mistake the fast-growing juveniles for the golden cichlid. Size: 20–25 cm.

▲ *Cichlasoma octofasciatum*

For a long time sold commercially under the name *C. biocellatum*, the **Jack Dempsey** (named after the boxer) is properly called ***C. octofasciatum***. A bad character, this, and likely to savage the decor! On the plus side, it spawns prolifically, producing 500–800 eggs. An interesting subject for the more experienced aquarist moving on to Cichlids. Size: 20–25 cm.

▲ *Cichlasoma nicaraguense*

The males of the **spilotum** grow up to 25 cm in length, but the females are distinctly smaller, and display brighter coloration during spawning. The eggs are not adhesive – a rarity among Cichlids – and are deposited at the bottom of a nursery pit dug into the aquarium bed.

◄ *Cichlasoma cyanoguttatum*

The **Texas cichlid** has a color pattern which varies according to its origin. Because of its size and behavior – it is vigorously territorial – it requires a large aquarium. Water should be alkaline and reasonably hard. The female lays up to 600 eggs. Size: 30 cm.

▲ *Thorichthys meeki* (Old genus name *Cichlasoma)*

To intimidate other fish, *T. meeki* enlarges its opercles (gill-covers), deploying its brilliant red throat membrane, which has earned it the common name of **firemouth cichlid**. Despite its small size, it is actually quite belligerent. The dorsal and anal fins of the male are more pointed. The female lays up to 1,000 eggs, which hatch in 48 hours; the fry are free-swimming 4 days later. Size: 10–15 cm.

A *CICHLASOMA* FOR THE BEGINNER

Cichlasoma bimaculatum, the **two-spot cichlid**, has a fairly calm temperament and is a good subject for the hobbyist wishing to gain experience with Cichlids. Its relatively modest size (15 cm maximum) means it can be kept in a 200-liter tank with slightly smaller fish such as some of the Characins. The water should be soft and acidic. The female lays up to 200 eggs, and the fry grow rapidly.

Cichlasoma nigrofasciatum
The **convict cichlid** is a territorial fish which you will often find playing bulldozers in your aquarium! It is best therefore to avoid plants or delicately positioned rockwork. Selective breeding has gradually evolved a xanthochromic (golden) variety, which is just as belligerent. Both strains can interbreed with the redheaded cichlid, but the hybrids inherit the convict's behavior patterns. Size: 15–20 cm. ►

▲ ***Cichlasoma nigrofasciatum***
Xanthochromic variety.

◄ ***Cichlasoma synspilum***
Despite its considerable size, the **redheaded cichlid** is fairly well behaved with other species, provided they respect its territory. Obviously, it requires huge amounts of space, but spawns easily, with the female capable of producing 800 eggs. Size: 30 cm.

▲ ***Heros severum***
A native of the Amazon basin, the **severum** thrives in soft, acidic conditions. Relatively tranquil except during spawning, it is one of the least prolific species of Cichlid, with the female laying only a hundred or so eggs in a clutch. Size: 20 cm.

Angelfish

Angels are the most well-known and popular of all the Cichlids. Their original habitats are the soft, acidic watercourses of the Amazon basin; they need an aquarium with a great deal of space, including depth, where they can swim without restriction. Plants, however, are also essential to form refuges. Angels are peaceful species – except during spawning – and you can keep them with Characins and *Corydoras* species in a regional South American tank. You should not, on the other hand, introduce smaller species, which the angels are likely to regard as prey. Angels will accept manufactured foods, but they delight in small, live prey, which is the best option.

Both parent fish are involved in caring for their young. The female deposits her sticky eggs on broad-leafed plants (especially those of the genus *Echinodorus*) or on PVC pipe placed in the tank. She will sometimes choose other, surprising sites, such as the aquarium glass or the heating equipment! The male then joins the female in guarding the eggs and fanning them; hatching takes place in 1–2 days. Sometimes, especially with the first clutch, the parents fail to fulfil their role and ignore the eggs; remove the adults, and imitate their nursing behavior by positioning an airstone or diffuser near the nest: this will stir the water and aerate the eggs.

The fry, which do not resemble the adults, start to feed on *Artemia* nauplii a few days after hatching. Whether breeding is successful or not, both the parent fish are able to mate again soon afterwards.

◄ ***Pterophyllum scalare***
Currently bred both in Europe and Asia, a long way from its native waters, the **angelfish** exists in a large number of varieties classified according to the amount and intensity of black coloration. Further, there are veil forms of practically every variety, sporting fins that are distinctly longer than normal. Size: 10–15 cm.

Pterophyllum altum
The **deep angelfish** is caught in its natural habitat, and so is rarer and more expensive to buy. It is distinguished from its cousin by the sharp indentation just above eye level. Its care is not quite so straightforward; the quality of the water must be just right. Size: 15 cm. ►

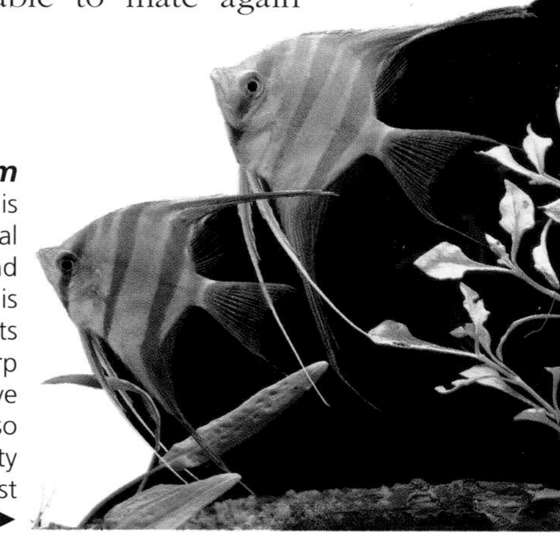

Discus

A native of the Amazon and Orinoco basins, the discus is often considered the most beautiful and regal of all freshwater fish. It lives in calm, clear waters with soft and acidic properties. Tranquil and peaceable, the discus is a leisurely swimmer, exhibiting stress reactions in the presence of livelier species. The best tankmates for it are Characins, species of *Corydoras* and *Apistogramma* or the various angelfish.

A large aquarium is necessary: allow 10 liters per adult, using a decor of suitably prepared bogwood, roots, and plants. Keep the temperature above 26°C and make regular partial water changes. Vary the diet, which should consist mainly of live or fresh prey. Breeding, considered extremely difficult, depends to a large extent on water quality: acidic, with a pH of 6, or even slightly less; very soft, using peat filtration; temperature must be consistently maintained at 28°C.

It is not easy to sex discus, but the adults pair off naturally into breeding couples. The female lays her eggs (up to 200) on a vertical support (PVC pipe, plant pot, aquarium glass), with hatching following in about three days; the fry remain attached by their heads and only start swimming two or three days later, under the supervision of the parent fish. The most extraordinary feature of these fry is that they derive nourishment from a mucus secreted from the parents' bodies – a virtually unique phenomenon in the entire fish world. Deprived of this critical feeding stage, they will not survive in the aquarium for very long. Ultimately they can be fed on *Artemia* nauplii.

Symphysodon discus discus
The **Heckel discus** has only three dark transverse bands. Unlike its cousins – the subspecies and varieties of *S. aequifasciatus*, which are mainly raised in captivity – the Heckel discus is usually procured from the wild. Tens of thousands of fish of these species are exported every year; there is little data concerning the influence of these culls on the natural population, but these Cichlids do not appear to be endangered. As a matter of interest, the Heckel forms a modest food resource, on a very localized basis, for certain native populations. Size: 10–15 cm. ▼

Symphysodon aequifasciata ▲
Brown variety. Size: 10–15 cm.

Symphysodon aequifasciata ▲
Breeding pair. Size: 10–15 cm.

► ***Symphysodon aequifasciata***
The black stripes vary in intensity according to mood and behavior.
Size: 10–15 cm.

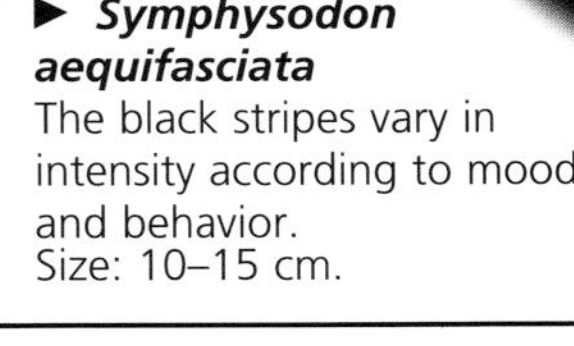

◄ ▲ ***Symphysodon aequifasciata***
There are several natural varieties of discus, technically known as subspecies:
– **brown**, basically brown, with blue streaks on head
– **green**, with a lighter body and blue-green belly; the head and upper back show blue, wavy stripes
– **blue**, much of whose body, especially the finnage, is covered with blue streaks.
Three other strains of discus have been bred selectively:
– **red**, which has a red back and belly; the pelvic fins are black, as opposed to red in other varieties
– **royal blue**, blue body with brownish-red streaks
– **azure**, a newcomer to the market, and apparently very hard to breed.
Size: 10–15 cm.

Symphysodon discus discus
(three transverse bands; central band always visible)

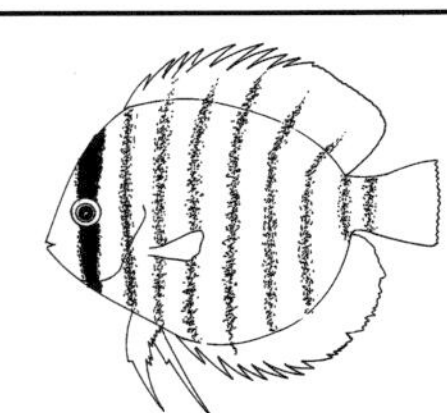

Symphysodon aequifasciata
(nine transverse bands; visibility varies)

Other American species

There are still more American members of this family. Some of the smaller ones are deservedly popular on account of their coloration and behavior, while others are giants requiring an aquarium of commensurate size.

► ***Aequidens maroni***

The **keyhole cichlid** is tranquil, even timid, and needs a well-planted tank with hiding places. Its breeding behavior is similar to that of *Aequidens curviceps*, though producing fewer eggs. Size: 12 cm.

Aequidens curviceps

The **flag cichlid**, not to be confused with ***Mesonauta festivus***, which shares its English name, is a small species from the Amazonian basin, and peaceful enough except at spawning time. The female deposits up to 1,000 eggs on a suitable surface; both parent fish then keep guard. The fry cling to their support by means of a substance secreted from glands on the head; when they become free-swimming, feed them on ***Artemia*** nauplii. Size: 8 cm. ▲

Aequidens pulcher

The **blue acara** is a territorial species and can be aggressive. The female lays 200–500 eggs on a flat stone. Size: 15 cm. ▼

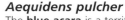

Papiliochromis ramirezi

Ramirez's dwarf cichlid is sensitive to water quality, so you will need to carry out regular, partial changes; it also prefers well-planted aquariums with plenty of hiding places. The female lays between 300 and 400 eggs on a flat stone. There is also a golden (xanthochromic) variety of this species, arrived at by artificial selection. Size: 6 cm. ►

Astronotus ocellatus

The **oscar** grows to 30 cm and has a bad reputation for wrecking the decor. Or, less uncharitably, it has plenty of character, and doesn't bother too much about the plants as it barges about. The answer is to use a very large tank (several hundred liters) and tough, well-anchored vegetation. Bronze and gold varieties of oscar have been evolved by artificial selection. ▼

Apistogramma agassizii

Tranquil and peaceable, **Agassiz's dwarf cichlid** demands regular water changes. The female cleans a solid support before laying up to 300 eggs. Size: 7 cm. ▼

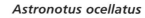

▲ ***Apistogramma cacatuoides***

Males of the **cockatoo dwarf cichlid** are mutually antagonistic. The female deposits her eggs on the roof of a natural cave or an artificial retreat such as a plant pot or piece of PVC pipe. She then keeps guard over them, driving off all intruders. The fry swim 5–7 days after hatching. Size: 7 cm.

◀ ***Nannacara anomala***
The modest-sized **golden dwarf cichlid** likes soft, acidic conditions. The female lays her eggs on a stone in a quiet place and then guards them, even against the male. Size: 8 cm.

Uaru amphiacanthoides
Rather slow and timid for its size, the **triangle cichlid** is more active at spawning time, when both parents guard and fan the 300 eggs. Care of this species demands a tank with a minimum capacity of 400–500 liters filled with soft, acidic water. Size: 25–30 cm. ▶

▲ ***Geophagus brasiliensis***
The **pearl cichlid** can exceed 20 cm in length and is highly teritorial; it is essential to keep it in a large tank with similar-sized species. Tolerates water with average pH and hardness levels, but you will need to carry out regular changes.

◀ ***Geophagus steindachneri***
The **redhump geophagus** is a placid species which loves to burrow in the sand. After laying, the female gathers the eggs in her mouth, whence the fry emerge in 2–3 weeks, though they will dart back inside when frightened. Size: 20 cm.

Cichlidae: African species

In view of their size and behavior, most of the African species require a tank of some considerable size, powerful filtration, and few plants – the latter are in any case quite rare in the natural habitats. The water should be distinctly alkaline (pH between 7.5 and 8, even higher for certain species) and hard. The best form of decor is an imitation scree offering plenty of hiding places; for the majority of species, you will also need to keep areas clear for swimming, though some prefer sandy zones. You can usually tell the males apart by their coloration. A large number of species practice mouthbrooding; the rest spawn in a cave or on a suitable surface.

Many of the Cichlids found in East African lakes are endemic, in other words, unique to the locality. The existence of localized populations sometimes gives rise to several strains of the same species, which are distinguishable by coloration.

Lake Tanganyika Cichlids

Some 80–90% of Cichlids found in this lake are endemic; certain species practice mouthbrooding, the rest are substrate-spawners, i.e. lay eggs on a suitable surface or support. Some of the smaller species shelter in the empty shells of *Neothauma*, an aquatic gastropod.

◀ ***Cyphotilapia frontosa***
The **frontosa** demands an aquarium containing a minimum of 400–500 liters, with a decor of rockwork. It feeds on quite large prey such as mussels or prawns. The adult males can be recognized by their bulging foreheads. Females are mouthbrooders. Size: 30 cm.

▲ ***Julidochromis dickfeldi***
Dickfeld's julie can be distinguished by its background coloration, often darker than that of its cousins, and by the blue border on the fins. Size: 8 cm.

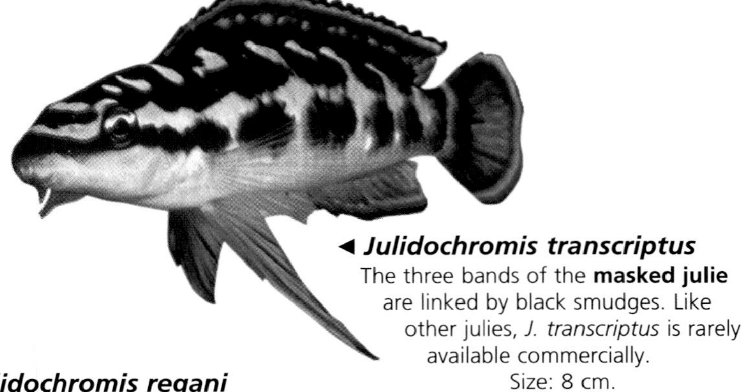

◄ ***Julidochromis transcriptus***
The three bands of the **masked julie** are linked by black smudges. Like other julies, *J. transcriptus* is rarely available commercially. Size: 8 cm.

Julidochromis regani
One of the largest julies, the **striped julie** or **convict julie** can grow to 15 cm; other species usually measure 7–9 cm. The English name derives from the four longitudinal bands. ►

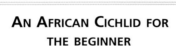

An African Cichlid for the Beginner

The behavior of *Neolamprologus brichardi* (**lyretail lamprologus**) makes it an ideal starter fish. It lives in shoals and is gregarious, save at spawning time, when it becomes territorial. The eggs are laid on the roof of a cave which the parent fish will hollow out, sometimes under a rock. The female cares for the eggs while the male stands guard over the nest; the fry are free-swimming some 8 days after hatching.

The female can give birth again after 1 month; consequently, you may find several generations of brothers, sisters, and male and female cousins all living together. The male looks after the older ones while the female tends the youngsters. When they are a few centimeters long, even the fry join in defending the territory.

In the wild, these species feed mainly on algae and plankton, but in captivity will take small live prey. Size: 10 cm.

▲ ***Julidochromis marlieri***
Marlier's julie is remarkable for its brown-and-white checkerboard patterning. Size: 10–12 cm.

Julidochromis ornatus
Males and females of the **ornate julie** pair-bond in a permanent, sedate relationship, even when not spawning. They seek out areas of rock with hiding places and shelters where they can reproduce. Several hundred eggs are attached to the roof of the spawning site; the female tends them while the male defends the territory. The fry are free-swimming after 8–10 days, under the watchful eyes of the adults. ***J. ornatus*** has three longitudinal bands on a light background. Size: 8 cm. ►

◄ ***Neolamprologus sexfasciatus***
Though not particularly aggressive, *N. sexfasciatus* should not share a tank with smaller species. The female lays her eggs in a shelter, on the underside of the roof, with the fry not emerging till a week or so later. Size: 8–10 cm.

▼ ***Neolamprologus tetracanthus***
The **tetracanthus** is a Cichlid which is likely to bully smaller species. It is fond of sandy areas furnished with plants – beds of *Vallisneria* for instance. It makes a tiny cave at the base of a rock by burrowing away the sand; the female then fixes her eggs (100–150) to the roof. Size: 15–18 cm.

▼ ***Neolamprologus leleupi***
Rather aggressive, this is a solitary dweller. The female of the **lemon cichlid** lays some 200 eggs in a cave hollowed out under a rock, with the fry hatching in 3 days and swimming freely a week later. Size: 8–10 cm.

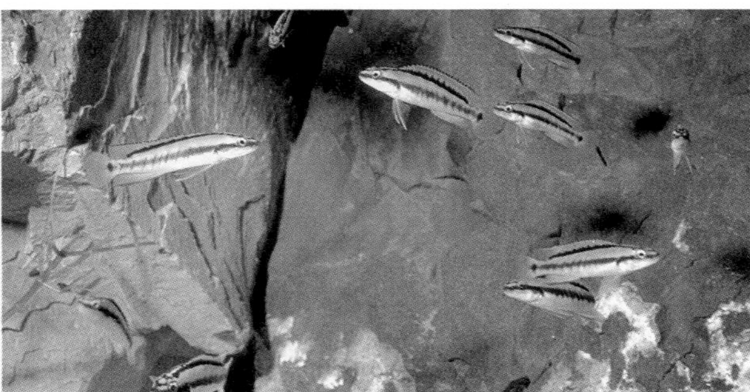

▲ ***Telmatochromis bifrenatus***
The **striped telmat** is distinguishable from its cousin *T. brichardi* by the presence of an extra longitudinal stripe, but sharing a virtually identical lifestyle; the female, for example, also lays in a narrow cavity. Size: 8 cm.

Telmatochromis brichardi
A small, gregarious species dwelling in rock zones. The female lays her eggs in a very small cave guarded by the male; the fry take several days to emerge. Its favorite food consists of live prey. Size: 8 cm. ►

THE SHELL-SQUATTER

Neolamprologus brevis (the **dwarf shell-dweller**) is a shy, even timid species. It spawns in the empty shell of *Neothauma*, a snail which shares its habitat. When the fry grow to about 2 cm they seek out shells of their own. In the aquarium, you will need to provide a fine sand substrate, which you should then scatter with different-sized snail shells (edible or marine species) placed with the opening upwards. This is not an easy species of Cichlid to obtain. Size: 5 cm.

▲ ***Neolamprologus tretocephalus***
The **five-barred cichlid** is belligerent and territorial, thriving, like all species of *Neolamprologus*, in tanks where there is abundant rockwork and the water is changed regularly. The female lays 200–300 eggs in a cave. Size: 10 cm.

◄ ► *Tropheus moorii*
The **moorii** seeks out rocky zones with clear water and a supply of algae, and so requires supplements of vegetable material in captivity. The males will fight for territory. The female incubates the eggs in her mouth; as they are larger than those of other species, she can only hold a small number, around 20 at most. The coloration of juveniles differs from that of adult fish, which, in any case, varies – as does the exact shape – according to their original habitat. Size: 12 cm.

Tropheus duboisi
The **blue-faced duboisi** juveniles are black with a scattering of white spots which disappear when the fish reach the adult stage, leaving a transverse white band halfway along the body. *T. duboisi* breeds in an identical manner to *T. moorii*. Size: 12 cm.

Cichlidae: Lake Malawi species

There are reckoned to be more than 200 species living in this lake, almost all endemic. The habitat consists of rocky zones with hiding places and shelters, surrounded by clear, shallow, and well-lit water. The Cichlids feed on the algae encrusting the rocks – practically the only vegetation present.

These fish require a fairly large tank (200–300 liters minimum for small species, 400–500 liters for the largest) fitted with a powerful filtration system. Rocks will form the main decor, but ensure the arrangement is stable, otherwise the more boisterous specimens will dislodge it. The water must be distinctly alkaline, with a minimum pH of 7.5 – even 8 and over – and fairly hard: 5.6–8.4° GH (100–150 ppm). Cichlids are very fond of live or fresh prey, but they will accept granulated artificial foods. Most species are mouthbrooders.

Until the last few years, a certain number of species were grouped within the genus *Haplochromis*. Scientists have now redistributed these across a variety of genera; however, the term "hap" (i.e. Haplochromine) is still commonly used as a catch-all designation for these endemic, mouthbrooding Cichlids.

***Aulonocara nyassae* ▲**
The **Nyassa peacock** is only aggressive towards conspecifics and until a hierarchy establishes itself among the males. It requires a tank large enough for unrestricted swimming, with rockwork and a sandy substrate. After laying her eggs on a stone, the female incubates them in her mouth, where even free-swimming fry will retreat if threatened. There are several varieties of *A. nyassae*, some of which could well be different species. Size: 12 cm.

Copadichromis boadzulu
On reaching 1–2 cm, fry of this species join groups controlled by a dominant male. The female incubates 30–50 eggs in her mouth for around 3 weeks. Size: 12 cm. ►

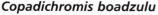

► ***Cyrtocara moorii***
The adults of the **blue lumphead** have a bulging forehead, more prominent in the males. Rather timid, *C. moorii* seeks out sandy areas of the lake bed with rocks to demarcate its territory. The female incubates the eggs in her mouth for 3 weeks. Size: 20 cm.

Sciaenochromis ahli ▲
A rather shy and timid "hap"; the male is blue, the female grayish with dark transverse stripes. Size: 12–15 cm.

▲ ***Copadichromis jacksoni* (female)**
Sometimes confused with *Sciaenochromis ahli*, this species is actually larger. Juveniles have two dark patches which usually disappear in adulthood. Size: 18–20 cm.

▲ ***Dimidiochromis compressiceps***
The long, flat head and slim, elongate body characterize the **Malawian eye-biter**, whose name derives from its reputation for devouring the eyes of other fish. It swims with head tilted slightly downwards ready to seize its prey. A typical habitat would be a sandy bed with plantations of *Vallisneria*.
Size: 15–20 cm.

▲ ***Nimbochromis livingstonii***
The **Livingstone's mbuna** is somewhat pugnacious and bullies smaller species. The dominant male takes on a blue, metallic coloration, while the females – who incubate their eggs for 3 weeks – exhibit brown spots on a light background. Size: 20 cm.

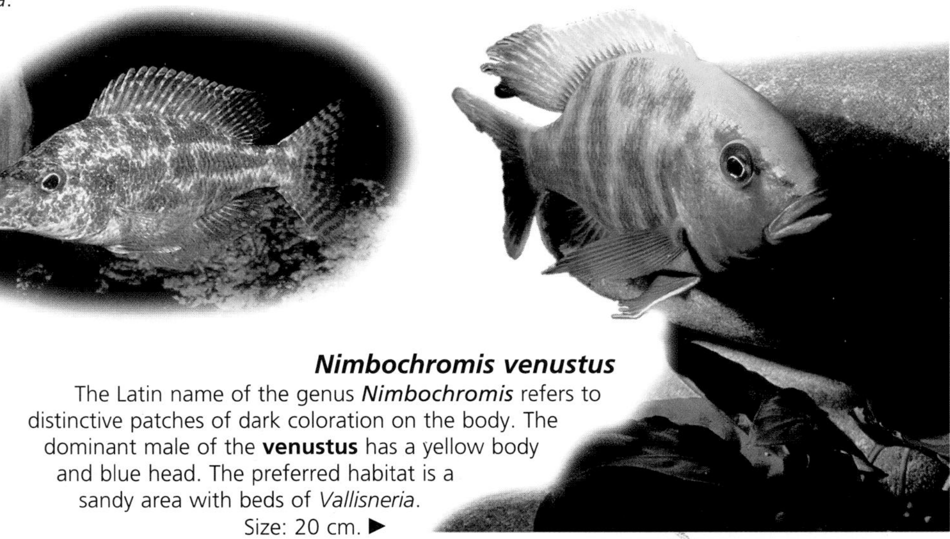

► ***Nimbochromis linni***
The **elephant-nose polystigma**, or **Linn's haplochromis**, a native of Pacific waters, is easily confused with a closely related species, *N. polystigma* (English name: the **polystigma**) but has a downward-tilted mouth. The female incubates up to 300 eggs for 3 weeks; the fry are free-swimming when they reach 1 cm. Size: 20 cm.

Nimbochromis venustus
The Latin name of the genus *Nimbochromis* refers to distinctive patches of dark coloration on the body. The dominant male of the **venustus** has a yellow body and blue head. The preferred habitat is a sandy area with beds of *Vallisneria*.
Size: 20 cm. ►

Protomelas annectens
A shy and timid species. The male of the **annectens** prepares a burrow in the sand for the female's eggs, which he then fertilizes. She incubates them in her mouth for 2–3 weeks; the fry emerge from their refuge when 7–8 mm in size. Size: 15 cm. ▼

◄ ***Protomelas similis***
The dark stripe extending longitudinally from the gill-cover to the tail of the **red empress** can lead to confusion with *P. annectens*.
Size: 15–20 cm.

Placidochromis electra
This species (**deepwater hap**) feeds on tiny particles which it extracts from the substrate by filtering it with its mouth. The eggs are laid in a burrow dug into the sand, with the female incubating them for 8 days in her mouth. The fry leave their refuge after 2 weeks.
Size: 15–20 cm. ►

Under the general name of **Mbunas** are grouped the genera *Pseudotropheus*, *Labeotropheus*, and *Melanochromis*, which display certain behavioral similarities. They are active fish, lively and quarrelsome, especially at spawning time or when defending territory: in the local African dialect *M'buna* means "stone-striker." In most cases, it is advisable to segregate them in a species aquarium and not to mix larger with smaller specimens. Mbunas are hardy, but sensitive to any reduction in oxygen level.

Breeding can take place in the community tank. The (polygamous) males are distinguishable by their coloration from the females, which incubate the eggs in their mouths for some 3 weeks. Mbunas are difficult to categorize owing to variations in color among local populations and to the more or less regular stream of new commercial imports.

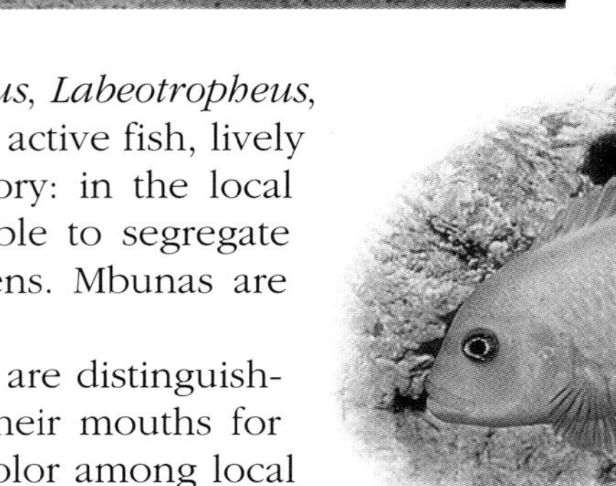

Labeotropheus fuelleborni
Fuelleborn's cichlid can be recognized by its curious parrot-beak snout. It requires supplements of vegetable material. There are several varieties or subspecies found in different parts of Lake Malawi.
Size: 10–15 cm. ▼

▲ ***Labeotropheus trewavasae***
The **Trewavas Malawi cichlid** – yellowside variety. *L. trewavasae* has a slimmer body than *L. fuelleborni* and will defend its territory vigorously. Its diet is essentially herbivorous, but it will also accept small crustaceans. Size: 8–10 cm.

▲ ***Melanochromis auratus***
The **Malawi golden cichlid** is the most belligerent of all Mbuna species, especially in the case of the dominant male. The female deposits her eggs in an out-of-sight nest while the male keeps guard; he is recognizable by two dark horizontal stripes on a light background, a patterning reversed in the female. Size: 8 cm.

Melanochromis johannii ►
Is very agressive – even the females attack each other. This fish readily accepts vegetable supplements. The male is dark with horizontal stripes, the female golden yellow. Size: 8–10 cm.

▲ _Melanochromis crabo_
A territorial and highly hierarchical species. The female **chameleon cichlid** lays her eggs on a flat stone, then retires to a quiet place to incubate them. Size: 8–10 cm.

▼ _Pseudotropheus elongatus_
The **slender Mbuna** has a more streamlined body than other **Pseudotropheus** species. The basic coloration is blue, but details vary extensively; the male has eye-spots (*ocelli*) on the anal fin. Size: 12 cm.

▼ _Pseudotropheus zebra_
The **Malawi blue cichlid** was one of the first Mbunas known to aquarists. Its diet is mainly herbivorous. There are several color morphs of *P. zebra* (blue or orange, for instance); some may in fact be closely related species. Size: 12–15 cm.

Pseudotropheus tropheops
The **tropheops** is one of the largest Mbunas and can measure up to 18 cm. The male displays a violet-brown coloration; the female is dark yellow. Supplements of vegetable material are desirable. ►

◄ ▼ _Pseudotropheus lombardoi_
The male **kennyi** is golden yellow, the female blue, with black transverse bands; unlike other Mbunas; juveniles assume these colorations on reaching 3–4 cm. The female retires to a quiet area of the tank to incubate her eggs. Size: 13–15 cm.

Pseudotropheus socolofi ►
Unlike other species in this group, the male and female **cobalt blue cichlid** are scarcely distinguishable. This Mbuna is aggressive and defends its territory ferociously. It appreciates supplements of vegetable material. Size: 13 cm.

Cichlidae: other African species

Besides the Cichlids of Lake Malawi and Lake Tanganyika, a few more interesting species are found in other, lesser-known lakes, and in certain rivers in East and West Africa.

Pelvicachromis pulcher

The **kribensis** is a native of Nigeria; it thrives in hard, even brackish waters with abundant vegetation. The female lays 200–300 eggs in a cave, tending them while the male defends the site, though he is less aggressive than other Cichlids. The fry are free-swimming 1 week after hatching.
Size: 10 cm. ▶

Astatotilapia burtoni

Burton's mouthbrooder is a species encountered in the Nile and East African lakes. It is more or less tranquil, but becomes territorial during spawning. The female lays her eggs in a hollow dug into the substrate and then incubates them in her mouth for 2 weeks in a secluded part of the tank.
Size: 10–15 cm. ▶

Hemichromis bimaculatus

Several related species are sold under the name of **crown-jewel cichlid**, the feral varieties having a more marked red coloration. The male will defend its territory vigorously; the female lays up to 500 eggs on a suitable surface, with the fry swimming within a week.
Size: 10 cm. ▶

Oreochromis niloticus

An algae- and plankton-eater in the wild, the **Nile mouthbrooder** becomes omnivorous in captivity. It grows fairly rapidly, and is very hardy: it can withstand a temperature range of 13–33°C and also survive in salt water after careful and progressive acclimatization.
Originally from the Nile, Chad, and Senegal, it has been introduced into practically the whole of tropical Africa, including Lake Victoria. Fishing for this species provides an important local source of food, but the largest specimens (often destined for smoking) are becoming rarer since the introduction of a voracious predator, the Nile perch or *Lates niloticus*. This fish, which can exceed 1 m and weigh more than 100 kg, is a notorious example of bad practice: importing a non-native species without proper precautions. However, the population levels of small Cichlids in Lake Victoria do not seem to have been affected.
O. niloticus has also been introduced into many of the world's tropical regions, where it is raised on a large scale to improve food resources. At the moment it is not in great favor with hobbyists.
Size: 30–50 cm.

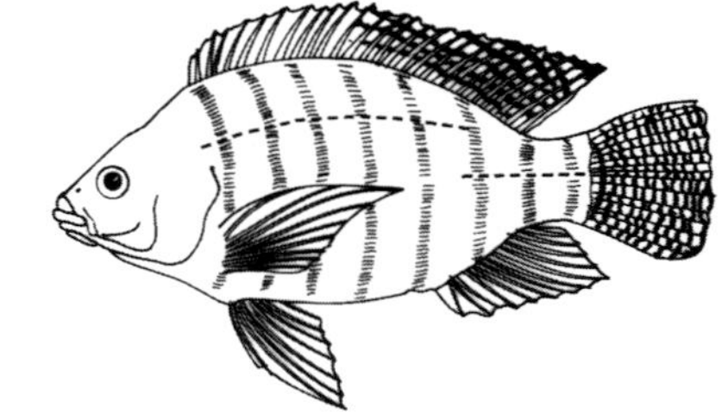

◀ *Oreochromis mossambicus*

The **Mozambique mouthbrooder** has been introduced into several tropical regions of the world. A large female can incubate several hundred eggs in her mouth for 3–4 weeks. The adults acclimatize well to seawater; the fry can withstand a progressive increase in salinity over 4–6 weeks from the time they are 1 cm long and are consequently useful for feeding as live prey, especially to marine species. Size: 50 cm.

▼ Tilapia mariae

The **tiger tilapia** can be extremely aggressive when defending its territory. The female lays up to 400 eggs on a suitable surface and then keeps guard until they hatch 2 days later. Size: 20 cm.

Pseudocrenilabrus multicolor

The **dwarf Egyptian mouthbrooder** is a small Cichlid dwelling in the Nile and Lake Victoria which will defend its territory against larger species. The female lays up to 100 eggs in a depression hollowed out of the sand and then incubates them in her mouth for around 10 days. Size: 8 cm. ►

▲ Tilapia buttikoferi

The female **hornet tetra** lays 200–400 eggs on a stone. The parents become very aggressive, defending both eggs and fry. Extra vegetable material should be added to the diet. Size: 30 cm.

Steatocranus casuarius

The bellicose **lionhead cichlid** or **African blockhead** has its home in fast-flowing, turbid waters. The characteristic protuberance on its forehead is larger in the male. The female lays 100–200 eggs in a hollow, which both parents will guard. Size: 10 cm. ▼

CICHLIDAE: ASIAN SPECIES

Very few in number; in fact, the hobbyist is likely to come across only two species.

***Etroplus suratensis* ▲**

In view of its size, the **banded chromide** requires a good-sized tank. It does best in hard, brackish water. Size: 20–30 cm.

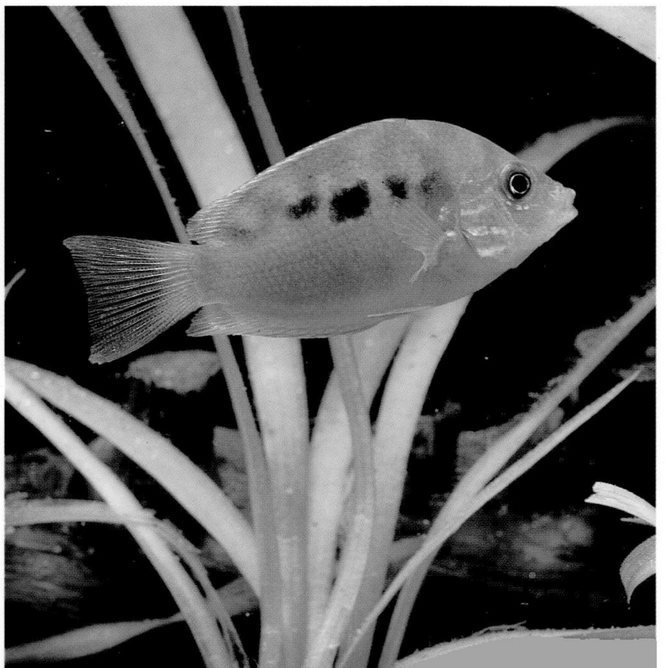

◄ Etroplus maculatus

The **orange chromide** also likes hard, brackish waters with abundant vegetation. A tranquil species which spawns quite prolifically, with the female laying 300 eggs on a suitable support. The newly hatched fry are then carried to a hollow dug out of the sand. There is also an all-gold variety of this species. Size: 8–10 cm.

BELONTIIDAE

These fish possess an unusual feature: located in the upper part of the head is a special organ known as the labyrinth – hence their earlier name of *Labyrinthidae*. They were also formerly known as *Anabantidae* (meaning "climbers"), since some can scramble out onto land. The labyrinth, in fact, allows them to breathe oxygen from the atmosphere. This process is supplemental to the normal function of the gills and represents an adaptation to their habitat, developing in juveniles during the first few weeks of life. The underlying reason is that *Belontiidae*, natives of Asia, live in environments deficient in oxygen: standing water, stagnant and often muddy, including pools and rice paddies. The pectoral fins of certain species have developed thread-like organs which have a tactile function and help the fish find its direction.

Betta splendens

The **Siamese fighting fish** only partly deserves its common name: the males are aggressive towards one another – and to females after spawning – but they do not interfere with other species. The females are always mutually tolerant. A handsome male (red, blue, or green) can therefore be kept in a regional or community tank. As soon as the female has laid her clutch of several hundred eggs, she must be removed, as she runs the risk that her mate will attack or even kill her. Incubation takes 2 days; remove the male after hatching. The fry will develop rapidly. Size: 6–8 cm.

◄ ***Betta splendens*** ▲
Males.

◄ ***Betta splendens***
A ripe female.

Colisa fasciata

Males of the **giant gourami** will battle for dominance. The females lay over 100 eggs in soft, acidic water. This species interbreeds with the thick-lipped gourami: dealers market the resulting hybrids under either name. Size: 10 cm. ►

◄ *Colisa sota (Colisa chuna)*

The **honey gourami** does not always construct a nest for spawning: the male carries the fry about until they are free-swimming. A gregarious but timid species. Size: 5 cm.

▲ *Colisa labiosa*

The timid **thick-lipped gourami** hides in the vegetation whenever it feels threatened. The female lays several hundred eggs in soft, acidic water. Size: 10–12 cm.

◄ ***Trichogaster leeri***

The male of the peaceful **pearl gourami** has a more pointed dorsal fin than the female, which can lay up to 1,000 eggs. The fry are slow to develop. Size: 13 cm.

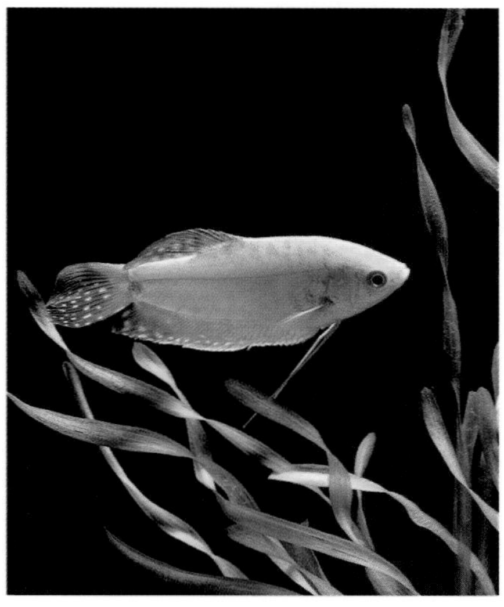

◄ ***Macropodus opercularis***

The **paradise fish** has been familiar to aquarists since the mid- 1800s. It is the "black sheep" of the family, but possesses the advantage of withstanding temperatures down to 15%C – sometimes even lower for short periods. The female lays several hundred eggs which hatch in 2 days or so. Size: 10–15 cm.

▼ ▲ ***Trichogaster trichopterus***

Trichogaster trichopterus

The tranquil **blue gourami** or **three-spot gourami** prefers to breed in seclusion from other fish. The current variety has only two black spots on its body – the third spot referred to in its English name is really the eye. These spots are not present in the Cosby strain. There is also a most beautiful golden variety, which is not albino. Size: 10 cm.

Helostoma temmincki

The **kissing gourami** is a near relative of the *Belontiidae* – it actually belongs to the family *Helostomatidae* – and like them possesses a labyrinth, and builds a bubblenest for its eggs. The "kissing" behavior observed between individuals probably has some social function; it is not necessarily linked to reproduction, though admittedly also occurring during the mating ritual. Size: 10–15 cm.▼

A GOURAMI FOR THE BEGINNER

The **Siamese fighting fish** (*Betta splendens*) is the traditional recommendation to the novice: the male makes a glorious sight in the aquarium. If your aim is to familiarize yourself with breeding procedures, it is better to try the **blue gourami** or the **dwarf gourami**. The latter (*Colisa lalia*) is tranquil and timid, retreating into the vegetation if disturbed. The female, less brightly colored than the male, is very prolific. The eggs hatch in 2 days, with the fry feeding on small live prey. There is also an orange-red version of this species – the **sunset**. Once again, the female is duller in color. Size: 5 cm.

CURIOSITY CORNER

Some species, often possessing unique anatomical features or biomechanisms, exist only as a single family in the world of the aquarist – and sometimes also in the wild. For these reasons we have grouped them together on this double page.

Notopterus chitala (Notopteridae)

The **Indian knifefish** or **clown knifefish** lives in Asia in slightly alkaline waters. It can swim both forwards and backwards, and tends to be nocturnal. Several species have proved marketable; one of them, *Notopterus notopterus*, which has only recently been successfully bred in captivity, is used as a food source in certain parts of the world. Size: 20–30 cm. ►

▲ *Gnathonemus petersii* (Mormyridae)

Peters's elephant-nose uses its "trunk" to sift the substrate for food, preferably in darkness, as it is rather timid. The elephant-nose can emit weak – and quite harmless – electrical discharges. Size: 15–20 cm.

Xenomystus nigri (Notopteridae)

The **African knifefish** is distinguishable from *N. chitala* by the absence of a dorsal fin, but resembles it in being a twilight species. Occasionally it emits a groan-like sound from the pneumatic duct, which links the swim bladder to the digestive tube. Size: 10–20 cm

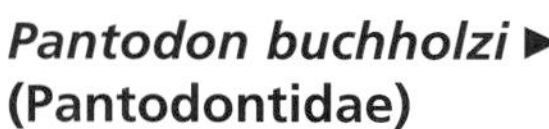

Pantodon buchholzi ► (Pantodontidae)

The **butterfly fish** is a surface-dweller, gulping down its prey (it has a preference for live food) with its yawning mouth. Sometimes aggressive, it can leap from the water. Its common name derives from its butterfly-like appearance as it swims with pectoral fins outspread. Size: 12 cm.

Eigenmannia virescens (Rhamphichthyidae)

The **green knifefish** originates from calm waters in South America, and therefore prefers soft, acid conditions. Another more or less twilight species, it appreciates live prey. Appears not to breed in captivity. Size: 20–30 cm. ►

▲ ***Chanda ranga* (Centropomidae)**
The natural habitats of the **glassfish** are hard, brackish waters in Asia. This is a peaceable species, but hard to breed. The female lays a hundred or so eggs in the fine-leafed foliage of certain plants. The tiny fry must be fed on infusoria of a suitable size. Size: 5–6 cm.

A DISGRACEFUL PRACTICE

The coloration of the back and belly is absent in feral varieties of the glassfish (*Chanda ranga*). A practice current in South-East Asia consists of injecting the fish with chemical dyes. This is more than questionable – it is downright unacceptable and ought to be stopped. We suggest very strongly that you boycott the purchase of such specimens; in any case, the coloration achieved is not permanent.

◄ ***Polycentropsis abbreviata* (Nandidae)**
The **African leaf fish** really does resemble a leaf – a camouflage used to outwit its enemies. Its deformable mouth means that it can swallow prey measuring up to half its own size. There are several related species; one of them, which belongs to the genus *Monocirrhus*, swims at an oblique angle, head down, and has a small barbel on its lower jaw. Size: 6–8 cm.

***Mastacembelus sp.* (Mastacembelidae)**
Several color variants are sold commercially under the name of *Mastacembelus* or **spiny eel**. The long snout acts as an organ of touch: only the head remains sticking out when the fish buries itself in the sand for protection. It is best to keep only one specimen, otherwise there will be constant fighting. Be careful too that this species does not escape from the tank, as it is very agile. Breeding in captivity is impossible without hormone injections. Size: 20 cm. ►

BRACKISH WATER SPECIES

Some species cope well with conditions where there are large variations in salinity. In the case of others, juveniles start their lives in fresh water before descending to estuaries, where they complete their development; once grown to adulthood, they live permanently in the sea. It is vital to keep such fish in special aquariums where the salinity is carefully adapted to suit their metabolisms. You will find several species available on the market; some possess really remarkable features and are regarded by aquarists as curiosities. However, few hobbyists think of actually keeping a brackish water aquarium, though this can be just as exciting as a freshwater or marine tank. Some of the species described below will coexist quite happily in the controlled environment of an aquarium.

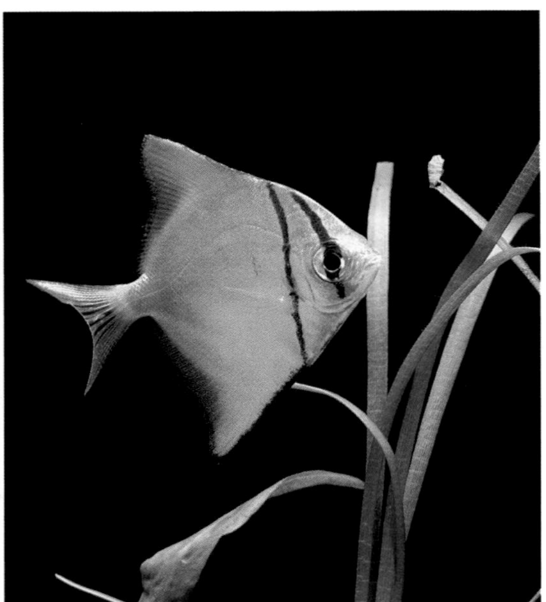

◄ ***Monodactylus argenteus*** **(Monodactylidae)**
The **mono** begins its life in fresh water, with the juveniles migrating to brackish regions as they mature. The adults are true sea-dwellers. This species requires a large tank with enormous amounts of space for group swimming. A timid species, it prefers live prey or fresh food. A near relative, *M. sebae* (the **fingerfish**), is partially herbivorous. When in poor health, or when the water quality is unsuitable, the coloration of both species darkens; normally, the silvery background predominates. Size: 15–18 cm.

Brachygobius xanthozona **(Gobiidae)**
The **bumblebee fish** comes from the coastal regions of South-East Asia. Its pelvic fins are modified into a sucker, which allows the fish to attach itself to a support and resist the current. It feeds on small, live prey and rarely breeds in captivity. Size: 5 cm. ►

◄ ***Periophthalmus sp.*** **(Gobiidae)**
The genus *Periopthalmus* contains some very bizarre fish which can leave the water and move around using their pectoral fins. They are found in all the world's tropical regions, except America, living in the sandy areas of estuaries. Caring for them in captivity requires an aquaterrarium rather than a simple aquarium; they need a bank of sand, with a gentle slope allowing them to emerge from the water, which should not exceed 15 cm or so in depth. Captive breeding is very rare. The two species most commonly available commercially are *P. barbarus* (**blotched mudskipper**) and *P. papilio* (**butterfly mudskipper**). Size: 10–12 cm.

Toxotes jaculator (Toxotidae)

The **archer fish** has its "hunting ground" just below the surface. To capture small insects for food, it shoots out a powerful jet of water, knocking down the prey, which it then snatches with its mouth. Its precisely aimed "shot" is made possible by excellent vision through both water and air; the jet can hit a target up to 1 m away. A territorial species, sometimes aggressive, and requiring hard, brackish water. Not known to breed in captivity. Food consists chiefly of living prey: preferably insects, otherwise tubifex or the fry of *Poeciliidae*. Size: 15 cm. ►

◄ *Scatophagus argus* (Scatophagidae)

Adults of the **spotted scat** can survive in fresh water, but are much less active than in salt conditions. This is a gregarious fish which requires vegetable supplements. The species *S. rubifrons* (**tiger scat**) is probably only a variety of *S. argus*. Scats are much more prone to disease if kept in fresh water, and thrive best in brackish or saltwater aquariums. Appears not to have been bred successfully by hobbyists; in any case, only reproduces in brackish water. Size: 20–25 cm.

Tetraodon fluviatilis (Tetraodontidae)

A few species of *Tetraodontidae*, a marine family for the most part, live in brackish water. The **round-spotted puffer**, the commonest, can become aggressive on reaching adulthood. It feeds voraciously on small snails, but will also take live prey. It appears that this puffer can be bred in captivity by using brackish water and keeping the temperature above 26°C. Size: 7–10 cm. ▼

▲ *Tetraodon palembangensis* or *T. biocellatus* (Tetraodontidae)

Several related species are marketed under the general name of **Tetraodon**; *T. palembangensis* is known as the **figure-eight puffer**. When threatened, all species can inflate their bodies with air and water to intimidate the enemy; they have teeth, and can feed on mollusks and crustaceans. *Tetraodon reticulatus* (**reticulated puffer**) is aggressive and frequents distinctly saline waters. It accepts live prey or meat-based foods; it is not known to breed in captivity. Size: 8–10 cm.

Marine fish

There are almost 20,000 species of marine fish in the world, but only a small minority is of any interest to the aquarist. Of these, most come from the Pacific and Indian oceans, although a few are native to Australia and the tropical Atlantic ocean.

Marine fish are usually collected in their natural environment and rarely reproduce in captivity. They find it more difficult to acclimatize than freshwater fish, particularly as regards feeding: some refuse to eat artificial food, and others have very special dietary requirements.

The smallest marine fish require a minimum water volume of 150–200 liters. Medium-sized species (around 20 cm) must be kept in tanks of 300 liters, or at least 400 liters if they are active. It is advisable to obtain juvenile (or sub-adult) specimens, as they are generally easier to acclimatize and feed.

Cohabitation of marine fish

Bearing in mind their behavior (aggression, need for territory, group life), not all marine fish can live together in the same aquarium, and any mistakes in this respect may prove tragic for your residents.

The table below therefore indicates how to fill a marine tank, on the basis of the characteristic traits of each species.

Fish to be kept as single specimens on account of their aggressive nature (generally linked to territory)	*Acanthuridae* (except *Paracanthurus hepatus*), *Balistidae*, *Canthigaster*, *Chaetodontidae* (with some exceptions), damsels (*Pomacentridae*), *Diodontidae*, *Labridae*, *Lutjanidae*, *Monacanthinae*, *Ostraciontidae*, *Plesiopidae*, *Pomacanthidae*, *Pseudochromis*, *Scorpaenidae*, *Serranidae* (except *Anthias*), *Siganidae*, *Tetraodontidae*, *Zanclidae* ◄ ***Lutjanus sanguineus*** **(Lutjanidae)**
Predatory fish, not to be kept with small species liable to turn into their prey 	*Balistidae*, *Diodontidae*, *Lutjanidae*, *Muraenidae*, *Scorpaenidae*, *Serranidae*, *Zanclidae* ◄ ***Cromileptes altivelis*** **(Serranidae)**
Fish that can live together in small groups ***Amphiprion ocellaris*** **(Pomacentridae)** ►	*Pacanthurus hepatus* (*Acanthuridae*), *Anthias* (*Serranidae*), *Blenniidae*, seahorses (*Syngnathidae*), clownfish (*Pomacentridae*), *Synchiropus* (*Callionymidae*), file fish (*Monacanthidae*)

Marine fish for beginners

The term beginners refers here not only to newcomers to fishkeeping, whose first tank will be a marine one, but also to aquarists who have already had experience with freshwater tanks. Beginners are recommended some species of clownfish (*Amphiprion clarkii* and *A. sebae*) and blue damsels, all of which belong to the Pomacentrid family. Also suitable are the smaller Labrids and the Blennies (family *Blenniidae*). The more experienced can try, in addition to these species, other clownfish and damsels, as well as some more regal species: queen angelfish (*Holacanthus ciliaris, Pomacanthidae*), auriga and raccoon butterfly fish (*Chaetodon auriga* and *C. lunula, Chaetodontidae*), clown and hippo tangs (*Acanthurus lineatus* and *Paracanthurus hepatus, Acanthuridae*).

For the experienced, more delicate marine fish

Once an aquarist is familiar with the problems of marine aquariums and how to deal with them, he or she can investigate other, more delicate species: annularis angelfish (*Pomacanthus annularis*), some dwarf angelfish such as *Centropyge acanthops* (yellow and blue angelfish), all from the Pomacanthid family, the *Naso* and *Zebrasoma* genera (*Acanthuridae*), yellow boxfish (*Ostracion cubicus, Ostraciontidae*), foxface fish (*Lo vulpinus, Siganidae*).
On the other hand, some species can be recommended only to the most experienced hobbyists: the Pakistani butterfly (*Chaetodon collare*), the copperband butterfly (*Chelmon rostratus*), the yellow longnose butterfly (*Forcipiger flavissimus*), all from the Chaetodontid family.
Also considered delicate are the *Acanthuridae, Balistids* and *Pomacanthidae* not mentioned above, and the *Zanclidae*.

HOLOCENTRIDAE

These are most active at night, their large eyes endowing them with good vision to detect their animal prey. They remain hidden by day, and so must be provided with shelters, and a tank of at least 300 liters capacity.

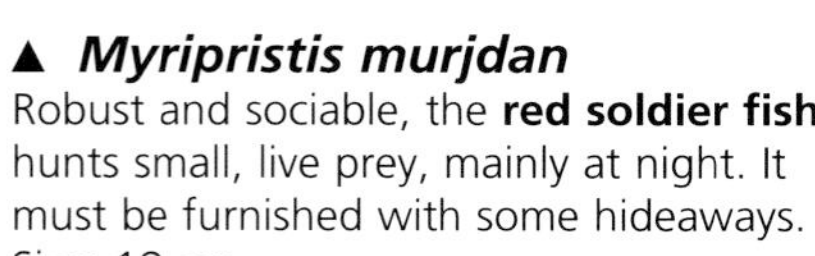

▲ ***Myripristis murjdan***
Robust and sociable, the **red soldier fish** hunts small, live prey, mainly at night. It must be furnished with some hideaways. Size: 18 cm.

Adioryx cornutus
The **squirrel fish** is a placid species which lives alone. It is easy to keep, though it must be given live food, such as small fish. Size: 14 cm. ►

Myripristis jacobus
Species related to *M. murjdan*. Size: 18 cm. ▼

◄ ***Adioryx spinifer***
Its bright red coloring distinguishes it from the *Adioryx cornutus*, but its lifestyle is very similar.
Size: 20 cm.

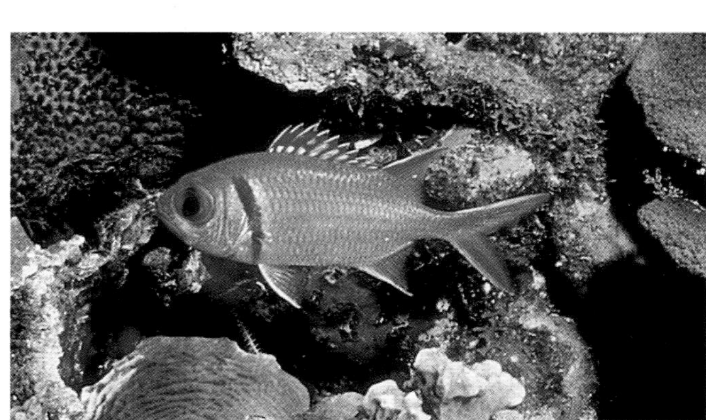

LUTJANIDAE

The Lutjanids (or snappers) frequent coastal waters, but not necessarily reefs. They are voracious fish, equipped with strong, pointed teeth, and need a large tank and enough space to enable them to swim in small groups. Lutjanids enjoy live food but can also be given pieces of fish, mussels, or shrimps.

▲ ***Lutjanus sebae***
The **red emperor snapper** lives close to corals. The adults, which are often solitary, are not always able to tolerate each other. This species must be put in a large tank with suitable hiding places. Size: 20–30 cm.

◄ ***Lutjanus sanguineus***
The **blood red snapper** has a good appetite and appreciates small fish. The juveniles have a dark band running from the eye to the base of the dorsal fin, but this is not very evident in adults. Size: 30–35 cm.

▲ ***Ocyurus chrysurus***
The **yellowtail snapper** is native to the tropical Atlantic. This strong swimmer likes to eat fish and small crustaceans. Rarely found in aquariums (regrettably, because it is a magnificent species), it needs a large tank, proportional to its size. It must be kept alone. Size: 30–40 cm.

◄ ***Lutjanus kasmira***
The juveniles of the **eight-stripe snapper** have less vivid coloring than the adults and a black spot on the body. Its diet consists of small fish and crustaceans. Size: 35 cm.

PLECTORHYNCHIDAE

The young live in groups; their coloring differs from that of adults, which are more solitary. They are bottom-feeders, often sifting the sand to capture small, live prey. In aquariums they can be gradually adapted to artificial food. They need a large tank with shelters.

▲ ***Plectorhynchus gaterinus***
The young fish sport horizontal bands, while the adults are bright yellow with dark dots. The **black-spotted sweetlips** is a peaceful fish that feeds on adult brine shrimp or other animal products. Size: 20 cm.

Plectorhynchus chaetodontoides
The **spotted sweetlips** lives alone (or in very small groups) in coral reefs. The white spots on the juveniles disappear when they become adults. They are barely active by day, and need a big tank to feel at home. Size: 20 cm. ▼

Plectorhynchus orientalis
The *zebra sweetlips* acclimatizes easily when young. It is quite voracious, and relishes shrimps, morsels of fish, or other animal products. There are several related species with horizontal bands. Size: 20 cm. ▼

SERRANIDAE

There are more than 400 species of Serranids in the world (including the groupers found in European seas) and some are easy to keep in a large aquarium (at least 400 liters). Serranids are robust and live alone once they become adults. The mouth of these voracious carnivores allows them to swallow small fish or large pieces of fresh food.

► ***Cephalopholis argus***
You can train the **black grouper** to eat out of your hand. It can be recognized by its brown coloring speckled with white dots. Size: 20–30 cm.

Cephalopholis miniatus
The solitary **red-spotted grouper** lives somewhat hidden in corals. It can live for over 5 years in an aquarium. The coloring grows darker in adults. Size: 20–30 cm. ►

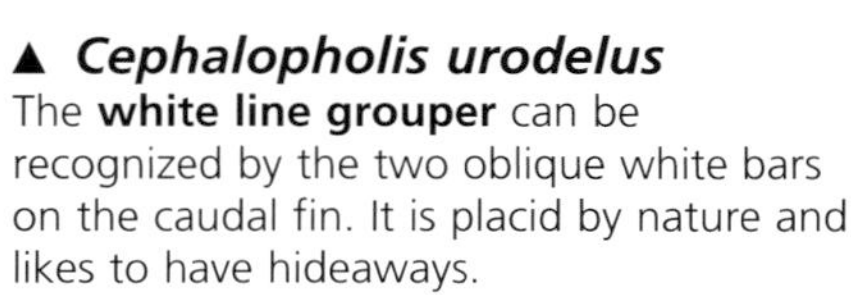

▲ ***Cephalopholis urodelus***
The **white line grouper** can be recognized by the two oblique white bars on the caudal fin. It is placid by nature and likes to have hideaways. Size: 20–25 cm.

Cromileptes altivelis ▲
The patches on the young grow less pronounced in adults. The **panther snapper** can grow up to 65 cm in the wild, and in an aquarium it can reach 30–40 cm. It stalks its small, live prey and suddenly pounces on them. This species does not succumb easily to common parasitic diseases. Several specimens can live together in a large tank.

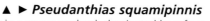

▲ ► ***Pseudanthias squamipinnis***
The **scalefin anthias** lives in a group or shoal, dominated by a few males. This pretty little fish can live in a fairly small tank (minimum of 200 liters) furnished with hiding places. It feeds on plankton in the wild and prefers small items of food, particularly live prey. This fish is sometimes classified in the Anthiid family. Size: 12 cm.

Hamlets

The Serranid family includes the species belonging to the *Hydroplectus* genus, native to the tropical Atlantic, that are small in size and therefore much appreciated by aquarists who have only a 200 liter tank. These fish live alone and hide in crevices in the decor. They feed on crustaceans, worms, and small fish.

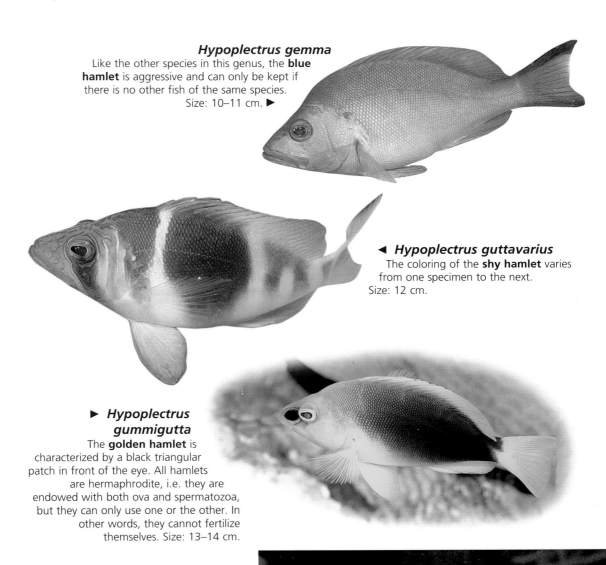

Hypoplectrus gemma
Like the other species in this genus, the **blue hamlet** is aggressive and can only be kept if there is no other fish of the same species. Size: 10–11 cm. ►

◄ ***Hypoplectrus guttavarius***
The coloring of the **shy hamlet** varies from one specimen to the next. Size: 12 cm.

► ***Hypoplectrus gummigutta***
The **golden hamlet** is characterized by a black triangular patch in front of the eye. All hamlets are hermaphrodite, i.e. they are endowed with both ova and spermatozoa, but they can only use one or the other. In other words, they cannot fertilize themselves. Size: 13–14 cm.

Hypoplectrus indigo
The **indigo hamlet**, bigger than the blue hamlet, is distinguished by its vertical bands, which are paler than its background color. Size: 15 cm. ►

CHAETODONTIDAE (BUTTERFLY FISH)

The butterflies are some of the most beautiful of all marine fish, on account of their vivid coloring. They are widespread in the tropical seas, where they live in coral reefs, either singly or as couples, generally staying close to the coast. The juveniles often have a different coloring from adults, which can cause some confusions between species. Butterfly fish generally have a specialized diet, according to the species: some graze on algae, some eat the tentacles of anemones or coral polyps, while others prefer different kinds of invertebrates. This sometimes leads to acclimatization problems, as they will not accept a normal diet. They must therefore be trained to eat other food: adult brine shrimps, worms, pieces of mussel, small shrimps. If they refuse this type of food they will soon die. The Chaetodons are considered the most demanding of fish as regards living conditions. This means the water must be of excellent quality – thoroughly stirred, filtered, and oxygenated – and regular changes, in small quantities, are beneficial. The temperature must be a minimum of 26°C, and the specific gravity 1.022–1.023.

Generally speaking, it is only possible to keep one Chaetodon per tank: they are territorial and do not really get along with each another, although they do accept fish from other species. Nevertheless, invertebrates are out of the question as cohabitants. The decor should consist of blocks of coral, through which they can weave about in comfort, thanks to their body form, but they must be given sufficient free space for swimming and feeding.

Chaetodon chrysurus
The **red-tailed butterfly fish** seems to tolerate other species from the same genus. It is an active fish that grazes on the algae in the decor and eats pieces of worms and mussels. Sometimes, however, it can refuse all food in its first few days in the aquarium. Size: 16 cm. ▼

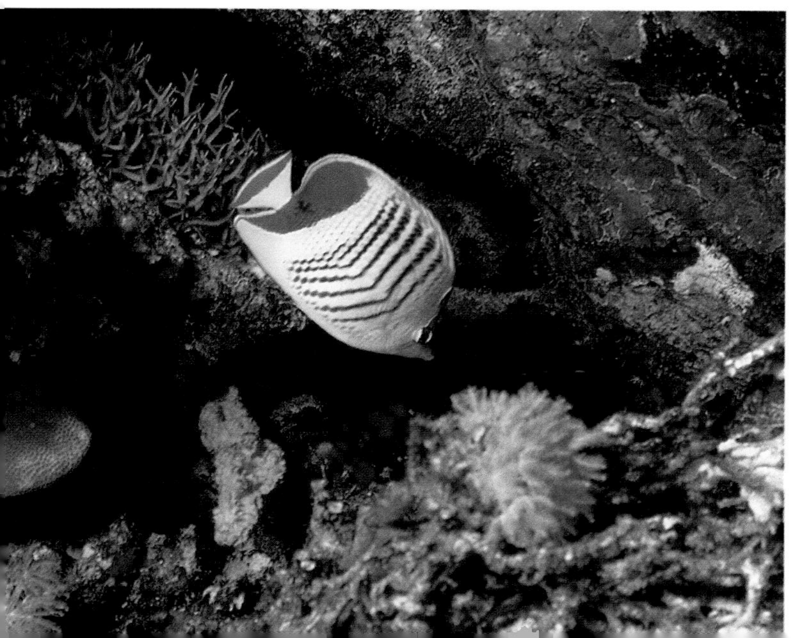

▼ ***Chaetodon auriga***
One of the best-known butterflies, the **auriga** is characterized by the adult's filamentous extension of the dorsal fin. Active and not prone to shyness, it is easy to acclimatize. Feed it with living or frozen food, backed up by vegetable material if there are no algae to graze on in the decor. Size: 14 cm.

◄ *Chaetodon capistratus*
Acclimatizing a **four-eye butterfly fish** can be complicated, as it normally feeds on the tentacles of anemones and corals, but it soon becomes easy to keep. It is one of the rare species emanating from the tropical Atlantic, where it is common. Size: 10 cm.

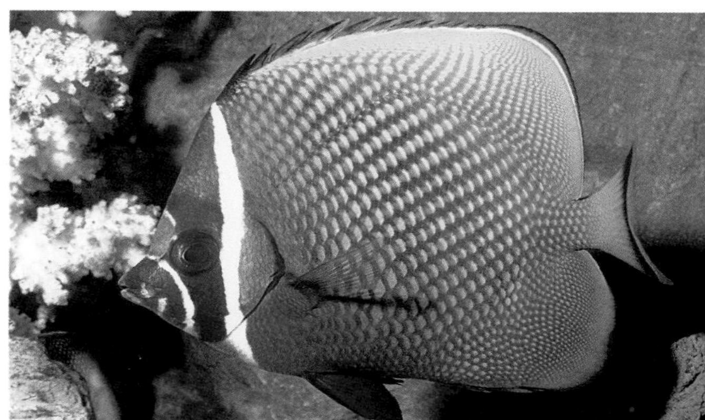

▲ *Chaetodon collare*
The **Pakistani butterfly fish** will tolerate fish of its own species. Undemanding as regards diet, it accepts both frozen and live food and also feeds off algae in the decor. It has a reputation for being easy to keep. Size: 17 cm.

▼ *Chaetodon miliaris*
In its natural habitat, the **lemon butterfly fish** feeds on the soft parts of corals. In captivity, it has to grow accustomed to small, live prey, then frozen ones (brine shrimps, tubifex worms).
Size: 13 cm

▼ *Chaetodon melanotus*
There are few differences between the juveniles and adults of the **black back butterfly fish**. This somewhat nervous species appreciates brine shrimps, worms, and small pieces of mussel, as well as small anemones of the **Aiptasia** genus that sometimes "spontaneously" appear in marine aquariums. Size: 15–17 cm.

▲ *Chaetodon lunula*
Easy to acclimatize, the **raccoon butterfly fish** accepts food of animal origin backed up with vegetable material. The black patches on the young (dorsal area and rear) get bigger in adults once they have reached 7 or 8 cm. Size: 20 cm.

► *Chaetodon meyeri*
Rarely found in the aquarium trade, **Meyer's butterfly fish** proves very difficult to acclimatize as it feeds on coral. Even if it does accept substitute food, it is not unusual for it to die in captivity. Size: 15 cm.

Chaetodon fasciatus
The **Red Sea butterfly fish** is considered very difficult to acclimatize, because it feeds on anemone tentacles and the soft parts of coral. This species can be confused with *C. lunula*. Size: 15–17 cm. ►

Chaetodon punctatofasciatus

Placid, little prone to aggression, but a vigorous swimmer, the **dot-dash butterfly fish** can accept artificial food, after first adjusting to small animal prey. It is considered difficult to keep. Size: 10 cm. ▼

Chelmon rostratus

The elongation of the "beak" of the **copperband butterfly fish** (more pronounced than that of the **Chaetodon** genus) has evolved to enable it to pick out food from crevices in the coral. This robust species swims slowly, except when it is alarmed. It feeds on small, live prey, notably crustaceans. Size: 17 cm. ◀

Chaetodon semilarvatus

The highly active **masked butterfly fish** searches out small prey near the substrate or in the algae, but it also swims in open water. Its maintenance can pose problems, as it is sometimes considered to be delicate. Size: 20 cm.◀

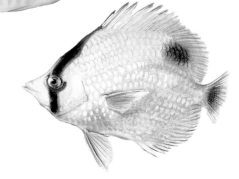

Chaetodon quadrimaculatus

In its natural habitat, the **four-spot butterfly fish** feeds on corals or small anemones. It does accept brine shrimps and frozen food in captivity, making it easier to keep. Size: 15 cm. ▶

▲ *Chaetodon ocellatus*

The placid **spot-fin butterfly fish** feeds on small live and frozen prey. It seems to accept the presence of other specimens from the same species. Size: 11–12 cm.

Butterfly fish coloring

The coloring of adults is often slightly different from that of juveniles (size less than 5 cm), the black patch on the rear of the dorsal fin sometimes disappearing in adults. It seems to act as a false eye (the real one being surrounded – and hidden – by a band or black patch) to deceive an enemy and surprise it by fleeing "in reverse." However, this theory has yet to be proven. Once the fish are fully grown, the juvenile bands can fade or disappear completely, although some, in contrast, can get bigger.

▲ ***Chaetodon striatus***
The **banded butterfly fish**, like the *C. capistratus* and the *C. ocellatus*, is native to the tropical Atlantic, while the other butterflies come from the Indo-Pacific region. It does not pose any problems once it has become used to small food items (crustaceans and anemones of the *Aiptasia* genus). Size: 15 cm.

Chaetodon vagabundus
The color of the young **vagabond butterfly fish** differs from that of adults. This species is not given to shyness and is easy to feed, with live prey and vegetable supplements. Its acclimatization is relatively smooth. Size: 15 cm. ▼

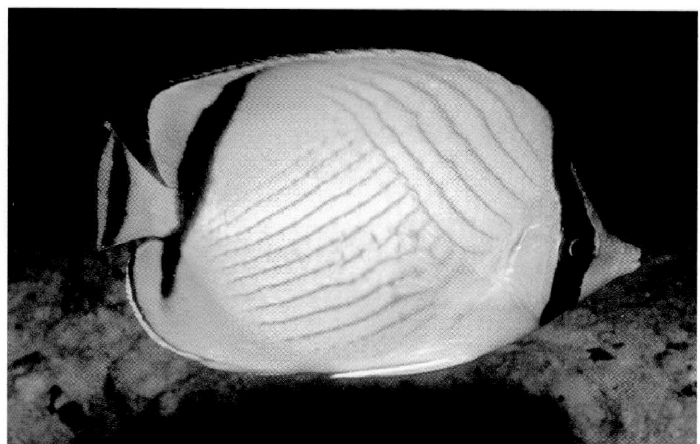

Forcipiger flavissimus
This is an easy species to acclimatize if it has not suffered too much during its importation. Not inclined to be aggressive (except against members of its own species), the **longnose butterfly** likes to have some hiding places. Its diet comprises mussels, tubifex worms, or fish flesh. Size: 15 cm. ▶

◀ ***Heniochus diphreutes***
The first spokes of the fins of the *Heniochius* genus are elongated to a greater or lesser extent, depending on the species. The **pennant butterfly fish** is peaceful and easy to keep in a spacious tank. Small, live prey is its favorite food. Size: 20–25 cm.

Heniochus intermedius
The background coloring of the ***black and white butterfly fish*** can vary from white to yellow, except on the upper part of the body. At night, when it can swim as actively as by day, it gets darker. Size: 15 cm. ▼

▲ ***Heniochus varius***
The **brown butterfly** is distinguished by a protuberance between the eye and the base of the dorsal fin, and by small tentacles above the eyes, which are more developed in the adult male. Size: 20 cm.

POMACANTHIDAE

The Pomacanthids are reef-dwelling fish, although they can also be found in the rocky coastal areas where algae grow. They can sometimes be difficult to feed in captivity, although younger fish adapt more easily to the food offered by aquarists. The Pomacanthids include both angelfish and dwarf angelfish.

Angelfish

Angelfish can be distinguished from butterfly fish by their protractile mouth and the presence of a spine at the base of the operculum.

They are good swimmers and live alone or in small groups, close to shelters such as caves and coral overhangs. As angelfish are highly territorial, they react badly to other members of their own species. The coloring of the juveniles gradually changes when they reach 8–10 cm (though this is not a general rule), and turns into that of the adults.

Juveniles adapt more easily to captivity, but only one angelfish can be kept in a 500 liter tank.

Their diet should consist of brine shrimps, mussels, and shrimps, along with cooked and chopped vegetable material.

▲ ***Chaetodonplus melanosoma***
The **black velvet angelfish** respects other species but chases members of its own species off its territory. It is shy, a good swimmer, and reckoned to be hardy. It devours large prey (nereis, also known as rag worms), but also eats tubifex worms and brine shrimps, as well as grazing on algae. Its skin is very sensitive to parasites. Size: 18 cm.

Chaetodonplus mesoleucus
The **Singapore angelfish** resembles a Chaetodon; the young are very similar to the adults. It is relatively easy to acclimatize if it is first fed live prey; it will then go on to accept artificial food. Size: 17 cm. ►

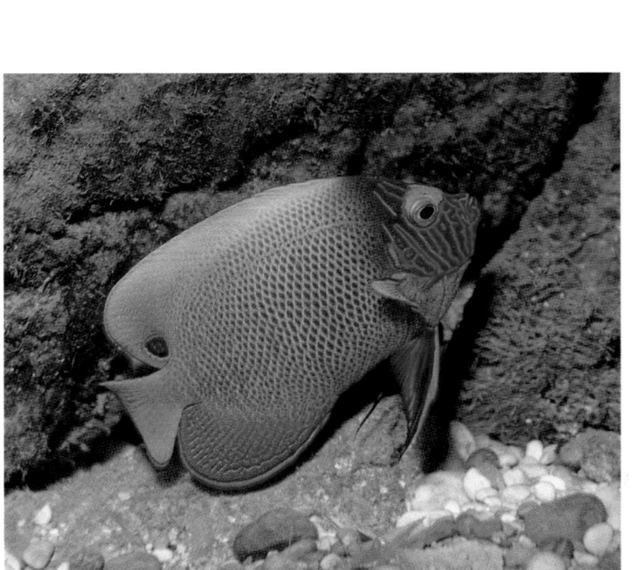

Euxiphipops xanthometopon
Young **blueface angelfish** acclimatize more easily and can adopt a "cleaning" role with other fish. The adults, territorial and fearful, prefer small items of food, with some vegetable material. Size: 30–40 cm. ►

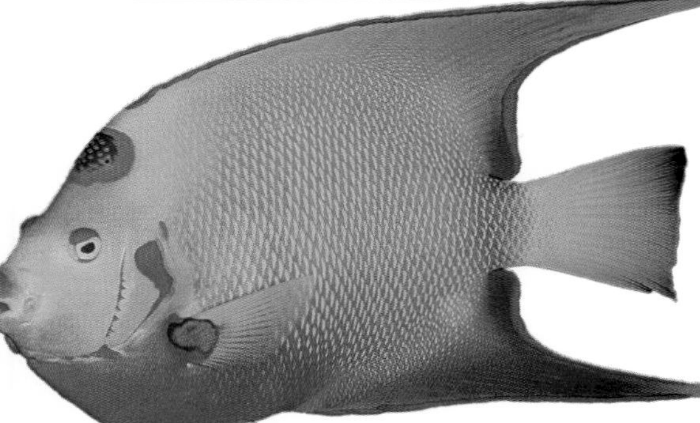

◄ *Holacanthus ciliaris*

Even the juvenile **queen angelfish** are territorial, which can cause cohabitation problems. They are easy to acclimatize, but demanding as regards the quality of the water. Their diet comprises brine shrimp, sponges, algae, and mussels. Size: 20 cm.

Pomacanthus annularis

Adult **annularis angelfish** can grow to 30 cm. Their acclimatization is more difficult than that of younger fish, below 7 or 8 cm, which adapt to captivity better. These fish graze on the algae in the decor but also appreciate meat dishes: reddish food seems to attract them, so it is worth trying to make them a "pâté" in this color. ▼

Holacanthus tricolor

The black patch on the juveniles of the **rock beauty angelfish** enlarges as they grow, until, by the time they are adults, it covers their entire body. Famous for being difficult to acclimatize, they feed on algae, brine shrimps, and small pieces of fish. Size: 15 cm. ►

◄ *Pomacanthus chrysurus*

The **African angelfish** is rarely seen in aquariums. It needs vegetable components in its diet. When it is young, its yellow-orange tail distinguishes it from the queen angelfish. Size: 20 cm.

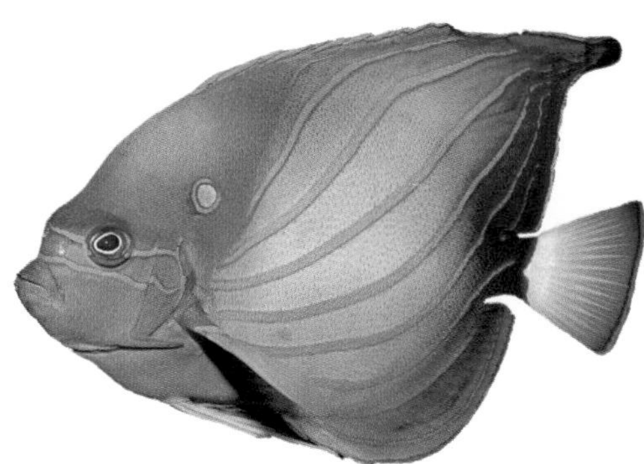

Angelfish juveniles' coloring: how to avoid being taken for an intruder

The coloring of angelfish juveniles (usually consisting of lines) is markedly different from that of adults. This enables them to avoid being considered as intruders on their own patch, as the adults rebuff fish of the same species, or those with similar coloring, in order to defend their territory and its resources: food and shelters. Both juveniles and adults share the same goal: to survive and perpetuate the species.

◄ ***Queen angelfish***
Juvenile.

Queen angelfish
Adult. ►

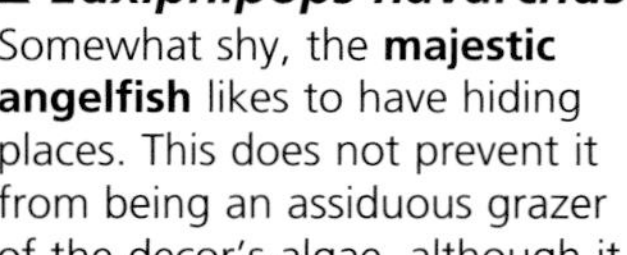

▲ *Euxiphipops navarchus*

Somewhat shy, the **majestic angelfish** likes to have hiding places. This does not prevent it from being an assiduous grazer of the decor's algae, although it does also accept small prey. Size: 20 cm.

Pomacanthus imperator

This is one of the most beautiful of all the angelfish. However, the territoriality of the **emperor angelfish** can make it aggressive towards other occupants of the tank. The juveniles display several white circles against a blue background. This fish eats raw or cooked mussels, nereis, tubifex worms, fish flesh, shrimps, lettuce, and plenty of filamentous algae. Size: 20 cm.▼

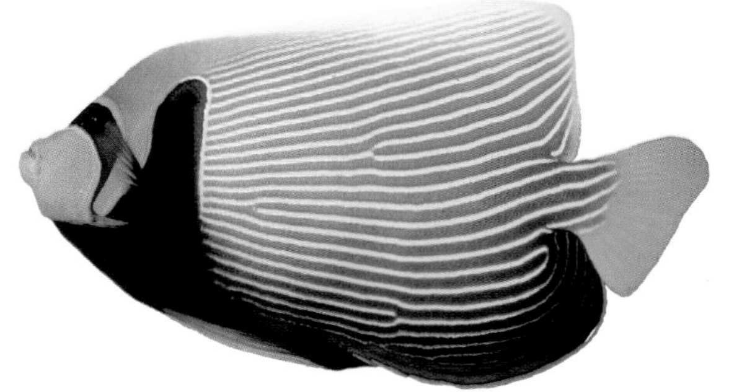

▲ *Pomacanthus maculosus*
In its natural environment, the **purple moon fish** feeds on sponges and coral, so these should be avoided in its aquarium. In captivity it can adjust to eating small, live prey, and can then move on to commercial food. Size: 30 cm.

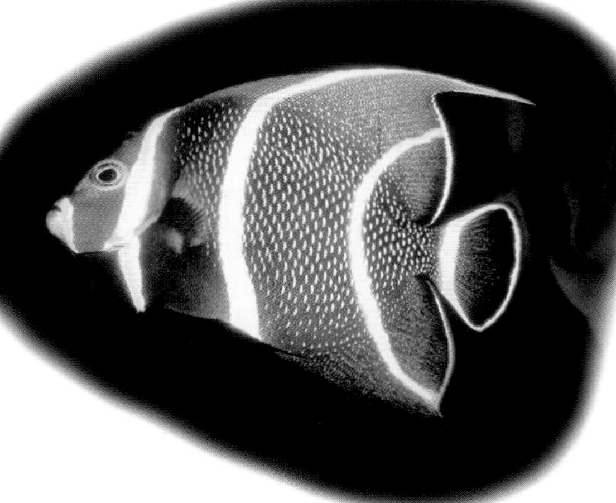

◀ *Pomacanthus paru*
Sub-adult.

Pomacanthus paru
Young. ▼

▼ ▲ *Pomacanthus semicirculatus*
The young have a dark blue body set off by fine white lines curving towards the rear. The territorial **raccoon angelfish** leaves its shelter to eat nereis, raw or scalded mussels, shrimps, pieces of fish, and tubifex worms, as well as algae, lettuce, and riccia.
Size: 40 cm.

Pomacanthus paru

Active by day and night, the **French angelfish** will eat brine shrimps and mussels, and can sometimes be tamed. The adult resembles that of the *Pomacanthus arcuatus* (gray angelfish), but the ends of its scales glow with luminous yellow dots. The young of both species can similarly be confused; they are markedly different from the adults, with curved yellow stripes against a black background. Size: 25 cm. ▶

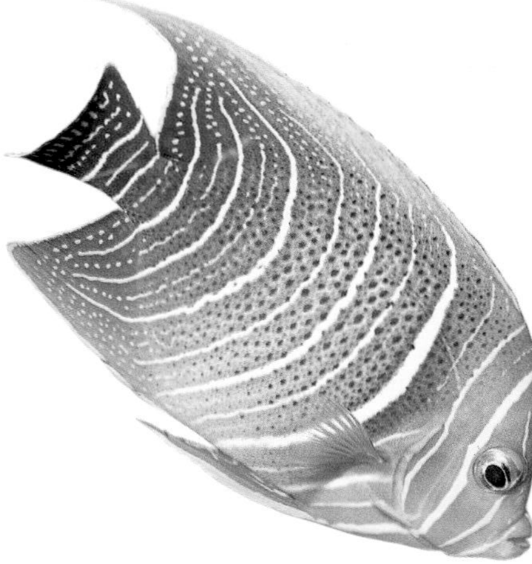

Genicanthus caudovittatus
The **Japanese swallow** can be distinguished from the *G. lamarck* by its vertical stripes. Shy, but often on the move, it eats the same as the *G. lamarck*: prey small enough to fit into its mouth. Size: 20 cm. ▼

◄ ***Genicanthus lamarck***
The male has a yellow patch on the underbelly and its pelvic fins are black. The **Lamarck angelfish** is sociable, despite its shyness; it lives in small groups and tolerates other angelfish. Size: 20 cm.

► ***Apolemichthys trimaculatus***
The spine characterizing this family is blue, as is the mouth, and both stand out against the yellow background. The black patch on the caudal fin of the young disappears in adults. The **flagfin angelfish** appreciates a vegetable component in its diet. It is a vigorous swimmer which needs a large tank. Size: 25 cm.

Apolemichthys xanthurus
An easy species to keep, the **gray poma angelfish** nibbles at algae, but it also eats mussels, shrimps, and brine shrimps. Size: 10–13 cm. ▼

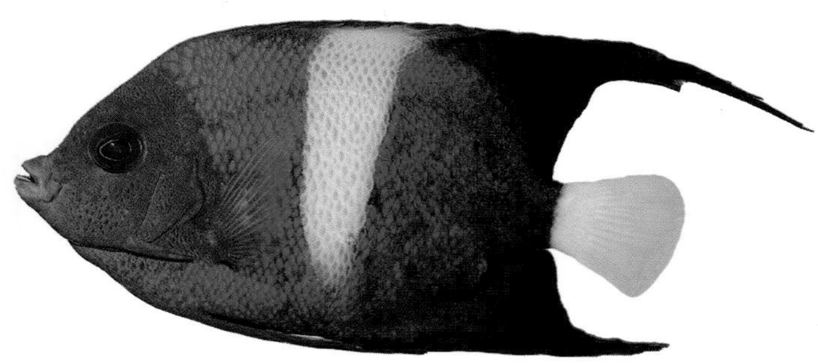

▲ ***Arusetta asfur***
The **asfur angel** is an active swimmer, but likes hiding among rocks. It feeds on mussels, lettuce, and animal foodstuffs. Sometimes confused with *Pomacanthus maculosus*, it can be distinguished by its yellow caudal fin, and the patch on its sides, also yellow, is further forward. It grows very slowly in an aquarium. Size: 20 cm.

Pygoplites diacanthus
Somewhat unassuming, the **regal angelfish** loves to take shelter in nooks and crannies. In the wild it feeds on sponges; in an aquarium, it must be supplied with small food items: brine shrimps, mussels, and chopped shrimps. Size: 25 cm. ►

Dwarf angelfish or Centropyges

These also belong to the Pomachantid family and share its characteristic spine. They are mainly native to the Indo-Pacific region, where they frequent the coral reefs taking shelter in caves or under overhangs. Territorial, they can be aggressive with members of their own species, or with Centropyges with a similar coloring. They are sociable with other fish and respect invertebrates. They are rarely longer than 12 cm and require an aquarium of at least 200 liters, equipped with places to hide. Their natural diet mainly consists of algae; in captivity, a vegetable diet of spinach and lettuce can be topped off with small, live prey, especially crustaceans.

Centropyge ferrugatus
The medium-sized **rusty angel** can be confused with other species. However, it is recognizable from the fine blue stripes on the dorsal and anal fins. The caudal fin is not convex. Size: 10 cm. ►

◄ ***Centropyge bicolor***
In nature, the peaceful **bicolor angel** live in groups, but this is not possible in captivity, except in very large aquariums. It is sometimes difficult to keep in a tank and has a reputation for being a fussy eater. Its basic diet consists of brine shrimps, tubifex worms, and chopped mussels. Size: 10 cm.

Centropyge eibli
Eibl's angelfish, aggressive towards all the other species in the genus, is easy to keep in captivity. Its vegetable diet can be complemented by small invertebrates. Size: 12 cm. ▼

◄ ***Centropyge acanthops***
This is a small species, relatively easy to keep, but rarely found in the aquarium trade. The **flame back angelfish** likes hideaways and feeds on algae and small invertebrates. In some specimens, the eye is surrounded by a blue circle. Size: 7 cm.

◄ ***Centropyge loriculus***
One of the most beautiful dwarf angels, the **flame angelfish** appreciates hiding places in an aquarium. It feeds on algae and brine shrimps, but may also accept commercial food. Size: 7 cm.

▼ ***Centropyge heraldi***
The **yellow angelfish** resembles the lemonpeel angel, although it does not have the blue marks on the eye, operculum, and fins. This delicate species is rarely imported. Size: 10 cm.

▲ ***Centropyge potteri***
The **Potter's angelfish** is placid and accepts a wide range of food. Nevertheless, it is sometimes considered delicate for an aquarium. Size: 10 cm.

▲ ***Centropyge flavissimus***
The eye of the **lemonpeel angelfish** is framed by a blue circle; the juvenile has an ocellus (eyelike spot) in the middle of each side. It accepts small items of food, but keeping it in captivity has its complications. This species is fragile and is rarely imported. Size: 11 cm.

Centropyge vroliki
This is one of the largest fish in this genus: the **half-black angelfish** acclimatizes well and flourishes in captivity, accepting both live and dead prey. It is particularly aggressive towards other dwarf angelfish when it is deprived of sufficient space. Size: 13 cm. ►

POMACENTRIDAE

These are undoubtedly the most popular marine fish found in aquariums. Modest in size and brightly colored, they are active and easy to keep. Most species reproduce without any problem. These fish are recommended for beginners, who can put them in a tank with a minimum of 200 liters of water. They feed on small animal prey, both live and dead.

Clownfish or Amphiprions

These fish owe their name to their coloring. Several species are commercially available nowadays, often with their associated sea anemone, because their life is generally intertwined with this invertebrate, which offers them protection. In return, the anemones can take advantage of the clowns' leftover food, although this is not always the case, and they can also live without the company of their tenants. The Amphiprions are not affected by the action of the anemone's venom; they protect themselves by progressively rubbing themselves in it, which grants them a kind of immunity. If a clownfish is separated from its anemone for any length of time, on its return it has to gradually rehabituate itself.

Anemones also play an important role in the reproduction of Pomacentrids for, without them, they breed less often. The fish mark out a territory (around 0.25 m²) close to the anemones, lay their eggs on a support, and defend the site. The parents, which stay faithful to each other – the males are generally monogamous – can reproduce every 2–4 weeks. Clownfish, at first males, later become females, which are then bigger. Feeding them in captivity does not present any problems: they like small live and frozen prey, mussels, and chopped shrimps, and they sometimes accept commercial artificial food.

▲ ***Amphiprion akallopisos***
Easy to keep in captivity, the **pink skunk clownfish** can live in small groups. It is sometimes dominated by other species. It lays its eggs close to an anemone. Size: 10 cm.

Amphiprion bicinctus
The **two-banded clownfish** is among the biggest of the genus. It is a robust species, which is sometimes aggressive towards other Amphiprions. Size: 15 cm. ▼

▲ ***Amphiprion ephippium***
Territorial and sometimes aggressive, the **red saddle clownfish** lives alone or in couples. It lays eggs without any problems and can live without an anemone. Size: 15 cm.

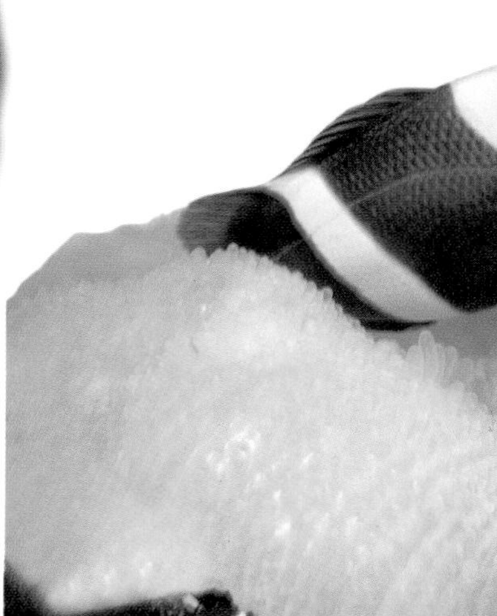

Premnas biaculeatus
The **maroon clownfish** is distinguished from the *Amphiprion* genus by the spine on its operculum. It is quite aggressive, towards both its own species and Amphiprions. Size: 13–15 cm. ▼

Amphiprion frenatus
The juvenile's small white band in the middle of its sides disappears in adulthood. Highly territorial, the **tomato clownfish** lives in couples; it reproduces easily. Size: 15 cm. ▼

▲ ***Amphiprion perideraion***
It is best not to keep more than one couple of this small species, without any other clownfish. The dorsal and anal fins of the male **skunk clownfish** display a fine orange band; the females are white or translucent. Size: 9 cm.

Amphiprion ocellaris
Several couples can live in the same anemone, if it is big enough. Easy to keep, the **ocellaris clownfish** is nevertheless fragile in its acclimatization period (1–3 months); after that, it is highly robust. It lays eggs without problems and accepts artificial food. It is sometimes confused with the true clownfish (*Amphiprion percula*), but its white bands are fringed with black. Size: 11 cm. ◀

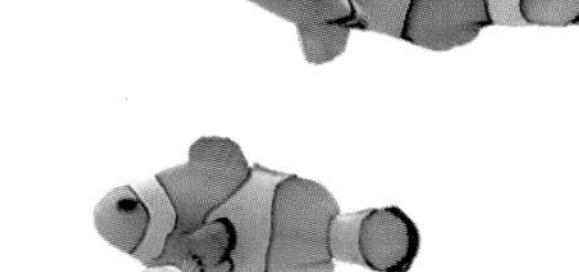

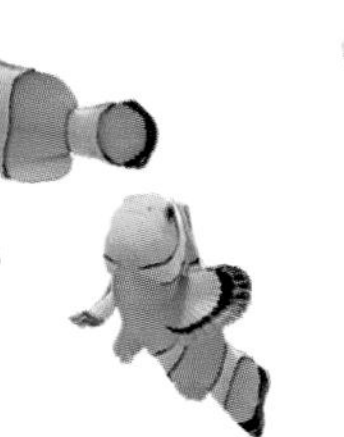

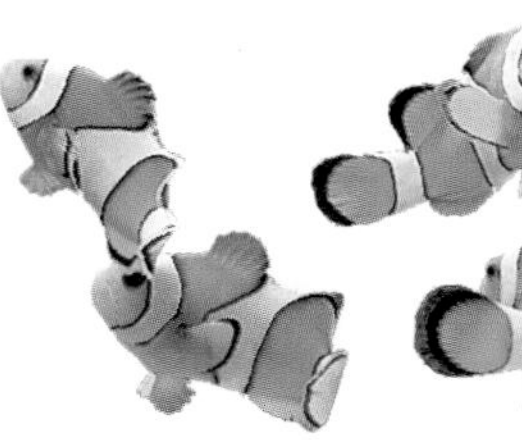

▲ ***Amphiprion sebae***
Seba's clownfish, easy to keep in an aquarium, is one of the biggest *Amphiprion* species, as the female grows to 12 cm. An anemone houses a single couple, sometimes with the fry.

◀ ***Amphiprion clarkii***
Clark's clownfish lives in couples, occupying several different anemones and straying some distance from them. It is one of the easiest to acclimatize. The male is distinguished by its yellow caudal fin (white in the female). Size: 15 cm.

Anemones associated with clownfish

Even though some clownfish can live without anemones, in captivity it is best to provide them with one – but not just any one. In fact, the associations concern exact species, although there may be confusion because the scientific names of anemones changed some 10 years ago. Some anemones can house several species of clownfish, others are more exclusive.

ANEMONES		ASSOCIATED CLOWNFISH
Current names	**Former names**	**Current names**
Cryptodendrum adhesivum	–	*Amphiprion clarkii*
Entacmaea quadricolor	*Physobrachia douglasi, Radianthus gelam*	*A. bicinctus, A. clarkii, A. ephippium, A. frenatus, Premnas biaculeatus*
Heteractis aurora	*Radianthus simplex*	*A. akallopisos (1), A. bicinctus (1), A. clarkii*
Heteractis crispa	*Radianthus malu*	*A. akallopisos (1), A. bicinctus (1), A. ephippium, Premnas biaculeatus (1)*
Heteractis magnifica	*Radianthus ritteri, R. paumotensis*	*A. akallopisos, A. ocellaris, A. percula, A. perideraion*
Stichodactyla gigantea	*Stoichactus kenti*	*A. bicinctus (1), A. clarkii, A. ephippium, A. ocellaris, A. percula, A. perideraion (1), A. sebae*
Stichodactyla haddoni	*Stoichactus sp.*	*A. clarkii, A. ephippium, A. ocellaris, A. sebae*
Stichodactyla mertensii	*Stoichactus giganteum*	*A. clarkii, A. ephippium, A. ocellaris*
Actinia equina (2)	–	*A. clarkii*
Condylactis gigantea (2)	–	*A. clarkii*

(1) Possible association, if no other anemones are available.
(2) Mediterranean anemones, to be used if no others are available.

Amphiprion percula in an anemone of the *Stichodactyla* genus. ▼

DAMSELS

Damsels are pretty fish that are easy to raise, and some live in association with anemones. They adapt well to captivity and often accept artificial food (though live prey, mussels, and ground shrimps are clear favorites); they lay eggs quite easily. With these characteristics in mind, and not forgetting their modest price, damsels are recommended for aquarists making their first venture into sea water.

▲ ***Pomacentrus coelestis***
The **electric blue damsel** can live in groups in a large tank. In a smaller aquarium it is wise to keep only a single specimen. Size: 8 cm.

▲ ***Glyphidodontops cyaneus***
Like the other species known as damsels, this is one of the least expensive of aquarium marine fishes. The **blue damsel** (syn. *Chrysiptera cyanea*) is territorial and can sometimes be aggressive. It accepts commercial foods. Size: 8 cm.

Abudefduf saxatilis
This is more aggressive than the other damsels. The **sergeant-major** can live to an age of 5 years or more in captivity. It eats mainly brine shrimps, mussels, and chopped shrimps. Size: 15–17 cm. ◄

DAMSELS FOR BEGINNERS

Novices are advised to start with the "blue damsels" group. *Chromis caerulea* (the blue-green damsel) is active and lives in groups, sometimes dominated by the males. It accepts artificial food. *Chrysiptera parasema* (azure damsel, syn. *Glyphidodontops hemicyaneus*) is a robust species which lays eggs in captivity. The female can sometimes lay more than 200 eggs, and is then ejected from the nest by the male, which takes on the task of guarding it. Hatching occurs after 1 week. This fish will accept commercial food.

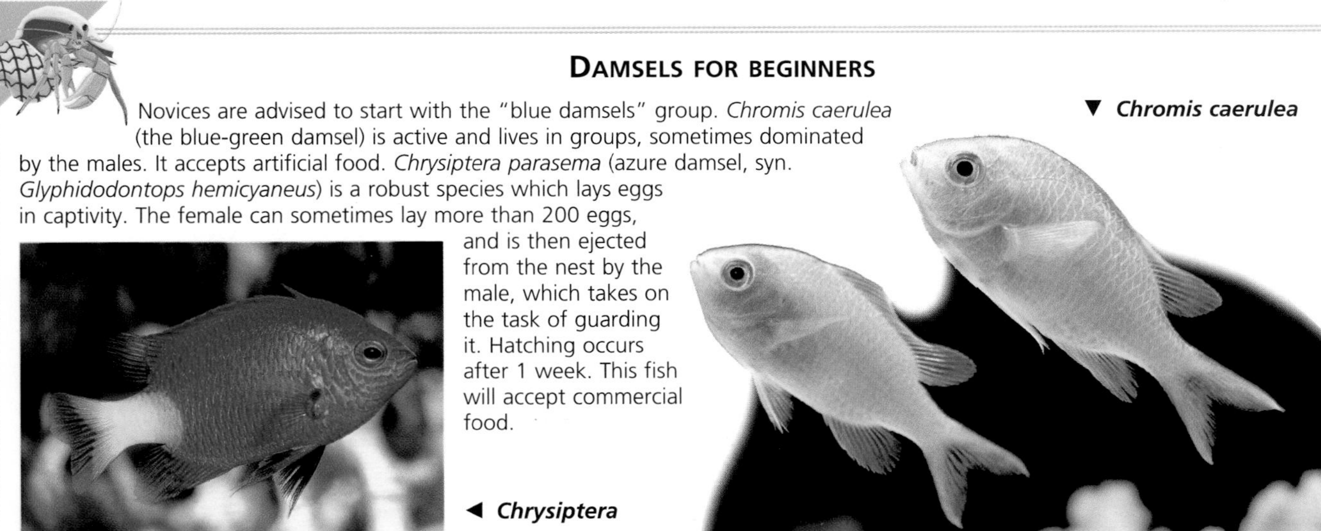

◄ ***Chrysiptera parasema***

▼ ***Chromis caerulea***

CLARIFICATION

Occasional variations in color and name changes can lead to confusions in this group, especially in the species that are predominantly blue.
The latter includes a blue-green damsel, while the blue damsels can present yellow coloring on the tail and belly, although this varies from one specimen to another. They are all easy to acclimatize and feed, and they reproduce in captivity – all these factors endear them to beginners.
The second group of damsels is distinguished by its vertical black bands (genus *Dascyllus*; 6 or 7 species are currently imported).
The third group covers the **Abudefduf** genus – including the species sometimes known as "devils" – which are less common in aquariums.

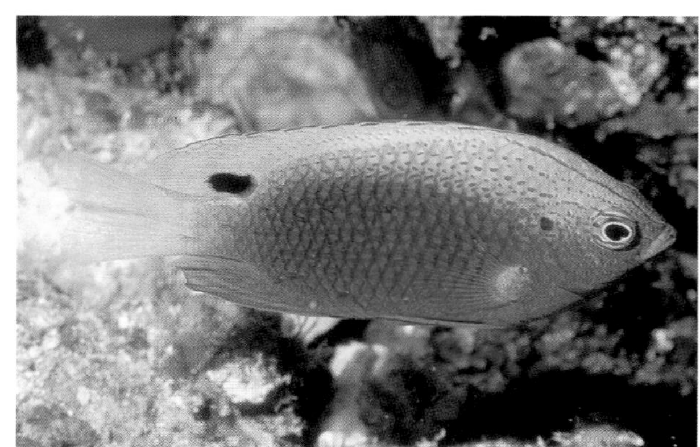

Dascyllus trimaculatus

The young **domino damsels** live in groups, while the adults gradually isolate themselves. The white spots disappear in older fishes. Their reproduction is easy; the male watches over the eggs. Size: 14 cm. ▶

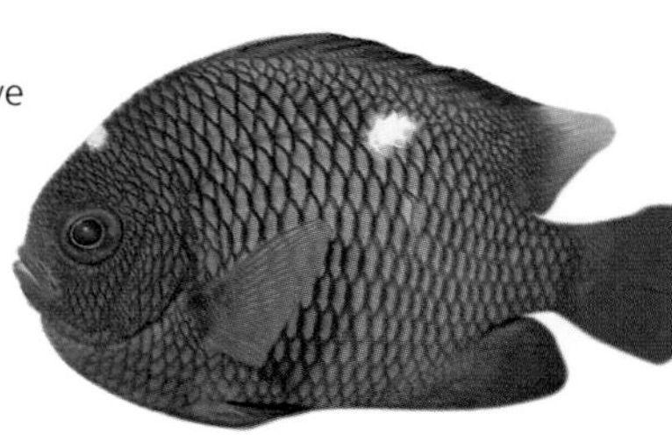

Dascyllus aruanus

The **three-stripe damsel** does not exceed 8 cm in length as an adult and prefers to live in isolation; the young live in groups. A closely related species, *D. melanurus* (black-tailed damsel), is distinguished by a vertical black band on the tip of the caudal fin. ▼

LABRIDAE

The Labrids constitute one of the major fish families (several hundred species divided among 70 genera). These highly active, colored fish with fusiform (tapering at each end) bodies often live alone. Some species bury themselves in the sediment at night, and this must be taken into account when planning the aquarium: provide them with a sandy bed. Their sturdy teeth allow them to feed on invertebrates (which must, therefore, be kept away from them). In captivity they accept live prey, but will become accustomed to deep-frozen (sometimes commercial) food. The coloring of the juveniles is often very different from that of the adults.

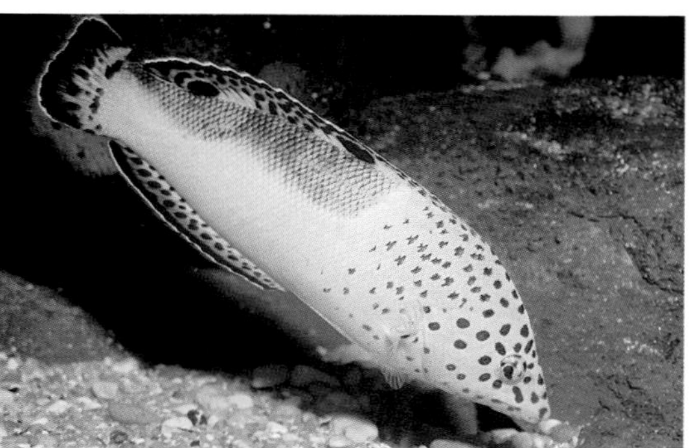

Coris angulata

The **Coris clown wrasse** grows to 1 m in the wild but does not exceed 30 cm in an aquarium. The juveniles are characterized by their large, red dorsal patches, which fade when they reach a length of 10–15 cm. The adults are a uniform brown-black. Aggressive towards other wrasses, this fish buries itself at night, or when in danger. ▲ ▶

▲ ***Coris formosa***

The adult **Formosa wrasses** are dark brown with dark patches; the paler juveniles have big white spots. Size: 20 cm.

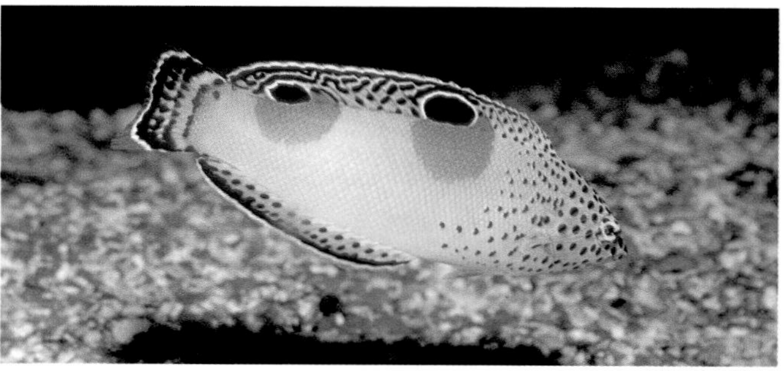

Gomphosus coeruleus

The **birdmouth wrasse** can live in couples, but two males will not tolerate each other. It is easy to keep and its feeding poses no special problems. The adult male is green-blue, the female brown-purple. Size: 30 cm (male), 20 cm (female). ▼

The false cleaner (*Aspidontus taeniatus*)

This is not a Labrid – in fact, it belongs to the Blenniid family – but it closely resembles the true cleaner, although the position of its mouth is different (it is terminal in the true version). It takes advantage of this resemblance by tricking fish into getting cleaned and then tearing off pieces of their skin, or even their branchiae. False cleaners are raised in specific aquariums and fed on crustaceans. On very rare occasions they attack fish belonging to the Labrid family. Size: 10–12 cm.

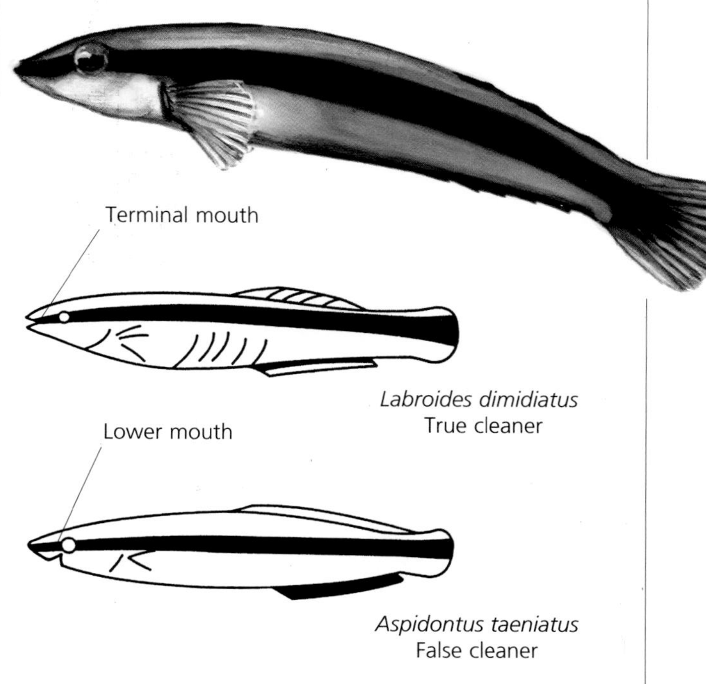

◄ ***Labroides dimidiatus***
This **wrasse** is "cleaning" an *Acanthurus leucosternon*.

▲ *Labroides dimidiatus*

The **cleaner wrasse**, with a reputation for being difficult to acclimatize, lives in couples as an adult. It feeds on live prey and it has a highly distinctive habit: it "cleans" other fish. It puts on a show in a specific part of the tank to attract them, and it then frees them of their external parasites or pieces of dead skin. When there are no males available, a female can change sex. Size: 10 cm.

▲ ◄ *Coris gaimard*

The adult **red coris wrasses** sport bright blue dots on a brown-red background; the young are red with white dorsal patches which gradually fade with age. This fish buries itself in the sand, although it is a good swimmer. It feeds on mussels, shrimps, worms, and artificial food. Size: 20 cm.

Bodianus mesothorax

The young are brown-black with dark patches on the fins that disappear in the bicolor adult. The **harpfish** swims continuously, and it must therefore be given a large space with room to move about, although the aquarium must also provide it with shelters. The adults do not tolerate members of their own species. Size: 20 cm. ▶

▲ *Bodianus rufus*

There is barely any difference between the young and the adults, which are somewhat aggressive. This **Spanish hogfish** has carnivorous tastes. Size: 25 cm.

▲ *Thalassoma lunare*

The **lunar wrasse** is aggressive towards other members of its own species. It is easy to acclimatize, although it requires large open spaces in which it can swim freely. Size: 20 cm.

Lienardella fasciata

The **Harlequin tusk wrasse**, aggressive even toward bigger fish, likes eating mollusks, worms, and crustaceans, and it needs shelters. Size: 15 cm. ▶

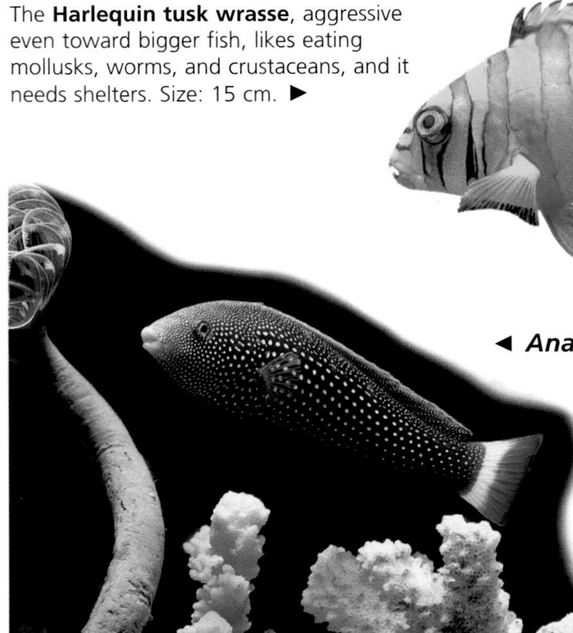

◀ *Anampses chrysocephalus*

The active **red tail anampses** spends its time looking for food of animal origin. It buries itself in the sand and needs hiding places. The coloring of the young resembles that of the female shown in the photo, but the males are very different. Size: 20 cm.

MURENIDAE (MURENAS)

These usually nocturnal fish stalk small prey. They camouflage themselves in rocks and crevices, with only their head sticking out. An aquarist must be careful, because a murena's bite can be dangerous.

Echidna nebulosa

The **snowflake murena** is an attractive species which sometimes makes an appearance by day, especially at mealtimes. It can live for quite a long time. Its tail can also be very long, so plan on a big tank. Size: 90 cm. ▶

SIGANIDAE

These are distinguished by spiny spokes which secrete a venomous substance. A prick is painful for an aquarist, although not as much as one caused by a lionfish (but it is still advisable to consult a doctor). These small-mouthed fish are herbivorous.

Siganus
Several of these species are commercially available. The peaceful **rabbitfish** graze algae in the decor but also accept small pieces of animal food. When they are frightened they take refuge in the hiding places that are indispensable for these fishes. Size: 20 cm. ►

▲ ***Lo vulpinus***
Hardy and easy to acclimatize, the **foxface** feeds on small, live prey and vegetable material. It will accept mussel pieces but what it really relishes is ground spinach. It is placid but active, and needs room to swim, along with somewhere to hide. Size: 20 cm.

ZANCLIDAE

The Zanchlids have a very compact body: one of the spokes of the dorsal fin is extended in a fine filament. Considered fragile and delicate, they feed on small, live prey and can sometimes attack invertebrates (corals, worms). Even if their form suggests otherwise, they are closely related to the Acanthurids, although, unlike these, they do not have a spine on the caudal peduncle. These fish are sensitive to chemical treatments and can die suddenly, without any apparent reason. In their native habitat (the Indo-Pacific region), they are respected, and even sometimes venerated, by local fishermen, who often return them to the sea.

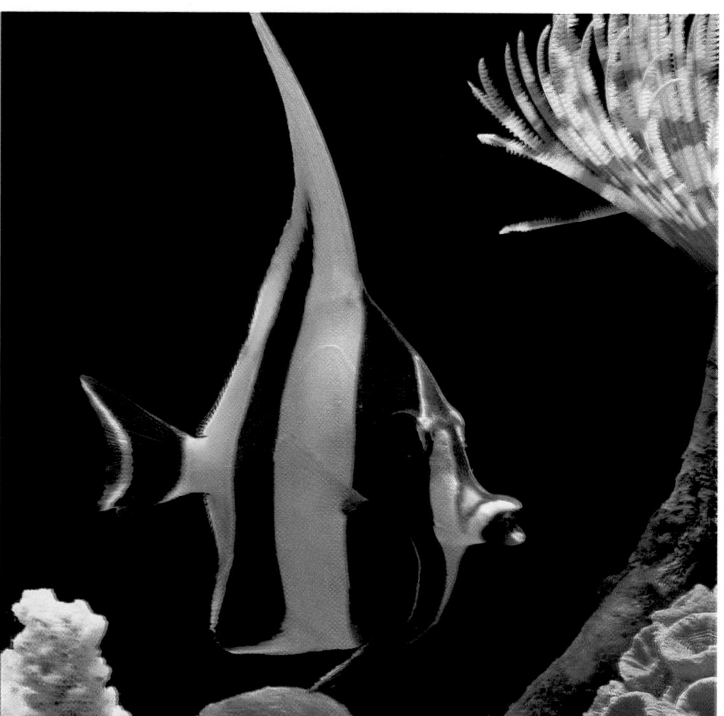

◄ ***Zanclus canescens***
The **Moorish idol** normally feeds on algae and sponges. In captivity it must be given a wide range of food so that it can make its own choice. It does not tolerate the presence of other Zanclids. *Z. cornutus* is considered a closely related species, but is distinguished by the absence of small spines in front of the eyes. Size: 25 cm.

ACANTHURIDAE (TANGS)

Native to the tropical waters of the Indian and Pacific oceans, the tangs are less common in the Atlantic ocean. An upright spine on the caudal peduncle has earned them the alternative name of surgeonfish, as this spine resembles a scalpel. It plays a defensive role and can represent a danger for the aquarist. Despite their squat bodies, which seem to have been squashed sideways, they are good swimmers, and they live in groups in a natural setting. They feed on algae and small prey which fit into their mouths. These fish are active and require a tank of at least 300 liters, with only one tang, because in such a limited space they do not get along with each other. It is also advisable not to put any invertebrates into the aquarium. Tangs feed on brine shrimps or other live prey, but they also require a vegetable complement. The water must be well filtered and stirred, with fairly bright lighting, to favor the growth of algae.
The young are easier to acclimatize. Their reproduction, which, in their natural environment, seems to be connected with the lunar cycle, has never been observed in an aquarium.

Acanthurus achilles
A very delicate species to keep, the **Achilles tang** appreciates partial (but small) changes of water on a regular basis. It accepts vegetable foodstuffs and small animal prey. Size: 15–18 cm. ▼

▲ *Acanthurus japonicus*
The **powder brown tang** is a good swimmer. It keenly grazes the algae on the decor, but also accepts small prey. It is very delicate to keep in captivity. Size: 18 cm.

Acanthurus lineatus
This is a fairly easy species to keep in captivity, if it is supplied with vegetable foodstuffs. A good swimmer, the **clown tang** behaves extremely aggressively towards other tangs. Size: 18–20 cm. ▼

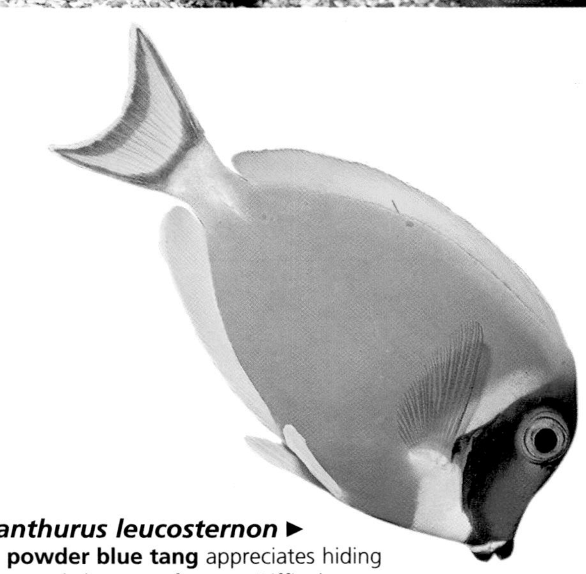

Acanthurus leucosternon ►
The **powder blue tang** appreciates hiding places and changes of water. Difficult to acclimatize, it can however accept commercial foodstuffs if they are predominantly vegetable. Size: 15 cm.

◄ *Acanthurus sohal*

The **sohal tang** is one of the most beautiful of the Acanthurids. It can accept artificial vegetable food, but it prefers to feed on brine shrimps and ground mussels. Its territorial behavior sometimes makes it aggressive. Size: 25 cm.

Naso brevirostris

Young **longnose unicorn fish** do not have a horn. A related species, *N. unicornis*, only has a hump on its forehead. These two species are vigorous swimmers and mainly feed on algae; the adults are more carnivorous than the young. Size: 25–30 cm. ▼

▲ *Naso lituratus*

The **smooth-headed unicorn fish** is a relatively easy species to keep. Although generally placid, they can become aggressive if they are upset. The adults in this species have fine extensions to the tips of the caudal fin, while the juveniles have white patches. Size: 25 cm.

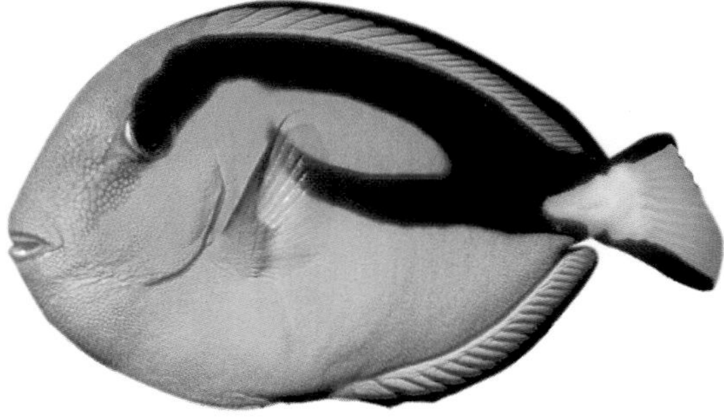

Paracanthurus hepatus ▲

The blue coloring of the young turns gray on their belly and back once they reach adulthood. Somewhat unobtrusive, the **hippo tang** likes having hiding places. Size: 18 cm

▲ *Zebrasoma flavescens*

The anal and dorsal fins of the zebrasomas are more developed than those of other tangs. These timid species must be provided with shelters. The coloring of the **yellow tang** varies according to its geographical origins. Size: 18 cm.

Zebrasoma veliferum

When the **sailfin tang** is in motion, this beautiful swimmer tucks its fins along its body, although it does open them to "impress" other members of the same species and to chase them off its territory (the yellow tang does the same). Size: 30 cm. ►

SCORPAENIDAE (LIONFISH)

Lionfish are not only stunning to look at, but they can also constitute a real danger for an aquarist: some of their spiny spokes emit a venom similar to that of certain snakes. They are placid and majestic fish, easy to keep in an aquarium of at least 300 liters. The tank must be furnished with elaborate and convoluted decor, complete with grottoes and overhangs: lionfish swim through them flat or at an angle. Their large mouth is equal to their voracity: they devour live prey, often small fish (take care with their roommates!). Nevertheless, these remain amongst the most deirable subjects for the amateur aquarist and repay without any doubt any amount of trouble.

▲ ***Pterois antennata***
The **antenna lionfish** has four dark bands on its head. A close relative, *P. sphex,* has less intense coloring. The latter is hard to find in Europe, but is frequently imported into the United States. Size: 20 cm.

WHAT TO DO IF YOU ARE STUNG

Consult a doctor immediately. The very intense pain increases for 20 minutes, reaches a peak, and gradually subsides over a period of 4–24 hours. Bleed the wound and immerse it in the hottest water possible to partially inhibit the action of the venom. Obviously, the best idea is to avoid getting stung; take care when putting your hand into the tank and wear protective gloves that are water-impermeable.

Pterois volitans
The **volitan lionfish** is the one most often found in the aquarium trade. It gets accustomed to dead foodstuffs. The membrane linking the spokes of the pectoral fins runs to the rear end of their body, which is not the case with the other species of the *Pterois* genus, where the rear is unencumbered. Size: 35 cm.▼

Pterois radiata
Two white horizontal bands on the caudal peduncle distinguish the **radiata lionfish** from the other species. Easy to keep, it gets used to eating dead prey. Size: 25 cm. ▶

◀ ***Dendrochirus zebra***
The **dwarf lionfish** does not grow longer than 15 cm, in contrast to the *Pterois*. It is also distinguished by the absence of a membrane between the spokes of the pectoral fins. Size: 15 cm.

BALISTIDAE (TRIGGERS)

Triggers live in reef areas where the water is in constant movement, so you must plan a large aquarium for them (at least 400 liters) with highly agitated and well-oxygenated water. Their jaws and teeth allow them to graze on coral, crabs, and mollusks. In captivity they accept animal food, such as small mollusks (cockles, mussels), complete with their shells. They are fairly aggressive and must be kept singly, away from small fish and invertebrates. One of the distinguishing features of this family of marine fish is its ability to stick out the first spoke of its dorsal fin, and then block it with the second one (explaining their alternative name of crossbowmen).

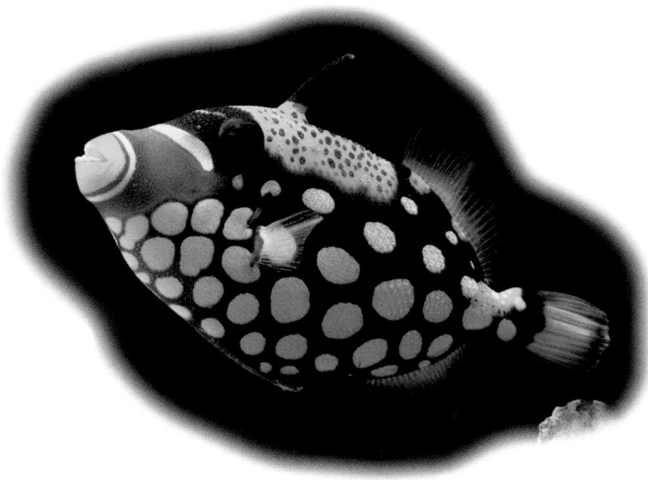

▲ ***Balistoides conspicillum***
The **clown trigger** is not only voracious – it is also fast, usually reaching any food before other fish. It is not slow to rearrange the decor, either, although it is easy to domesticate. However, it is best to acclimatize it before it measures more than 10 cm. Size: 25 cm.

▲ ***Balistapus undulatus***
The **undulated trigger fish** is so resistant that it can survive for over 10 years in an aquarium. It is easy to acclimatize and keep, although it is prone to knocking over bits of decor. Size: 20 cm.

▲ ***Rhinecanthus aculeatus***
Its common name, the **Picasso trigger fish**, comes from its distinctive coloring. It defends its territory fiercely. Some related species (*R. asasi*, *R. rectangulus*, *R. verrucosus*) are sometimes commercially available, often under the same name. Size: 20 cm.

Balistes vetula
The **queen trigger fish**, native to the tropical Atlantic – the others come from the Indo-Pacific region – is one of the most placid. It is easy to acclimatize and grows quickly – sometimes up to 50 cm. Size: 30–50 cm. ▼

Odonus niger

The **blue trigger fish** can live for more than 10 years. If you have a couple, reproduction may be possible in a very large aquarium, in a nest dug into the sand. Size: 20 cm. ►

Pseudobalistes fuscus

The coloring of juveniles is paler than that of adults. The **blue line trigger** is fairly aggressive but can get to know its owner. It sometimes looks for its food by "spitting" water to lift up the sand. Size: 35 cm. ▼

Xanthichthys auromarginatus ▲

The **magnificent blue throat** trigger requires a large tank, with shelters where it can take refuge at night. It is aggressive towards both fish smaller than itself and members of its own species. Size: 30 cm.

HAEMULIDAE – NEMIPTERIDAE

The Haemulids (grunts or pork fish) make sounds by grinding their teeth, with the swim bladder acting as a resonator. Rarely found in aquariums, they are nevertheless robust.
The Nemipterids live near reefs and are vigorous free-swimmers. They feed on small prey captured on their journeys or in the sediment.

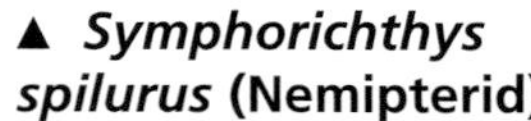

◄ *Anisotremus virginicus* (Haemulidae)

The **pork fish** lives in schools when it is young. The adults gradually become loners as they grow older, and their coloring becomes brighter. In captivity, they can be fed small animal prey, dead or alive. Size: 30 cm.

▲ *Symphorichthys spilurus* (Nemipterid)

The large **long fin** or **blue and gold snapper** requires a lot of water to be able to move around freely. It prefers to live in calm areas and accepts a wide range of food. This brightly colored fish is rarely found in the aquarium trade. Size: 30 cm.

OSTRACIONTIDAE (BOXFISH)

Their body form renders their swimming clumsy, but these fish are nevertheless highly active. Their skin is fragile and very sensitive to parasites. In an aquarium it is best to keep only one specimen, which can sometimes be "tamed" to eat out of your hand. Their small mouth means that they can only eat tiny prey and algae. If they are alarmed, boxfish secrete a toxic substance, with deadly effects for other fish in the vicinity.

▲ ***Lactoria cornuta***
The form of the **long horn cowfish**, with "horns" on its head, is highly unusual. It is a placid species, easy to feed with small live or dead prey. Size: 10 to 15 cm.

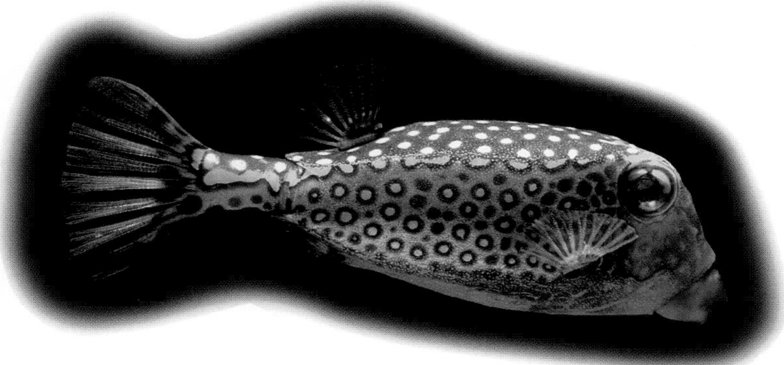

▲ ***Ostracion meleagris***
The magnificent **spotted boxfish** is considered tough, although it only acts aggressively towards its own species. It must be supplied with animal foodstuffs and a vegetable complement. The coloring varies according to the fish's age and sex. Size: 15 cm.

Ostracion cubicus
Easy to keep, the **yellow boxfish** is aggressive towards all other boxfish. It swims slowly in and out of the decor, hiding in a shelter when disturbed. Size: 25 cm. ▶

PLOTOSIDAE

This is one of the few catfish families that live in the sea. Their anal and dorsal fins are long, and the pectoral fins have a spiny spoke connected to a venomous gland. The barbels around the mouth have a tactile function and help to detect food. Their elongated body enables them to weave their way skilfully through natural obstacles in their path.

◀ ***Plotosus lineatus***
The young live in shoals where they form a ball, with their heads facing outwards, when they are faced with danger; the adults are more solitary. They feed on animal foodstuffs or small prey appropriate to the size of their mouth. This fish has a reputation for being fragile and an avid consumer of oxygen. Size: 30 cm.

CANTHIGASTER

This is a small family, closely related to the Tetraodontids; like them, they are commonly known as puffers because they can blow up their bodies. Easy to keep, they feed on crustaceans and mollusks. They are aggressive towards members of their own species, but are placid in the company of other fish.

◄ ***Canthigaster margaritatus***
The **peacock puffer** is distinguished by a black patch framed in pale blue. It adapts well to an aquarium, though its animal food supply must be complemented by vegetable material. Size: 12 cm.

Canthigaster valentini
The **Valentini puffer**, which can be recognized by its two black bands, is less common in the aquarium trade than the peacock. If Canthigaster are not fed properly they may start nibbling at the fins of other fish. Size: 20 cm. ►

DIODONTIDAE (PORCUPINE FISH)

Their skin is dotted with spines, which stick out in response to danger, and the effect is enhanced by the fish puffing out its body to impress its foe. Porcupine fish are considered easy to acclimatize, but they do not tolerate members of their own species. They feed on mussels and small shellfish – complete with shell – which they can munch thanks to their strong teeth.

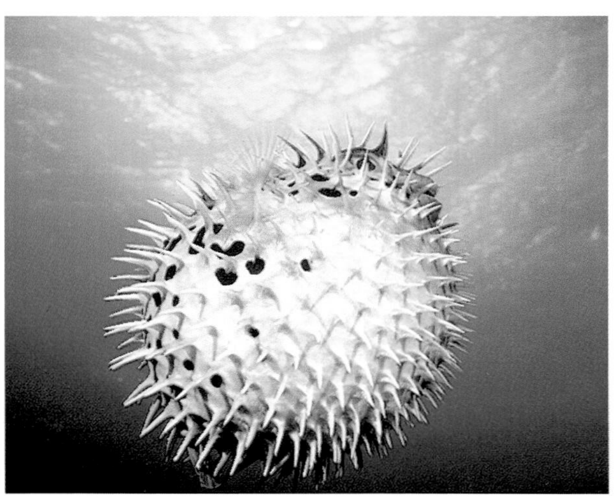

◄ ▲ ***Diodon hystrix***
It is best not to put invertebrates in a tank with the **common porcupine fish** as there is a chance it might find them appetizing. It may eat shrimps, small crabs, or mussels out of your hand – but watch out for its teeth! Sadly, this fish is sometimes sold, dried and bloated, as a decorative object, or even as a lampshade! It can grow to 90 cm in the wild.

TETRAODONTIDAE (PUFFERS)

Their skin is highly sensitive as they have no scales, but they can puff themselves up with air and water in the event of any danger. Their teeth, joined together like a parrot's beak, enable them to break corals and the shells of crustaceans. Do not be tempted to feed them out of your hand, to avoid getting bitten. They are easy to keep in captivity, but it is best to keep them singly as they cannot stand other puffers, and invertebrates should obviously be ruled out.

Arothron nigropunctatus
The gray color of the **dogface** or **hushpuppy** gets darker with age. It can get so accustomed to an aquarist that it will even allow him or her to scratch its back! There are other puffers on the market, particularly the meleagris puffer, *A. meleagris*. Size: 20 cm.▼

▼ ***Arothron citrinellus***
The **yellow puffer** is easy to acclimatize. It is active and needs space for swimming, along with hiding places in which to shelter. It appreciates a vegetable complement to its animal food. Size: 20–25 cm.

Arothron hispidus
The **stars and stripes puffer** is not only aggressive towards other puffers but can also turn against smaller species if the aquarium is too small. It is easy to acclimatize and can sometimes be tamed. Size: 50 cm. ►

SYNGNATHIDAE

This family includes both temperate and tropical seahorses. They are bad swimmers and feed, in motion, on small planktonic crustaceans.
In the same family, related species, known as sea needles, are sometimes available. They are easy to keep in captivity with the same diet, and are particularly suited to aquariums for invertebrates.

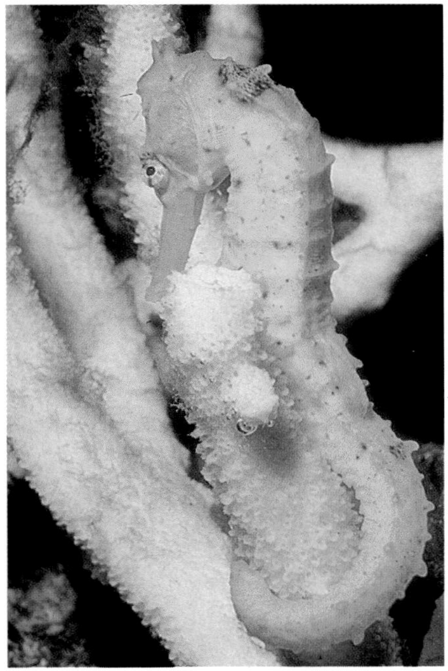

◄ ***Hippocampus kuda***
The **yellow seahorse** is, as its name suggests, usually yellow, but its coloring gets darker in poor environmental conditions. It stays in a vertical position, with its tail serving to cling on to the decor (which must be free of Coelenterates). In captivity, it feeds on brine shrimps or other small, live prey. Reproduction may be possible in captivity: the male incubates the eggs in its ventral pocket. Size: 15 cm.

GRAMMIDAE

Known as dwarf bass, due to their similarity to the true bass, the Grammids are small and colorful. They are ideal fish to include in an aquarium with invertebrates.

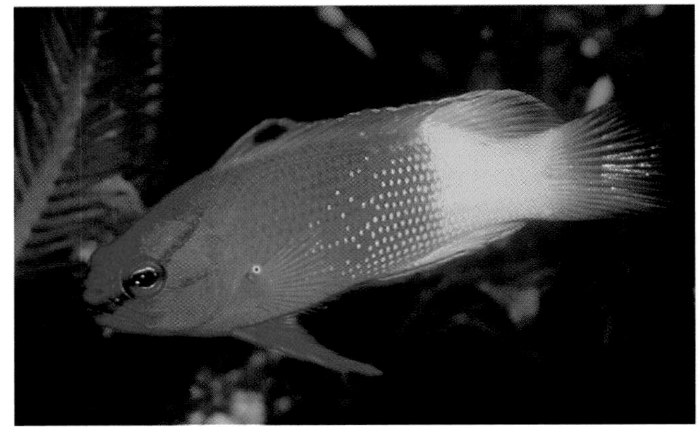

Gramma loreto
The **royal gramma** takes refuge in hiding places, often with its head inside. As an adult it lives alone and can be aggressive towards members of its own species. It feeds on brine shrimps, pieces of mussel, or small fish. Size: 8 cm. ►

PSEUDOCHROMIS

These are solitary, active fish which quickly go into hiding when they are disturbed. They must cohabit with species of the same size, in a decor furnished with hiding places.

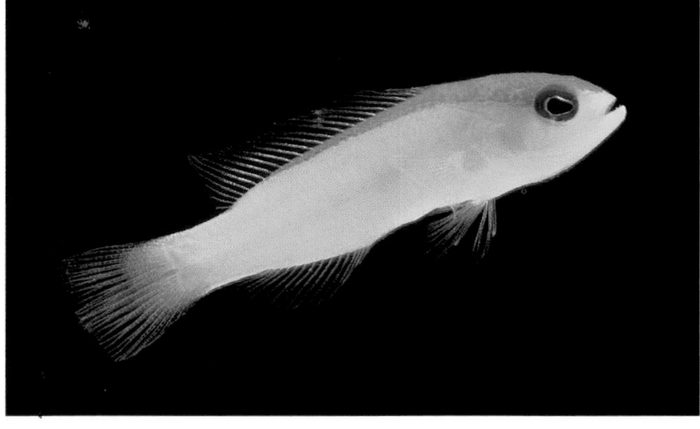

◄ ***Pseudochromis diadema***
This resembles the royal gramma, with which it can cohabit – which is not the case with members of its own species. It flaunts a golden yellow coloring set off by purple. It feeds on small, live prey and pieces of mussel. This fish is recommended for invertebrate aquariums with enough space for it to hide. Size: 7 cm.

PLESIOPIDAE

The Plesiopids, related to the Pseudochromis, can be distinguished by their large dorsal and ventral fins. This family of coral-dwellers numbers only a few species, of which only one is found in the aquarium trade. They live in reefs, where they hide in the crevices. This has led them to be considered as somewhat rare, although there are probably more of them than is generally

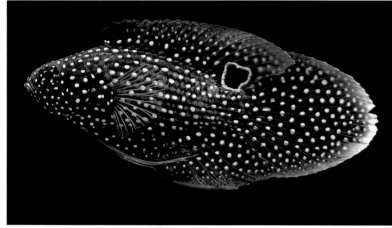

Calloplesiops altivelis
The **marine beta grouper** has a majestic bearing, in keeping with its placid, rather shy nature. It cohabits with species of the same size and feeds on live prey, ground mussels, and small fish. In aquariums, it seeks out dark nooks and crannies. Its eyesight is exceptional. Size: 15–18 cm. ►

EPHIPPIDAE (BATFISH)

The dorsal and anal fins of young batfish are disproportionately large, making their body higher than it is long. As they reach adulthood, they gradually adopt a circular form. Slow and easy to acclimatize, they are, however, aggressive toward other batfish. They grow very quickly, with some adults reaching heights of 75 cm and weights of around 25 kg.

◄ ***Platax pinnatus***
The **red batfish** must be kept with peaceful species if its fins are to remain intact. Its diet consists of small live or frozen prey. Some related species are also widely available.

APOGONIDAE (CARDINALS)

The cardinals, diminutive and brightly colored, prefer darkness (as their large eyes suggest). They live in groups and are not too keen on active fish. The male incubates the eggs in its mouth (rare among marine fish). Hatching is possible in captivity, but feeding the fry brings new problems.

Sphaeramia nematoptera
The **pajama cardinal** can live in groups and respects invertebrates. It is sometimes confused with the closely related species *S. orbicularis,* which is also commercially available. They must both be fed with small animal foodstuffs. Size: 10 cm. ►

CALLIONYMIDAE (DRAGONETTES)

Their life is inextricably linked with the bed, where they look for the live prey that make up their diet. They are usually found in fairly shallow water. They can raise themselves slightly by supporting themselves on their ventral fins. Their cylindrical body is covered by a scaleless skin.

◄ ***Synchiropus splendidus***
The **blue mandarin** accepts small morsels of fish or mussels, which it will only take from the bed. Even when raised in couples, they will fight to the death, especially if the tank is too small. These fish are well suited to invertebrate aquariums. Size: 10 cm.

MONACANTHIDAE (FILE FISH)

These are somewhat more pacific than the triggers, to which they are scientifically related. These rather timid fish feed on very small prey (brine shrimps, pieces of mussel).

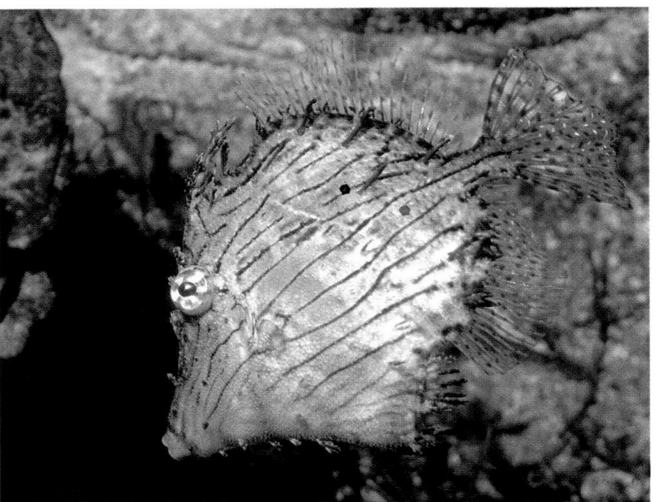

▲ ***Oxymonacanthus longirostris***
The **orange-spotted file fish** likes nooks and crannies but is also an active swimmer. It can live in groups and is recommended for invertebrate aquariums. Size: 10 cm.

◄ ***Chaetoderma penicilligrum***
The **tassled file fish** stands out due to the protuberances on its skin. It relishes algae, even more than live prey. The adults are loners and can attack some invertebrates. Size: 11–25 cm.

OPISTOGNATHIDAE

This family digs vertical burrows in the sand, and barely venture out, hiding themselves completely if there is any danger. Their large mobile eyes enable them to detect their small prey.

▲ ***Opistognathus aurifrons***
The **pearly jawfish**, an easy fish to keep, is recommended for invertebrate aquariums. It must have at least 15 cm of sediment. It feeds on mussels, shrimps, and fish flesh, but all its food must be broken up into small pieces. Reproduction is possible, but is best left to experienced fishkeepers. Size: 10–15 cm.

CIRRHITIDAE

These generally live in shallow coastal waters. In captivity, they prefer to share with peaceful fish that do not penetrate into their strictly demarcated territory.

Oxycirrhites typus
The **longnose hawk**, a delicate species to keep, is suitable for an invertebrate tank. It accepts brine shrimps, then small animal foodstuffs appropriate to the size of its mouth. It is rarely captured or imported. Size: 10 cm. ▼

GOBIIDAE (GOBIES)

Gobies live in coastal waters. When they are away from their shelters, they resist the movement of the water by clinging on to rocks with their pelvic fins, which are turned into suckers (although there are exceptions to this). They are easy to raise and feed on small, live prey.

Lythrypnus dalli
The **Catalina goby**, a small species native to California, can be distinguished by its vertical blue bands. It lives in harmony with invertebrates. Size: 4 cm. ▶

◀ ***Nemateleotris magnifica***
The **fire goby**, native to the Indo-Pacific region, more than lives up to its Latin name of *magnifica*. It adapts well to captivity but remains somewhat timid, and so it must be kept with placid species, or in an invertebrate tank. It accepts artificial food. Several species from the same genus, with similar vivid coloring, are sometimes found on the market. Size: 10 cm.

BLENNIIDAE (BLENNIES)

Blennies live in rocky coastal spots, or in sheltered reef areas. These robust little fish, easy to raise, are well suited to a tank for marine invertebrates. They are characterized by their abundant mucus and their often bright coloring. Blennies are not common in the aquarium trade, although it is possible to find some species belonging to the *Ecsenius* genus.

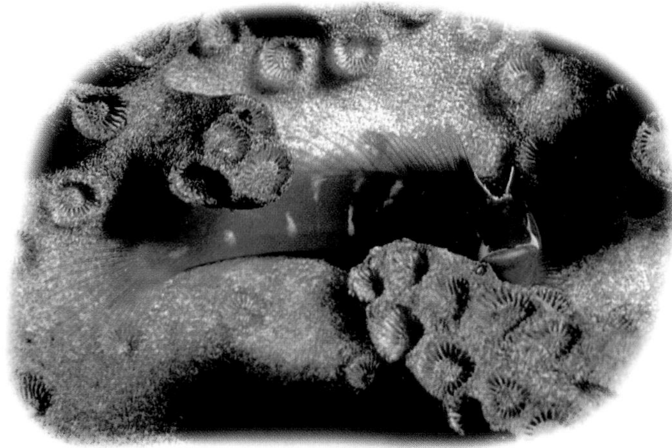

◀ ***Ecsenius sp.***
The **blennie** defends its territory, so the presence of other fish from the same family is not advisable. It moves around, but often remains stationary to observe its surroundings, or hides among the decor. It feeds on algae taken from the decor and also accepts small animal foodstuffs. Size: 8–10 cm.

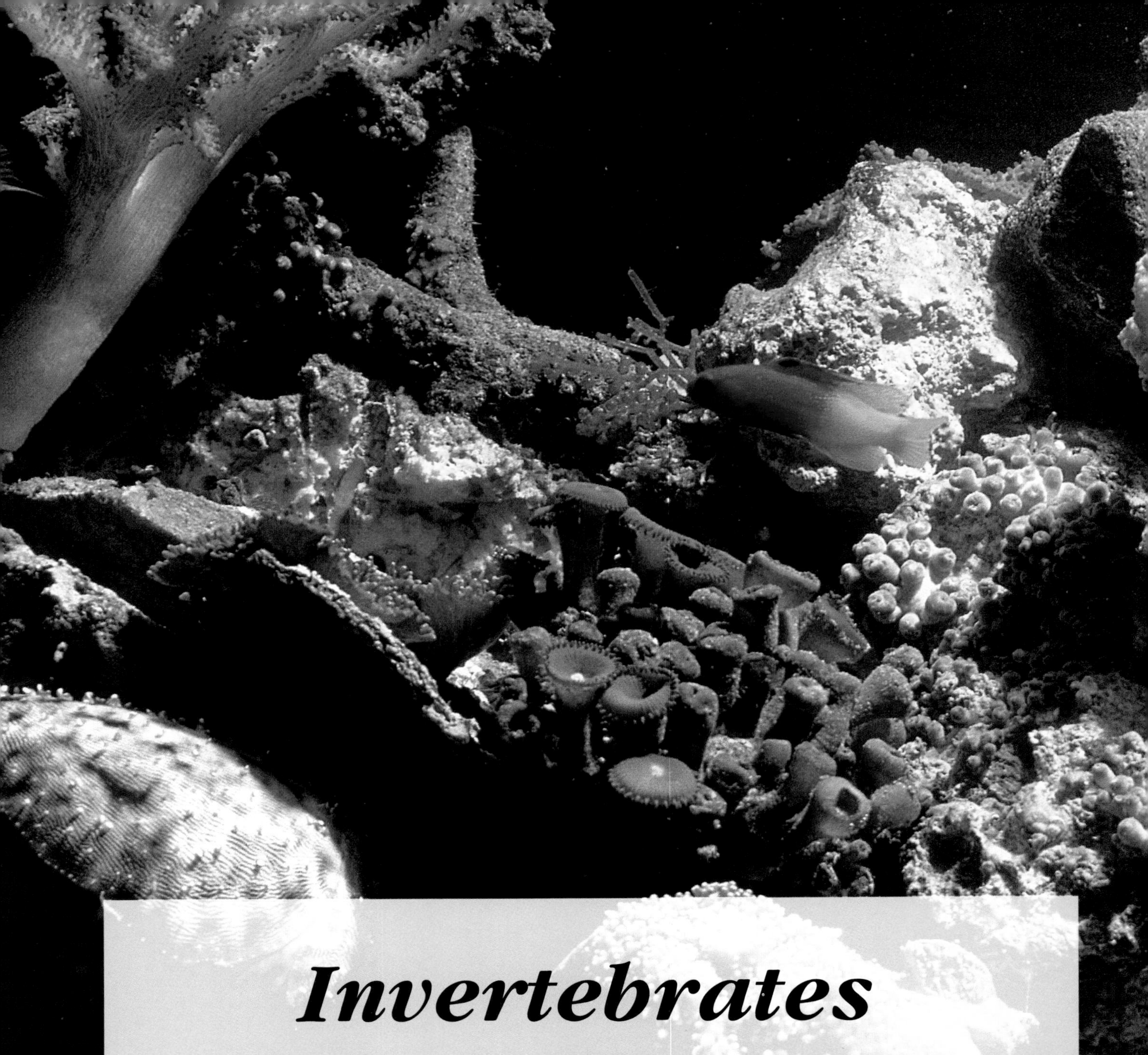

Invertebrates

Some species of invertebrates play a significant ecological role in an aquarium by feeding on detritus and helping to maintain the plants. These animals present a huge biological and ecological diversity, and this is one of the reasons why they are so attractive to aquarists. Most invertebrates are very demanding as regards water quality, especially the marine species. They can therefore be difficult to keep, although there are some hardy species suitable for hobbyists, and even novices.

THE MAIN INVERTEBRATE GROUPS

The invertebrates, as their name indicates, have no backbone. Their body is soft, but it is protected on the outside, by a carapace in the case of the crustaceans, or by a shell in mollusks, or it is supported by an internal calcareous skeleton, as in corals.
Although they are considered less evolved animals than the vertebrates – the group to which fish belong – invertebrates sometimes adapt in surprising ways to ensure their survival. The crustaceans, for example, can walk or swim to look for food or flee an enemy, while corals and anemones unfurl to capture microparticles, such as plankton, in open water, or retract to escape their predators.

SPONGES

Up until the 19th century, naturalists hesitated when classifying sponges: animal or vegetable? It must be admitted, however, that their field of research was extensive, as there are around 10,000 species of sponges.
These very old animals were among the first to appear on earth or, more exactly, in the sea. Freshwater species are rare and are not found in aquariums, but some marine species can be kept in captivity.

COELENTERATES

These animals, slightly more evolved than sponges, were also classed as vegetables for many years; even now the term animal-flowers is used to describe them. The Coelenterates comprise medusas ("jellyfish") – rarely seen in aquariums, apart from a few public ones – and the *Anthozoa*, which include anemones and corals, some of which are found in aquariums.

WORMS

Worms are barely evolved soft-bodied animals. They are more common in aquariums as live food than as residents, but are never found in freshwater aquariums.
A few specific species can be kept in captivity in sea water. They live in a tube and are often sedentary. The coloring of worms can vary enormously, but they are usually blue or purple, flecked with white, and almost always bicolor.

Mollusks

Their limp body is protected by a shell, which has two parts – these are the bivalves – or a single part – as in the case of the gastropods.

The **bivalves** half-open their shell – formed, as their name suggests, by two valves – to filter water. In this way they absorb oxygen and capture food particles, particularly vegetal plankton. Keeping them in an aquarium does not, therefore, pose any problems.

The **gastropods**, related to land snails, have a spiraled shell which varies in shape, according to the species. An organ in the mouth in the form of a grater, the radula, allows them to graze micro-algae on the decor, glass sides, or plants. This cleaning function constitutes their main attraction for aquarists. Do not, however, expect them to gobble up all your unwanted algae, as they play a more preventive role to restrict their untimely growth. They can sometimes attack the leaves of plants or eat a surplus of the food intended for fish. Some species are carnivorous.

Crustaceans

The crustaceans' bodies are protected by an articulated carapace. The animal abandons its carapace when it becomes too small due to body growth; this phenomenon is called the molt. The crustacean is particularly vulnerable to attacks from predators during the formation of the new carapace. The crustaceans found in aquariums belong to the decapod group, which have five pairs of walking legs, the first of which are used as pincers, with varying degrees of strength. The two pairs of antennae, highly developed in shrimps, play a tactile and sensory role. Crustaceans are carnivorous, and can feed on live or dead prey – they are not difficult to feed in an aquarium.

Echinoderms

These possess a symmetry based on five, which is extremely rare in nature, as most animals have a binary symmetry, meaning that, if they are cut down the middle, two identical parts can be observed. This is not possible with echinoderms, because they have to be cut into five sections to obtain identical pieces. Echinoderm means spiny skin: this is highly appropriate in the case of sea urchins, less so in relation to the rough starfish. Generally speaking, echinoderms will not survive for long outside water. They are found only in sea water.

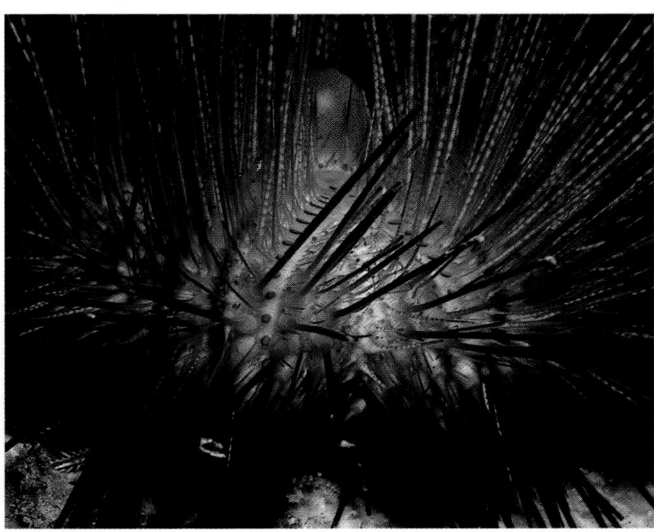

FRESHWATER INVERTEBRATES

Although freshwater invertebrates play a significant ecological role in their natural habitat, they are not popular with aquarists, and this is a great shame. They are represented by two main groups: the mollusks and the crustaceans.

MOLLUSKS

Bivalves commonly known as freshwater mussels can be found in some tropical waters. Although they differ as regards their anatomy, they are in fact distant cousins of the mussels on our coasts. They live buried, or partially buried, in the sediment. They eat by filtering micro-algae or vegetal plankton dissolved in the water. This can be a useful attribute in an aquarium, as it helps contain the proliferation of this type of algae. On the other hand, if there is not enough food, they will eventually die – which is not always noticeable at first, and therefore entails a risk of pollution from their dead bodies lingering in the water. Bivalves therefore have a somewhat limited appeal to fishkeepers, especially as few tropical species are available in the aquarium trade.

▲ Ampullaria sp., *like this golden variety, are one of the most effective gastropods against algae.*

As regards the gastropods, some species are considered pests – physas, for instance – while others, such as the *Planorbidae*, *Ampullaria*, and Malaysian snails, play a positive ecological role, above all by feeding on unwanted algae. In good conditions, they proliferate rapidly; they can be removed by hand or by trapping them with a leaf of lettuce or boiled spinach: if you put one of these in a tank at night, the next morning it will be covered in snails. If a population of gastropods disappears from an aquarium, this is probably a sign of imbalance.

CRUSTACEANS

In freshwater tanks, these are mainly represented by several species of shrimps, although it is occasionally possible to find a tropical crawfish, and even small crabs. As crustaceans' carapaces mainly consist of calcium carbonate ($CaCO_3$), it is advisable to keep them in hard water, and some crabs can even live in brackish water. Carnivorous fish are obviously out of the question as roommates. Small species of fish are not normally at risk from crustaceans, but a weakened or sick fish may be captured and devoured. Crustaceans' role in the wild as environmental regulators can be reproduced in captivity.

Whatever species you may choose, all crustaceans feel more at home if they are provided with shelters, especially during the molt. If they are fed properly, this process will occur regularly, but the animal is vulnerable while it is forming a new carapace. It is during this critical period in their lifecycle that crustaceans usually attack each other.

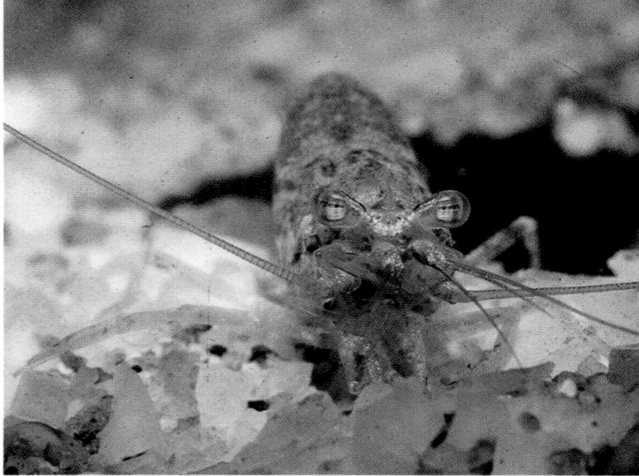

▲ *Shrimps from the* Macrobrachium *genus are becoming increasingly common in freshwater aquariums.*

MARINE INVERTEBRATES

Marine invertebrates are sometimes more difficult to keep in an aquarium: on the one hand, they are very sensitive to the quality of the water, which must be as faultless as possible, and, on the other, feeding them is complicated, particularly in the case of sponges, Coelenterates, anemones, and corals. It is also important to consider the compatibility of invertebrates, not only with each other but also with fish – as invertebrates are the favorite meal of some fish!

For all these reasons, the best option is a specialist tank, which will provide a spectacle just as fascinating as that of a fish aquarium, although those fish which can cohabit with invertebrates represent a logical complement to this type of aquarium. The invertebrates which are most robust and easiest to acclimatize can reproduce in captivity (especially some species of anemones), but success in this area requires a solid background in marine aquariums on the part of the hobbyist.
Nevertheless, some marine aquarists hesitate to cross the threshold from fish to invertebrates, on the grounds both of cost and risk. However, these days there is a craze for this type of aquarium, but you must not get carried away: it is not feasible to reconstitute a coral reef, although it is possible to achieve satisfying results, both in terms of ecological equilibrium and an engrossing spectacle.

General maintenance conditions

The aquarium

The bigger it is, the easier it is to acclimatize the invertebrates. Do not consider a tank of under 300 liters for a medium-sized anemone, accompanied by its clown fish. A volume of 400–500 liters is the absolute minimum for a tank containing several species of invertebrates. A maximum height of 50 cm is recommended to allow the light to penetrate, as well as making it easier for the aquarist to intervene. It makes sense anyway to install as large a tank as possible, as your enthusiasm for these creatures is bound to grow.

Mounting a tank almost entirely composed of invertebrates, with a few fish added, requires ample knowledge of these animals. ▼

Lowering the pH in a marine invertebrate tank

The pH in a coral tank sometimes undergoes slight but regular decreases. When it drops to under 8.3, it can be raised with sodium carbonate. Dissolve 5 g in 1 liter of water, and add 1 ml of this solution to each liter of clean water. This process is repeated every day until a pH of 8.3 is obtained. There are also some ready-to-use solutions for this purpose available in the aquarium trade.

▲ *Easy-to-use tests make it possible to control water quality, which must be perfect in an invertebrate tank.*

Water

This must be stirred vigorously: use a pump with an outflow equal to at least five times, and up to ten times, that of the volume of the aquarium. Do not forget that the water in an invertebrate tank will never be as agitated as in a natural setting. The water must be very clear, to facilitate the penetration of light. It is therefore vital to have good mechanical filtration, possibly in conjunction with an air pump. Invertebrates are extremely sensitive to nitrates (NO_3-).

A box filter is indispensable, and its volume must equal at least 10% that of the aquarium.

It must be pointed out, however, that tanks containing true corals, or madreporites, which form reefs can sometimes work well without this type of filter. In order to facilitate the operation and reduce the burden of the filter, thus increasing its efficacy, put the protein skimmer in its first section. As a complement to these techniques, you are strongly advised to perform partial water changes, at a rate of around 10% of the volume, once a week.

It is advisable to change the water the day after the weekly feeding session, as this will help to reduce pollution. The specific gravity of the water must be around 1.024, although it can go up to 1.026.

Light

This is extremely important, both as regards quantity and quality. Apart from the aesthetic effect, lighting serves to enhance the development of *Zooxanthellae*, the micro-algae which live in the animals' tissues and contribute to their equilibrium.

If the water is less than 50 cm deep, use fluorescent tubes as day lighting, in conjunction with a blue tube. Deeper water requires powerful HQI lamps, again combined with a blue tube. The lighting must be strong (around 1 W per liter of water) and should be left on for about 13 hours every day. UV lamps are not recommended for invertebrates.

More detailed information on lighting can be found in the chapter Equipment and Accessories (page 226).

The substrate

Fine-grained soils are to be avoided, a size of 2–5 mm being perfect. The bed must be calcareous and comprise sand made from corals and marine algae, which can be complemented by crushed oyster shells to guarantee a moderate supply of calcium carbonate.

▲ *The substrate in marine tanks consists of coral elements in fairly large grains.*

ZOOXANTHELLAE

These are green micro-algae which live in the skin of *Anthozoa* and other organisms, such as sponges or giant clams, a type of bivalve mollusk. They exchange substances with the cells of their hosts. The carbon dioxide (CO_2) resulting from the metabolism of the cells – i.e. the oxidation of the foodstuffs – is collected by the *Zooxanthellae*. These, in their turn, absorb nitrogenous and phosphorous substances, carry out photosynthesis, and produce organic substances that enhance both their own growth and that of their host. This type of mutually beneficial association taking place inside an animal is known as endosymbiosis. The *Zooxanthellae* contribute, to some extent, to the feeding process of *Anthozoa*, which therefore need only a very scanty external supply of nutrients: some organisms, such as the anemones, need to be fed only around once a week in an aquarium.

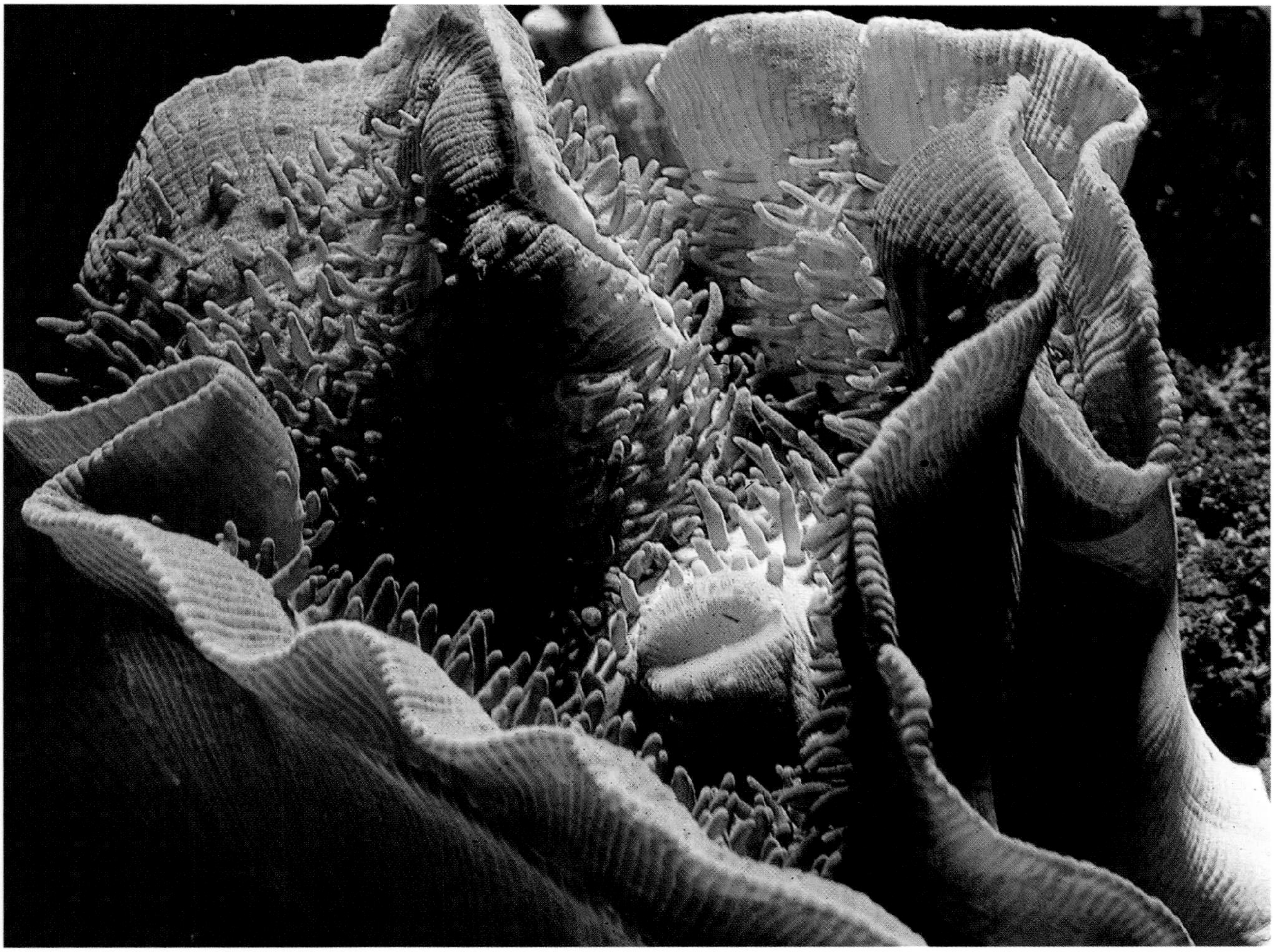

▲ *The green coloring of this* Anthozoa *indicates the presence of a significant number of* Zooxanthellae*: this animal must therefore be placed under fairly intense lighting.*

The decor

This serves as a support for some animals. Create an aquascape in tiers or with steps, and place the species on it according to their need for light. This is easy to do with artificial materials, and the decor can be finished off with dead coral and rocks.

◀ Caulerpa prolifera *is a common alga in marine invertebrate tanks.*

▲ *When well acclimatized, the Coelenterates soon deploy their tentacles, which is a sign of good health.*

Vegetation

Plants release substances that have a beneficial effect on invertebrates, although as yet we still know relatively little about the mechanism of this process.

Use algae of the *Caulerpa* genus, but do not allow them to become too dense.

In addition, remain on the lookout for the growth of certain filamentous algae, as there is a danger that they might smother some sponges and delicate Coelenterates.

Acclimatizing invertebrates

As the characteristics of invertebrates' native waters are radically different from those of the tank in which they will be placed, great care must be taken with respect to their acclimatization. The container in which the new arrival has been transported must be gradually filled with water from its future aquarium, to enable the invertebrate to slowly adapt before it is carefully transferred into its new habitat. The whole process takes about 1 hour. A quarantine period in an acclimatization tank is recommended. When handling invertebrates, be aware of the stinging capability of some species (such as anemones and madreporites).

Sponges

Sponges enjoy shadows or darkness as they can only tolerate a small amount of light. They do not like water with a high content of nitrates or filamentous algae, which smother them. They reproduce, either sexually – rarely achieved in an aquarium – or through asexual division, with a detached piece of sponge evolving into a new specimen.

A sponge is a kind of "sack" devoid of any specialized organs. Water penetrates the walls, circulates in the canals, as a result of the movements of thousands of strands protecting the cells, and leaves via the opening in the top. The water provides oxygen and the particles on which the sponge feeds, particularly the micro-algae of phytoplankton.

Removing a sponge from water has fatal consequences, as air bubbles enter the canals where the water circulates and block them. The sponge, unable to eliminate the bubbles, eventually dies.

Sponges are fed in the same way as Coelenterates, with a preparation based on mussels, or special liquids available commercially from specialist suppliers.

Coelenterates

The Coelenterates constitute a complex group (see table, page 171). They include the *Anthozoa*, which are divided into hexacorals, where the number of tentacles is a multiple of 6, and octocorals, where the number of tentacles is a multiple of 8.

The hexacorals are divided into:

– *Actiniaria* (true anemones);
– *Ceriantharia*;
– *Zoantharia* (colonial anemones);
– *Corallimorpharia* (discus anemones);
– *Scleractinia* (madreporites or true corals).

These invertebrates are characterized by tentacles attached to a foot, and the whole organism is called a polyp. Anemones and *Ceriantharia* are isolated polyps, while the other *Anthozoa* are colonial polyps, connected to each other at their base, which end up by spreading out over large areas like certain plants.

Darts for defense

The bodies of Coelenterates, particularly the tentacles, are covered with urticant (stinging) cells, equipped with a strand that is sensitive to contact with other organisms. When a Coelenterate is touched, thousands or even millions of cells open and eject a filament with a microscopic dart at the tip which injects venom; in this way, a prey is quickly paralyzed before being eaten. Care should be taken when handling, therefore.

Introducing Coelenterates to an aquarium

Coelenterates must of course present all the necessary signs of good health before being introduced to an aquarium: they should be unfurled, swollen, and full of water. If they are in a bad state, they look wilted and may not be viable.
Anthozoa like clear and well-lit water, as it benefits both them and the *Zooxanthellae* to which they play host. They must be placed close to the surface of the aquarium. The water quality is, of course, very important, and in addition the calcium

What if you touch a coelenterate?

Some species have a greater stinging capability than others. Serious reactions, such as cramps or breathing difficulties, rarely encountered among aquarists, can be provoked by certain medusas (jellyfish), due to a phenomenon known as anaphylaxis: the body is sensitized to the venom after an initial contact and becomes more vulnerable. In the event of an accident, detach the tentacles and, above all, do not rub your eyes. Treat the stung area immediately with diluted ammonia, but it is best to consult a doctor.

How to classify coelenterates

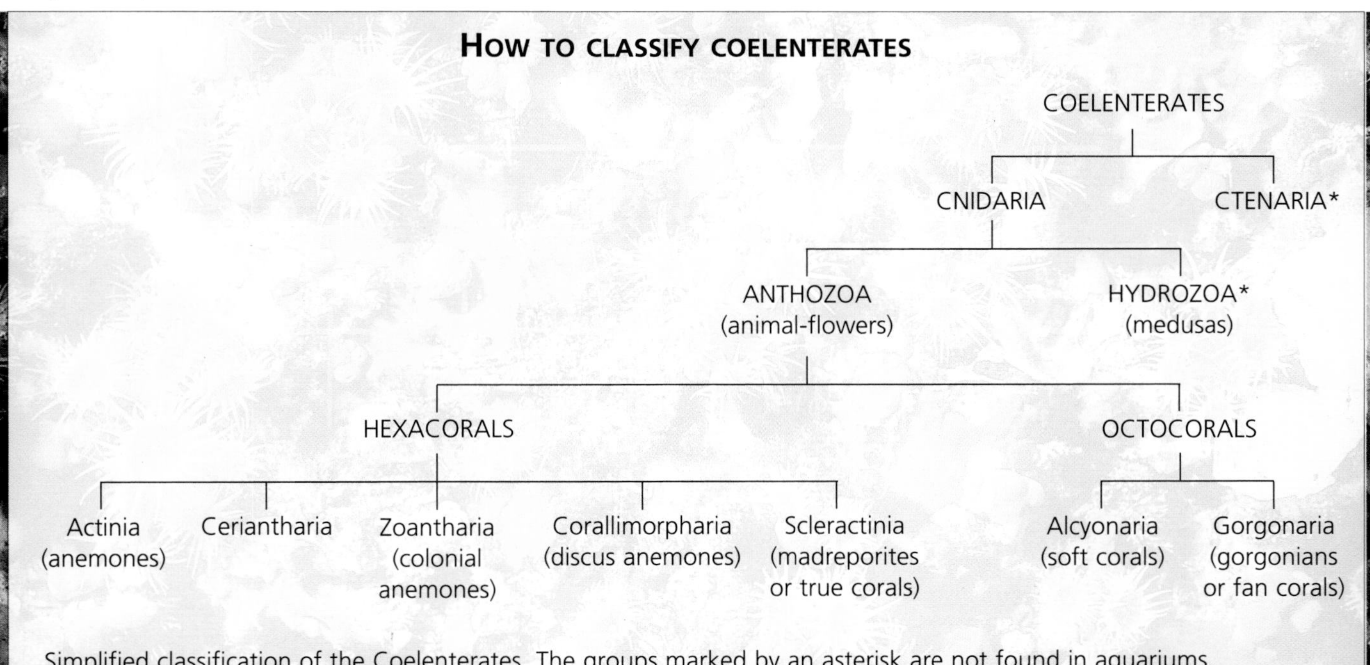

Simplified classification of the Coelenterates. The groups marked by an asterisk are not found in aquariums.

levels must be monitored with particularly close attention.

The skeleton of corals is mainly composed of calcium carbonate, which is abundant in the natural habitat – up to 500 mg/liter – and so an aquarium that is to be inhabited by corals must also have the same level.

The concentration in an aquarium can sometimes fall below 300 mg/liter, depending on how many organisms there are in the tank, and in these cases calcium must be added. Several relatively simple methods for raising the calcium level are detailed in the box on page 173.

Coral reefs

The accumulation of calcareous coral skeletons gradually forms reefs, of which the most famous is the Great Barrier Reef, stretching north-eastward from south Australia for almost 2,000 km. It is the biggest structure of animal origin in the world! This ecosystem, one of the richest and most diverse in existence, is also fragile and constantly subject to attack. The last few decades have witnessed the destruction of some reefs, the coral being used to build houses, roads, and even airport runways! Obviously, aquarists have been accused of taking part in this pillage, which seems grossly exaggerated: the removal of corals from their natural habitat for the aquarium trade does occur, but it is negligible compared to other large-scale extractions. Furthermore, some species are protected by law and never reach hobbyists' tanks.

Public marine aquariums can, on the contrary, make a contribution to the study of invertebrates. The aquarium of the Monaco Oceanographic Museum, for

Certain species of fish and marine invertebrates found in aquariums come from coral reefs. ▼

When must calcium be added?

Calcium is added when the concentrated measured is less than 400 mg/liter. There are tests on the market to measure the quantity of this parameter. Remember that the measurement of CH, in sea water, reveals the quantity of carbonates and bicarbonates. When this is less than 7°CH (128 ppm), it can be concluded that a lack of calcium carbonate is more than likely and steps should be taken to remedy this.

How to supply calcium to a coral aquarium

Method 1

From the start, i.e. when you put the first water in, use commercial salts enriched in calcium. Then, add the same salts over the course of regular partial water changes, at the rate of 10% per week.

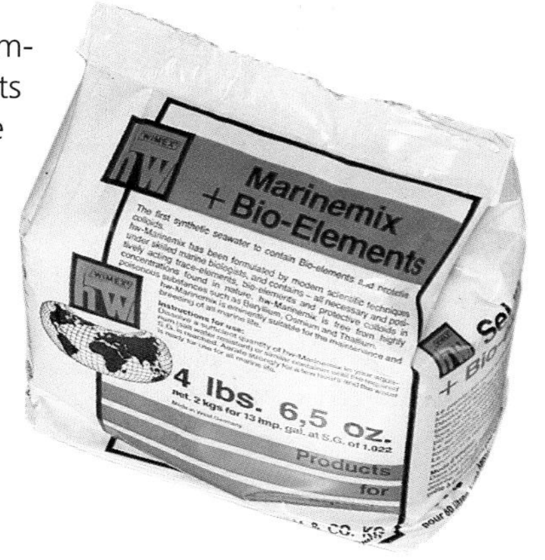

Some commercial salts are specially designed for marine invertebrates. ▶

Method 2

Use commercial products specially prepared to increase calcium levels.

Method 3

Place a calcareous element, such as calcareous rock, or crushed and washed oyster shells, in the filter, and this will gradually release calcium. However, this method will not give rise to any rapid or significant increase in calcium levels.

Method 4

Prepare a solution of slaked lime, Ca $(OH)_2$, available in aquarium stores, at a rate of 1.5 g/liter. Pour in 1 ml of this solution per liter of sea water.

Proceed gradually, monitoring the pH constantly to ensure it does not rise above 8.5.

Method 5

This is the most complicated, but also the most effective.

Prepare two solutions:

– one of dehydrated calcium chloride ($CaCl_2$, $2H_2O$) at a rate of 15 g/liter, which will provide the calcium;

– the other of sodium bicarbonate ($NaHCO_3$), at a rate of 17 g/liter, which will provide the carbonates.

Then calculate the difference between a carbonate hardness of 130 ppm (7.2°CH) and the one measured in the aquarium. Multiply the result by the net volume of the tank, and divide the result by 10. This will give the amount of each solution required, in milliliters, to pour into the aquarium.

Example: for a tank with a net volume of 500 liters, with a carbonate hardness of 100 ppm (5.6°CH), the result is:

Amount of each solution (in ml) = 500 x (130–100) ÷ 10 = 1,500 ml.

The following table gives you the required amount of each solution (in ml) for specific cases.

When adding calcium, the pH value must not rise above 8.5; regular control is necessary. ▼

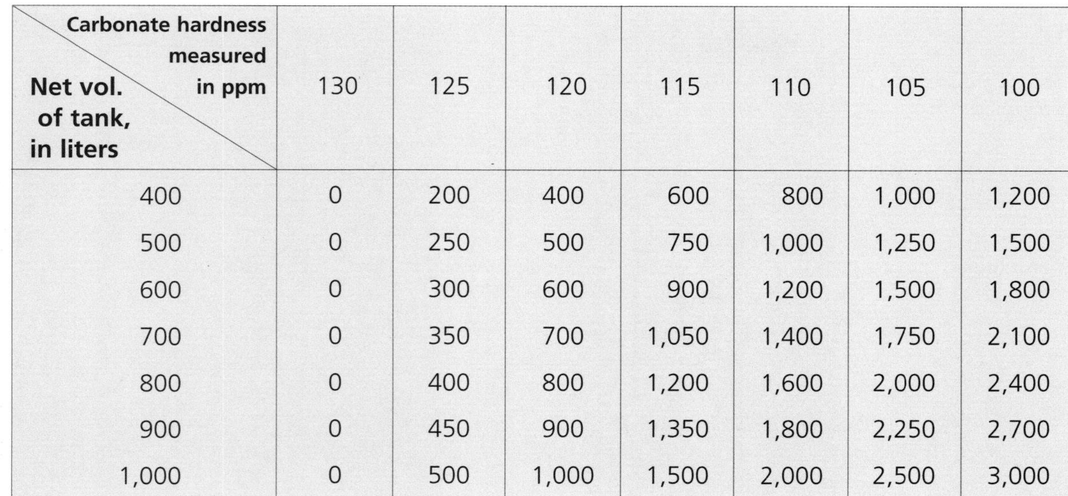

Net vol. of tank, in liters \ Carbonate hardness measured in ppm	130	125	120	115	110	105	100
400	0	200	400	600	800	1,000	1,200
500	0	250	500	750	1,000	1,250	1,500
600	0	300	600	900	1,200	1,500	1,800
700	0	350	700	1,050	1,400	1,750	2,100
800	0	400	800	1,200	1,600	2,000	2,400
900	0	450	900	1,350	1,800	2,250	2,700
1,000	0	500	1,000	1,500	2,000	2,500	3,000

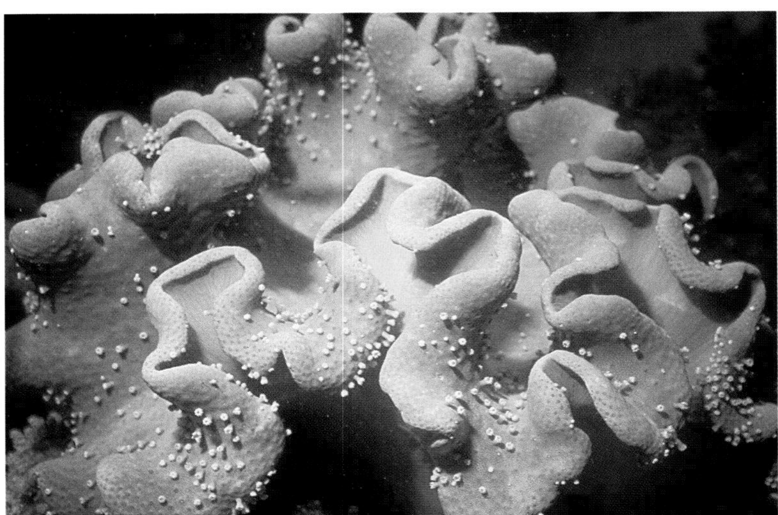

▲ *The leather corals of the* Sarcophyton *genus will not tolerate being close to Coelenterates highly prone to stinging.*

example, is carrying out research in this field, using a 40 m³ tank containing several tons of corals, which are nurtured and bred. Until recently, raising corals on this scale in captivity was impossible, above all because of their very great sensitivity to nitrates (NO_3-). Scientists solved this problem by allowing these nitrates to turn into nitrogen gas (N_2), thanks to the anaerobic bacteria which survive at the bottom of the tank, where the oxygen levels are low. The nitrogen produced by the metabolism of these bacteria then passes into the atmosphere.

This complicated technique is beyond the reach of most aquarists, however experienced they may be.

Feeding Coelenterates

By filtering the water, the Coelenterates trap small suspended particles, particularly the crustacean zooplankton. Collecting, keeping, and distributing plankton is not a task to be taken lightly, and it is best to look for other solutions.

However, it must be made clear that commercial foods on the market provide little more than a stopgap.

It is possible to use rotifers or freshly hatched brine shrimp nauplii, normally used as the main food for fish, but not everybody breeds these animals. There is another food which is available to all hobbyists, as it is inexpensive, easy to make, and can be frozen: it is usually called mussel choppy. Mussels are not only cheap but also rich in proteins, carbohydrates, mineral salts, and vitamins. Other possi-

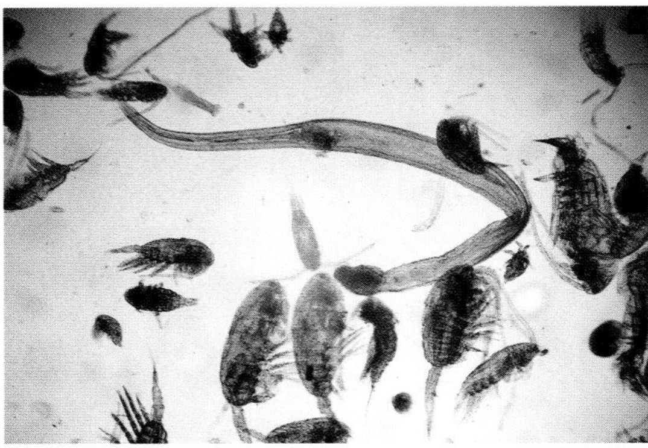

In their natural habitat, Coelenterates feed on animal plankton, but these are difficult to supply in an aquarium. ►

Food for Sponges and Coelenterates: A Recipe

Ingredients:

- mussels or cockles;
- white fish, i.e. lean and free of lipids;
- shelled shrimps in cans (optional).

Cook the mollusks and fish. Put the shrimps in boiling water for 1–2 minutes.

Remove the mollusks' shells.

Mix all the ingredients thoroughly. You can add a vitamin solution, flakes or granules of fish food, boiled spinach, or the special foods for invertebrates available commercially. If the paste is too thick after mixing, thin it with sea water.

Pass the mixture through a sieve. What is left behind in the sieve can be distributed to anemones or small fish; this purée can also be frozen. Allow the purée to stand for several hours in the refrigerator, then discard any excess water.

The resulting paste can be used straightaway for feeding, or can be frozen.

It is best to put the food into the aquarium at night, 1 or 2 hours before switching off the lights. Switch off the filters, pumps, and aeration for a moment. Thaw the food, if necessary, and distribute the equivalent of one tablespoon of the prepared liquid for every 200 liters of water. Deposit the food above the invertebrates with a narrow, rigid tube. The filtration and aeration systems can be switched back on a few minutes afterwards.

◀ *The Coelenterates can cohabit with algae – encrusting or otherwise – and even with small fish.*

bilities are cockles, the flesh of lean fish, or cans of shelled shrimps, which are produced in large quantities in Asia, cost little, and are readily available.

The other problem is establishing a feeding schedule. It must be remembered that the majority of organisms being fed play host to *Zooxanthellae*, which often satisfy a significant proportion of their dietary needs, and so a weekly feed is more than sufficient. Do not forget that the best time for this is the night before a water change, to reduce the risk of pollution.

The larger anemones feed on adult brine shrimps, small pieces of mussel, fish, or shrimps or a mixture of these.

Compatibility between Coelenterates

Urticant (stinging) Coelenterates must be kept apart from the more delicate species: a safety margin of 10–15 cm is often recommended. The madreporites and anemones are among the most urticant, and they must not be put alongside a leather coral from the *Sarcophyton* genus, for example. Other alternatives for a Coelenterates tank are algae – whether encrusting or not – supported by live rocks, or even caulerpae. Their development must be controlled so that they do not end up smothering the *Anthozoa*. The introduction of certain fish is possible, even desirable, but there are cases of classic incompatibilities (see table, page 178). Specially designed artificial decor can be colonized quickly, depending on the organisms' rate of growth and reproduction. This can sometimes make it difficult for even a practiced eye to spot the difference between artificial and natural decor in an aquarium which has been in operation for several months.

WORMS

Some species belonging to the *Annelida*, a group that includes the sea worms used as bait in fishing, live in a tube which they build themselves: these are known as

◀ *In an invertebrate tank the development of algae must be restrained, so that they do not smother the Coelenterates (left,* a Cerianthus*).*

▲ *This cowry has withdrawn its mantle into its shell.*

sedentary *Annelida*. The brightly colored branchial plume which sticks out of it traps oxygen, as well as the organisms which make up zooplankton. At the sign of any danger, or if the tank or its support are knocked, this branchial plume retreats into its tube. The feeding of *Annelida* in captivity is identical to that of Coelenterates. When you buy one, make sure that the branchial plume is functioning correctly and its tube is intact. It is best to buy a worm fixed to a piece of rock.

Mollusks

Few mollusks are found in aquariums, and they are not often available commercially. Among the gastropods, the cowries, well known to collectors of shells, can be kept in captivity. Some fish may nibble the "mantle", the part of the animal's body used outside the shell.
Of course, in the event of any danger the animal retreats into its shell. Hobbyists enchanted by the beauty of this shell can put a specimen in a tank containing small Pacific fish (Gobiids, Blenniids, Grammids, *Pseudochromis*, for example). In the bivalve group there is the famous giant clam, which can sometimes grow up to a length of 1 m in the wild, where it feeds on vegetal plankton. Some smaller species can be acclimatized in an aquarium. However, these animals are only recommended for experienced hobbyists.

Crustaceans

It is easy to keep a few species in a marine aquarium, to take advantage of their bright colors. These invertebrates are carnivorous: in an aquarium they should be fed on mussels, fish, or white meat.

▲ *Hermit crabs are highly striking invertebrates which run around the aquarium in all directions to look for their food. They withdraw into their shell when frightened.*

Shrimps play an ecological role by feeding on fishes' leftovers. ▼

Shrimps

These rarely swim and prefer to get about by walking on the decor. If they are disturbed they abruptly recoil by tucking up their abdomen. Several specimens can live together, but it is vital to keep them away from carnivorous fish.

▲ Enomotoplus sp., *the lobster crab, related to the langoustine, is an attractive and placid resident.*

Crabs

The small abdomen is tucked under the lower part of the body. Their pincers are particularly well developed. The larger specimens, which can be aggressive, must not be put into marine aquariums, as they can attack other invertebrates, and sometimes even fish.

Pagurids

These are better known as hermit crabs. Some tropical species can be found commercially, some of them bearing a small anemone on the gastropod shell which houses them. The shell is discarded when it becomes too small for the growing animal, so it is vital to provide bigger ones, as, unlike other crustaceans, a pagurid's abdomen is not protected by a carapace that it makes itself.

Echinoderms

Sea urchins

These are not very easy species to acclimatize. It is possible to keep one small specimen at most, which will often live away from the light. They are herbivores that sift the substrate looking for algae to eat. In among the prickles it is possible to see the articulated pedicellariae, which end either in a tiny pincer for trapping food or a sucker. The latter allows sea urchins to develop on rigid supports or the glass sides of the tank.

▲ *Some species of sea urchins with varying sizes of prickles can be found in marine aquariums.*

Starfish

These are not recommended for a marine invertebrate tank, as they attack other species, such as sponges. Starfish are in fact either carnivorous, gripping their prey with their long arms that emerge from a central disc, or microphages, in which case they feed on small organisms on the bed.

The ophiuroids, sometimes called brittle-stars and closely related to starfish, have articulated arms which allow them to move around quite quickly. These arms, like those of the starfish, can regenerate themselves if they break off.

"Live rocks"

These are pieces of rock or fragments of dead coral (madreporites), that are bound together by calcareous rocks or various pieces of debris from invertebrates. They

"Live rocks" *are covered with many small organisms (worms, Coelenterates) which would be difficult to introduce into an aquarium in any other way.* ▶

Compatibility and incompatibility between fish and invertebrates	
Total incompatibility with all invertebrates	Triggers (*Balistidae*), snappers (*Lutjanidae*), murenas (*Murenidae*), groupers – except *Anthias* (*Serranidae*), wrasses (*Labridae*), porcupine fish (*Diodontidae*), puffers (*Tetraodontidae* and *Canthigasteridae*), scorpions (*Scorpenidae*), zebras (*Plectorhynchidae*), other fish longer than 10–15 cm with a lively nature.
Incompatibility with worms, crustaceans, mollusks, echinoderms	Predatory fish from other groups, such as squirrel fish, soldier fish (*Holocentridae*) and batfish (*Ephippids*).
Incompatibility with sponges and Coelenterates	Butterfly fish (*Chaetonidae*), angelfish (*Pomacanthidae*).
Compatibility with practically all invertebrates	*Anthias* (*Serranidae*), sea horses (*Syngnathidae*), hawks (*Cirrhitidae*), *Opistognotidae*, lime fish (*Monacanthidae*), mandarin fish (*Callionymidae*), cardinals (*Apogonidae*) – except with small shrimps, rockets (*Plesiopidae*) – except with crustaceans, *Grammidae,* and *Pseudochromis*, *Blenniidae*, *Pomacentrids*, small tangs (*Acanthuridae*). This amounts to more than 20 species, generally under 10 cm in length, easy to acclimatize.
An aquarist does not in fact reconstitute a biotope in an invertebrate tank, since it unites species which do not necessarily live together in a natural setting. Common sense will make it possible to obtain satisfactory results, pleasing to the eye, in which fish and invertebrates live together in harmony.	

are sometimes removed from their natural setting and sold commercially. "Live rocks" harbor various organisms: bacteria, algae, sponges, small Coelenterates, and sometimes even small crustaceans, hidden in crevices. They can therefore be considered as living pieces of decor which contribute to the equilibrium of the aquarium. If, before sale, they have been suitably transported, cared for, and housed, then they are worth acquiring, despite their high price, as they permit the introduction of a variety of beneficial organisms into the aquarium, in the most "natural" way possible.
Another option is to collect these types of rock yourself, off the shores of Florida, for example. Organisms capable of surviving in a tropical tank grow there in summer, when the water temperature is higher. There is always a chance, however, of introducing an undesirable organism or of finding that some residents of the "live rock" deteriorate and die, with an ensuing risk of pollution. It is therefore best to proceed with caution and isolate the rock in a quarantine aquarium.

Compatibility between invertebrates and marine fish

Invertebrates cannot cohabit with just any fish, for a number of reasons. The first is that they are liable to become prey for carnivorous fish. Coelenterates are completely incompatible with angelfish (Pomacanthids), for example. Secondly, some lively and active fish, of over 10–15 cm in length, can jostle and disturb invertebrates in the aquarium.
Furthermore, the bigger and more active a fish, the more it excretes nitrogenous substances, leading to the accumulation of nitrates (NO_3-), which are harmful to invertebrates. It is therefore best to avoid the presence of this type of fish. Too many fish produce the same result and the same degree of harm for invertebrates.
Finally, there is another problem when a sick fish has to be treated, particularly with substances containing metals, which are toxic for most invertebrates. Remember that it is always preferable to nurse a fish in a hospital aquarium.

INVERTEBRATES

These days, more and more aquarists seem to be taking an interest in these animals. Ecologically speaking, invertebrates represent a natural complement to fish and plants; in visual terms, you can put on a spectacle of luminous beauty, particularly in sea water, using anemones and corals, to which can be added small fish, either lively or placid, but always brightly colored. There are also a few species of freshwater mollusks and crustaceans which are easy to keep in captivity, although they are little known and often overlooked.

GASTROPODS

These are often unintentionally introduced into aquariums, usually via plants containing eggs or small juveniles which are difficult to spot. Gastropods lay their eggs in a small, transparent, gelatinous mass.

▲ ***Ampullaria gigas***

Ampullaria

Some species of the **apple snail** can grow to 20 cm in the wild, but those found in an aquarium (belonging to the *Ampullaria* genus) do not exceed 7 cm. They eat vegetation and detritus, helping to restrict the development of algae, and like fairly hard water. Unlike many other gastropods, they are sexed and lay their eggs outside the water. Size: 6–7 cm.

Planorbis

These are water snails with a flattened shell. Their orange-red body contains plenty of red globules to establish a high oxygen concentration, as they live in environments lacking in oxygen and breathe through their lungs, sometimes rising to the water surface. They graze on both short and filamentous green algae, whose growth they help to restrict. Size: 3–4 cm.

◀ ***Planorbis sp.***

Malayan snails

They breathe through their branchiae and can retreat into their tapered shell, which closes with an operculum. They relish the tiny algae which encrust the decor; if they are well fed, they proliferate quickly. They are considered less effective than the planorbis, but as they bury themselves, they contribute to the equilibrium of the aquarium by turning over and aerating the bed. If you want to get rid of them, introduce a fish from the *Tetradon* genus, which will appreciate these mollusks. Several Malayan snail species belonging to the *Melanoides* genus (such as *Melanoides tuberculata*), native to South-East Asia, can be unintentionally introduced into tanks along with plants. Size: 1–2 cm.

◀ ***Melanoides sp.* (Malayan snail)**

Physas

Their spiraled shell is markedly less elongate than that of Malayan snails and they are also slightly bigger. They do not play an important role in the control of unwanted algae. As they reproduce rapidly, it is best not to introduce them into an aquarium. Size: 1–2 cm.

Physa sp. ▶

CRUSTACEANS

The word crustaceans usually brings marine species to mind, and it is often forgotten that they also live in fresh water. Less colorful than their marine cousins, they are nevertheless interesting to observe. They prefer hard water, on account of the calcium carbonate that forms their carapace.

▲ ***Atya moluccensis***

Shrimps

Few species are commercially available, even though they are abundant in certain tropical regions. Several specimens can live together, if there are a sufficient number of shelters to provide hiding places in the aquarium.

Atya

These shrimps are found in many tropical regions in the Americas, Africa, and Asia, sometimes in brackish water. They are bottom-dwellers that feed on leftover food – both natural and artificial – and fish, and so their ecological role is quite substantial. These shrimps from the *Atya* genus (particularly *Atya moluccensis*, native to South-East Asia) are only occasionally found in the aquarium trade. They like lively, well-oxygenated water and are sociable, and so can be kept in small groups. Size: 6–7 cm.

Palaemonidae

This family includes the familiar pink shrimp, as well as a large number of freshwater tropical species, such as the genus *Macrobrachium* (which covers some 200 species). These long-pincer shrimps are sometimes raised for restaurants: this is the case with *M. rosenbergii*, which grows to 25 cm, without counting its pincers.

It is the smaller species that are sold in the aquarium trade, with *M. lanchasteri* being the most common at the moment. Native to South-East Asia, it acts as a garbage collector in a tank by eating the particles left behind by the fish. This shrimp likes filtered light and shelters for taking refuge if it is disturbed. When it is really frightened, it can jump out of the water to escape from danger. It is prone to attack the fish fry, which it easily detects with its acute sense of smell. Size: 7–8 cm.

▲ ***Macrobrachium sp.***

Crawfish

There are around thirty species of crawfish in the world, distributed across the temperate and subtropical zones. Although some European species can adjust to tropical aquariums, it is advisable to let them remain in the wild as the regulations concerning their entrapment are strict.

▲ ***Procamburus clarkii***

One crawfish, *Procamburus clarkii*, the **Louisiana crawfish**, has been imported by a number of countries. It can cause a great deal of damage as it is fossorial and burrows in river banks.

It grows quickly (starting to reproduce at the age of 7 or 8 months) and is highly adaptable, as it tolerates a wide range of temperatures and requires little oxygen. Many of the imported specimens come from South-East Asia, where there are red and blue varieties.

It is omnivorous and can attack plants and fish, as well as other crustaceans. It is therefore best to keep a single specimen, even if the aquarium is very big and endowed with hiding places. Size: 15 cm.

SPONGES

The form and color of sponges are extremely diverse: balls, mats, or tubes, in red, orange, yellow, brown, or gray. They attach themselves to a support (rocks, but also dead coral or mollusk shells) and shy away from the light. Sponges seem to proliferate spontaneously in marine tanks, as they can be introduced, in sizes invisible to the naked eye, along with other invertebrates, live rocks, or in water. Both the common and scientific names are little known and it is difficult to ascertain with any exactitude which species are found in the aquarium trade in the absence of detailed research.

▲ **Red Sea sponge**

COELENTERATES

These are the favorites among aquarists that specialize in invertebrates, although their availability – and their price – can vary enormously. Furthermore, there is sometimes confusion over their names: some species may not even have one as they have yet to be systematically studied and described!

▲ *Anthozoa* sometimes provide a refuge for shrimps, protecting them from their predators.

Hexacorals

This group covers the majority of the Coelenterates found in marine aquariums, particularly anemones and corals. Do not forget that most of them need strong light, as they contain *Zooxanthellae*, and that they can be fed on small morsels of animal origin. The aquarist must take care when handling some species, as their capacity to sting can be considerable. The great majority of these animals are imported from the Indian or Pacific Oceans, but they are only sporadically available in the aquarium trade.

Sea anemones *(Actinia)*

These live on the substrate, attached by their single foot, which acts as a sucker, but they can move around and find the place that suits them best (sometimes the tank's front pane). Some rare species live in the sand and can retreat into it. They are fairly robust in an aquarium if in water that is well lit and aerated (some anemones have *Zooxanthellae*). A large living space must therefore be planned for them, as other *Anthozoa* do not appreciate their tentacles; moreover, they sometimes excrete filaments of mucus that can pollute the water. Only clownfish can accustom themselves to contact with their tentacles. Anemones eat small pieces of mussel, shrimp, fish, or a choppy made from these ingredients. Sexual reproduction is a possibility, and some anemones are livebearers; asexual multiplication can take place via budding, which will go on to produce a young anemone. When buying anemones, make sure that they are puffed out and unfurled, as these are signs of good health.

Heteractis (formerly ***Radianthus***)

This has a large number of tentacles, which are quite long (up to 10 cm) and somewhat rigid. Species of this genus can achieve a diameter of several dozen centimeters, and they are appreciated by several species of clownfish. Diameter: 30–40 cm.

◀ ***Heteractis magnifica***

Stichodactyla (formerly ***Stoichactus***)
In its natural habitat a species of the *Stichodactyla* reaches lengths of 1 m. The tentacles are arranged in dense ranks, particularly round the edge of the anemone.
Diameter: 20–50 cm.

Entacmaea
This genus was created a few years ago to cover some species from the old *Radianthus* genus (the remainder being included in the *Heteractis* genus).

Aiptasia
The **glass anemones** are often introduced to an aquarium along with rocks or water. They are livebearers that can quickly colonize a tank, to the detriment of other *Anthozoa*. However, they do have advantages in an aquarium with butterfly fish (Chaetodontid family), as they constitute these fishes' staple diet. Diameter: 5–10 cm.

▲ ***Stichodactyla mertensii***

▲ ***Entacmaea quadricolor*** sheltering the clownfish *Amphiprion bicinctus*.

Ceriantharia

These resemble anemones, although they can be distinguished by their non-retractable tentacles. Moreover, they are not attached by a single foot but live in a self-secreted tube, whose support requires a layer of not too rough sand, 15–20 cm thick.
Ceriantharia feed on finely ground mussels, fish, shrimps, or brine shrimps. Certain species can sometimes be found in the aquarium trade, although their name is often unknown or incorrect. Height: 20–30 cm.

◄ ***Cerianthus sp.***

▲ ***Aiptasia sp.***

▼ ***Parazoanthus sp.***

Zoantharia (colonial anemones)

These are neither anemones, as they live in colonies, nor corals, as they have no calcareous skeleton. These animals colonize rocks, mollusks' shells, and sometimes sponges, corals, and Gorgonians. They can harbor *Zooxanthellae*, and therefore need the appropriate light level.

Parazoanthus sp.
This colonial anemone consists of small polyps which can reach a height of up to 2 cm, with tentacles that do not exceed 5 mm in length. They must be placed 10 or 20 cm under the water surface in an aquarium to take maximum advantage of the light, due to the presence of *Zooxanthellae*. They must not be put close to stinging *Anthozoa*. Like many other animals in this group, their food consists of a fine choppy based on mussels. When buying this encrusting anemone, make sure that it is attached to a rock.

Corallimorpharia

These invertebrates, which are not corals – they have no skeleton – are known as **discus anemones**. They live attached by a foot that is less powerful than that of the anemone. The diameter of the disc-shaped polyp varies from one species to another. The presence of *Zooxanthellae* demands strong light. Asexual reproduction through budding is possible in captivity. Size: 10–30 cm.

Actinodiscus

Several species from this genus are available on the market, and they are easy to keep. Their feeding, identical to that of the animals above, should take place on a weekly basis, as *Zooxanthellae* supply a part of the substances they need to live and they sometimes reject the food offered by the aquarist.

▲ ***Actinodiscus sp.***

Scleratinaria

True corals or **madreporites** live in a calcareous skeleton, into they which they can withdraw. This skeleton means that they make the most significant contribution to the building of coral reefs in tropical seas. These are the most difficult invertebrates to keep in a marine tank, as they require well-aerated water of the highest quality, with no suspended particles – and therefore crystal clear – and an extremely low nitrate content. As they are very sensitive to nitrates, it is essential to partially change the water on a regular basis, in small volumes. The tentacles, often drawn in by day, unfurl at night to capture food. This does not mean that corals like darkness; on the contrary, they must be provided with a great deal of light, on account of the presence of *Zooxanthellae*. They are carnivorous, feeding on animal plankton in their natural habitat and a choppy based on mussels or fish in captivity, once a week. A supply of calcium carbonate is desirable for the growth of the skeleton. Take care when placing them in an aquarium, as they should not come into contact with other *Anthozoa* once their tentacles have unfurled.

▲ ***Acropora sp.***

***Acropora* (Acroporidae)**

They are rarely imported alive but their skeletons are often used as decor in domestic aquariums. In the wild, their growth is rapid (a few centimeters per year) and they can exceed 1 m in height. Height: 20–50 cm.

***Fungia* (Fungids)**

These solitary (and therefore non-colonial) corals generally live on the sediment and do not take part in the construction of reefs. The distinctive skeleton can be used as a decorative feature. Diameter: 20 cm.

▲ ***Fungia sp.***

***Goniopora* (Poritidae)**

The species from this genus are imported on a fairly regular basis, and are some of the easiest to keep in an aquarium. They prefer moderately aerated water. Size: 20–30 cm.

***Favia, Platygira* (Favidae)**

These are easy to keep in captivity and accept small, live prey. The colored tentacles are drawn in by day. Size: 20 cm.

▼ ***Goniopora sp.***

***Leptosammia* (Dendrophylliidae)**

One temperate species in this genus also tolerates tropical temperatures: *Leptosammia pruvoti*.
Its yellow-orange color and small size make it good for decoration. It is preferable – in fact, essential – to put it into the aquarium already attached to a support. Size: 5 cm.

***Plerogyra* (Caryophylliidae)**

The species in this genus, known as **bubble corals**, are quite easy to keep in an aquarium. The daytime "bubbles" withdraw at night to give way to stinging tentacles 1–5 cm long. In the wild, the bubbles provide the coral with a certain degree of protection, as the tentacles are not attacked by fish (butterfly fish, for example). The color of the bubbles varies depending on the presence of *Zooxanthellae*, and these mean that this coral requires strong lighting. It is best to feed it at night – when the tentacles are unfurled – with relatively large, live prey. It is also possible to accustom it to eating a fine choppy based on seafood between the bubbles by day. Avoid allowing the bubble coral to touch other invertebrates, on account of its capacity to sting. Size: 20–30 cm.

Half-open ***Plerogyra sp***. Some tentacles are visible; the green color is the result of *Zooxanthellae*. ▼

Octocorals

These live in colonies in both temperate and tropical seas. They are able to build a skeleton, but it is not the same as that of the madreporites. Their tentacles, numbered in multiples of eight, are 1–5 cm long. Their reproduction is either sexual or asexual, through budding. As with the hexacorals, some species can house *Zooxanthellae.*

▲ ***Sinularia sp.,*** soft coral from the Indo-Pacific region.

Alcyonarians (or soft corals)

These live attached to the substrate by a horny secretion, and their polyps can be withdrawn. The presence of *Zooxanthellae* means that they require strong lighting.

***Sarcophyton* (Alcyoniidae)**

When they expel water from their tissues to renew it, they look like leather, hence their name **leather corals**. They are easy to keep in well-aerated water and they grow quickly. Their color varies according to the concentration of *Zooxanthellae* present.

Their weekly diet consists of a fine choppy of mussels and other seafood. They must be positioned with care in the aquarium, well away from other stinging species. Two leather corals are most commonly found in the aquarium trade: *Sarcophyton glaucum* and *S. trocheliophorum*.

Size: 20–30 cm.

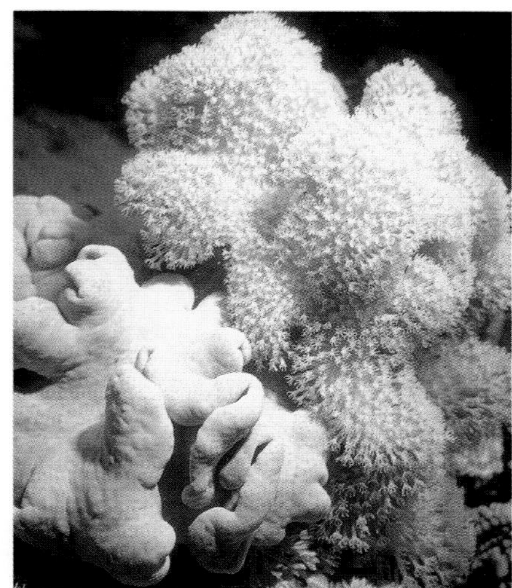

Sarcophyton sp., closed (left) and with the polyps extended (right). ►

Gorgonians

The species in this group, which comprises several families, present a ramified, fan-like form and can grow to a height of 2 m. Their skeletons can be used for decorative purposes. These animals prefer a fairly dark environment, where they live attached to a support. They sometimes have a tendency to be colonized by other organisms, such as sponges or filamentous algae. Their food must be very fine and distributed daily. Size: 15 cm.

A FALSE CORAL, A TRUE GORGONIAN

The red coral *(Corallium rubrum)* found in the Mediterranean, up to a depth of 200 m, is in fact a Gorgonian. These days there are no colonies over a few dozen centimeters, and their disappearance can be attributed to fishing off the coasts of France, Sardinia, and Tunisia that is so intensive it is best described as pillage! Such demand is explained by the fact that the bright red skeleton of this species is used in jewelry (particularly so in Italy).

▲ **Gorgonian and Alcyonarian**

WORMS

Worms belonging to the genus *Sabellastarte* are sometimes imported. The branchial plume (in a double crown) can reach 15 cm in diameter. It is best to keep them away from stinging *Anthozoa.* Their diet is the same as that of the Coelenterates.

◄ ***Sabellastarte sp.***

MOLLUSKS

Certain species of mollusks can be kept with fish, and sometimes with other invertebrates, so they are popular among hobbyists.

▲ *Cypraea tigris*

Gastropods

The species found in the aquarium trade are mainly carnivorous and feed on mussels or fish. There are others which graze the algae on the decor.

Cypraea

The highly decorated shell of the **Cypraea** is much prized by collectors. In aquariums the porcelain-like shell is only visible when the mollusk is at rest; when they are active, it is covered by the mantle (the most external part of the body), containing the sensitive organs. Two species are sometimes found on the market, both with a carnivorous tendency: the **tiger Cypraea *(Cypraea tigris)***, over 10 cm in length, and the **geographical Cypraea *(C. mappa)***, which rarely exceeds 7 cm. They are mainly active at night.

Other species

Small gastropods can sometimes be introduced on live rocks; they are not difficult to keep, as they are herbivores. In contrast, the species belonging to the *Murex* genus eat by piercing the shell of other mollusks, so they can be fed small mussels, shelled or intact.

Bivalves

It is sometimes possible to come across small specimens of the giant clam (*Tridacna* genus) that can be fed on mussel choppy. Most species have *Zooxanthellae* on the outer part of their mantle, and they must therefore be placed close to a strong light source. Giant clams are demanding as regards water quality. Generally speaking, they need a certain amount of protection, nevertheless, they can be sold legally, although they are rarely found in the aquarium trade. Those that do appear on the market are mainly raised in tropical areas – and they are expensive. Size: 5–25 cm.

◄ *Tridacna sp.*

Stenopus hispidus ►

CRUSTACEANS

The most common species in marine aquariums are shrimps – usually brightly colored, although more subdued species are also found – and they are imported on a fairly regular basis. These animals pick up food left over by fish and in this way they contribute to the equilibrium of the aquarium.

Shrimps

These very brightly colored animals are much appreciated by hobbyists for the theatrical flourish they add to a tank. They are relatively easy to keep if the water quality is good and the aquarium is equipped with hiding places. New species regularly crop up on the market.

Stenopus hispidus

This is one the most common shrimps in the aquarium trade. In their natural habitat (several tropical seas), the **barber shrimps** live in couples and serve as cleaners, especially for angelfish (Pomacanthids). They abandon this role, totally or partially, in an aquarium if they are well fed. Like many shrimps, they pick up the food rejected or ignored by fish. The male searches for food and gives it to the female. It is best to keep a couple in a tank and provide them with hiding places, where they will take refuge by day, as they are most active in the dark. In good conditions, this shrimp molts several times in a year, particularly if it is well fed. Size: 7–8 cm.

Lysmata amboinensis (formerly *L. grabhami*)

This very sociable **cleaner shrimp** tolerates the presence of other shrimps and can also live in groups. It cleans the skin of certain fish with its antennae, which also detect the presence of the specimen to be "cleaned." Apart from the usual food, you can also try providing filamentous algae for this shrimp, as it searches for microorganisms in them. Size: 7–8 cm.

◄ *Lysmata amboinensis*

Lysmata debelius
This is a timid species that lives in couples and prefers temperate waters to tropical ones. The **red shrimp** is still rarely found on the market, like other species of the same genus, such as *Lysmata wurdemanni*. The latter resembles the *L. seticaudata*, which is native to the Mediterranean and also to tropical regions, and is very popular in Europe.
Size: 7–8 cm.

◄ ***Lysmata debelius***

Crabs
Some small species can occasionally be found in the aquarium trade. In captivity, it is best to keep a single specimen, which can be fed on nauplii of brine shrimps or very fine slithers of mussels. Species of the ***Neopetrolisthes*** genus (porcelain crabs) live in symbiosis with anemones (for example, *Stichodactyla gigantea*) and feed on small particles using a pair of claws equipped with tiny fringes. Size: 4–5 cm.

▲ ***Neopetrolisthes sp.*** cannot live without an anemone, such as one from the *Stichodactyla* genus.

Hermit crabs (or pagurids)
These are sometimes considered the garbage collectors of the aquarium as they eat a wide range of detritus. It is not advisable to introduce them into a tank with other invertebrates (except, perhaps, the smaller species), although there is little risk in an aquarium inhabited by fish, as they can withdraw into their shell. The names of the species found on the market are often not known. Size: 4–6 cm.

Other crustaceans
Odontodactylus scyllarus
The aggressive **mantis shrimp** spends much of its time prowling and swimming in search of food, but, even though it can bury itself in sand, it also needs a hiding place. In the light of its behavior and feeding habits (small crustaceans and fish), the mantis shrimp must not be kept in an invertebrate aquarium. Its size and agility make it suitable for cohabitation with certain fish. Size: 10–15 cm.
Enoplometopus occidentalis
Contrary to what may be inferred from its common name of **lobster crab**, this decapod, closely related to the langoustine, is not aggressive. By day it remains hidden in a shelter, coming out at night to feed on the bed of the aquarium (leftover fish food, especially mussels, and sometimes filamentous algae). This is a crustacean worthy of a place in an invertebrate tank. Size: 10–15 cm.

ECHINODERMS

These invertebrates are the hardest to find in the aquarium trade, although they are fairly resistant and survive well in a tank.

▲ ***Linckia laevigata,*** a microphage starfish that can cohabit with other invertebrates.

Sea urchins
These crawl over the decor to graze on the algae which form their diet. Be careful, because they are highly prized by Balistids, puffers, and some Labrids, which have teeth strong enough to break the internal calcareous skeleton of sea urchins, and do not seem to be put off by their stings. The names of the extremely few species available are not known with any precision.
Size: 10 cm.

◄ ***Eucidaris tribuloides,*** native to the Caribbean.

Starfish
These survive well in an aquarium. Worthy of note among the carnivores are the *Protoreaster* and *Oreaster* genera, which feed on other invertebrates, especially the bivalve mollusks. They must not be kept in a tank with other invertebrates. Feed them with raw or cooked mussels. Other genera, such as the *Echinaster*, *Linckia*, and *Fromia*, are microphages and feed on the assorted debris found on the aquarium bed. They are preferable to the carnivorous starfish in an aquarium. The ophiuroids are attractive echinoderms in a marine invertebrate tank; they can be accidentally introduced with live rocks. Size: 10–15 cm.

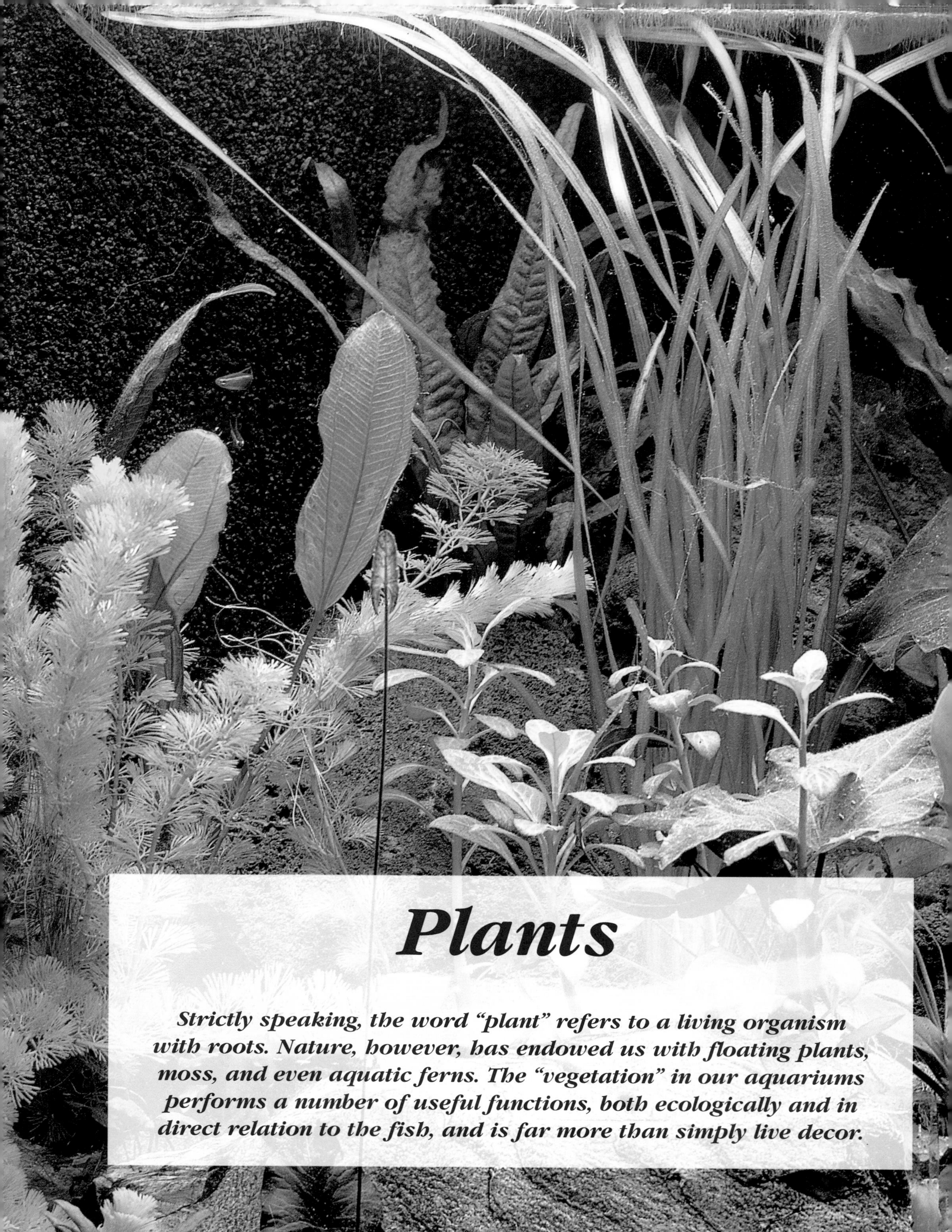

Plants

Strictly speaking, the word "plant" refers to a living organism with roots. Nature, however, has endowed us with floating plants, moss, and even aquatic ferns. The "vegetation" in our aquariums performs a number of useful functions, both ecologically and in direct relation to the fish, and is far more than simply live decor.

ORIGIN AND VARIETY OF PLANTS

The vast majority of aquatic plants are not taken from the wild but are grown by specialist firms. These plants serve as decorative elements in the aquarium, but this is not their only role, as they also contribute to its ecological balance, especially via their production of oxygen when in the light.

THE ORIGIN OF AQUARIUM PLANTS

All aquarium plants will reproduce in tanks, so there is no point in collecting them in their natural setting, unless you want new species or a pure variety. Some plants sold in aquatic stores are mere hybrids bearing the name of one of its two "parents", which can sometimes lead to confusion. The collection of certain plants from the wild is prohibited.

Aquarium plants are cultivated by specialist companies, mainly in South-East Asia but also in Europe and the United States. Agricultural greenhouses are used, partly heated by solar energy, or sometimes geothermically, using hot water pumped into irrigation canals. Sunlight may be complemented by artificial lighting if the plants demand this.

Most species are raised with a large part of the plant – or even all of it – outside the water, although the environment is extremely humid. They adapt to the aquarium setting, but tend to change the shape of their leaves when introduced into this different environment.

An enormous variety of plants can be cultivated, in this case under glass, in an extremely hot and humid atmosphere. ▼

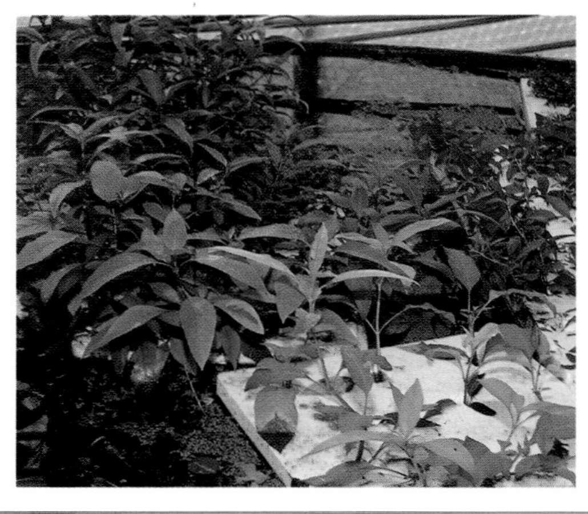

▲ *Most aquarium plants are raised out of water.*

DIFFERENT TYPES OF PLANTS

Contrary to what one might expect, most of the plants found in aquariums are not really aquatic. They generally live partly out of the water, with only the lower portion permanently submerged. Their leaves are sturdy, unbroken in form, and quite big. When the level of rivers and ponds rises due to rain – sometimes very heavy in tropical regions – the plants end up almost entirely, or sometimes even completely, covered by water. They develop submerged leaves, which are different from those which appear outside the water, being finer and more delicate. At the end of the rainy season, the water returns to its initial level, and the plant reassumes its previous form.

Other plants are totally aquatic, with the upper part of their stems only rarely seen above the water level – usually to produce a flower.

There are also amphibian or totally aquatic mosses, that are very useful in aquariums, as they provide a place for some fish to lay

Different types of plants in freshwater aquariums

Types	Characteristics	Observations
Stemmed plants.	Leaves of varying degrees of fineness, on either side of the stem.	Fairly rapid growth, easy to take cuttings. They are generally truly aquatic, but can survive outside water.
Plants without any apparent stem, with roots and sometimes a bulb.	The petiole (leafstalk) grows directly from the base. Sturdy and often large leaves.	Fairly slow growth, reproduction by runners or by separation of the base. Amphibious plants adapt to total submersion.
Floating plants.	The leaves spread out over the surface, with the roots visible to some extent under the water.	Rapid growth if the light is intense. They provide a refuge for fry. Swept along by currents in the water.
Plants without buried roots.	Rhizome (aerial root) developing on a support, with leaves growing out of it.	Slow growth. They attach themselves to various supports (rock, wood, artificial decor).
Mosses.	No stem visible, somewhat tufted appearance. They attach themselves to a support.	Useful for some fish species to lay eggs.

Some types of ferns can adapt to freshwater aquariums. ▼

Floating plants are useful for providing shade, as well as a shelter for fry. ▼

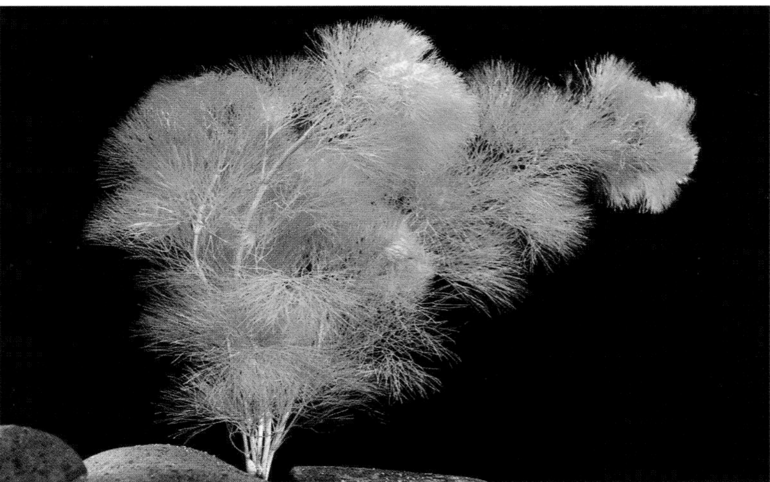

▲ *Plants with fine leaves are prized both by herbivorous fish and other species that lay their eggs on them.*

their eggs. Another option is ferns, not only the best-known species from temperate regions but also those from the tropics that can survive entirely submerged by water.

Plastic plants

It is possible to find excellent imitations of natural plants, but as an aquarium is a reconstitution of a piece of nature, it is easy to see why they are totally off limits for many aquarists, who prefer their plants to be natural. Some of these artificial plants, however, can serve as a support in a rearing tank for those species of fish that lay adhesive eggs.

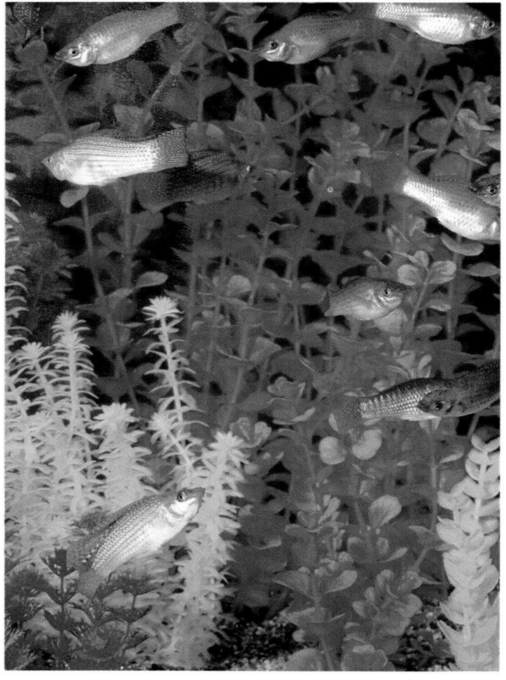

The effect created by plastic plants is not always in exquisite taste! ▶

Plants in a marine aquarium

There are substantially fewer marine plants suited to an aquarium than freshwater ones. The most common are from the *Caulerpa* genus, which grow quickly under the right conditions. These algae attach themselves to the floor and decor with a runner. They are highly recommended in a marine tank, as they are bound to enhance the overall balance. Their exuberant growth, however, can sometimes interfere with fixed marine invertebrates, such as anemones and corals. This anarchic behavior must therefore be restrained by regularly eliminating a certain amount of this vegetation.

The role of plants in an aquarium

Contrary to what is often thought, plants do not merely serve as decoration but also make a major contribution to the equilibrium of the aquarium (see page 196 on the mechanism of photosynthesis): by day, they absorb carbon dioxide (CO_2) given off by fish and produce oxygen (O_2). Moreover, they absorb nitrates, the end product of the nitrogen cycle (see page 19), and thus reduce the concentration in the water.

Plants are similarly useful for fish. Some species (like *Ancistrus* and *Gyrinocheilus*) feed on algae that grow on the decor, or even on fine-leafed plants (as in the case of livebearers from the Poeciliid family), though this can spoil the visual effect. Others, such as South American Characins, lay their eggs on the foliage, which helps to keep them out of sight of predators. Fish such as scaklares, watching over their eggs, use large leaves to fan them. When the fry are born, they find shelter in the vegetation – particularly plants with floating leaves – as well as nourishment there, as the plants enhance the development of microorganisms like infusorians, which are a valuable food source.

Finally, if the vegetation is sufficiently lush, it can also provide welcome shade and hiding places for adult fish.

ALGAE PROBLEMS

The large majority of aquarists have found themselves confronted with undesirable levels of algae that are sometimes difficult to combat. Generally speaking, it is better to avoid excess growth in the first place than to have to try to fight it – often with varying degrees of success.

ALGAE OVERGROWTH

This overgrowth can be recognized by its greenish or yellow-brown color, (while whitish or gray filamentous masses, made up of bacteria and fungi, may also be mixed in with algae). This type of growth can form quite thick layers on the glass panes, the bed, and the decor, appearing as filamentous tufts or even completely covering other green algae.

While a modest presence of algae can be considered a sign of equilibrium, this overgrowth is evidence of a degree of imbalance, and so algae are often referred to as biological indicators. You must be careful, however, as every aquarium is a special case, and applying a generalization to a specific situation could ultimately lead to the wrong conclusions.

The disadvantages of algae

Apart from being an eyesore, excess algae grow on the panes, reducing the visibility. They attach themselves to plants and proliferate, with the subsequent risk of suffocating their hosts, as the plants are prevented from exchanging gases and absorbing the salts in the water. Finally, they incrust themselves on the slightest details in the decor, which does nothing to enhance the visual effect.

... and their advantages

These are substantial. Algae consume nitrogenous substances, particularly nitrates, and sometimes ammonia. This is the normal role of plants in fresh water, and algae can therefore complement this action or, on the contrary, exert an antagonistic effect by diverting nutritious salts away from the plants. The vegetation is less abundant in marine tanks, and so algae – particularly the filamentous green ones – can play an important role.

▲ If due care is not taken, micro-algae can rapidly cover the decor and panes of an aquarium. This does not necessarily have a negative effect on the fish, but the visual effect is seriously undermined.

Algae can also be grazed or ground by some fish. In fresh water, this applies to the Poeciliids and the species known as "suckers" or "washers" (*Gyrinocheilus, Ancistrus, Hypostomus, Panaque, Otoclinchus, Epalzeorbynchus*). In sea water, algae form part of the diet of fish families, such as the Chaetontids, Centropyges, and Acanthurids; their presence in an aquarium can help these fish acclimatize themselves to the artificial environment of the domestic aquarium.

COUNTERING ALGAE PROBLEMS

Mechanical methods

Algae can be removed by hand, by sliding the leaves of the plant between the thumb and index figure, by rolling filamentous algae around a stick, or, finally, with a scraper equipped with a razor blade or a small scouring pad (available commercially, although you can also make one yourself). Any rocks, sand, coral skeletons, branches, or roots infested by algae can be treated, outside the aquarium, in a 10% bleach solution, to which these algae

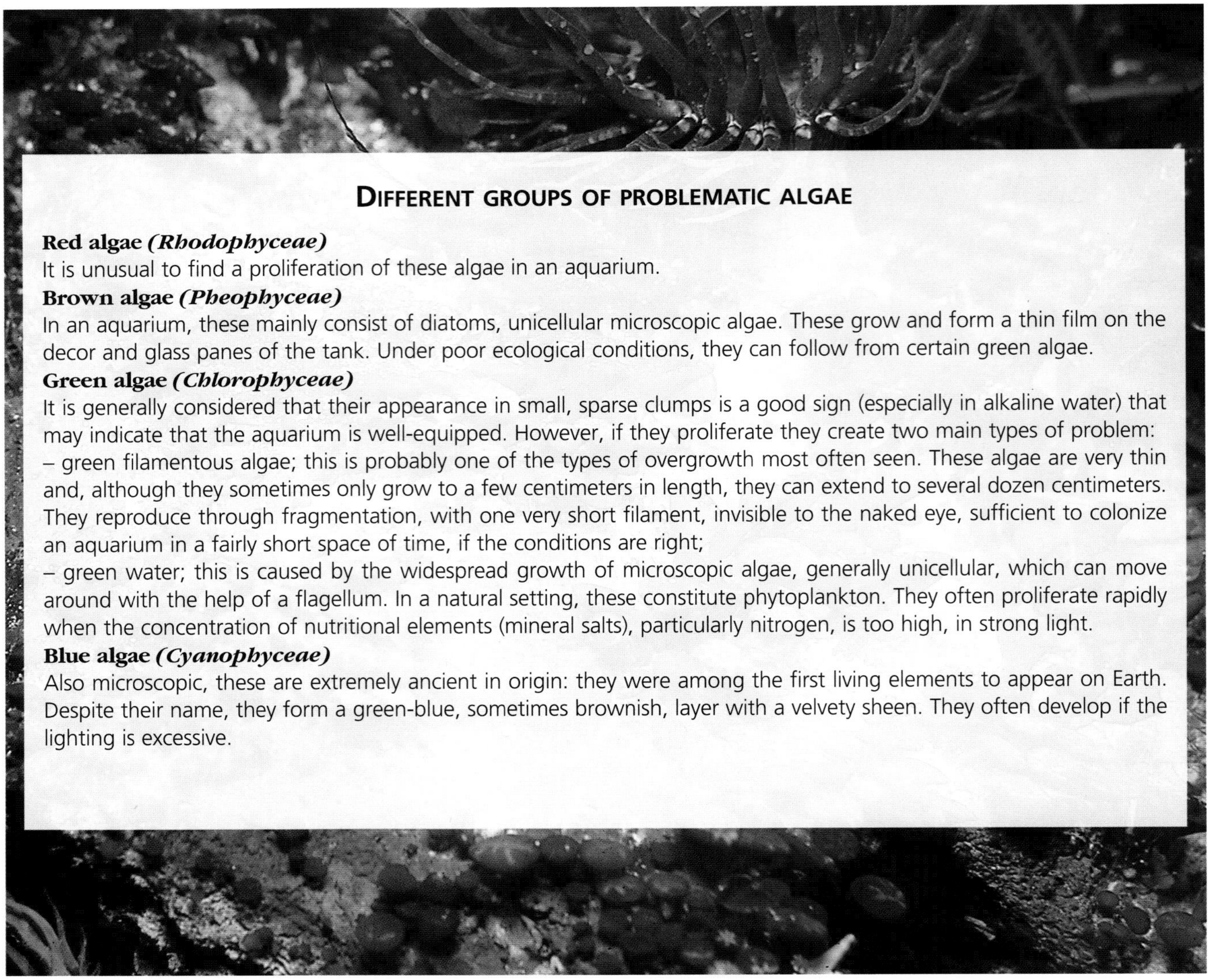

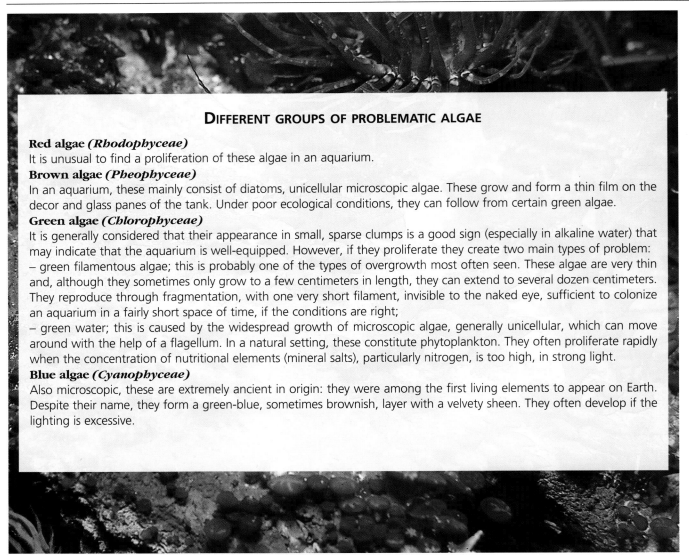

Different groups of problematic algae

Red algae *(Rhodophyceae)*
It is unusual to find a proliferation of these algae in an aquarium.

Brown algae *(Pheophyceae)*
In an aquarium, these mainly consist of diatoms, unicellular microscopic algae. These grow and form a thin film on the decor and glass panes of the tank. Under poor ecological conditions, they can follow from certain green algae.

Green algae *(Chlorophyceae)*
It is generally considered that their appearance in small, sparse clumps is a good sign (especially in alkaline water) that may indicate that the aquarium is well-equipped. However, if they proliferate they create two main types of problem:
– green filamentous algae; this is probably one of the types of overgrowth most often seen. These algae are very thin and, although they sometimes only grow to a few centimeters in length, they can extend to several dozen centimeters. They reproduce through fragmentation, with one very short filament, invisible to the naked eye, sufficient to colonize an aquarium in a fairly short space of time, if the conditions are right;
– green water; this is caused by the widespread growth of microscopic algae, generally unicellular, which can move around with the help of a flagellum. In a natural setting, these constitute phytoplankton. They often proliferate rapidly when the concentration of nutritional elements (mineral salts), particularly nitrogen, is too high, in strong light.

Blue algae *(Cyanophyceae)*
Also microscopic, these are extremely ancient in origin: they were among the first living elements to appear on Earth. Despite their name, they form a green-blue, sometimes brownish, layer with a velvety sheen. They often develop if the lighting is excessive.

are very sensitive. Any submerged equipment colonized by algae (heating, pipes, diffuser, filter) can be treated in the same way. It is important to rinse and dry them thoroughly before putting them back into the tank. Sometimes, however, the proliferation of algae can be so extensive that the only option is to create a whole new aquarium from scratch.

Ecological methods

Try to regulate the factor provoking the algae overgrowth by adjusting the amount of light, which should be reduced in the case of green or blue algae. Changing the position of the tubes, or the addition of deflectors, to keep algae off the front of the tank, produces good results. In freshwater aquariums, you can make partial water changes, on a fairly regular basis, using water with a low hardness containing few mineral salts.

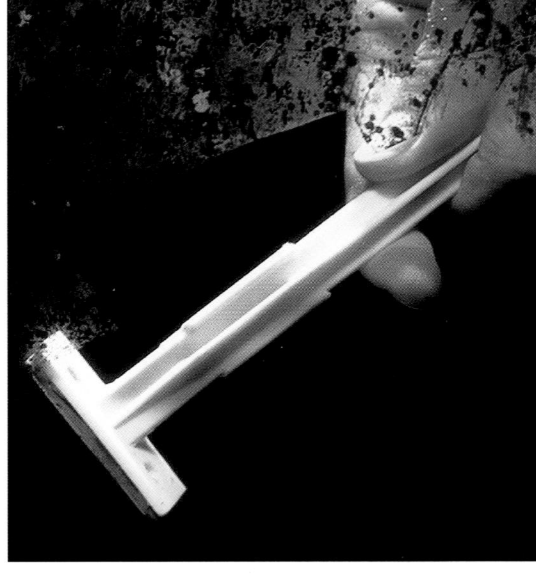

A disposable razor is useful for eliminating algae that grow on the aquarium panes. ▶

Be careful, however, not to make any drastic alterations to the quality of the water if this has been specially adjusted to specific plants and fishes.
In seawater tanks, change the water, replacing it with reconstituted water of the same salinity.

Biological methods

These can involve the use of herbivorous animals only interested in certain types of algae, such as the fish mentioned above or gastropods (rare in sea water).
The battle on the biological front is sometimes fought without any intervention on the part of the aquarist, as larger aquatic plants release substances that can inhibit the development of algae.
The extent of this phenomenon is very difficult to appreciate in an aquarium, as it is invisible to the human eye.

Chemical methods

There are special products on the market designed to kill algae. As their effect has not been fully established, it is best to be cautious with the dosage, as these substances probably also affect other plants. For the same reasons, the use of copper sulfate is not recommended, as it is dangerous for invertebrates.
There is no miracle solution. The use of several techniques at the same time sometimes has positive results, but it is not unusual to find that the algae reappear after a while. It is best to get used to partially eliminating them on a regular basis.

Several fish can be used in the biological battle against algae in fresh water: Epalzeorhynchus siamensis *(right) and* Gyrinocheilus aymonieri *(left).* ▼▶

CARING FOR PLANTS

Plants need light, mineral salts (fertilizer), and carbon dioxide (CO_2) to grow, and their survival and reproduction depends on the right proportions of these elements. A fishkeeper also needs to be an aquatic gardener and have "green fingers" to cultivate his or her live decor.

You must respect the needs of plants to obtain optimal growth and reproduction. ▶

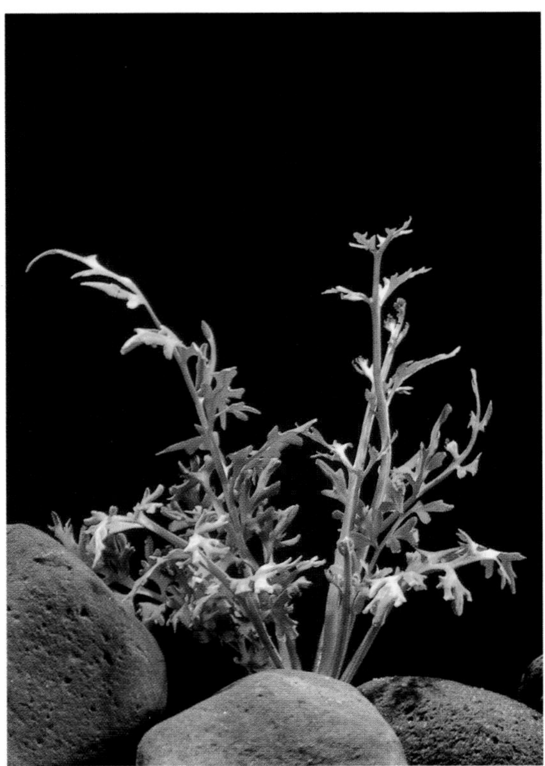

WHAT PLANTS NEED

Water

Aquatic plants are in general very sensitive to the water quality.

Although some plants, such as the floating fern, are easy to keep, and seem indifferent to the quality of the water, others require water that is soft and acid or, alternatively, alkaline and hard, and will only flourish in water that is adapted to their specific needs.

Plants have an overwhelming need for light, whether natural or artificial, to grow and produce oxygen, once they have absorbed carbon dioxide. ▼

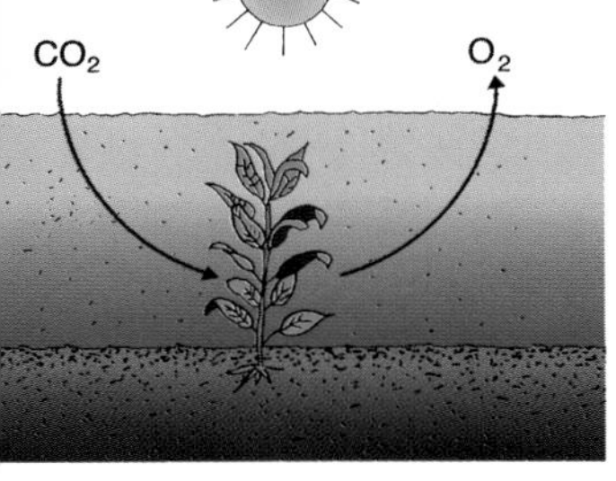

Light

Aquarium plants usually need strong lighting, produced by special fluorescent tubes for 12 or 13 hours a day.

For information concerning lighting see page 226.

If the lighting is deficient in either quality or quantity, the plants will turn yellow and eventually die.

Carbon dioxide (CO_2), oxygen (O_2), and photosynthesis

Like all living beings, plants are continuously respiring. They consume oxygen and expel carbon dioxide, thereby affecting the oxygenation of the water, both in a natural setting and an aquarium.

By contrast, in reaction to light – therefore only by day – they absorb the carbon dioxide from fish respiration and produce oxygen: it is this photosynthesis that enables them to grow. This phenomenon has a beneficial effect on the equilibrium of the aquarium, as it results in the production of more oxygen than the plant consumes in its respiration.

There may be slight variations in the oxygen levels from day to night, with the minimum levels being reached in the last third of the night. An aquarist (preferably an insomniac!) can verify this by measuring the pH every hour in a cycle of 24 hours (see diagram on page 14).

An increase in the water's oxygen level pushes up the pH, while the production of CO_2 at night acidifies the water and the pH goes down.

> **MAGNESIUM, CHLOROPHYLL, AND IRON**
>
> Magnesium is an important element, as it makes up part of the chlorophyll pigment that absorbs light. Iron plays a role in the chemical reactions of photosynthesis. If plants are deficient in iron, their growth slows down and they turn yellow; specialists refer to this as chlorosis – a condition also seen in agriculture.

This phenomenon, which is only really visible in heavily planted and densely populated aquariums, rarely entails any problems for fish.

Fertilizers

When an aquarium is put into operation, the bed and the water contain mineral salts. These gradually run out and the plants are therefore in danger of mineral deficiency. Faced with this situation, an aquarist has three options:
– regularly change part of the water (generally 10% of the volume per week), to obtain "new" water containing salts;
– add liquid fertilizers specially designed for aquatic plants;
– add solid fertilizers, in the form of sustained-release mineral salt capsules placed at the base of the plants.
You can also make a solid fertilizer at home, based on clay. Knead it, form small balls, then have them soak up liquid fertilizer. Placed at the base of plants, these balls gradually release their nutrients.

Mineral salts

This name covers all the substances needed for the growth of aquarium plants. They are in fact the equivalent of the fertilizers that are used in agriculture, or for house plants.
Plants' needs vary according to the substance: some are only required in tiny amounts (metals, for example) but they must be constantly available. Mineral salts are absorbed by the roots and leaves in truly aquatic plants, and by the roots in amphibian plants.
In the natural environment, some aquatic areas are considered fertile, as the renewal of the water and the equilibrium of the natural cycles provide sufficient amounts of mineral salts for plants to prosper. Those regions lacking these vital elements are characterized by sparse vegetation, or none at all.
In an aquarium, which is a self-contained environment, the water and the bed contain mineral salts that will gradually run out, at a rate determined by the quantity of the vegetation. You must therefore make plans to reinforce the mineral salt level on a regular basis, as you would for house plants. Some aquarists provide, from the very beginning, an enriched soil that will gradually release these mineral salts. This is particularly useful when

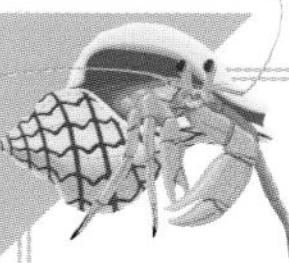

A FEW RULES FOR A NOVICE "AQUATIC GARDENER"

1. Choose plants suited to aquarium water.
2. Choose hardy species, some rapid growers and other slower.
3. Satisfy their needs, especially as regards special lighting.
4. Check the supply of nutrients.
5. Do not hesitate to ask for advice, from your aquarium store owner or from clubs and associations.

A LACK OF CO_2

There is usually enough carbon dioxide in the water, but it can sometimes be deficient, even in a tank that is profusely planted and well lit. If this occurs, the carbon dioxide that has been trapped by the bicarbonates is used in its turn: the pH often rises above 7.5, sometimes even up to 8, in fresh water, and the calcium forms a fine layer on leafy plants and "suffocates" them. Deposits can also be seen on the glass panes, at water level. Carbon dioxide diffusers are available in the aquarium trade to remedy this problem. You must also bear in mind that aeration and stirring of the water, which contribute to its oxygenation, help expel the CO_2 dissolved in the water into the atmosphere. This means that excessive stirring can sometimes have dire consequences for plants.

Nowadays specialist aquarium stores stock equipment designed to supply plants with the CO_2 they need. ▶

MINERAL SALTS REQUIRED BY PLANTS

– Nitrogen, contained in nitrates.
– Phosphorus, contained in phosphates.
– Potassium, which is a component of other salts.
A few other substances are also needed, sometimes in very small quantities:
– Metals, such as iron and magnesium (see page 196);
– Vitamins.

extensive planting is envisaged for the aquarium (in the case of a Dutch aquarium, for example – see page 33).

GENERAL CONDITIONS FOR GROWING AQUATIC PLANTS

Many aquarists treat plants as mere decorative elements; others cultivate them in the same way as they raise fish: they make them grow and even reproduce. It is possible to find veritable "aquatic horticulturalists" who obtain astonishing results.

How do you know if your plants have a growth problem?

A plant lacking any of the elements it needs to live turns yellow or brown and rapidly dies. The leaves get covered with a fine layer of filamentous algae and eventually fall off. However, in some species it is not easy to tell when the growth process is slowing down.

Vegetation can thrive in an aquarium, if it is provided with good lighting and nutrient salts. ▼

REPRODUCTION OF PLANTS

In the wild, the most common mode of reproduction among plants is sexual, involving flowers and seeds. When the conditions in a setting are inauspicious, however, sexual reproduction gives way to asexual reproduction, know as vegetative multiplication. Pieces of plants that have broken off or been uprooted, and then swept along by the movement of the water, settle and take root. It is this vegetative multiplication method that is used in aquariums. The techniques used, which vary according to the type of plants, are similar to those of horticulture.

TAKING CUTTINGS

Cuttings can be taken from a stemmed plant, which is cut cleanly with a razor blade or scissors. The upper part, about one third of the length, is replanted. Some aquarists prefer to remove the leaves from the lower third of the cutting before planting it, while others recommend leaving them in place, on the grounds that they will gradually be converted into mineral matter as they are degraded. Roots form and the new plant normally grows quickly. The lower part of the mother plant produces lateral shoots that can be used for cuttings later on. Adventitious roots (those growing sporadically away from their normal location) make it easier to take cuttings from most stemmed plants (like *Cabomba, Hygrophila).*

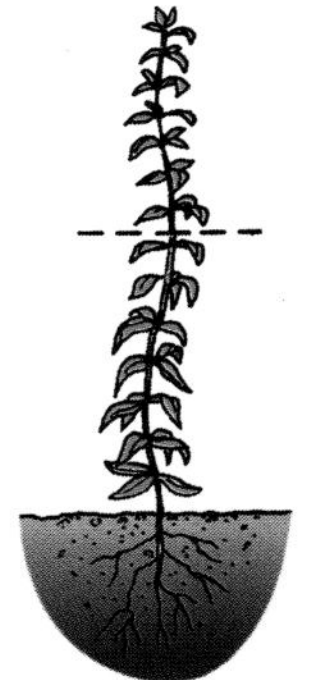

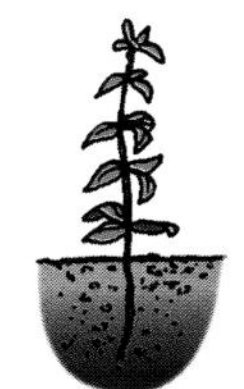

◀ *To take cuttings from a plant, cut the upper part (top) and replant it (center). This provides the opportunity for lateral shoots to emerge on the original stem (below).*

How to encourage cuttings?

The upper part of a stemmed plant produces substances that inhibit the growth of side shoots. If this section is cut off or firmly squeezed, these substances do not reach the lower part of the plant, and lateral shoots suitable for cuttings can grow. This technique is widely used when the stem of a plant reaches the surface of the water.

To take a cutting from a stemmed plant, it is advisable to make a clean cut. ▼

Cuttings can be easily taken from most stemmed plants, provided a few precautions are taken. ▼

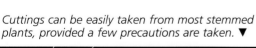

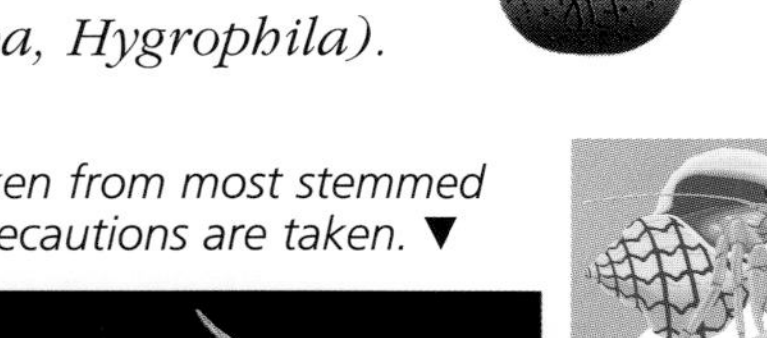

A FEW HINTS FOR SUCCESSFUL CUTTINGS

If the lower part of a stemmed plant loses its leaves, this means that light is having difficulty in penetrating right to the bottom of the aquarium. In this case, cut the plant a few centimeters from the bed and transplant the healthy upper part.

If you have small rearing tanks, these can be used as aquatic "greenhouses" for the cultivation of stemmed plants. It is best to use fertilizer, in the form of liquids or clay balls. Some fish need to be added to ensure the supply of CO_2 to the plants. Aeration is not strictly necessary, and filtration should be moderate.

Dividing the base

Plants without stems thicken at the base, sometimes forming smaller, secondary feet with roots. These can be carefully removed with a razor blade and replanted.

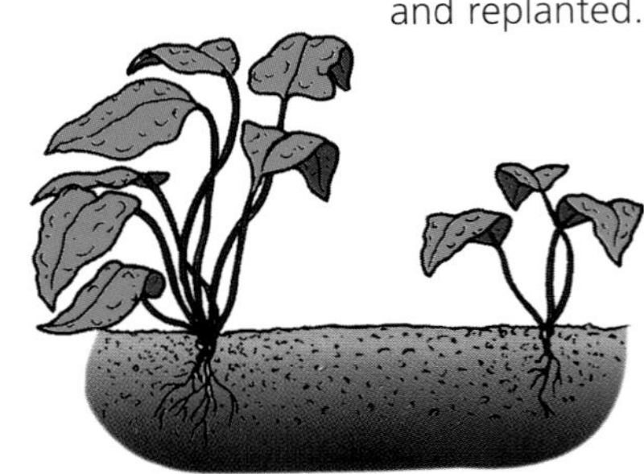

◀ *The division of the base is a technique applicable to many plants, such as the cryptocorynes.*

Layering

Some plants, such as the *Echinidorus* species or the marine algae from the *Caulerpa* genus, produce a horizontal aerial stem, known as a runner (or stolon). A young plant then grows out of this, producing roots that enable it to establish itself in the bed, either spontaneously, or with added help from the aquarist, who may have to encourage it to take root. After about a week, the roots will have grown sufficiently to allow the runner to be cut off. In the case of the Congo fern, this produces a rhizome that grows slowly, with new leaves appearing on it. If you cut off this rhizome between two leaves, you are left with two independent plants.

▼ *Top right:* Valliseneria *and* Sagittaria *reproduce spontaneously via runners (top). The new plant must be made to take root (center) before cutting the runner (below).*

A "rearing tank" for plants?

Why not? Some aquarists sometimes manage to get plants to reproduce sexually, when they bloom. They use one or several cultivation tanks, in which cuttings, layering, and division of the base are regularly performed. When they are fully grown, the plants are then transplanted into a community aquarium.

A reproduction tank for plants must have specially adapted and fairly strong lighting. The water level should not be too high, to assist the penetration of light, and the bed should be given appropriate enrichment. Miniature *jardinières* can even be constructed, using jars or ice cream or yogurt cartons, for example. The filtration should be gentle, and there should be no oxygenation at all, to avoid the CO_2 dissolved in the water being let off into the atmosphere. If there is not enough carbon dioxide, equipment to provide moderate diffusion of this gas into the tank is available in aquarium stores. A few fish will add the finishing touches to the equilibrium, and if you choose specimens from the same species, they can reproduce as well. These days many aquarists are enthusiastic about the reproduction of fish, but few are interested in cultivating plants, although this can be just as fascinating. The propagation of aquatic plants is easy and you can quickly build up large stocks to pass on to, or exchange with other enthusiasts.

▲ *Marine algae of the* Caulerpa *genus multiply by extending a runner, which sprouts new leaves*

Aquarium plants

Of the thousands of plants that are genuinely aquatic, or only amphibian, only a few hundred are to be found in the aquarium trade. The vast majority of these come from tropical fresh water, with the remainder coming from northern climes, and therefore suitable for temperate aquariums and garden ponds. The most common plants are generally the most robust, and are therefore specially suitable for beginners. Others are best left to committed aquarists keen to create a veritable aquatic garden. The special plants – the floating species, mosses, and ferns – have been grouped together, on account of their exceptional lifestyle; they should be of interest to all aquarists.

MOST POPULAR PLANTS

They could also be called "the classics," as they have given great pleasure to both veteran and novice aquarists for generations. Some are of particularly interest to beginners, as they are not only easy to cultivate but also inexpensive.
They are mainly stemmed plants which provide cuttings without any difficulty and grow rapidly provided they are given the appropriate level of light. Some are species that adapt to different types of water, others are more suited to a regional aquarium.

Acorus (Araceae, Asia)

The *Acorus* genus, native to temperate and cold waters, is widely distributed outside its original breeding grounds. It will not tolerate temperatures over 22°C and is therefore exclusive to temperate aquariums. These plants reproduce by dividing a rhizome between the buds. They are generally paludal (marsh plants) and are equally suited to aquaterrariums and garden ponds, although they will also survive totally submerged.

Acorus gramineus
There are two varieties of this species. The biggest, the **green acorus**, grows to a height of 30 cm; the smallest, the **dwarf acorus**, at around 10 cm, is ideal in foregrounds.

Acorus calamus
The **sweet flag** or **muskrat root** is found in Europe. As it can grow to a height of over 1 m, it is reserved for garden ponds.

▲ ***Acorus gramineus***

Bacopa monnieri ▶

▼ ***Bacopa caroliniana***

Bacopa (Scrofulariaceae, southern United States, Central America)

These hardy plants, with their paired oval leaves, can be made to flower in an aquarium, but taking cuttings is the best way to propagate. They prefer water that is neutral or slightly acid and not too hard, and are best planted in groups, with small spaces between their stems.

Bacopa caroliniana
The hardy **water hyssop** tolerates temperatures as low as 20°C, but will not stand those above 24–25°C. Size: 30 cm.

Bacopa monnieri
There is more space between the leaves than in the above species. The **snowflake hyssop** grows quite slowly and is very easy to keep but it requires good lighting. Size: 30 cm.

▲ *Cabomba aquatica*

Cabomba (Cabombaceae, southern United States, South America)

Some fish, such as South American Characins, take advantage of the fine foliage of the cabomba to lay their eggs, while other partially herbivorous fish graze on it. These plants need good lighting, water that is not too hard, and a more or less neutral pH. For reproduction take cuttings from the side shoots, or from the top.

Cabomba aquatica

If the light is weak, the **water cabomba** spreads out on the surface of the water. It grows quickly, unless the water is lacking in carbon dioxide; this means that you must avoid circulating it too vigorously. Size: 30–40 cm.

Cabomba caroliniana

More robust than its cousin, the **fish grass** or **water shield** can tolerate temperatures of 20°C but its soil must be fairly rich. The form of its leaves depends on the conditions under which it is cultivated. Size: 30–40 cm.

▲ *Cabomba caroliniana*

Ceratophyllum (Ceratophyllaceae, cosmopolitan)

Ceratophylls can be found all over the world, but only one species is common in aquariums.

Ceratophyllum demersum

The **water sprite** is found in Europe and Central America, though this temperate water plant can adjust to tropical aquariums. It is well suited to tanks with goldfish or garden ponds, where it can sometimes grow in profusion. It is easy to cultivate, although its stem breaks easily. It does not have any true roots and finds it difficult to establish itself in the substrate; it therefore has to be "wedged in" by rocks or branches, or float on the surface. It is easy to take cuttings from the main stem, or from side shoots. It is relatively indifferent to the hardness and pH of the water, but it does require strong lighting. Size: 30–40 cm.

▼ *Ceratophyllum demersum*

Elodea and *Egeria* (Hydrocharitaceae, cosmopolitan)

These are known as water pests, on account of their tendency to proliferate. Under an intense light they produce a great deal of oxygen. They put down roots but can also live afloat, preferably in hard, alkaline water.

Elodea canadensis

Originally from North America, **Canadian pond weed** has been introduced into temperate regions all over the world, although only the female has been present in Europe since the middle of the 19th century, and it can obviously only reproduce through cuttings. It is a plant for temperate aquariums or garden ponds, with an optimum temperature range of 15–20°C.

***Egeria densa* (formerly *Elodea densa*)**

Both sexes of the **dense elodea** were, similarly, introduced into Europe, although it is highly unusual to find reproduction through flowering in an aquarium. It is suited to temperate aquariums, but can tolerate temperatures of up to 25°C. Size: 30–40 cm.

◀ *Egeria densa*

▲ ***Eleocharis vivapara,*** a species closely related to *Eleocharis minima*

Eleocharis (Cyperaceae, tropical regions)

These plants, resembling tufts of grass, live in swamps, and are therefore suited to aquaterrariums, although they can also be cultivated in aquariums under strong lighting, in hard, alkaline water.

Eleocharis minima

When the stems of the **spiked rush** reach the surface, they spread out and do not emerge above it. Vegetative multiplication occurs with the help of runners or the division of a clump. Size: 20–30 cm.

Heteranthera (*Pontederiaceae*, Central or South America)

These plants are totally aquatic, requiring intense light and a fairly rich soil. They are sensitive to any deficiency in iron. The water must be slightly alkaline and moderately hard.

Heteranthera dubia

The **yellow-flowered heteranthera** can be reproduced with cuttings, a process that is facilitated by adventitious roots on the stem. The stem is quite fine and can float on the surface of the water. Size: 40 cm.

Heteranthera zosterifolia

The **stargrass** can live totally submerged. It multiplies through cuttings of the side shoots; it can also grow as a creeper. Size: 30 cm.

► ***Hygrophila guianensis***

▲ ***Hygrophila difformis***

◄ ***Hygrophila corymbosa***

Hygrophila (Acanthaceae, South-East Asia)

More than 10 species are found in the aquarium trade, although the existence of different varieties and the modifications made to scientific names can lead to confusion. They live half-submerged, but can tolerate immersion in a moderately hard acid or neutral water. They need intense light to grow well, and should be planted in groups, but with sufficient spaces between the stems. It is easy to take cuttings: just chop off the head of the stem as soon as it reaches the surface.

***Hygrophila corymbosa* (formerly *Nomaphila*)**

The **giant hygro** tolerates temperatures as low as 15°C. The presence of adventitious roots is an advantage when taking cuttings. Size: 30 cm.

***Hygrophila guianensis* (formerly *H. salicifolia*)**

The **willow leaf hygro**, recognizable by an almost square stem, is sensitive to excessively hard water or a lack of iron. When the light is insufficient, the leaves at the bottom of the stem fall off. Size: 30 cm.

***Hygrophila difformis* (formerly *Synnema triflorum*)**

Considered a weed in its native region, the **water wisteria** is prized by aquarists for its pale color and finely serrated leaves, although when these first appear their form is less delicate. This plant tolerates fairly wide ranges of hardness and pH. When the leaves drop off the stem, young shoots appear in their place. Size: 30 cm.

▲ *Limnophila heterophylla*

Limnophila (Scrofulariaceae, South-East Asia)

Its fine foliage is much appreciated by certain fish which lay their eggs on it or, depending on the species, munch on it. These amphibian plants can live submerged, and when they reach the surface of water they spread out on top of it. At this point cuttings should be taken and transplanted. Good lighting is essential. A lack of iron causes their leaves to turn yellow.

Limnophila aquatica

The **aquatic ambulia** grows well in soft or slightly hard and acid water, providing it has an adequate supply of mineral salts. Small shoots from its base are perfect for cuttings, although removing the top is equally effective. This ambulia must be planted in clumps, with the stems slightly separated to take advantage of the light. Size: 30 cm.

Limnophila heterophylla

The **heterophyllous ambulia** is less tufted than the above, but its tips must nevertheless be removed regularly. Size: 30 cm.

Ludwigia (Onagraceae, tropical regions)

Ludwigs thrive on light, iron, and fairly rich soils. Cuttings are taken by lopping off a stalk under the adventitious roots. Another option is to cut off the top of the plant, which avoids the loss of any of the lower leaves. Size: 30 cm.

Ludwigia ascendens

The totally aquatic **large-petaled ludwig** can sometimes appear above the surface. It tolerates a wide range of hardness and a pH of around 7. It is especially recommended for beginners.

Ludwigia alternifolia

As its name indicates, the leaves of the **alternate leaf ludwig** are arranged alternately along the stem, and not directly opposite each other. It prefers soft, acid water. Size: 30 cm.

Ludwigia brevipes

A fairly resistant plant, the **false lusimakhos** tolerates hard, alkaline water and temperatures slightly below 20°C. It can therefore be used in a temperate aquarium. Size: 30 cm.

Ludwigia repens

The **rampant ludwig** is found in both a green variety and a reddish variety. Both require good lighting but are considered hardy. Size: 30 cm.

▲ *Ludwigia sp.*

▼ *Ludwigia repens*

Myriophyllum (Haloragaceae, North and South America)

Around a dozen species from this genus, both amphibian and totally aquatic, constitute some of the most popular aquarium plants. Their soft foliage is appreciated by fish with herbivorous tastes, while others use it to lay their eggs. The aquatic milfoils thrive on light and relatively hard water, although this must be clear, as small suspended particles get trapped in the foliage. The main method used for reproduction is that of taking cuttings.

Myriophyllum aquaticum

In contrast with the other species, the **water milfoil** prefers soft, acid water. Cuttings are taken by removing the top or the tiny branches. You can achieve a stunning decorative effect by planting a copse of these plants. Size: 40 cm.

Myriophyllum spicatum

The **spiked milfoil** is a hardy, fast-growing plant that needs fairly hard alkaline water. It must be pruned regularly to ensure that it remains sturdy. Several other species of milfoils are available on the market, some with reddish hues; they all require good lighting. Size: 40 cm.

Myriophyllum aquaticum ►

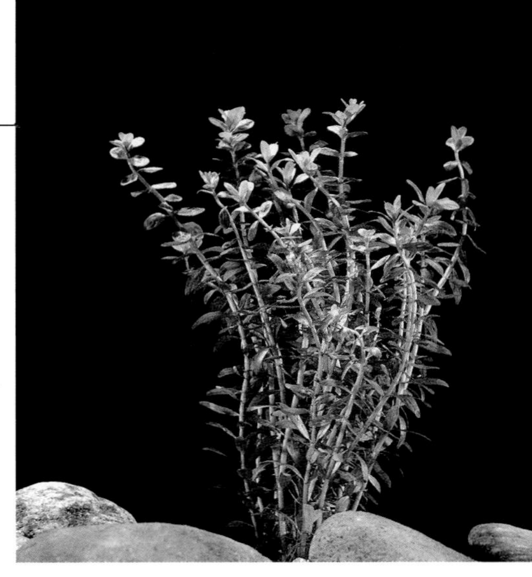

▲ *Rotala rotundifolia*

Rotala (Lythraceae, South-East Asia)

The leaves of these species are reddish in color, especially on the underside, but their shape varies according to the setting. They grow in soft, acid water, under strong lighting, and need plenty of iron. The formation of adventitious roots makes it easy to take cuttings. They can produce a striking visual effect if they are planted in a grove, as they stand out well against green plants.

Rotala macrandra

The coloring of the **giant red rotala** varies according to the intensity of the lighting, but, as is name suggests, red usually sets the tone. It grows quite quickly, but pruning encourages the growth of lateral shoots which can be used for cuttings. Size: 30 cm.

Rotala rotundifolia

The upper face of the leaves of the **round-leaf rotalia** is green, the lower one a reddish color. When the leaves emerge from the water they turn completely green. It is beautiful in clumps, though you must leave sufficient spaces between the stems when planting. Size: 30 cm.

▼ *Sagittaria sagittifolia*

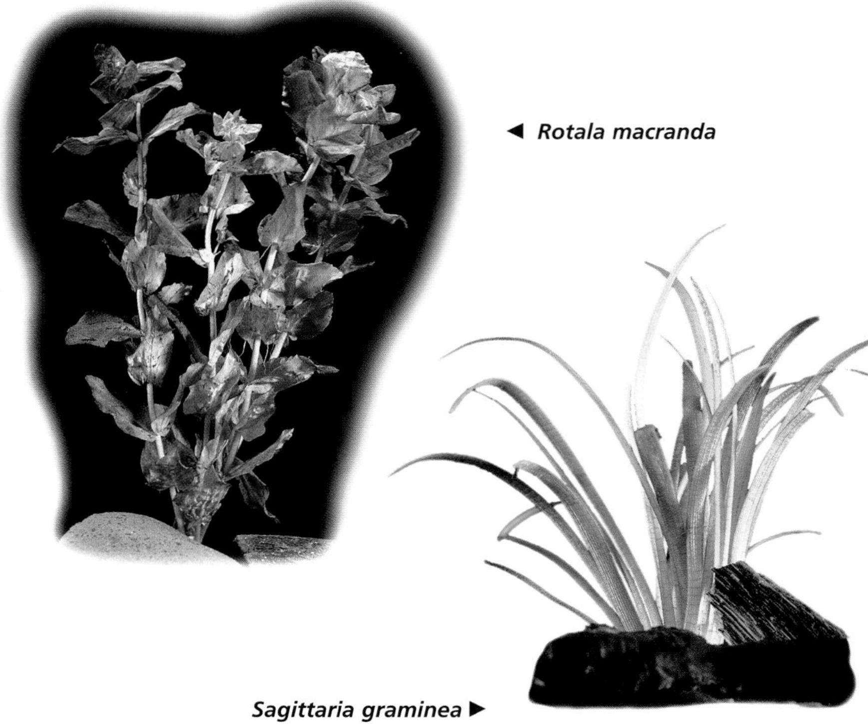

◄ *Rotala macranda*

Sagittaria graminea ►

Sagittaria (Alismataceae, North and South America, and Europe)

The leaves of these paludal plants that are above water are arrow-shaped, while the submerged ones take the form of thin ribbons. Take care not to push the rhizome too far into the soil: the plant can be held in place by a curved piece of wire. Vegetative multiplication occurs by means of seedlings formed on a runner, which can took root on their own, or with the help of the aquarist. The runner can then be cut off.

Sagittaria graminea

There are several varieties of the **narrow leaf arrowhead**, which differ in the length and width of their leaves. They all prefer moderate lighting, soft or slightly hard water, and an approximately neutral pH. Size: 40 cm.

Sagittaria sagittifolia

The amphibious **arrowhead** is quite common in calm waters in Europe, especially in garden ponds, where it resists the winters, although it prefers sunny areas. Size: 40–50 cm in water.

How to distinguish between sagittarias and vallisnerias

Sagittarias and vallisnerias can be distinguished by the tips of their leaves.

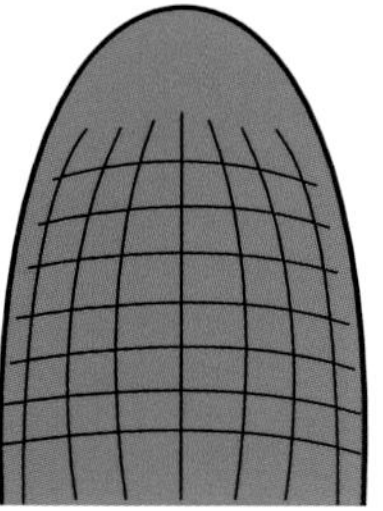

Sagittarias

The longitudinal veins do not reach the tip. The transversal veins are perpendicular and numerous.

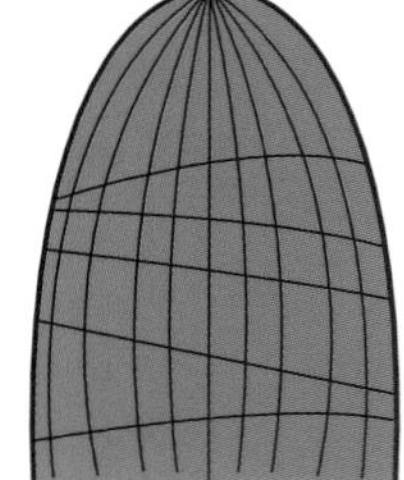

Vallisnerias

The longitudinal veins reach the tips. Few transversal veins, sometimes at oblique angles.

Vallisneria (Hydrocharitaceae, Asia)

The vallisnerias are often confused with the sagittarias. Like them, they reproduce through runners, need plenty of light, water that is not too hard, and a slightly acid pH.

Vallisneria asiatica

The **eel grass** is found in several varieties. Its leaves are spiraled. It can exceed 40 cm in height, which makes it ideal for decorating the sides or rear of an aquarium. Size: 40–50 cm.

Vallisneria spiralis

The term *spiralis* refers to the floral peduncle and not the leaves. The **spiraled eel grass** is very popular in aquariums and reproduces actively under good conditions. Size: 40–50 cm.

Vallisneria gigantea

Its leaves, which can grow to 1 m in length and 3 cm in width, rest on the surface of the water. The **giant vallisneria** prefers intense lighting and a slightly enriched soil. It is obviously only suitable for large aquariums. Size: 1 m.

◄ ***Vallisneria gigantea***

Vallisneria spiralis ►

PLANTS FOR THE MORE EXPERIENCED

Once you have gained experience with the above species, you can move on to other less common plants. Those that take the form of tufts tend to grow quite slowly, which may be frustrating for more impatient aquarists. However, they are a beautiful sight if their requirements are satisfied, especially with respect to the water quality and the intensity of the lighting.

Alternanthera (Amaranthaceae, South America)

These plants prefer soft, acid water and multiply with the help of cuttings. Their reddish color stands out among the other plants in an aquarium.

Alternanthera sessilis

There are two varieties of **sessile alternanthera**. The first, with totally red leaves, does not last for more than a few months if it is fully submerged. The second can be distinguished by the brown-green coloring of the upper part of the leaves, and can adapt more easily to a totally aquatic life. Size: 30–40 cm.

Alternanthera reineckii

More hardy than the above species, **Reineck's alternanthera** is not so eye-catching as it does not share the red coloring. It produces lateral shoots under intense lighting, which make it easy to take cuttings. Size: 30–40 cm.

◄ ***Alternanthera reineckii***

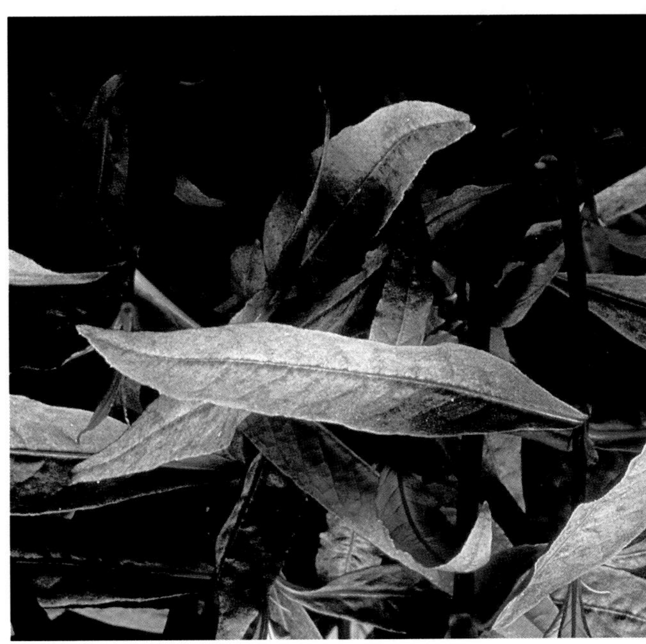

▲ ***Alternanthera sessilis***

Anubias (Araceae, West Africa)

These grow slowly, under weak lighting, in soft, acid water. Multiplication takes place through a division of the rhizome, which must never be covered with soil.

Anubias barteri

There are two varieties: the smallest, the **dwarf anubias**, is ideal for foregrounds; the biggest, **Barter's anubias**, has spear-like leaves and can be placed a little further back. Size: 30 cm.

Anubias heterophylla

The **Congo anubias** can exceed 35 cm in height and is therefore only suitable for large aquariums. The shape of the leaves can vary considerably but, broadly speaking, they are oval or lanceolate. Size: 30–40 cm.

▲ ***Anubias barteri***

Cryptocoryne cordata ►

◄ ***Anubias heterophylla***

Cryptocoryne (Araceae, South-East Asia)

Several dozen species of this genus are used in aquariums, which sometimes gives rise to confusion. Some are genuinely aquatic, others amphibious. The quality of water required varies according to the species: soft to moderately hard, slightly acid to alkaline; the soil must always be quite rich. Sexual reproduction with flowers is rare; vegetative multiplication occurs by means of runners or the division of the clump.

Cryptocoryne balansae

Balansa's cryptocoryne prefers intense light and a temperature over 25°C. It should be kept as a single specimen, to highlight it. Size: 40 cm.

Cryptocoryne beckettii

Beckett's cryptocoryne, paludal in the wild, is very resistant and can live totally submerged. Size: 40 cm.

Cryptocoryne ciliata

The **ciliated cryptocoryne** is one of the species in this genus that tolerates hard water, and it requires fairly rich soil. It is amphibious in its natural environment. Size: 40 cm.

Cryptocoryne cordata

The ***Siamese cryptocoryne*** exists in several varieties, which differ from each other in the shape of their leaves. It adjusts well to hard water. Size: 15–20 cm.

Cryptocoryne crispatula

A large hardy species, the **undulated cryptocoryne** is reserved for big aquariums, where it deserves to be shown off. It dislikes water that is too hard. Size: 50–70 cm.

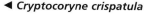

▼ ***Cryptocoryne beckettii***

◄ ***Cryptocoryne crispatula***

Hottonia inflata ►
(foreground)

Echinodorus (Alismataceae, South America)

Most echinodorus are paludal plants, but they can also survive underwater. The shape of the leaves depends on the conditions under which they are cultivated, which can range from slightly acid to neutral water, and low to moderate hardness. These plants turn yellow when they lack iron, so you must ensure that there is an adequate supply. You can reproduce them by taking a cutting of a rhizome on which seedlings have appeared.

Echinodorus amazonicus

Under good conditions (moderate to strong lighting), the **Amazon** grows to 40 cm. If the water is too hard it is markedly smaller and appears to stop growing.

Echinodorus maior

The **giant echinodorus** reaches the same height as its Amazonian cousin and, like it, is worth highlighting in a large aquarium if it is the only representative of its species. Size: 30–40 cm.

Echinodorus quadricostatus

The **dwarf Amazon** serves to decorate the foreground of an aquarium. It prefers a moderately rich soil, and tolerates temperatures under 20°C. The shape of the leaves varies according to the lighting. Size: 10 cm.

Echinodorus tenellus

The **pygmy Amazon**, the smallest of the genus, prefers soft water. It can rapidly accumulate an extensive covering of runners. It does not like too many fine muddy particles round its base. Size: 10 cm.

▲ *Echinodorus tenellus*

◀ *Echinodorus amazonicus*

◀ *Echinodorus sp.*

Hippurus (Hippuridaceae, cosmopolitan)

These plants are found in the temperate regions of the northern hemisphere. They are most common in garden ponds.

Hippurus vulgaris

Its aerial leaves differ in shape from those underwater. The **water spruce** can be cultivated in a tropical aquarium. Size: under 50 cm submerged, 10–15 cm above water.

Hottonia (Primulaceae, Central America)

Some species from this genus are native to the northern hemisphere, and so they can resist water temperatures down to 15°C.

Hottonia inflata

A totally aquatic plant with finely serrated leaves, the **featherfoil** likes soft, acid water. Adventitious roots on the knots of the stem make it easy to take cuttings. It is highly attractive when planted in groups. Size: 20–30 cm.

Lobelia (Lobeliaceae, North America)

The plants in this genus, native to tropical regions, are either terrestrial or paludal. One of the latter types can adjust to tropical aquariums, although it grows very slowly.

Lobelia cardinalis

This amphibious plant can resist temperatures of 10–20°C in moderately hard, approximately neutral water. The **cardinal flower** is appropriate for temperate or tropical aquariums, though it requires intense light in a tropical tank. It multiplies by means of cuttings. Size: 30 cm.

▼ *Lobelia cardinalis*

SPECIAL PLANTS

These plants are not rooted and complement the classic vegetation on both the aesthetic and ecological fronts. floating plants provide shade and shelter for fry; mosses are used by some fish to lay their eggs, and slow-growing ferns colonize solid supports. Moreover, floating plants are renowned for the speed with which they grow.

Bolbitis (Lomaropsidaceae, Africa and Asia)

These ferns live either wholly or partially submerged. One species is particularly popular among aquarists.

Bolbitis heudelotii

The species from this genus most often found on the market, is a true fern and its rhizome must never be buried as it naturally attaches itself to a support (such as a rock, root, or artificial decor). This attachment can be temporarily encouraged by tying the rhizome with nylon line, or wedging it between small stones. It grows slowly and requires normal lighting, water of a moderate density, and a pH of around 7. It can be made to reproduce by cutting off the rhizome when new shoots appear. Size: 20–30 cm.

Ceratopteris cornuta (Parkoriaceae, cosmopolitan)

This floating fern makes an ideal shelter for new-born fry, or a support for the bubble nests of the Belontiid family. It grows quickly under strong lighting: when it takes root – which it does with ease – its coloring turns paler and its leaves change shape.

Ceratopteris thalictroides

The **Sumatran fern** prefers to be rooted, but it can also survive floating, though its leaves grow thicker. It is a fast-growing, hardy species. Size: 50–60 cm.

◄ *Ceratopteris thalictroides*

Lemna (Lemnaceae, cosmopolitan)

Water lentils float on the surface and grow very fast. If they are introduced into a tank, either deliberately or accidentally, they can colonize the entire surface, so they must be eliminated regularly.

Lemna minor

The **duckweed** is often confused with *L. gibba*, but its leaves do not exceed 1 cm in length. It can be used to provide shade in one part of the aquarium, or a refuge for fry. Size: around 1 cm.

◄ *Lemna minor*

▼ *Microsorium pteropus*

Microsorium (Polypordiaceae, South-East Asia)

This genus includes ferns with a clear predilection for humid environments. Only one species is of any great interest to aquarists.

Microsorium pteropus

The **Javan fern** grows slowly, under moderate to intense light, but it is very hardy. Like all ferns, it can reproduce sexually with spores, but vegetative reproduction is much more common in an aquarium. The rhizome can be cut off when young fronds appear, and can attach itself to a support with the help of small roots. This process can be encouraged by wedging the rhizome between stones – taking care not to squash it – or tying it down with a nylon line. Size: 15–20 cm.

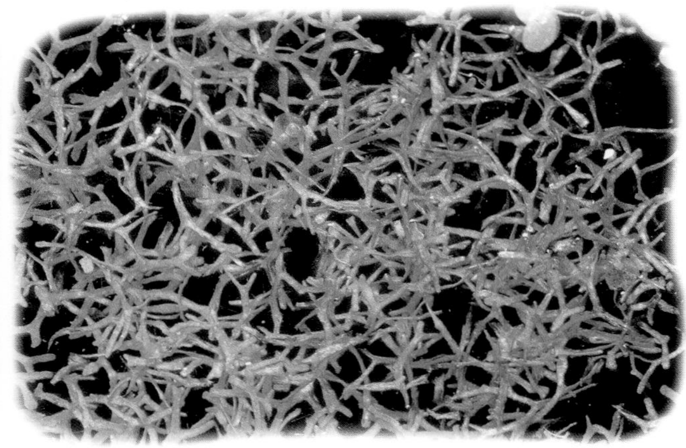

▲ *Riccia fluitans*

TRUE TERRESTRIAL PLANTS AND FALSE AQUARIUM PLANTS

Some house plants that require plenty of humidity, such as *Aglaonema*, *Dracaena*, and *Chlorophytum*, are sometimes sold as aquarium plants. They do not last very long when they are completely submerged, but, at a pinch, they can be put into the bank of an aquaterrarium. They are usually bicolored, with leaves combining green with either red or white. You are strongly advised not to buy them for an aquarium.

Riccia (Ricciaceae, Europe, North and South America, and Asia)

Single specimens of these plants are tiny (1–2 mm), but they spread to form a floating carpet. They grow quickly, especially under strong lighting, and so they must be cleared on a regular basis.

Riccia fluitans

The **floating riccia** provides shelter for fry, and a breeding ground for the infusorians that often constitute their first food. This plant prefers moderately hard water, with a pH of around 7.

Pistia (Araceae, tropical regions)

The *Pistia* genus appears to contain only one species. It is a floating plant which grows rather slowly, but it is of great interest to aquarists.

Pistia stratoites

The leaves of the **water lettuce** have a velvety sheen. This plant needs strong lighting to grow and for seedlings to form on the runners. It provides an aquarium with shade and a refuge for fry. It is badly affected by drops of water formed by condensation on the lid of the tank. Diameter: 5–6 cm.

▲ *Salvinia auriculata*

Pistia stratoites ►

▲ *Vesicularia dubyana*

Salvinia (Salviniaceae, South America)

Despite their distinctive appearance, the salvinias are floating aquatic ferns. The leaves are usually rough and arranged on either side of a floating horizontal axis. They reproduce by means of runners, and can rapidly invade a tank, although they are sensitive to drops of condensation falling from the lid.

Salvinia auriculata

The floating leaves of the **salvinia** are more than 1 cm long, which distinguishes it from the closely related, and otherwise biologically identical, *S. minima*. If the lighting is good, it grows quickly in neutral, soft water. It is recommended as a haven for fry in rearing tanks. Size of a floating leaf: 2 cm.

Vesicularia (Hypnaceae, South-East Asia)

This genus includes a large number of species native to continental tropical regions. Most are terrestrial, while some are amphibious or aquatic.

Vesicularia dubyana

Javan moss is very popular among hobbyists as it attaches itself to all types of decor, whether artificial or natural (wood, rocks). When introducing it into an aquarium you can help it to establish itself by wedging it with small rocks or pieces of wood. It likes soft, acid water, with moderate lighting. It offers an excellent support for the eggs of certain fish, as well as a shelter for fry. It can sometimes be invaded by filamentous algae. A close species, Bogor's moss *(Glossadelphus zollingeri)*, is also on the market.

Saururus (Saururaceae, North America)

The vegetative reproduction of these plants can be achieved by taking cuttings or dividing the rhizome. They live in marshy areas and so are often only partially submerged.

Saururus cernuus

Leiden's plant can acclimatize to an aquarium: it is not fussy about water quality, but it does need plenty of light. This paludal plant is hardy and grows slowly; it is possible to take cuttings from the stems. Size: 40–50 cm.

▲ ***Saururus cernuus***

Spathiphyllum (Araceae, South America)

These are amphibious plants that can be cultivated in flowerpots. Their leaves are sturdy and their growth is slow but regular.

Spathiphyllum wallisii

The **spathy** usually dies within a few months if it is permanently underwater. However, some aquarists manage to keep them alive for longer periods, without any apparent explanation. Nevertheless, it is best to cultivate this plant partly outside water – which should be soft and slightly acid – for a few months if you have kept it totally submerged. Size: 40 cm.

▲ ***Spathiphyllum wallisii***

PLANTS FOR THE AQUATIC GARDENER

Less commonly available (and often too expensive for many aquarists), these species demand the utmost respect for their requirements. The cultivation conditions for some of them are quite unusual, and they need a long "wintering" period every year. You should have extensive experience of aquatic plants before tackling these specimens, otherwise you might be rapidly disappointed. If they are set off well, these plants can quickly becomer the focus of attention in a tank, particularly in Dutch aquariums.

Aponogeton (Aponogetonaceae, Africa, Madagascar, and Sri Lanka)

These very beautiful plants are by no means easy to keep in an aquarium, as they have to pass through a "wintering" period lasting a few months, at a temperature of around 15°C. Their bulbous rhizome, with no leaves, must be kept in a separate tank in shallow water. After wintering, the water level and temperature are increased. The aponogetons like strong lighting and moderately hard water. Sexual reproduction with flowers is possible in an aquarium. Vegetative multiplication occurs if the rhizome is divided, and buried once leaves and roots have appeared.

Aponogeton crispus

A. crispus grows quite quickly. Like the other species of this genus, it looks best if it is grown as a single specimen, highlighted against other plants. Size: 40–50 cm.

▲ ***Aponogeton ulvaceus***

Aponogeton ulvaceus

With its wavy, translucid leaves this specimen is considered to be one of the prettiest aquarium plants. Size: 40–50 cm.

Aponogeton madagascariensis

The leaves of the **Madagascar laceleaf** consist of veins, which give it a striking appearance but also make it especially vulnerable to invasions by filamentous algae.

It is often sold under the names *Aponogeton fenestralis* or *Aponogeton henkelianus*, but has a reputation for being difficult to cultivate. Size: 40–50 cm.

◀ ***Aponogeton crispus***

▼ ***Aponogeton madagascariensis***

▲ *Crinum sp.*

Barclaya (Nymphaeaceae, South-East Asia)

The *Barclaya* genus contains only three species, all native to South-East Asia. Although the relationship is not immediately apparent, the barclayas are closely related to water lilies and are included in the same family.

Barclaya longifolia

The only species found in the aquarium trade, *Barclaya longifolia,* demands strong lighting – otherwise its leaves will remain small – and a neutral or slightly acid, barely mineralized water. Growth can slow down during the wintering period, but new leaves appear afterwards. It is difficult to make it reproduce by cutting the rhizome, and so it is best to wait for young leaves to sprout. This plant needs to be kept on its own to highlight its distinctive coloring. Size: 40 cm.

Crinum (Amaryllidaceae, Asia, Africa, and South America)

There are several species of crinums scattered round the tropical regions of the world, and all have a bulb. Only one of these, native to West Africa, is available to the aquarium trade.

Crinum natans

The **aquatic crinum** is hardy and can reach a height of 1 m when its growth is enhanced by intense lighting and hard, alkaline water. Size: 50 cm.

Eichhornia (Pontederiaceae, South America)

This genus includes both submerged and floating paludal plants. They are rarely found in aquariums, but are suitable for garden ponds.

Eichhornia azurea

When the **azure water hyacinth** is submerged, its fine leaves are round at the tips. It needs soft water and good lighting. It can be reproduced by means of cuttings. Size: 40 cm.

Eichhornia crassipes

This magnificent floating **water hyacinth**, ideal for garden ponds, has also been successfully introduced into many tropical areas to purify the water, as it gobbles up nitrates. However, in large bodies of water it grows so profusely that it has caused problems for boats, although there are plans to alleviate this by producing methane from water hyacinths through fermentation. Size: 10 cm.

▲ *Eichhornia crassipes*

▲ *Eichhornia azurea*

Nymphaea (Nympheaceae, South-East Asia, Africa)

The nymphaeas, better known as lotuses, are basically pond plants: one plant can sometimes cover up to 1 m^2. Two species can be kept totally submerged in an aquarium. Size: up to 50 cm under water.

Nymphaea lotus

There are two colored varieties of **lotuses**: one is predominantly green, the other mainly red. It must be kept in fairly soft water, with a covering of floating plants to provide shade. The leaves that reach the surface must be cut to enhance the growth of the ones underneath the water. When it reproduces, young plants appear on the rhizome shoots. Diameter: 50 cm.

Nymphaea rubra

This species has exactly the same requirements and biological characteristics as *N. lotus*, but has a strong purple coloring. The **purple lotus** therefore stands out dramatically when surrounded by green plants. Size: up to 50 cm under water.

◄ *Nymphaea lotus*

CLASSIFICATION OF PLANTS ACCORDING TO THE TYPE OF AQUARIUM	
TYPE OF AQUARIUM	**SUITABLE PLANTS**
North and Central America (water slightly hard and alkaline)	*Bacopa, Cabomba, Heteranthera, Hottonia, Ludwigia, Myriophyllum, Sagittaria, Saururus*
South America (soft, acid water)	*Alternanthera, Cabomba, Echinodorus, Eichhornia, Heteranthera, Myriophyllum, Salvinia*
West Africa (variable water characteristics)	*Anubias, Bolbitis, Crinum, Nymphaea*
Asia and South-East Asia (slightly soft, acid water)	*Acorus, Barclaya, Cryptocoryne* (some species in hard, alkaline water), *Hygrophila, Limnophila, Microsorium, Nymphaea, Rotala, Vallisneria, Vesicularia*
Madagascar (moderate hardness)	*Aponogeton*
Cosmopolitan plants, relatively indifferent to water quality	*Acorus, Ceratophyllum, Ceratopteris, Elodea, Egeria, Eleocharis, Lemna, Ludwigia, Pistia, Riccia*
Plants for temperate water aquariums	*Acorus, Ceratophyllum, Elodea, Egeria, Hippurus, Lemna, Riccia*
Plants for ponds	*Eichhornia, Elodea, Egeria, Hippurus, Lemna, Sagittaria sagittifolia*
Plants for aquaterrariums	*Acorus,* some *Cryptocorynes, Eleocharis, Hippurus, Lemna, Microsorium, Nymphaea, Pistia, Riccia, Salvinia, Vesicularia*

MARINE VEGETATION IN AQUARIUMS

No plants are found above the water (or with flowers) in a marine tank; only a few algae can be cultivated, but the results can often be highly attractive. Unlike the undesirable microscopic or filamentous algae, these species can be quite big and do not present any problems. These hardy plants take in nutrients over practically all their surface area.

▲ ***Halimeda tuna*** (in the foreground)

Mediterranean algae

Some species native to the Mediterranean coasts can acclimatize themselves to tropical aquariums. If you remove them from their natural setting, it is advisable to take not only the alga but also part of its support, usually a rock.

Codium bursa **(Codiaceae)**
The **felt ball codium** forms a sphere with a diameter that can exceed 25 cm. It grows very slowly and the biggest specimens unfurl. This species likes strong light.

Codium vermilara **(Codiaceae)**
Its felt-like appearance and bottle-green color are the distinguishing features of the **felt codium**. This species prefers well-lit areas. Size: 20 cm.

Halimeda tuna **(Udoteaceae)**
The **Halimeda** likes a murky environment and grows more quickly when the temperature is high, provided this does not exceed 25–26°C. Size: 1–10 cm.

Udotea petiolata **(Udoteaceae)**
Like the above, the **udotea** prefers poorly lit settings and grows on sand or rocks. Size: 3–20 cm.

Ulvas and enteromorphs (Ulvaceae)

These algae are common on European coasts. They do not last for long in an aquarium, but are useful as food for marine fish with herbivorous tendencies.
The **ulvas** or **sea lettuces** (several species belonging to the *Ulva* genus) resemble translucent lettuce leaves. Leaf size: 25–30 cm.
The **enteromorphs** are filamentous, also translucent, and pale green (*Enteromorpha* genus, several species). Size: 40–50 cm. It is worth noting that in the wild Ulvaceae thrive in areas rich in nitrates.

▲ ***Ulva* and *Enteromorpha***

Caulerpas (Caulerpaceae)

The caulerpas are green algae (*Chlorophyceae*) found in the tropics. There are several dozen species, but only a few are found in aquariums. They consist of a filamentous runner, which attaches itself to a support by means of rhizoids (or anchoring feet). The fronds extend from these rhizomes, their shape varying according to the species. Caulerpas grow quickly in an aquarium; the runner can sometimes increase its size by several centimeters per week.

▲ ***Caulerpa sertularoides***

Caulerpas like moderate lighting and clear, well-circulated water. Vegetative multiplication takes place through the division of the runner, where young fronds appear. In addition, a fragment of this alga can give rise to a small seedling. Sexual reproduction is rare in an aquarium.

Caulerpa prolifera

The **Mediterranean caulerpa** is found not only in the Mediterranean but also in other temperate regions around the world. The frond takes the form of an narrow, elongated leaf. It is very adaptable, as it tolerates temperatures of 14–30°C, and is therefore suitable for temperate marine aquariums. Size: 10 cm.

Caulerpa sertularoides

The **feathery caulerpa** grows just as rapidly. The shape of the fronds varies according to the setting and, most especially, the light. Size: 15 cm.

***Caulerpa prolifera* (full leaves) and *C. sertularoides* with *Hippocampus kuda* ▼**

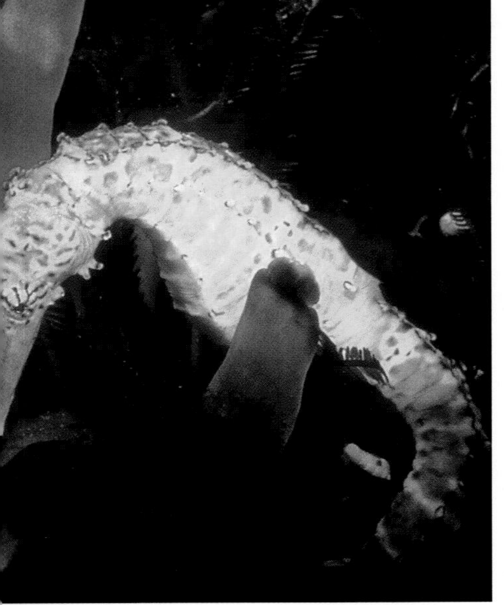

THE TROPICAL CAULERPA ARRIVES IN TEMPERATE WATERS

It was thought that tropical caulerpas could not tolerate northern climes (around 10–23°C). In 1984, however, the *Caulerpa taxifolia* species was found off the coast of Monaco, occupying a few square meters. Since then it has proliferated wildly and, according to some estimates, now covers over 80 km^2 in the Mediterranean, stretching from the Spanish island of Majorca to Croatia. Furthermore, the plant grows up to six times the size found in the tropics!
The morphology of *C. taxifolia* is similar to that of *C. serularoides*, and it grows quickly, often to the detriment of other plants, particularly *Posidonia oceanica*, a genuine but increasingly rare flowering plant. *C. taxifolia* contains toxins that could cause food poisoning in humans, although no case has yet been reported. This is logical, as this alga is only eaten by a few fish, and these are not eaten by humans. The caulerpa invasion can be held in check – at the moment it seems impossible to eliminate it completely – by sending down divers to collect it by hand or with suction pumps, but this involves vast expense. Other solutions proposed include releasing copper ions toxic to these plants, dumping tons of salt on them, or sending in a fleet of caulerpa-eating snails. A huge research program is underway to evaluate the propagation, distribution, and influence of this alga in the Mediterranean. Where does it come from? The aquarist community has been blamed, on the assumption that it was accidentally thrown into the sea, but (like other tropical algae) it could also have been introduced on ships' anchors and hulls. This invasion shows that certain species, especially the tropical ones, can survive elsewhere, and so aquarists must be careful when they throw out water; in any case, it is best not to use this alga in aquariums, the other two species being good alternatives.

Techniques

Creating an aquarium and putting it into operation do not demand any great expertise. These days even novice aquarists have easy access to a wide variety of techniques. Choosing the right equipment and understanding the basic rules will enable you to get the most out of your aquarium.

Tetra Test
Tetra Test

ASSEMBLING A TANK

If an aquarist is unimpressed by the range of aquariums on the market, then there is always the alternative of constructing a home-made tank. This requires only patience and precision: the most important thing is to follow the sequence of operations. The hobbyist thus has the chance to choose a tank according to his or her requirements or the setting within which it will be placed.

▲ *An aquarium can only be fully appreciated when it is integrated into its environment.*

The aquarium

Different models

Aquariums come in various shapes and sizes so that they can fit into the interior design of any home.

Traditionally, most tanks take the form of a horizontal rectangle, but these days it is also possible to find cubes, vertical rectangles, or panoramic aquariums, all specially adapted to a specific setting.

The basic model – and the cheapest – consists of a tank with a lid. It is also possible to equip it with a lighting hood. There are other models with an integral hood and minimal external decoration, i.e. a strip, of varying widths, that goes round both the base and the top, hiding the surface of the water. This type of aquarium can be sold on its own or with a support. It can sometimes be fitted with a filtration unit. Finally, in the top range, there are aquariums built into a piece of furniture, normally containing a filtration unit and lighting hood. The supporting furniture often has shelves or closets that serve to hide the pumps and other equipment, and the aquarium is framed by decorative elements that leave it visible from three sides.

Materials

Commercial aquariums are almost always made of glued glass, with silicone joints. These materials are suitable for water volumes of around 500 liters – volumes rarely exceeded in the aquarium trade.

The generalized nature of the materials and the relative simplicity of the gluing mean that any careful hobbyist can build a glued glass aquarium him or herself.

For bigger volumes, polyester resin or cement are used, with only the front part of the tank made of glass. These are the materials found in public aquariums. Plexiglas, which is light but also scratches easily, is used for the rarer round forms.

Small plastic tanks are also available for use as rearing or quarantine tanks.

Dimensions

The most harmonious form is obtained when the length is equal to the height multiplied by 1.5–2.5. The height will be slightly greater than the width, except in built-in tanks, where the contrary is the case. These proportions can be adhered to up to a length of 1.5 m, but they are impossible after that, as the height must never exceed 0.5 m (see table).

It is not advisable to use very narrow aquariums, as a trick of the eye means that a tank seems one-third narrower when it is filled with water, producing an unfortunate visual effect. Narrow tanks can be attractive, however, if they are put on narrow pieces of furniture, such as a mantelpiece or a divid-

◀ *"Diamond" tank. An original shape providing a striking visual effect. (La Rochelle Aquarium)*

ing wall between two rooms. It is also important to take into account the weight of the tank. A solid support is required, because an aquarium is heavy when it is put into operation: the weight of the water and decor must be added to that of the tank itself.

Positioning

An aquarium must be positioned with care, as once it is filled it will be impossible to move it anywhere else. It is a complicated decision, involving the visual impact on the room, practical considerations, and ecological criteria.

• *Visual impact*

Obviously, a big tank fits better into a large room, and a narrow tank into a small room. Choose a fairly dark spot to highlight it, well away from the television, to avoid any competition between these two centers of attention.

An aquarium traditionally has its longest dimension set against a wall, but there are other ways of setting it off. It can occupy a corner, be placed on a partition between two rooms, or be built into a wall.

• *Practical considerations*

You must plan on having an electrical

Dimensions, volumes, and weights

You must consider the gross volume (that of an empty aquarium) the net volume (when the tank is full, the sand and decor take up a certain amount of space) and the final weight of the aquarium when in operation. This depends on the bed and the extent of the decor; as these vary from one tank to another, the weight is therefore only indicated as a rough guide.

Length	Width (dimensions in meters)	Height	Gross volume (in liters)	Net volume (in liters)	Weight (in kg)
0.80	0.30	0.40	96	77	125
0.80	0.40	0.45	144	115	194
1	0.40	0.50	200	160	280
1.20	0.45	0.50	270	216	400
1.50	0.50	0.50	375	300	550
2	0.50	0.50	500	400	700

▲ *There are a huge number of original ways of setting off an aquarium.*

socket at an easy distance. A nearby tap would also be an asset, but if this is not possible make sure you have a hose for filling and draining the tank. When the aquarium is set against a wall, it is advisable to leave a space of a few centimeters at the back to make room for cables and pipes. The height of the aquarium also has to be planned with care, as it should be at eye level to be seen to advantage. Therefore, when it is placed in a main room, its base must be around 1 m from the floor, and in this way children will also be able to see it without any problem.

• *Ecological criteria*

It is essential that sunlight, especially that coming from the south, does not strike the aquarium directly, as there is a danger that green algae will grow, not to mention an excessive increase in temperature in summer. It is therefore best to face the tank towards the north or east. Do not hesitate to try out different positions with an empty tank before taking a decision with lasting consequences.

The support

As we have already seen, the weight of an aquarium is quite considerable. It is therefore vital to set up a sturdy and perfectly horizontal support (check the latter with a spirit level). Special furniture is available in the aquarium trade, but you can just as well build one yourself, the essential point being that the weight is distributed on intermediary beams. The support can be the same size as the tank or bigger, but it should never be smaller, either in length or width. Put a sheet of water-resistant marine plywood – 10–15 mm thick, according to the dimensions and weight of the aquarium – on the support, and then cover this with a 15 mm thick polystyrene sheet, which will compensate for any irregularities in the support. If you are a do-it-yourself enthusiast and have patience, you can set the aquarium, together with its support, into a piece of wooden furniture, so that it can only be seen through its front pane.

The lid

The lid, placed directly above the tank, is necessary for several reasons:
- to avoid water spilling on the lighting hood;
- to stop dust falling into the water;
- to prevent any possible jumping fish escaping from the tank;
- to reduce evaporation.

The lid must be made of glass to allow light to enter the tank, and so it must be cleaned regularly. On a practical level, small pegs stuck to the top make it easier to handle, and some corners can be cut away to make room for pipes and electrical cables. Also for practical reasons, it is advisable to have several small lids which fit together, especially in big tanks.

Avoid:

- placing any decorative objects immediately above the aquarium, as this makes using the lid impractical;
- putting any electrical devices under the aquarium: this is dangerous, due to the possibility of water spilling;
- installing the aquarium near a radiator.

MAKING AN AQUARIUM OF GLUED GLASS

Making an aquarium with glued glass is not the exclusive domain of professionals; these days it is also an option for hobbyists. The crucial factor is the care taken in the operation, along with a good organization of the work plan and respect for the sequence of the operation. It is advisable to practice first with a small rearing tank or hospital tank before taking the plunge and building a large aquarium. Hanging out in aquarium clubs can be useful, as it will give you a chance to meet experienced aquarists who can provide advice or give you a hand when you come to glue your first aquarium.

▲ *Marine tank built into a wooden closet, made by an aquarist.*

Materials and tools

• *Glass*

The fundamental material for your aquarium, the element which underpins its existence, is obviously glass. It can be cut to measure in glass merchants or do-it-yourself stores. This operation must be performed correctly, as any slight mistake in the cutting can have serious consequences, especially if the corners are not perfectly square.

The calculation of the dimensions of the panes must therefore be made with care, and do not forget to take into account the thickness of both the glass and the layer of glue (around 0.5 cm). The table below gives you the dimensions of the glass required for two tanks of different volumes. You need a base, two small sides, the front, and the back. There are also provisions for longitudinal reinforcements, which prevent the glass panes from curving due to the weight of water and support the two-section lid. In larger

◀ *Tank 3.7 m long, reconstituting the biotope of Lake Malawi.*

CUTTING THE GLASS FOR TWO DIFFERENT TANKS

We have chosen one tank of 96 liters and another of 200 liters (the gross volume in both cases) that can easily be built by two people.

Characteristics of the tank	Tank 80 cm long	Tank 1 m long
Dimensions (l x w x h in cm)	80 x 30 x 40	100 x 40 x 50
Gross volume (liters)	96	200
Thickness of the glass (mm)	6	8
Base (cm)	1 x (80 x 30)	1 x (100 x 40)
Small sides (cm)	2 x (28.7 x 40)	2 x (38.3 x 50)
Large sides (cm)	2 x (80 x 40)	2 x (100 x 50)
Longitudinal reinforcements (cm)	2 x (78.7 x 2)	2 x (98.3 x 2)
Lateral reinforcements (cm)	–	1 x (38.3 x 2)
Lids (2 or 3 mm thick, dimensions in cm)	2 x (39.2 x 28.5)	2 x (49 x 38)

Do not forget to cut a piece off a corner of each section of the lid and have some pegs (around 2 x 5 cm) ready to use as handles.

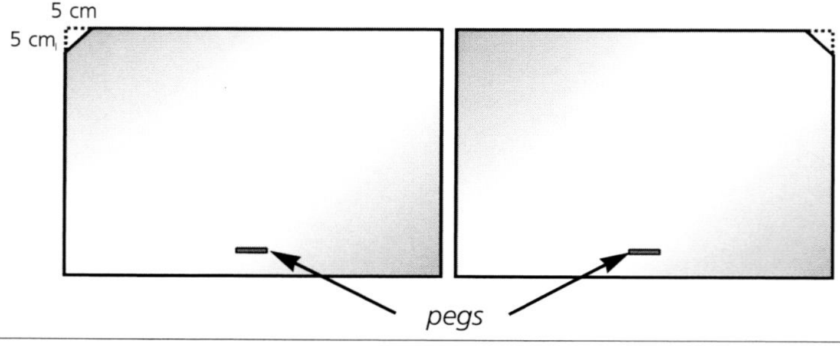

Squeezing the silicone glue onto a sheet of glass. ▼

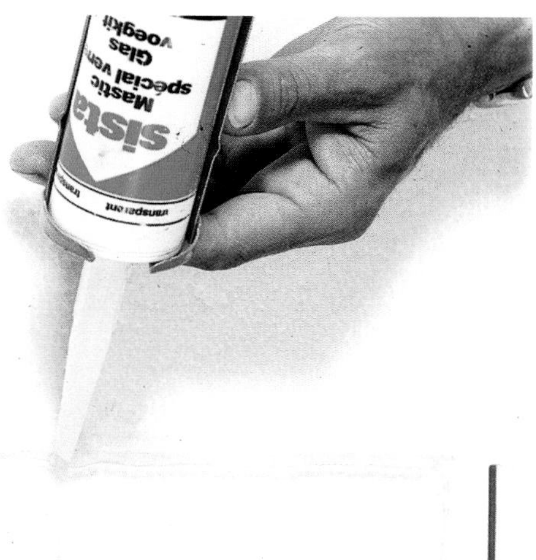

tanks, where the length is equal to or greater than 1 meter, one or sometimes several lateral reinforcements are also required to consolidate the unit.

Offcuts of glass can be used as pegs for lifting off the lids. After the cutting, remember to ask for the edges to be sanded down lightly, to avoid any unfortunate accidents from splinters or sharp edges.

• *Glue*

A good glue is needed for sticking the glass walls together effectively: transparent silicone glue for this purpose is available. When exposed to the air it hardens to form a watertight join. The speed of hardening depends on temperature, so special care must be taken in summer. At a temperature of 19–20°C, the glue stays soft for around 3 minutes, which allows time for working. The hardening is sensitive to the touch for 1 or 2 hours afterwards, and is complete in 48 hours.

You are advised to be very careful when handling the glue. If you happen to spill or smear some, a dried run-off on a smooth surface can be easily scraped off with a cutter. It is a lot more difficult if clothing becomes impregnated with it. Above all, make sure not to rub your eyes when handling it and, in the event of any accident, consult a doctor immediately.

This glue gives off a characteristic vinegary smell which disappears after a little while. It keeps well if the tube is closed with its original cap and stored in a cool, dark, dry place.

• *Supplementary materials*
You will require the following materials for the gluing process:
– methylated spirits or acetone, for cleaning the panes before gluing;
– clean rags or absorbent paper;
– cutter with a fine blade;
– sticky tape;
– small receptacle for water;
– set square and tape measure.

When you have assembled all the necessary materials, you are ready to go on to the construction.

Prepare a work surface large enough to allow you to spread out the panes and move around freely. It is advisable to get somebody to help you by holding the panes.

Sticking the various elements together
(see panel overleaf).

Installing the box filter

There is very little left for you to do, for the moment, apart from installing a box filter. The filtration system can be planned at the gluing stage or added afterwards. It can be placed on the right or on the left and must be hidden by exterior trim, such as a wooden facing that matches the aquarium and its support. Its volume must not be less than 1/10 of the total volume of the aquarium, if it is to be completely effective. Inside the tank, you must add the following parts, cut from 3 mm thick glass:
– a glass panel separating the filter from the rest of the aquarium, with a perforation to allow the water to flow through.

Going back to the example of the two tanks which served to illustrate the gluing of an aquarium, the dimensions of this panel would be:
• 28.7 × 38 cm for the 96 liter tank
• 38.3 × 48 cm for the 200 liter tank.

– four strips of glass intended to hold the filtering material (3 cm wide and 38 cm long for the 96 liter tank; 48 cm long for the 200 liter tank).

These elements must be mounted in accordance with the diagram below (if the filter is to be on the left of the aquarium), with the glass strips in pairs facing each other. They must not be more than 8 cm apart. The distance between the perforated panel and the closest side is 8 cm for the 96 liter tank and 10 cm for the 200 liter one. Note that the box filter is slightly lower than the main tank, to allow the water to circulate.

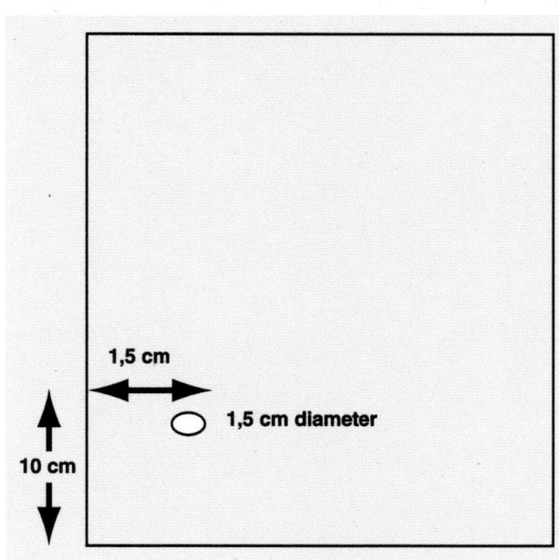

▲ Panel dividing off the box filter.

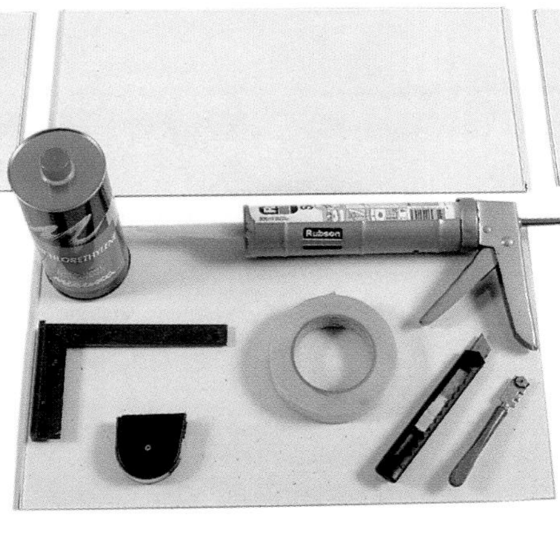
▲ To work efficiently, you must be able to spread the panes out on a sufficiently large work surface.

Front view of aquarium. ▼

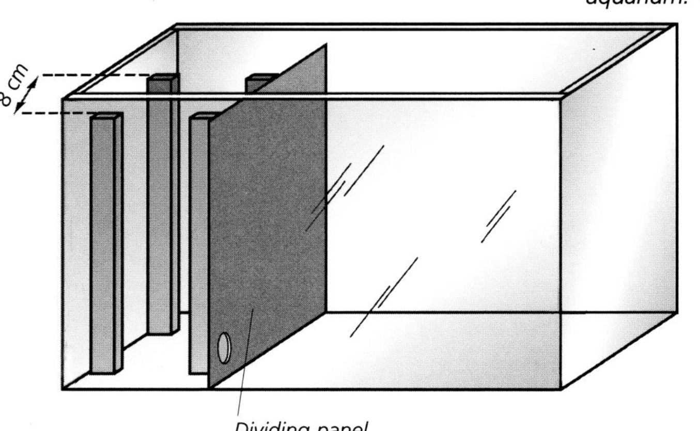

STICKING THE VARIOUS ELEMENTS TOGETHER

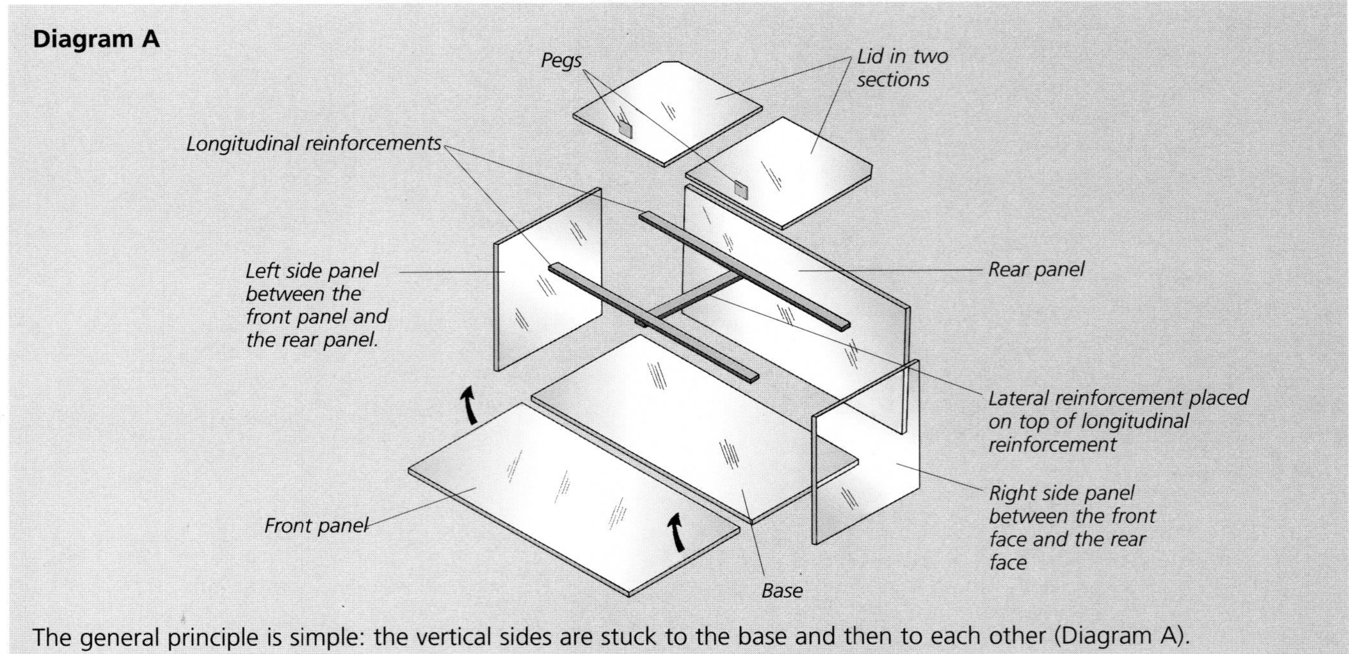

The general principle is simple: the vertical sides are stuck to the base and then to each other (Diagram A).

Diagram B

Rear panel

Left side

Base

Right side

Front panel

The dotted lines indicate the position of the glue.

The sequence for the operation is as follows:

1. Even if the glass panes were sanded when they were cut, run a piece of fine sand paper along the edges, then wipe them clean.

2. Lay the panes flat, as in diagram **B**.

3. Clean the parts to be glued with the acetone or methylated spirits. These areas must not come in contact with your hands, so the panes must only be handled by their future top edge.
Then allow to dry (it dries quickly).

4. Apply the glue parallel to the edge of the pane (diagram **C**).

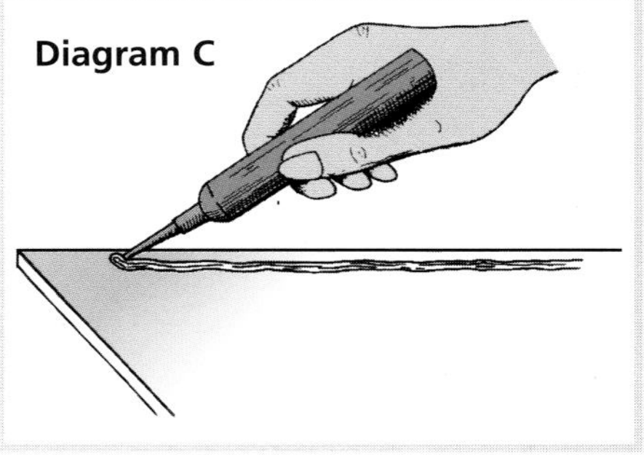

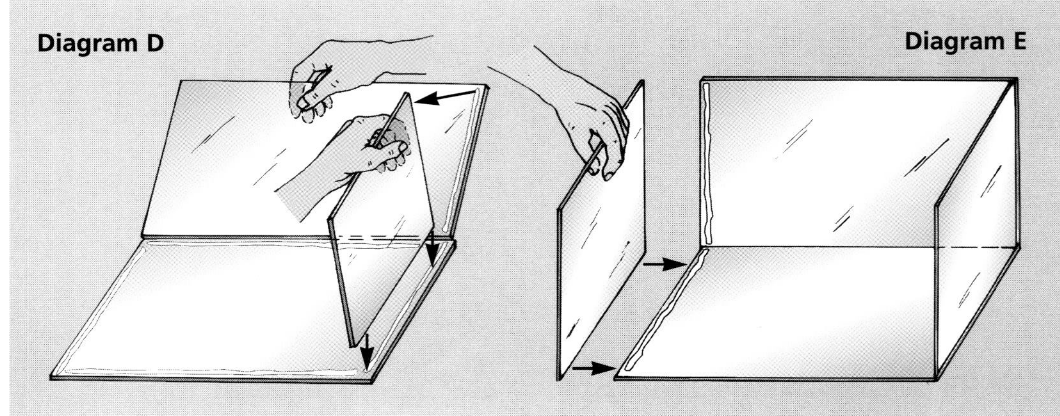

5. Put one of the two large panels in place, then the two small ones (diagrams **D** and **E**). Note the position of the hands on the top edge of the panels.

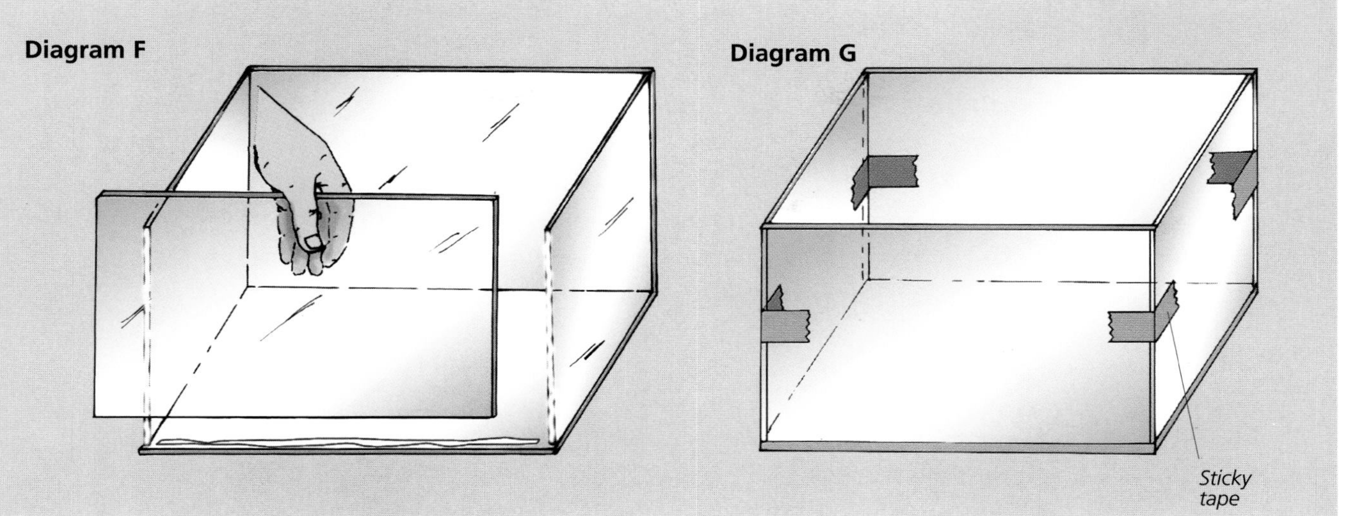

6. Finish off by putting the second large panel in place (diagram **F**). If you are planning to use decoration made of synthetic materials, do not put the front pane in place straight-away, so that you can add it in greater comfort. Once you are through, finish off the gluing of the tank.
7. Apply pressure to the areas which have been glued, to eliminate any air bubbles – this is extremely important. It is quite normal for the glue to squeeze out on both the inside and outside.
8. Use the sticky tape on the outer side to keep the four vertical panes upright (diagram **G**).

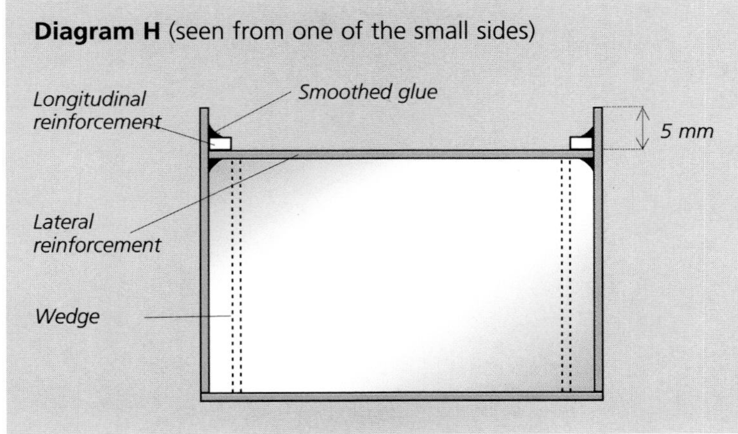

Once the gluing has been finished, it must be inspected by looking down on the aquarium. The four sides of the tank are represented by hatching, the reinforcements by filled areas.

Diagram I

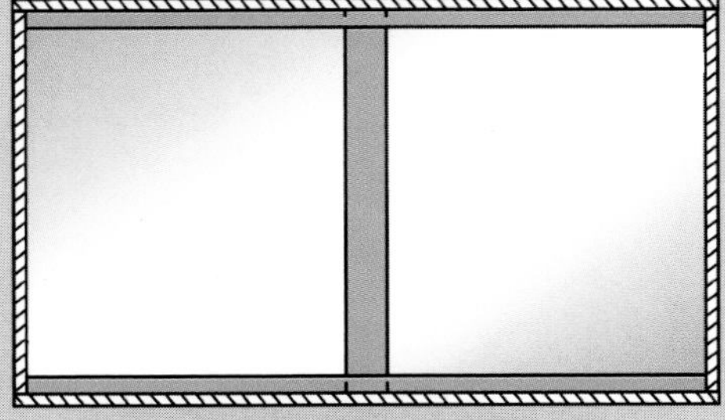

9. Moisten a finger in the receptacle containing water, then smooth down the glue on the inside of the aquarium. The result must be concave.
10. Glue the reinforcements, wedge them, and smooth down the glue (diagram **H**).
11. Stick the pegs on the lids.
12. Leave to dry for 48 hours. Carefully trim any excess glue on the outside and any smudges on the inside. Make sure you do not damage the parts you previously smoothed down.
13. Place the aquarium on an absolutely flat surface and pour in water, to check whether it is watertight.
The whole gluing process must be finished in 3 minutes, but there is no point in rushing: bad gluing can have disastrous consequences for the stability and watertightness of the tank.
Of the possible problems that may emerge during this procedure, the three main ones are:
– a pane may break when you are handling it;
– you may make a mistake in the mounting, especially with the small sides, if their length and breadth are almost the same;
– the pieces may not fit together properly.
In the latter two cases, leave to dry, unstick, scrape off the glue with a cutter, clean, and then mount the tank again. If the aquarium leaks, indicate the source with a felt pen or sticky tape, then empty the tank and leave it to dry. Clean the defective area and reapply the glue on the inside, making sure to extend beyond both edges of the source of the leak.

EQUIPMENT AND ACCESSORIES

An aquarium can only function properly with reliable equipment. It must be easy to put into place and to use and it must offer every possible guarantee of safety, paying particular attention to the potentially dangerous combination of water and electricity. There is sufficient variety in the aquarium trade to supply hobbyists with a reasonable choice, on the basis of their particular needs and means. It is pointless (and expensive) to think big; besides, simplicity is often the byword for efficiency and success.

LIGHT

Light not only serves to provide visual pleasure and highlight the aquarium, it is also essential to its equilibrium, as fish, like most living beings, need the alternation of day and night, which acts as a biological clock. The action of light also makes it possible for plants to perform photosynthesis and grow. Marine invertebrates that play host to micro-algae (see page 169) require strong lighting.

An aquarium must therefore be equipped with a light source which resembles as far as possible the one found in their natural habitat, as regards quantity and, most important, chromatic quality.

Quality of the light

Obviously, the best light would be that of the sun, which permits life on our planet. It is unfortunately impossible to take full advantage of it in an aquarium, for two main reasons.

Firstly, it cannot be quantitatively dosed. This means that too much light often causes the growth of unwanted algae, and so it is important not to directly expose a tank to natural light, especially if it is facing south. On the other hand, if the direct influence is deficient, the aquarium does not receive enough light to ensure that the plants grow satisfactorily.

Secondly, sunlight does not adequately highlight the aquarium and fish.

It is therefore essential to resort to artificial lighting placed above the aquarium, usually in a hood specially designed for this purpose. This lighting must satisfy certain conditions, as regards:

– the type of bulb used and the quality of the light produced;

– the intensity of light supplied to the aquarium;

– the duration of the lighting.

You must be realistic as regards what you can achieve: no artificial light is going to be the same as sunlight. It is, however, possible to get close, ideally with a combination of different complementary light sources.

Intensity of the light

The total intensity provided by the lighting is an extremely important factor, as plants must be provided the amount of light they need to grow in this artificial environment.

It is inevitable, however, that some light is lost, particularly if the beams have to travel long distances. The importance of the intensity of light (expressed, for the sake of simplicity, in watts) is often underestimated, and as a result many aquariums are under-lit. It is unusual to find cases of overlighting.

The tables on the following pages give the indications required for obtaining an optimum amount of light for your aquarium. As a general rule, the use of fluorescent tubes is generally recommended for water up to a height of 0.5 m.

Loss of light

The further away the light source, the greater the loss in:

- the lighting hood;
- the glass lid covering the aquarium;
- the water.

Part of the light is reflected by the surface of the water, another part is absorbed (the deeper the aquarium, the greater the importance of the absorbed light), and a final part is diffused by suspended sediment. It is estimated that the bed only receives 20–30% of the total light, which can be detrimental to the growth of small plants.

In order to reduce the loss of light, you must:

- recover as much as you can in the hood through reflection;
- keep the aquarium lid spotless;

◄ Light is recognized as being important for plants, and also for marine invertebrates. It must be sufficiently strong to reach the bottom of the aquarium.

– make sure that the water is clear;
– maintain the depth of the water below 0.5 m if you are using fluorescent tubes.

Light sources

A whole host of light sources, each with its own distinguishing features, is available to aquarists.

• *Incandescent lamps*

These are what we use from day to day in our homes, but they are absolutely out of the question in aquariums: the quality of light is poor, and this type of bulb gives off too much heat.

• *Fluorescent tubes*

Incorrectly known as neons, these tubes contain a gas that turns fluorescent under the action of an electrical discharge. They give off little heat and are available in various lengths and intensities. They last for 3,000–4,000 hours, or around a year. The quality of the illumination decreases over the course of time, however, and this can be clearly seen if an old tube is replaced by a new one. For this reason, never change all the tubes in a tank at the same time, as plants may be traumatized by this abrupt change in the intensity of the light. A used tube can be recognized by its black or dark ends. Fluorescent tubes come in various colors: firstly, the cold white or industrial white tubes, which are to be avoided, and the daylight tubes. The latter approximate sunlight the most closely and provide well-balanced lighting. Also available are colored tubes with a variety of dominants, including the tubes with a pink dominant used in horticulture, which are particularly effective for the growth of plants, as they mainly emit blue and red rays, which are trapped by plants and used in the photosynthesis process. Some aquarists do not appreciate their somewhat unnatural color, which tends to exaggerate the red and blue tones of fish. Sometimes tubes with a blue dominant are combined with white to create a light reminiscent of that found in deep waters. Such tubes are beneficial for corals and other animals from the same group, and have therefore acquired the name of actinia tubes.

Other colors are available, but they are less common. It is sometimes possible to find tubes with a yellow dominant, which are combined with blue tubes to achieve a more balanced light.

A fluorescent tube is not plugged directly into the mains: you must insert a transformer, the ballast, and a starter which produces the electrical discharges required. If you buy a well equipped aquarium, or one with a lighting hood, the tubes will be provided. This does not always mean that you can rest easy, as the intensity of the pre-installed tubes is sometimes insufficient.

• *Halogen lamps*

The tungsten filament of incandescent bulbs is here replaced by another metal, which prevents them from turning black. These lamps can be equipped with a rheostat, but they are generally little used by hobbyists.

• *Discharge lamps*

An electrical discharge between two electrodes vaporizes a gas, such as mercury or sodium vapor – which emits an intense light. These lamps have a slight yellow dominant, imperceptible to the human eye, which is compensated by a blue fluorescent tube. They heat up and consume more electricity than fluorescent tubes. Some, known as HQI daylight, are prized by aquarists, but they are expensive and impractical for normal tanks. They are mainly used in seawater aquariums over 0.5 m in height, as they help to acclimatize Anthozoans with *Zooxanthellae* (see page 169).

Some blue fluorescent tubes can compensate the dominant yellow of HQI bulbs, resulting in a balanced lighting which is as pleasing to the inhabitants of the aquarium as it is to the eye of the beholder. ▼

Some examples of fluorescent tubes

Manufacturer, brand	Type, model	Dominant color	Use	Observations
Philips	TLD18	Blue	– Used with daylight lamps, it creates a light resembling that found in deep waters (sea, East African lakes). – It compensates the yellow dominant of HQI lighting.	– The darker TL03 has beneficial effects on Anthozoans (actinic tube). It must be used with daylights or HQIs. – The Bluemoon (Interpet) is roughly equivalent to the TLD 18.
Pennplax	Ultratrilux	Daylight	– Fresh or sea water. – It can be combined with pink tubes when the vegetation is dense.	– Less common than the other daylight lamps. – Another model, the Trilux, is slightly pink and roughly corresponds to the Aquastar. It lasts a long time but is more expensive.
Sylvania	Daylight	Daylight	– As above.	– One of the most common and versatile. It is recommended to beginners for any purpose.
Interpet	Beauty light	Rose	– Growth of plants. – It can be combined with daylight lamps.	– Uncommon
Sylvania	Aquastar	Daylight, with very slight pink tone	– Fresh water. – It can be combined with pink tubes. – Some aquarists consider it slightly less suitable for sea water.	– One of the tubes considered as giving the best results for light that looks natural, and for the growth of plants.
General Electric	Triton	Daylight	– Fresh and sea water. – It can be combined with pink tubes.	– Many aquarists consider it roughly equivalent to the Aquastar, but it is less common.
Osram	Fluora	Rose	– Growth of plants. – It combines with daylight lamps to resemble natural lighting.	– Slightly less pink than the Grolux, but with identical results for plants.
Sylvania	Grolux	Rose	– Growth of plants. – Its dominant color can be compensated by daylight lamps	– One of the oldest and most well-known, a starter for many novice aquarists. – Some hobbyists find it too pink and prefer the Fluora.

The fluorescent tube

Its connection sequence is as follows:

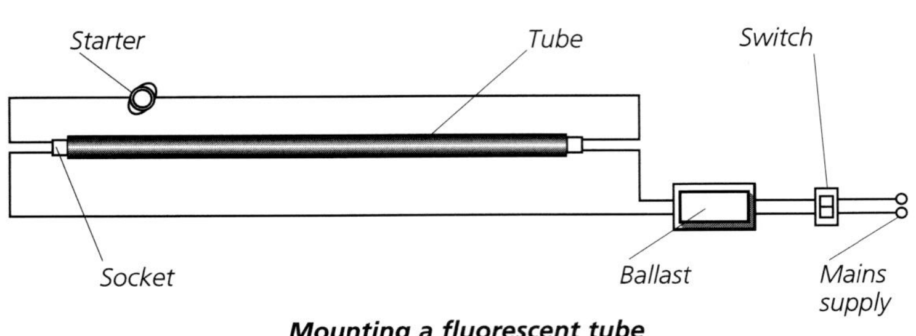

Mounting a fluorescent tube

Watertight caps are available to protect the ends of the tubes and to avoid any electricital accidents. The ballast gives off heat, so it should not be installed in the hood, although unfortunately this does occur in some commercial equipment.

Several different lengths of tube, with the wattage adjusted proportionally, are available.

Length and intensity of different models

Length (cm)	Intensity (watts)
36	14
44	15
60	20
75	25
90	30
120	40

- *The hood*

Whatever type of light source you choose, it requires a support: this is the hood. Fluorescent tubes must be included in a hood, out of reach of splashed water. It is often protected by a pane of glass but, if this is not the case, the aquarium lid serves the same function. To avoid any loss of light, any partition between the lighting and the water must maintain its shape when exposed to heat, as well as being transparent and, above all, clean. Glass is therefore the ideal material. Loss of light in the hood can be substantial, sometimes up to 20–30%. There are a few tricks which can resolve this problem, the main principle being to reflect as much light as possible towards the water. You can, therefore, line the inside of the hood with the smoothest possible aluminum foil, coat it with white or metallic paint, or make one or several semicircular metallic reflectors to fit round the tubes. Some galleries on the market use one of the last two techniques. As the intensity of the light decreases when it gets further away from its source, it is important for the latter to be as close to the water as possible. It should not be any closer than 5–8 cm, for technical and safety reasons, but even with these restrictions the illumination can be satisfactory. (This reduction in intensity has been taken into account in the calculations for the strength of the lighting and the number of fluorescent tubes.)

Duration of lighting

High-quality lighting serves no purpose if it is switched on only for a few hours a day; by contrast, there is no sense in providing illumination for 15 hours a day if the lighting is inappropriate. One will not compensate the other under any circumstances. Once the lighting is suitable, both qualitatively and quantitatively, you must decide for how long you are going to switch it on.

In tropical regions, the day lasts for approximately 11 to 13 hours, and this is what wild plants and fish are accustomed to. The situation is different for plants and animals raised in captivity, which can tolerate different lighting, but always within the bounds of reason. An aquarium can be lit for 13 hours a day, but some hobbyists exceed these limits, as they get used to turning the aquarium on when they get up and switching it off late at night. In this way the lighting can be on

Some, generally small, aquariums, include basic equipment. The lighting is therefore incorporated into a hood which cannot get splashed by the water.. ▶

◄ *A blue tube can be added to daylight lamps to recreate the lighting in reef areas.*

Which tubes for which aquarium?

The following examples all assume a maximum water depth of 0.5 m and a minimum of three tubes.

Type of tank	Type and combination of tubes	Observations
Classic freshwater tank, average number or few plants	– A pink tube, combined with daylight lamps	This respects the balance of the colors, with the pink enhancing the growth of plants. Low to medium intensity.
Freshwater tank with abundant vegetation	– At least 50% pink tubes, combined with daylight lamps	This encourages the growth of plants, but at the expense of natural-looking light. High intensity.
Regional East African tank	A blue tube (for example, TLD 18 or Bluemoon), combined with daylight lamps	This attempts to recreate the natural lighting of these waters. Medium to high intensity.
Marine tank, without any plants or invertebrates	– Daylight lamps, possibly with a blue tube	This attempts to recreate the natural lighting of clear reef waters. Low to medium intensity.
Marine tank with plants but without any invertebrates	– A pink tube, combined with daylight lamps	Balance between a natural-looking light and a light to enhance plant growth. Medium intensity.
Marine tank with invertebrates (particularly Anthozoans)	– An actinic blue tube (the TL03, for example), combined with daylight lamps.	For enhancing the maintenance and growth of invertebrates playing host to *Zooxanthellae*. High intensity.

Good lighting requires good installation

The positioning of fluorescent tubes in a hood

The fluorescent tubes must be distributed with, optimally, a distance of 8–10 cm between them (diagram **1**). In the fitted aquariums that are commercially available, the length of the tubes matches that of the aquarium, although it is noticeable that the sides of the aquarium receive a little less light than the center or the front and back. Problems arise when the tubes are markedly shorter than the tank, which can occur in commercial aquariums with unusual dimensions, or in homemade ones. If the tubes are all centered, then there is a space on both sides, which may disadvantage plants on the sides of the tank. A partial solution to this problem is alternating the position of the tubes along the sides (diagram **2**).

Diagram 1

Another option is the use of tubes of different lengths, making sure that they are arranged to cover the whole surface of the tank and that their total intensity is sufficient.

Diagram 2

How many fluorescent tubes are needed for good illumination?

• The number of tubes required depends on their intensity and the size of the aquarium. Here are some indications for water of a maximum depth of 0.5 m:

Normally planted freshwater tank, marine tank with plants	1 W/2 liters of water/ normal intensity
Densely planted freshwater tank (Dutch aquarium, for example), regional East African tank	1 W/liter of water/ high intensity
Sparsely planted freshwater tank, sea water without invertebrates or plants	1 W/3 liters of water/ fairly low intensity
Sea water with Anthozoans (corals, anemones) and plants	1 W/liter water/high intensity

• These are the data, according to some standard dimensions, for a normally planted tank:

Dimensions of tank (L x w x h in cm)	Volume (in liters)	Length of tube (in cm)	Power (in W)	Number of tubes
80 x 30 x 40	96	60	20	2
100 x 40 x 50	200	90	30	3
120 x 45 x 50	270	90	30	4
150 x 50 x 50	375	120	40	4 or 5

for stretches of 16 or 17 hours, which is far too much. It does not especially harm the fish, but it nevertheless changes the balance of the aquarium, and is particularly conducive to the development of algae. It is advisable to keep the lighting on for about 10 hours and switch it off at around 10 or 11 o'clock at night. The use of programmed electrical clocks facilitates this operation, and particularly avoids any abrupt and unnatural transition from dark to light, which can be harmful to some fish in the aquarium. In this way, the aquarium will receive the light of the new day first, followed by its own lighting. Once the artificial lighting has been switched off at night, the tank will still be able to take advantage of the ambient lighting.

It is also possible to create a program that switches the fluorescent tubes on and off, one after the other, using several timers, thereby recreating, to a certain extent, sunrise and sunset.

The ideal lighting program would therefore switch on the room's ambient lighting in the morning, or allow the dawn light to exert its influence, then turn on one tube about 1 hour later, and finally switch on the other tubes a little later. At night, it would first turn off some of the tubes – with just one remaining lit – then, a short while later, the final tube, and, finally, the ambient lighting in the room.

Last but not least: do not interrupt a daytime light. Several hours of darkness, whether total or partial, unbalances the growth of plants and the behavior of fish.

◄ *Good lighting must both cover the needs of plants and satisfy the visual sense of onlookers.*

HEATING

After the vital matter of lighting, there follows a second issue, which is no less important: heating. You must first establish your requirements. The aquatic animals and plants in tropical regions live in warm water in which the temperature hardly varies over the course of the year. Tropical aquariums must therefore be heated, with the temperature guaranteed at around 25–26°C, or even 27°C for sea water. These temperatures can be maintained with a watertight electrical heater connected to an adjustable thermostat that switches itself off once the desired temperature has been achieved. When the latter goes down by 1°C or less, the thermostat reconnects the current and the heater starts to heat up again. Classic thermostats for aquariums allow the temperature to be regulated with some precision, to around 0.5°C.

More precise electronic thermostats are also available. These react to variations of the order of 0.1°C, but unfortunately they are more expensive.

Heating equipment

Once you have established your requirements, the next step is to choose the problem of the heating equipment. There are independent elements available, attached to a thermostat, but they have

HEATING FOR BEGINNERS

A heater-thermostat is the most practical solution for beginners. Make sure to choose a model in which the temperature readings are clearly visible. They often have a small light which indicates when the element is heating up. The power depends on the volume of water the aquarium will hold: calculate around 1 W/liter, which means that a 100 liter tank requires a heater-thermostat of 100 W.

A heater-thermostat must always be totally submerged. ►

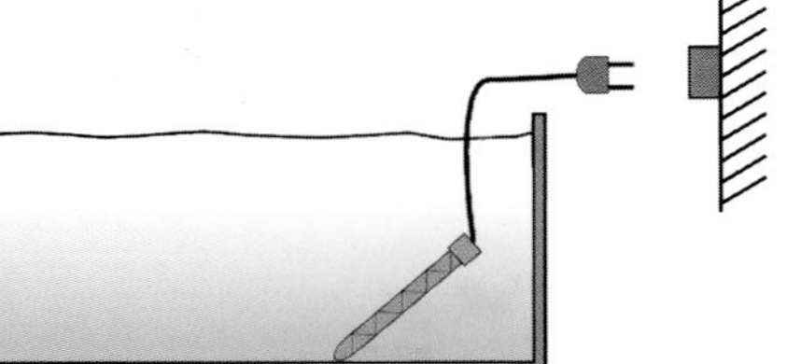

the disadvantage of multiplying the number of electrical connections and cables to be hidden.

Another option is a heater-thermostat – combining both a thermostat and a heater – which is completely watertight and submergible. This system is becoming increasingly popular as it is so easy to use.

Finally, a less common type of element consists of a heating cable sealed inside a flexible tube, which is placed in the sediment. Some aquarists, however, think that the diffusion of heat via the bed damages the roots of plants. Furthermore, there is a danger that the cable may be partially unearthed by a burrowing animal in the tank.

▲ *Independent thermostat and heater: practical, if you want to modulate the power of the heating, but unwieldy as regards electrical cables.*

A heater-thermostat comprises both thermostat and heater. It is therefore easier to hide than the two separate elements. ▼

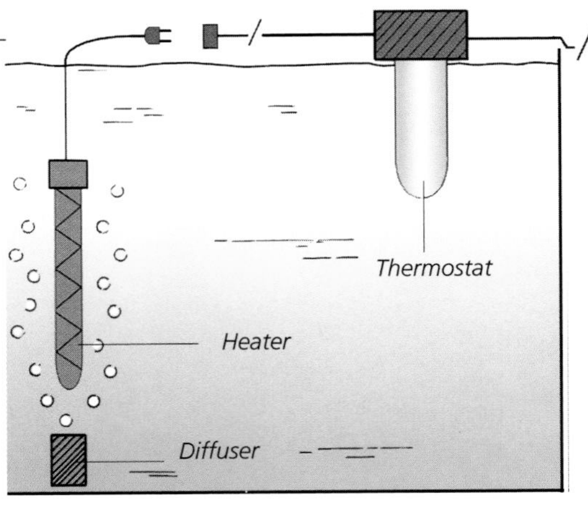

▲ *The thermostat must be placed some distance away from the heater for an adequate control of the temperature.*

▼ *A reliable thermometer is necessary for monitoring the temperature.*

The heating power level

The temperature in an inhabited room – a lounge or bedroom – rarely falls below 17°C. If an aquarium is installed, the heating must be sufficiently powerful to go from this room temperature, which will be the same as that of the unheated tank, to one of around 25–26°C.

A power level of 1 W/liter is generally sufficient to ensure this increase in temperature. Therefore, 100 W will be required for a 100 liter aquarium, and this will also suffice for a 150 liter tank.

In an uninhabited, and usually unheated, setting, such as a garage, cellar, or loft, a tank sometimes requires up to 2 W/liter, but rarely more than this.

There is a sufficiently wide range of heating devices and power levels to cover all your needs for volumes up to 500 liters (25, 50, 75, 100, 150, 200, and 500 W). Beyond that, it is cheaper and easier to heat the entire premises (as in the case of clubs and public aquariums) than to heat tanks individually.

Installing the heating equipment in the aquarium

It is important that the heat discharged by the heater is spread throughout the aquarium, in order for the temperature to be relatively uniform. Therefore, put the heater-thermostat in a turbulent spot, to help spread the heat and prevent any areas being warmer than others. Another alternative is to distribute the heat by dividing the overall intensity – two heat sources of 100 W instead of a single one of 200 W, for example – but this entails more cables to hide, both inside and outside the aquarium. The thermometer must be kept away from the heat source, to avoid being directly affected by it.

Possible problems

Sometimes, the glass protecting a heating apparatus may break, especially when

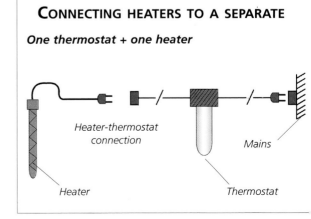

Connecting heaters to a separate

One thermostat + one heater

Heater-thermostat connection

Mains

Heater

Thermostat

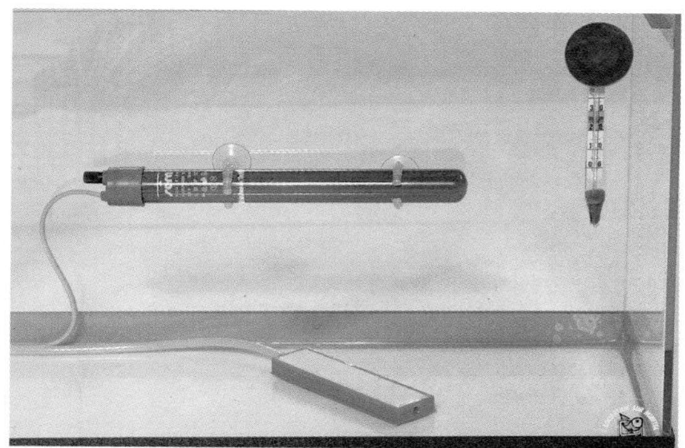

▲ *A diffuser placed under the heater-thermostat distributes heat throughout the aquarium.*

you are handling it, and so it must be replaced. However, before plunging your hand into the aquarium, it is essential to unplug the heating system, as there is a risk, however minimal, of getting an electric shock – water, particularly salt water, is an excellent conductor of electricity. The heater's heating wire can break, meaning that the water is no longer being heated and gradually cools. In this case, an internal black deposit appears in the heater, or on the heater component of the heater-thermostat.
Another common problem is the blocking of the thermostat in the heating position: the metal strip "sticks" to its contact, the element continues heating, and in a few hours the temperature of the tank can soar above 30°C. This can occur with well-used thermostats, although the problem can be avoided with a second thermostat, inserted as a safety measure between the first and the mains supply. If in doubt, consult a qualified electrician who has experience in dealing with domestic aquariums or your local supplier.

THERMOSTAT

One thermostat + several heaters

Adaptor
Thermostat
Mains
Heaters

Aeration

Here a question arises: should we speak of aeration or oxygenation? The two terms lead to confusion, and it is sometimes thought that aerating the water means introducing oxygen. In fact, when a volume of water is circulated, the agitation of the surface facilitates both the penetration of atmospheric oxygen into the water and the elimination of the carbon dioxide dissolved in the water. It is not therefore the bubbles produced that directly oxygenate the water, but the movement they create. Circulating also allows the heat given off by the heating apparatus to be diffused and thereby distributed evenly over the whole tank. The water expelled from the filter can also help to stir the water in the tank.
Obviously, if an aquarium is well balanced, there is no need to aerate it: this is often the case in small, normally planted, and quite densely populated tanks. However, gentle aeration does provide a degree of security.
For large aquariums, in contrast, aeration is recommended, especially when they house fish with high oxygen requirements, such as the large freshwater Cichlids. Strong aeration is similarly necessary in marine tanks, in the form of vigorous stirring of the water, to recreate the conditions of the natural setting.

▲ *There are several types of air pumps; some have controls to regulate their intensity.*

Aeration equipment

• *The pump*
A small pump, connected to the mains, draws in the atmospheric air surrounding it and pushes it along a narrow pipe to a diffuser. This forms the bubbles that will break on the surface of the water. There are several models of pump, of varying degrees of output, according to the volume of air required; the smallest are sufficient for aquariums of a maximum volume of 100–150 liters. Pumps make a certain

▲ A single pump can feed several diffusers, through the use of shunts, or also a filter-plate.

amount of noise, which may seem a nuisance, as an aquarium is generally appreciated for the impression of silence and serenity that it creates. The output of some pumps can be regulated, making it possible to increase or decrease the volume of air produced.

- *The air distribution pipe*

There are several types of air distribution pipes, of varying degrees of rigidity, of which the most common diameters are 4–6 mm. It is best to choose one that is fairly stiff, as, if it happens to get jammed, it will not be completely flattened and will still allow a little air to pass through. Always buy a piece of tube longer than you need, to avoid any unpleasant surprises.

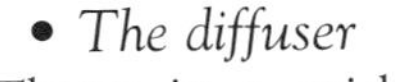

- *The diffuser*

There is a wide range of diffusers on the market: rectangular or cylindrical, in natural or artificial materials. The most practical ones are made of

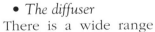

Reducing the noise of the air pump

Some pumps are noisier than others, and this can sometimes be irritating when the aquarium is situated in a bedroom or other inhabited room. There are several ways of reducing this noise:
– make a support for the pump, using a small wooden board on a block of foam;
– enclose the pump, in a cupboard, for example;
– place the pump away from the tank, with a sufficiently long aeration pipe (an air pump often goes unnoticed in a kitchen, where its noise blends in with other household appliances);
– if the output of the pump cannot be regulated, make a shunt with a faucet on the end, to allow a slight controlled escape of air (this solution is effective only in some pumps).

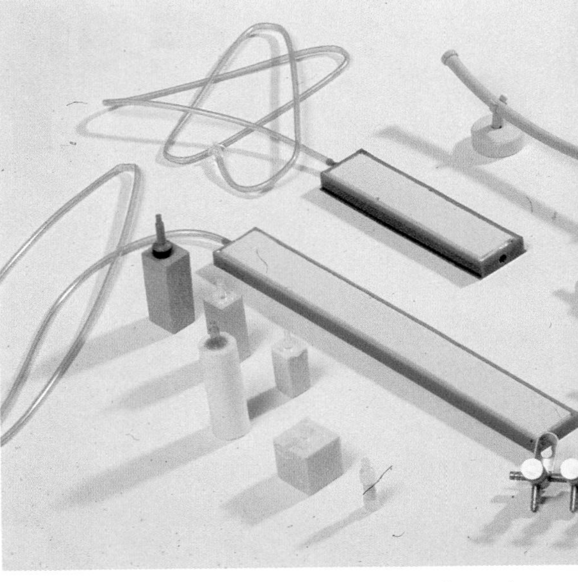

▲ There is such a huge range of aeration accessories that no aquarist will have any problem finding equipment suited to his or her individual requirements.

microporous or ceramic materials. These produce very fine bubbles and can be cleaned easily when they get clogged up. Do not forget that diffusers will become encrusted with calcium, salt, or algae after they have been in use for a while. They have the disadvantage of floating, so they must be held down, with a stone, for example. Be aware that diffusers that produce fine bubbles require stronger air pressure to maintain the flow.

- *Small accessories*

Various small accessories complement the main items. Connectors, shaped in the form of a T, Y, or X, make it possible for a single pump to supply several diffusers, in the same tank or in different ones.

How many diffusers in an aquarium?

This depends on the volume and type of aquarium.
– For a tank of 100–150 liters, normally planted, a single diffuser with a moderate output is sufficient;
– beyond that, in fresh water, calculate one diffuser for every 100–150 liters (one for every 100 liters, if the tank is sparsely planted, or not planted at all);
– in sea water, use one diffuser for every 75–100 liters, at top intensity.

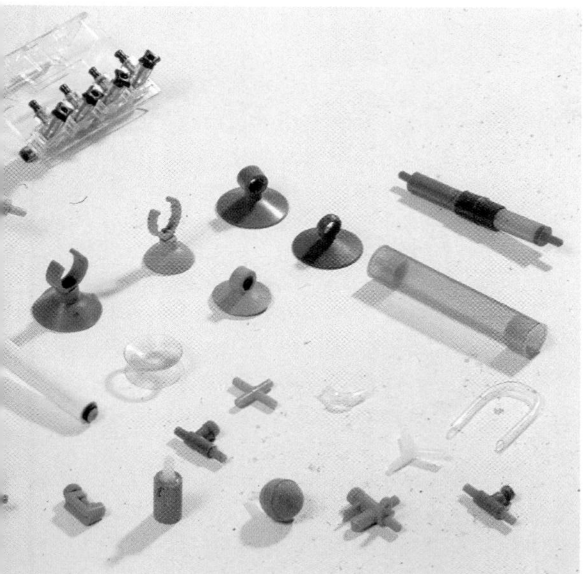

Faucets regulate the flow when there are several channels. There is a variety of models, in plastic or metal, single or in sets for large installations.

• *Positioning the aeration equipment*

It is best to place the pump above water level; this eliminates the possibility of water flowing back down the air pipe when the current is switched off.

A pump can sometimes be found below water level, especially in built-in aquariums, and so a small valve must be inserted to reduce the above risk.

Perfectionists place the air pump outside the room containing their aquarium, to avoid any possible diffusion inside the aquarium of toxic products, such as aerosol sprays or cigarette smoke.

Small filters are able partially to purify the air. These consist of active carbon that absorbs smells and fumes, which is placed in the air circuit after it leaves the pump.

Many aquarists consider that bubbles in a tank provide a somewhat unnatural appearance, so they hide their diffusers and pipes in the decor, and the bubbles are only noticeable when they break the surface of the water.

For the reasons mentioned above, the ideal position for a diffuser is close to a heating apparatus. However, make sure that no pipe comes into direct contact with an element.

Since a diffuser stirs the water, sometimes vigorously, it is possible that it also puts back into suspension various pieces of debris, such as excreta, uneaten food, and pieces of vegetation. If the suction of the filtration system is nearby, this is not a serious problem; if this is not the case, there is a risk that this debris will spread over the tank, with all the unappealing visual results that may be expected. To avoid this annoyance, do not put the diffuser on the bed, but to place it halfway up the aquarium. It is advisable to check that the lid fits properly at the point where the bubbles reach the surface, in order to avoid any splashing of water onto the lighting hood. The faucets regulating the air must obviously be placed outside the aquarium. Often, in the case of well planted aquariums, no aeration equipment is used, as the plants themselves produce enough oxygen.

Aeration for beginners

One of the smaller pumps on the market is sufficient, along with a few meters of pipe and a diffuser in microporous plastic. If the pump is placed below the water level of the aquarium, it is vital to acquire a valve to prevent the water flowing back.

▼ *It is not the bubbles from the diffusers that oxygenate the water, but the movement that they create.*

Installation of an aeration system

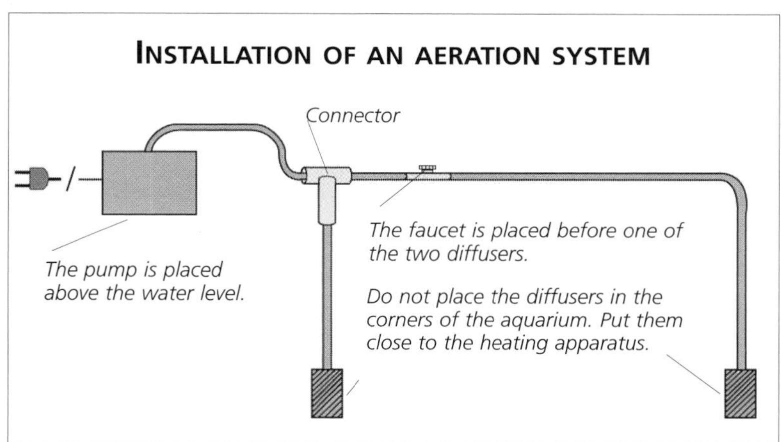

Connector
The faucet is placed before one of the two diffusers.
The pump is placed above the water level.
Do not place the diffusers in the corners of the aquarium. Put them close to the heating apparatus.

◄ *External filter with several filtration compartments.*

Filtration

Why filter the water?

Once an aquarium is put into operation, the characteristics of the water change fairly rapidly. These modifications are a result of the biological activity of living beings – plants, fish, and invertebrates – as well as various chemical reactions that occur in the water and sediment. In this way the water gradually becomes loaded with suspended matter – animal excrement, vegetable debris, surplus food, sometimes even dead bodies – and suspended solids produced by the activity of the occupants.

Of these, the most significant are the nitrogenous products released by animals' liquid excretion. These substances are very toxic, and so their accumulation is a cause for concern.

The suspended matter remains in open water, or ends up as sediment. In either case, it is visible. The suspended solids, on the other hand, are not visible, and therein lies the danger. It is however, possible to ob-serve a slow modification of the water color; in the long term, it takes on a yellowish color. This alteration can be detected very early on by immersing a white object.

Filtration therefore aims to trap the suspended matter, in order to attain clear water that is more receptive to the penetration of light and avoid any risk of intoxicating the residents of the tank. As we have already pointed out, filtration also contributes to good oxygenation. You must not, however, neglect to remove the biggest scraps yourself.

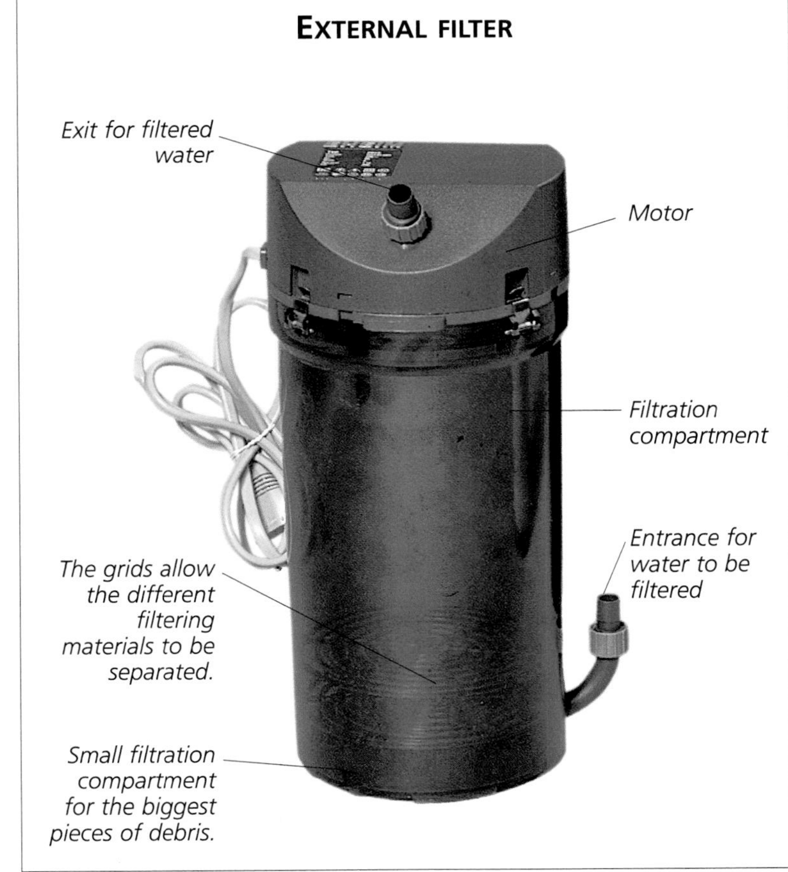

Principle of filtration

Several filters function by retaining suspended matter: this is mechanical filtration. The filtering media gradually become clogged and must be cleaned or changed. In order to transform nitrogenous substances and encourage the nitrogen cycle (see page 19), oxygen and good bacteria are required: this is biological or bacterial filtration. The biological filter therefore comprises a support that will be colonized by bacteria, with circulation of water to provide oxygen. The medium in mechanical filtration serves the same function as a biological filter once it has been colonized by bacteria.

The various filtration systems

- *The under-gravel filter*

The water travels from top to bottom through the sand and is taken back in under a platform that is slightly raised from the bottom of the tank. The water is then pushed out into the aquarium by means of an air-lift (see panel on page 239) fed by an air pump. Here, it is the sand which acts as the filtering medium, via a double action: first mechanical, as it retains the particles that are in suspension, and secondly biological, as the nitro-

The under-gravel filter

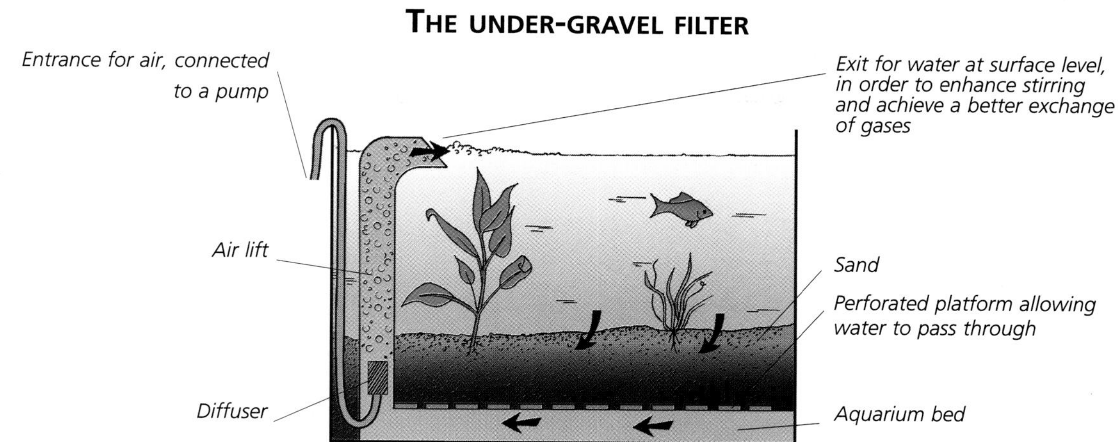

Advantages

– Inexpensive;
– easy to install;
– little or no maintenance;
– easy to camouflage;
– fed by an air pump (often the same as the one used by a diffuser);
– the water clears quickly

Disadvantages

– It must be put in before the bed, when the aquarium is being built;
– it can only, therefore, be removed by taking out all the decor, vegetation, and bed (which means reconstructing the aquarium);
– the sand builds up rapidly, according to its density, and must be cleaned (taking us back to the point above);
– draining the bed is not beneficial to most plants with roots;
– the base of the air-lift may become blocked if it is narrow (under 1 cm); it can be cleared by blowing down it, or by using a long thin rod;
– when the filter is inactive for a while, there is a risk of deoxygenating the bed, which can cause the development of toxic products.

The air-lift

This ingenious system allows water to be raised to a certain height and also helps to stir, and therefore oxygenate it. As a rough guide, an air-lift with a diameter of 3 cm, fed by an air pump, has a flow of several hundred liters per hour, with a water depth of 40 cm.
The air-lift makes it possible to use an under-gravel filter or a drip filter, or send water from a box filter into the aquarium. In order to reduce the noise of the bubbles and enhance the circulation of the water, its top section can be bent to be flush with the surface.

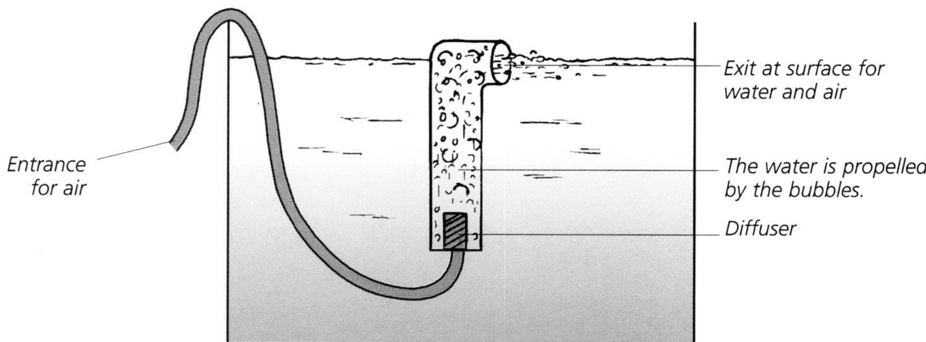

This type of air-lift is available in the aquarium trade. It can also be made at home, using a pipe and a PVC bend (2–3 cm in diameter). It is attached to the tank with suction pads.

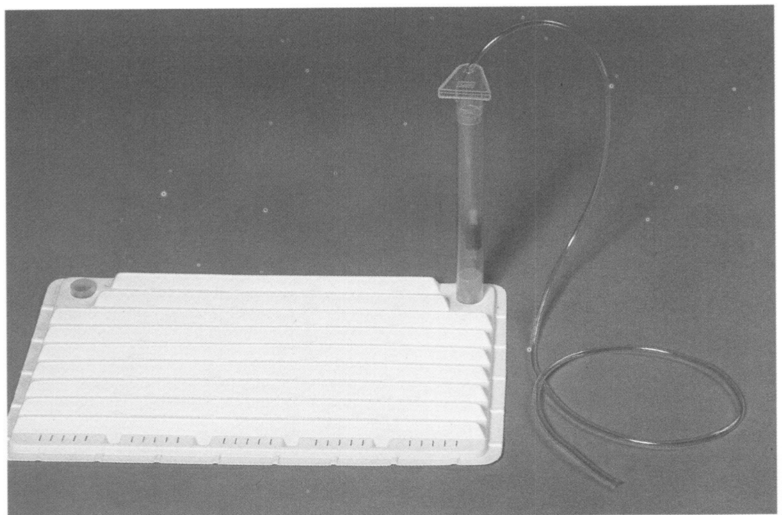

▲ *This under-gravel filter is used with a thick sediment that serves as a filtering medium*

gen cycle is created by the bacteria and the oxygen supplied by the circulation of the water. The size of the grains of sand is therefore important (for more detail, see Choosing the Bed, page 260), as it must allow both the water to pass through and the particles to be retained. This is why you should avoid sand that is too fine and, at the other extreme, sediment that is too thick.

The under-gravel filter used to be extremely popular, but these days it has given way to other techniques. However, it can be used in small temporary tanks or in a community tank, but with a slow and continuous flow, as a complement to another filtration system.

• *Small internal filters fed by air*

These also work with an air pump, but a small filtering medium, often made up of foam, replaces the sand. They are only effective in small aquariums with a capacity of 50 liters or less.

You can make this type of filter at home. Take a PVC receptacle that is easy to cut, ideally a bottle with a capacity of 1.5–2 liters. The use of foam tends to make the apparatus float to the surface, so you must insert a ballast to weigh it down. The upper part of the foam can be covered by coarse, heavy material, such as gravel or sand, serving not only as ballast but also as a pre-filtration element (see box below).

• *Small internal filters with an electric motor*

The motor makes it possible to draw up the water through a thick grid that blocks the passage of the larger pieces of debris. The water is then guided towards a filtering medium, such as foam or Perlon, before being expelled into the aquarium. This system works well but is insufficient for an aquarium with a volume of over 100 liters, although there are models available that can be adjusted according to the volume of water being treated and that will prove effective.

A QUICK WAY TO MAKE A SMALL INTERNAL FILTER

1. Diffuser
2. PVC pipe, with incisions all down one side, which will be set into the block of foam
3. Block of foam hollowed out in the center to allow room for the air-lift
4. Gravel (pre-filtration and ballast)
→ Direction of water

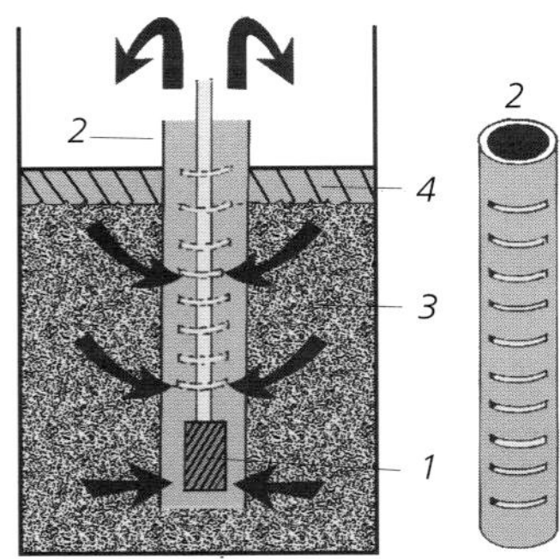

1. Diffuser
2. Air-lift
3. Block of foam
4. Water recovery chamber
5. PVC bottle
6. Gravel (pre-filtration and ballast)
→ Direction of water

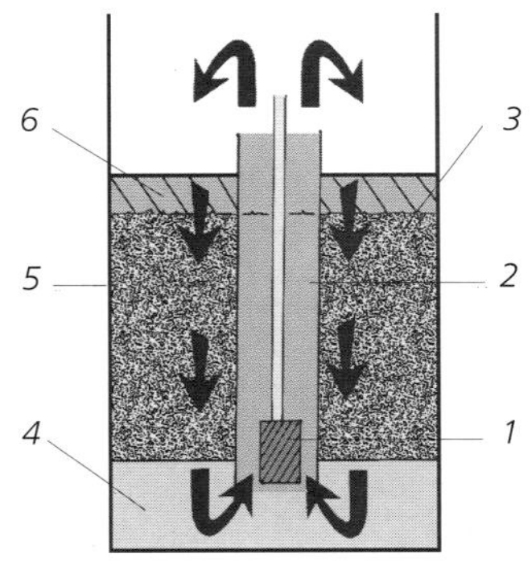

• *External filters*

The water siphoned into the aquarium passes into a filtration bay containing several filtering media and is sent back into the tank by means of an electric pump. There is a variety of models available, depending on the power of the pump and the volume of the filtration bay. It is even possible to find filters for garden ponds. These filters are highly efficient; their main disadvantage lies in the amount of

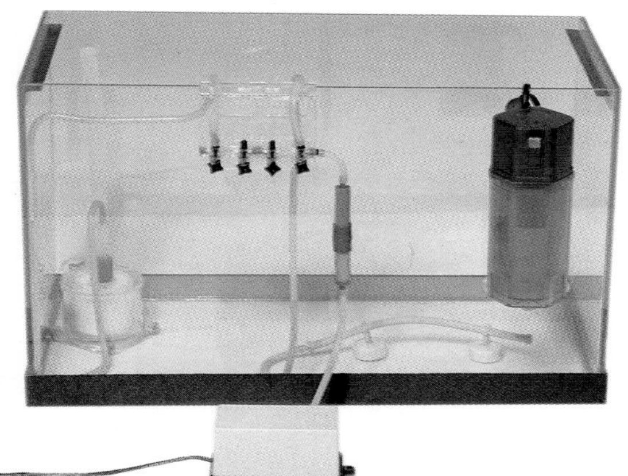

▲ *For a small tank, a small internal filter, using either an air-lift (left) or an electric motor (right) is sufficient.*

Small submerged filters with an electric motor

The outflow of the motor is sometimes excessive for the volume of the filtering medium. The latter must be cleaned regularly as it gets blocked up – it can be inspected through the PVC of the filtration compartment.

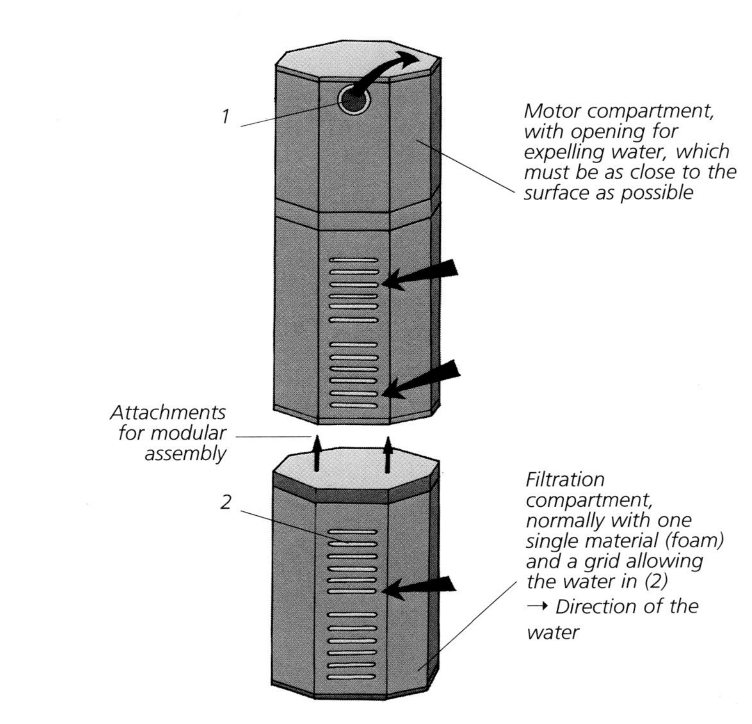

External filters with an electric motor

These are suitable for large aquariums – some have a flow of 1 m^3/hour – and contain materials with various particle sizes in the filtration compartment. They must be placed at the bottom of the tank to avoid any possible draining. These filters are more expensive than those already described, but, though they are mechanically very efficient, they are not effective in biological terms. The use of particles of different sizes prevents the apparatus from getting blocked up too quickly. It is easier to clean if you have the foresight to install faucets on the pipes.

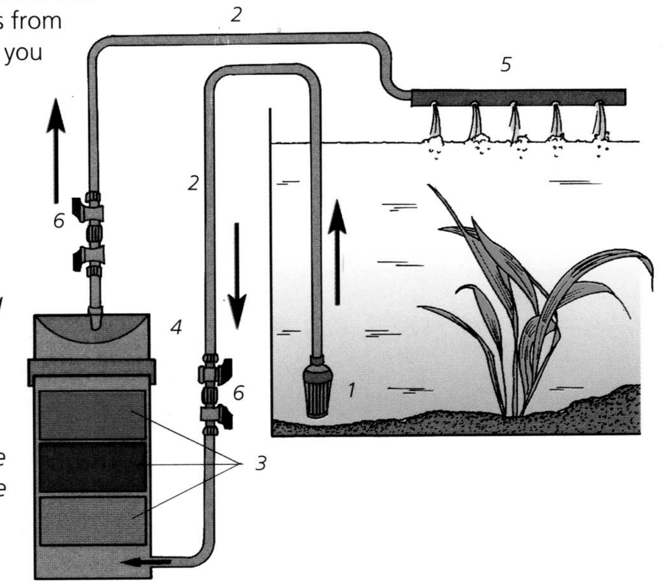

1. Strainer to prevent small fish or bits of debris getting sucked up and blocking the pipes
2. Semi-rigid pipes
3. Filtering media that get finer as the water advances
4. Motor compartment
5. Perforated rigid pipe which allows the water to be expelled at or above surface level, to enhance the exchange of gases
6. Faucets
Direction of the water

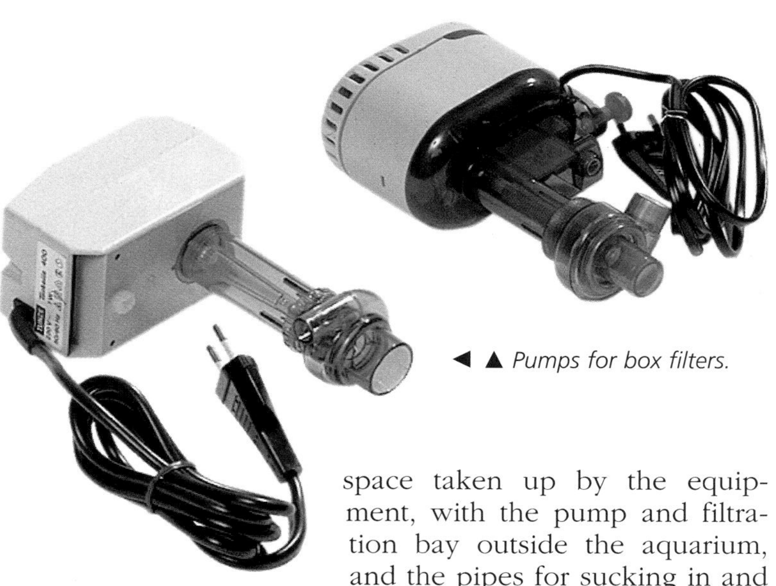

◄ ▲ *Pumps for box filters.*

▲ *A box filter integrated into an aquarium.*

space taken up by the equipment, with the pump and filtration bay outside the aquarium, and the pipes for sucking in and expelling the water inside.

• *Box filters*

These are sometimes built into some aquariums on the market, but they can also be added afterwards. In the latter case, they must be hidden by exterior fittings. The use of this type of filter is becoming more widespread, as it is easy to put into operation and maintain. In a large aquarium, however, its mechanism – the retention of particles – can prove insufficient, and so a complementary external filter must also be used.

Box filter

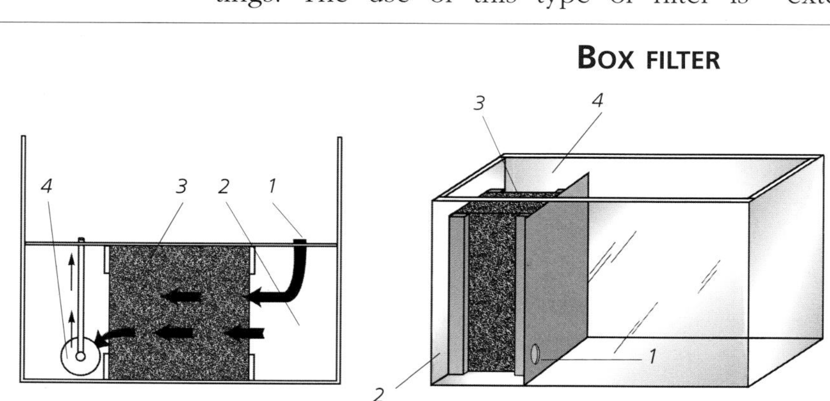

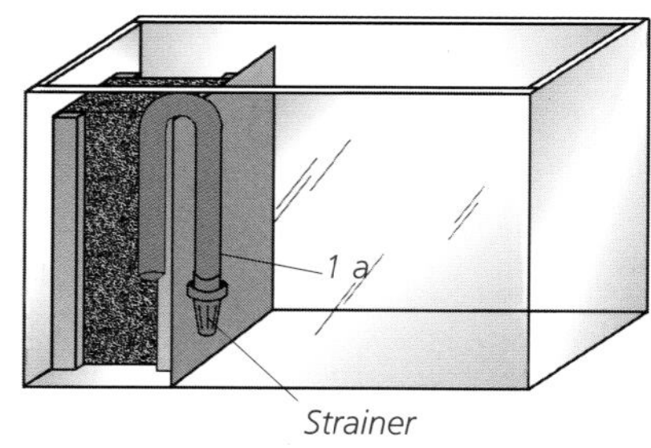

1. Entrance for water through a hole in the glass, protected by a grid. A siphon with a strainer on the end (1a) can also be used. The grid or strainer prevents fish passing through, apart from the smallest fry, which can sometimes be recovered in the box (2). Both must be maintained regularly, as various bits of debris, particularly vegetal matter, build up there, slowing down or even preventing the circulation of the water.
2. Box. This can contain a pre-filtration material, such as Perlon (page 248). In sea water, it is an ideal replacement for the protein skimmer (page 250).
3. Filtration foam (page 248). This retains fine particles and is the medium for the biological filtration. It is easier to maintain if it is divided into two approximately equal parts.
4. Sump for keeping water before it is sent back into the aquarium by a pump or air-lift. This part of the box filter can receive heating and aeration.
There is a variation on this system: the double box filter.

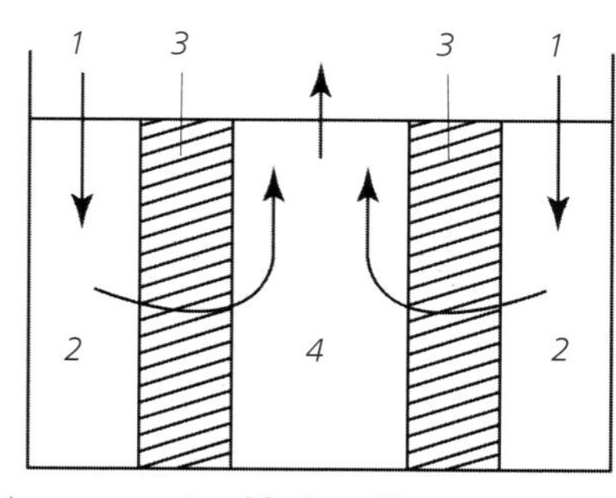

Double box filter

◀ Two box filters in the rear corners.

Box filter in central position, built into artificial decor recreating a cliff or rocky slope. ▶

The box filter is normally placed on one of the sides of the aquarium. Wherever it is put, it is vital that the volume of the filter is equal to at least 10% of the volume of the aquarium. In the diagrams above, the aquarium is seen from above, with the front at the bottom of the drawing; the foam is represented by hatching. The decor can be artificial.

• *Wet-dry filters*

Here, the filtering media are not totally submerged in the water, but are sprinkled by it.

This means that they are in permanent contact with the air, encouraging good oxygenation of the water and effective functioning of the nitrogen cycle. This technique is particularly popular among experienced fishkeepers with large freshwater or marine tanks.

There are two systems: the gutter filter, which has long been in use, and is easy to set up, and the more recent wet-dry filter, placed under the aquarium, which requires more space. In both of these cases, coarse pre-filtration media are desirable.

– Gutter filter: the water is pushed up from the aquarium by an electric pump or an air-lift to a horizontal gutter equipped with filtration material.

The water then passes along the gutter and falls as 'rain' into the tank, thereby enhancing the oxygenation. Chicanes can increase the time taken by the water's journey and, therefore, its oxygenation.

– Wet-dry filter under the aquarium: this is considered the ultimate filtration system by some aquarists. The main problem in setting it up lies in the incorporation of an outlet for excess water in a side wall or the back of the tank. The water descends into another tank and drains through the

Gutter filter equipped with thick filtering media (left) and finer ones (right). ▼

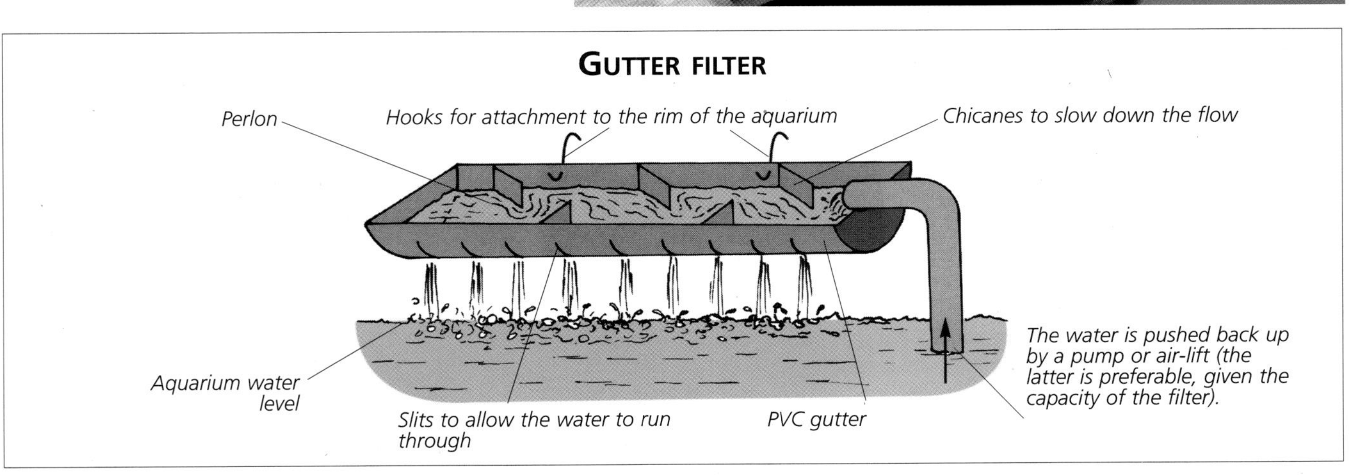

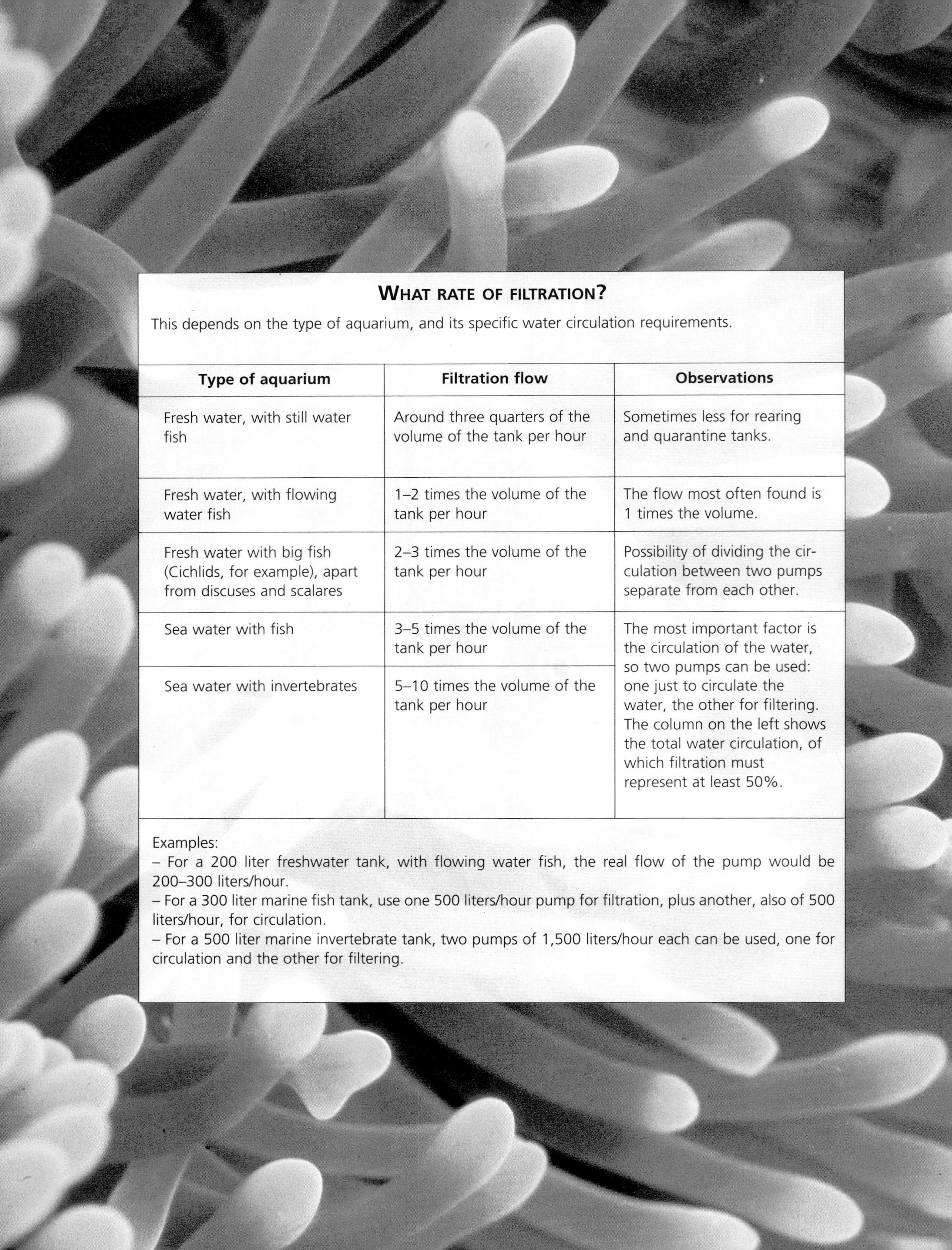

WHAT RATE OF FILTRATION?

This depends on the type of aquarium, and its specific water circulation requirements.

Type of aquarium	Filtration flow	Observations
Fresh water, with still water fish	Around three quarters of the volume of the tank per hour	Sometimes less for rearing and quarantine tanks.
Fresh water, with flowing water fish	1–2 times the volume of the tank per hour	The flow most often found is 1 times the volume.
Fresh water with big fish (Cichlids, for example), apart from discuses and scalares	2–3 times the volume of the tank per hour	Possibility of dividing the circulation between two pumps separate from each other.
Sea water with fish	3–5 times the volume of the tank per hour	The most important factor is the circulation of the water, so two pumps can be used: one just to circulate the water, the other for filtering. The column on the left shows the total water circulation, of which filtration must represent at least 50%.
Sea water with invertebrates	5–10 times the volume of the tank per hour	

Examples:
– For a 200 liter freshwater tank, with flowing water fish, the real flow of the pump would be 200–300 liters/hour.
– For a 300 liter marine fish tank, use one 500 liters/hour pump for filtration, plus another, also of 500 liters/hour, for circulation.
– For a 500 liter marine invertebrate tank, two pumps of 1,500 liters/hour each can be used, one for circulation and the other for filtering.

PRINCIPLE OF WET-DRY FILTER PLACED UNDER THE AQUARIUM

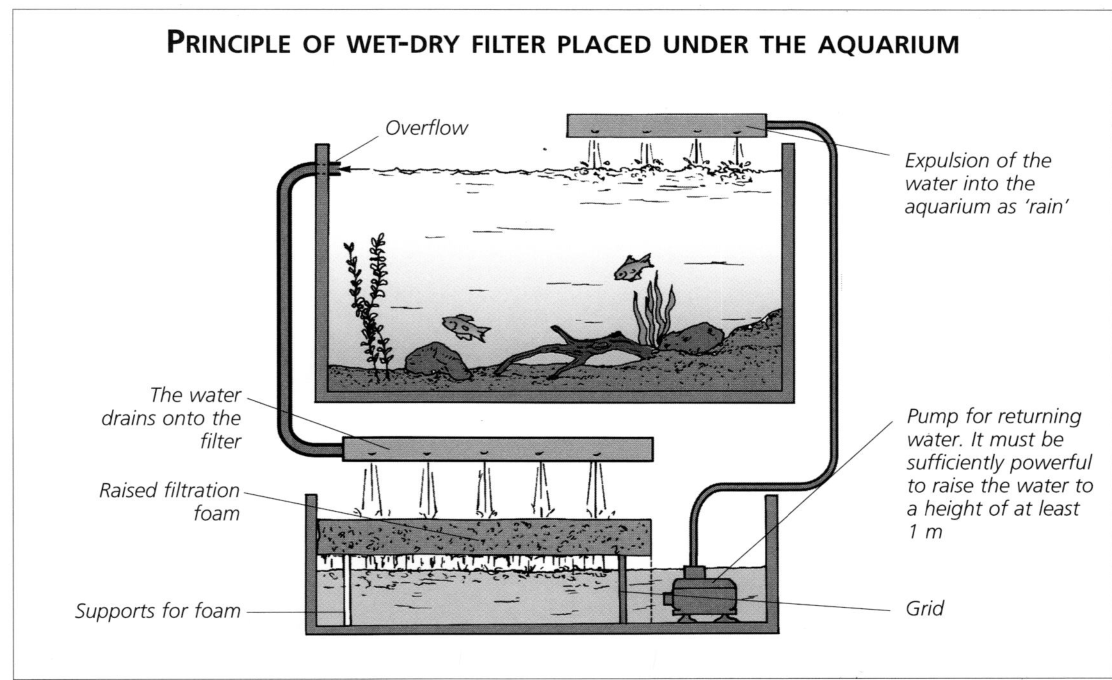

filtering medium, before being pumped back into the aquarium.
Some manufacturers market small internal wet-dry filters, which are intended for aquariums of a maximum volume of around 200 liters.

THE REAL POWER OF A PUMP

Here is an example based on a 1,000 liters/hour pump model, capable of reversing the flow to a height of 1 m:
In fact, a very slight curve should be visible,

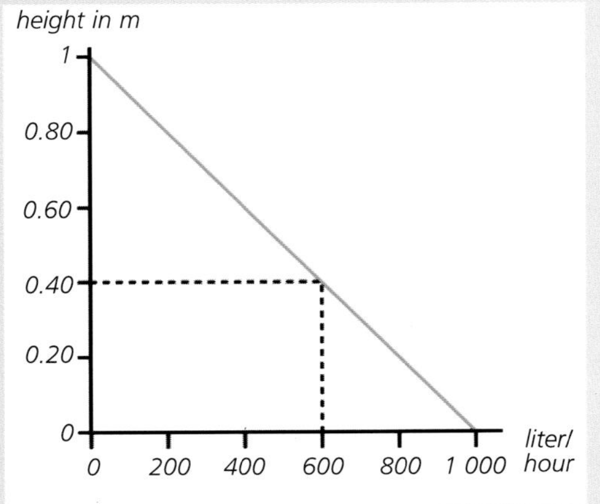

but the precision here is sufficient to see that the pump has a flow of no more than 600 liters/hour for transporting water to a height of 40 cm.

PUMPS

Pumps are used for box or wet-dry filters. In the case of marine aquariums, they are sometimes used merely to circulate the water, or simply surrounded by a block of foam.

• *A pump's power*

There are several brands of pump and various levels of power. The power level is calculated for the operation of a pump that does not raise the water level: the water is pumped and sent back to the same level.
Manufacturers supply two figures for every pump:
– the maximum flow, which corresponds to a flow reversal height of 0;
– the maximum water height to which the pump can take the water, corresponding to a flow close to 0.

The real power of a pump actually depends on the height of the water. ►

▲ The pre-filtration material is often coarse, in order to trap the bulkiest particles.

In some rare cases, the directions for use will include a graph that makes it possible to calculate the real power corresponding to each height of flow reversal, but on most occasions you will have to draw this yourself.

Uses, advantages, and disadvantages of the various filtering media

The filtering materials can be either natural – gravel, sand, clay, active carbon, peat, crushed oyster shells, rocks – or artificial – PVC, foam, Perlon, and various plastic materials.

Different materials correspond to specific functions.

For a coarse filtration, use gravel, rocks, sand, clay, or large pieces of PVC.

A fine filtration requires fine sand, foam, or Perlon; a biological filtration, sand, foam, cotton, or clay. Peat, active carbon, crushed oyster shells, or calcareous rocks are effective materials for exerting a chemical action.

With the exception of the last category, a filtering material must be chemically neutral, i.e. it must not modify the main characteristics of the water (pH, hardness, or density).

All the filtering media of variable volume (gravel, sand, earth, clay) are easier to handle if they are placed in a fine-meshed pouch (made from a net curtain or tights, for example).

• *Gravel and thick sand*

These are used as pre-filtration media to trap the largest pieces of debris, especially in the external filters. They are being increasingly replaced by artificial material, but fairly thick sand (grains of 2–3 mm) are still required in freshwater under-gravel filters.

• *Lava rocks*

These rocks, broken into pieces of various sizes, play a double role: mechanical, for suspended matter, and biological.The form and surface of the rocks encourage the presence of bacteria, as well as good water circulation of water.

• *Oyster shells and calcareous rocks*

These play the same role, but also release

Which filter for which aquarium?

The type of filter depends on how the tank is being used, but also on the hobbyist's budget; you must therefore look for the best quality/price ratio.

The use of two complementary techniques makes it possible to obtain the maximum efficiency in biological filtration. Also, this reduces the risk if one filter is affected by a technical or biological problem.

Type of aquarium	Volume	Filtration system	Observations
Rearing, quarantine	Under 100 liters	Under-gravel filter, small internal filter, powered by air or electricity.	The under-gravel filter is not the most practical solution.
Fresh water	100–200 liters	Box filter or external filter	If the tank does not have an in-built box section, choose the external filter.
Fresh water	Over 200 liters	Box or external filter	The two systems can be used together.
Sea water	Over 300 liters	Box filter, external filter, wet-dry filter	These three techniques can be used together.

▲ *Lava rocks provide a good bacterial support.*

▲ *Balls of clay can be used for pre-filtration.*

moderate amounts of calcium carbonate into the water going through them. They are therefore used to maintain a high degree of hardness in some types of tanks, such as regional East African aquariums, for instance.

They must be pounded and crushed, and then rinsed carefully, in order to eliminate the fine particles produced.

• *Clay*

Clay, in the form of balls of a few mm to 1 cm in diameter, provides a good bacterial support. It is rarely used on its own, but rather as a complement to another material, to ensure pre-filtration.

• *Peat*

Peat (see page 16) is placed in a filter to acidify the water passing through it; therefore, its main role is not filtration, although it can trap some particles. It is used in fresh water to obtain the low pH required to keep and reproduce certain species (see South American aquariums, page 35, and also Cyprodontidae, or killies, page 95). Be aware that peat turns water an amber yellow color.

It is, therefore, not at all advisable to apply peat designed for horticultural use, as it contains substances that can be dangerous in an aquarium. Suitable peat is commercially available, although you will have to proceed by trial and error and do some tests before finding the quantity needed to maintain a specific pH.

Perlon retains fine particles. It is an easy material to use. ▶

• *Active carbon*

Active carbon is obtained by calcining (burning) vegetable matter under very precise conditions. It is a very porous material with properties useful to fishkeepers. It fixes organic coloring substances, which makes it possible to obtain really clear water. It also fixes some medicines, especially those based on colorants. In this case, a filter is only used to eliminate a medicine, once the treatment has been completed. What is more, active carbon traps smells. Its main deficiency is that it loses these distinguishing properties quite quickly. It offers a good support for bacteria, but no more so than other more practical filtering media.

To sum up, active carbon is a material with very specific applications, to be used only in fresh water and not in sea water, and it must be rinsed in warm water before use.

• *Perlon*

This artificial material comes in the form of intertwined filaments. Be careful: it

▲ There is a very wide range of filtering materials; often the most desirable is the one offering the largest surface area for trapping bacteria.

must not be confused with glass wool, which is highly unsuitable for aquariums, as it can release tiny fragments into the water. It is generally used in association with foam as the first filtering material, especially so in box and wet-dry filters.

• *Foam*

This synthetic polyester foam has open pores, like that found in mattresses or cushions. This material is very fashionable in the aquarium trade these days and it seems to offer nothing but advantages: it is light, neutral, easy to handle and cut, as well as being cheap. Furthermore, it provides a highly effective bacterial support, and is also excellent for mechanical filtration. The foam generally used has a density of 20 kg/m^3, and its porosity is ideal both for retaining suspended particles and for allowing bacteria to develop. Generally speaking, the experience of a great many aquarists and public aquariums has shown that a thickness of 8 cm, divided into two more or less equal parts for easier upkeep, is usually sufficient for filtration.It is possible to find some commercially available, or else home-made, filters entirely composed of foam – small internal filters or external filters, both box and wet-dry – and these are also completely satisfactory.

► Polyester foam comes in various porosities, the ideal one corresponding to a density of foam of 20 kg/m^3.

• *Various plastic-based materials*

Different types of plastic material, such as PVC, can be used to make the filtration or pre-filtration elements: small pieces of pipe around 1 cm in diameter, balls, cubes with an openwork design, etc. The list is endless, and contains not only items found in the aquarium trade but also recycled domestic materials.

• *Combinations of filtering media*

When several filtering materials are found in the same filter, the water must successively pass through materials decreasing in grain size.
The coarsest materials serve as a pre-filter for large pieces of debris, while the others retain the finer particles. All these filtering media enhance the development of bacterial colonies that convert nitrogenous products, with pride of place being taken by foam and clay balls.

• *Cleaning the filtering media*

The filtering media progressively accumulate particles, at a rate depending on granule size, the speed at which the water flows through them and finally the amount of suspended matter it contains. When they are saturated, they can

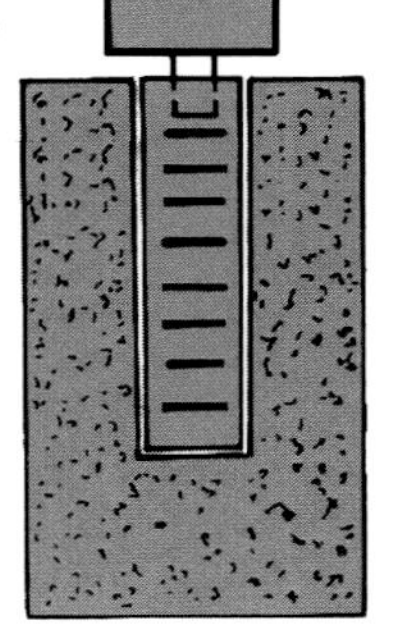

Making a foam filter in an emergency

The sucking nozzle of an electric pump is extended with a pipe – PVC or semi-rigid plastic, such as a garden hose – with a series of slits down the sides. This is inserted into a block of foam with the center already cut out with a knife or blade. The water has to pass through the foam, before being taken in through the slit pipe and returned to the aquarium. This quick and easy filter works well when improvisation is called for to keep an aquarium in operation.

▲ *A pump, a PVC pipe with slits down the sides, and a block of foam make up a filter that can be quickly put into operation.*

be cleaned with warm tap water, without any detergent or soap, until clear rinsing water is hence obtained.

Aquarists who have several tanks wash several pieces of foam together in a washing machine, though obviously without any washing powder. It is unfortunate that cleaning eliminates the large majority, or indeed all, of the useful bacteria. The filter will therefore be effective for particles but will no longer be able to play any biological role. To alleviate this problem, you can clean only half the filtering media each time: the bacteria living in the unwashed part will be sufficient to purify the water and will quickly recolonize the other half. If you are using two filters, you can, of course, clean one at a time. If the aquarium has to remain empty, in the meantime the filtering media can be put into the filter of another aquarium, and in this way they will still collect bacteria and can quickly be put back into service. It is vital not to interrupt the nitrogen cycle in a biological filter, as this may give rise to toxic compounds.

Filtration of sea water

Filtration of sea water: special points

It is necessary to discuss separately certain issues specific to sea water. The ideal solution would be to use two filters: one with a moderate flow, mainly for the conversion of nitrogenous matter (a box or wet-dry filter), the other with a stronger flow, primarily serving a mechanical function. An under-gravel filter can also be used to enhance the circulation of water in the generally fairly thick sediment, but it must not be used on its own. One effective combination consists of a reverse-flow under-gravel filter coupled with an external filter (see box).

The filtration flow must be 3–5 times the volume of the tank per hour for fish, and up to 10 times the volume for invertebrates, especially Anthozoans. Once again, foam is the perfect material, providing it is no more than 6–8 cm thick. If thick materials, such as crushed oyster shells or PVC materials, are used, then the foam can be thicker. Never use peat or active carbon.

Equipment specific to sea water

Marine fish are more sensitive to the quality of the water than freshwater species. This calls for the use of equipment to complement the filtration system, in order to obtain water of the highest quality.

Reverse-flow under-gravel filter

The water passes through the substrate from the bottom to the top, more for oxygenation than filtration. There are no particles to form sediment, as these are sent back in suspension into the water, which is filtered by an exterior system before being propelled under the sediment.

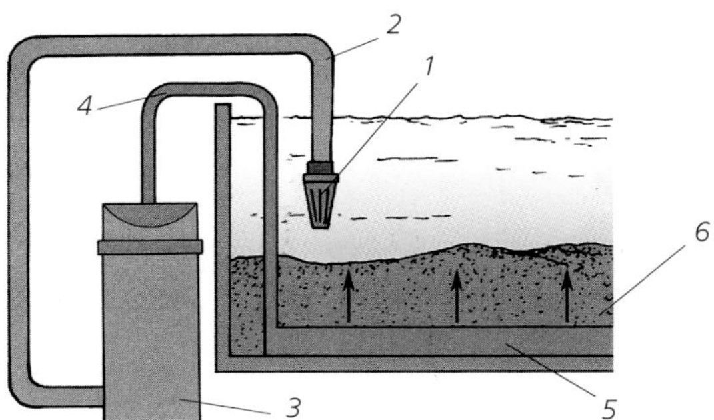

1. *Strainer*
2. *Suction of water*
3. *External filter with electric motor*
4. *Return of water under the filter*
5. *Under-gravel filter*
6. *Passage of water from bottom to top*

This type of filtration is sometimes used in large marine aquariums containing fish, thereby avoiding any possible problems resulting from a lack of oxygen in the bed.

• *The protein skimmer*

This system enables the aquarist to carry out partial chemical purification of the water by eliminating certain dissolved substances, such as proteins.

The principle is simple: the water is agitated in a confined space, leading to the precipitation of a number of substances. A frothy foam, often yellow-colored, is produced, and this is then eliminated via the overflow.

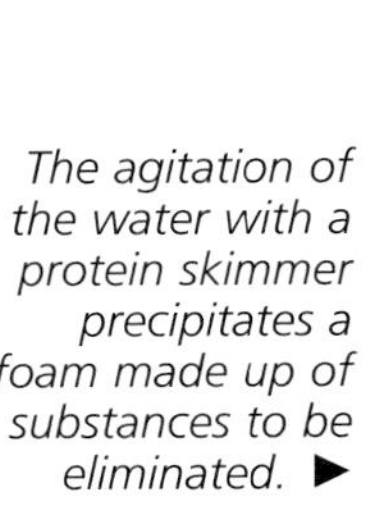

The agitation of the water with a protein skimmer precipitates a foam made up of substances to be eliminated. ▶

The protein skimmer is an independent element that can be placed anywhere in the tank. It can also complement the filtration system, reducing the burden of a box filter when it is installed in its first section.

Also very often employed as a preventive measure in tanks containing fish, the protein skimmer is not used if the tank is not overloaded, and if a biological filter is already working effectively.

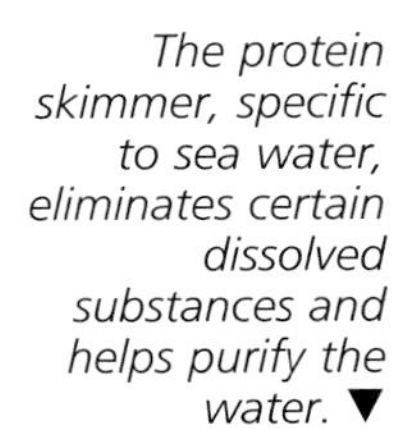

The protein skimmer, specific to sea water, eliminates certain dissolved substances and helps purify the water. ▼

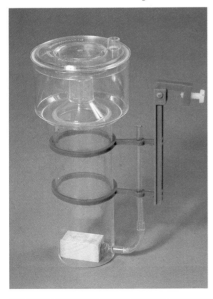

The protein skimmer is recommended for an invertebrate tank, especially one with corals and anemones, although it does eliminate some substances that are absorbed by invertebrates.

Aquariums of up to 300 liters use a protein skimmer fed by a fine-bubble diffuser, and therefore supported by an air pump. Beyond these volumes, plan on installing two protein skimmers, or invest in one fed by an electric injection pump.

• *The purifying action of UV rays*

Ultraviolet rays are luminous, but invisible to the human eye. Some of them are responsible for tanning (UV A and B), while others, with a shorter wavelength (UV C), have germicidal properties and kill a large number of bacteria and viruses.

These UV rays are used for the bacteriological purification of water, especially as their action is selective, as they do not destroy the "good" bacteria of the nitrogen cycle.

The field of action of these rays is limited – somewhere in the order of a few centimeters. The water must therefore pass close to the source of the rays, at a speed which allows it to receive sufficient amounts of their luminosity. In order for the rays to exert their maximum effect, the water must be clear, and therefore well filtered.

UV sterilizers are commercially available. Again, the principle is simple: a lamp, usually a tube, sends out rays, and the water is pumped around it. The power of a UV system and the flow of the water around the lamp vary according to the volume of water being treated. The lamp is completely watertight, thanks to a quartz sheath that allows this type of ray to pass through. The blue-violet color given off by the lamp only serves to show that it is functioning. Do not look directly at the source of the UV rays, as they are dangerous for the eyes – this is why the sterilizer usually has an opaque covering.

The lifespan of a lamp operating for 24 hours a day is around 5 or 6 months. However, the quality of the rays usually deteriorates after 4 months, and so they should be replaced three times a year.

Volume of water (in liters)	Power of the lamp (in W)	Flow of water (in liters/hour)
up to 100	8	50
100–500	15	200
500–1000	30	500

VITAL TOOLS FOR THE WELL-EQUIPPED AQUARIST

There are certain useful – indeed, indispensable – accessories that an aquarist always needs at hand for everyday chores or the upkeep of the aquarium: a tool kit, in fact.

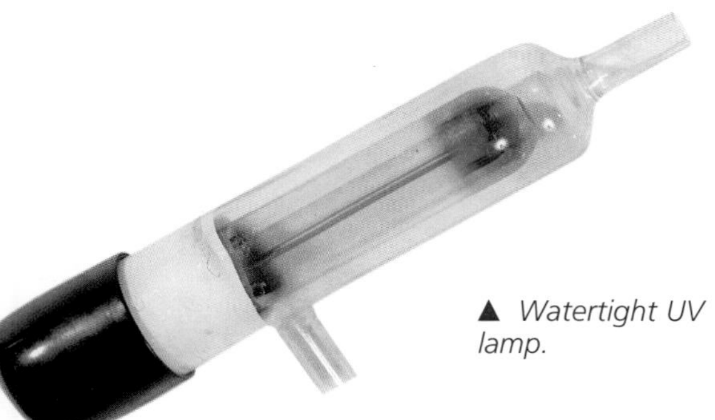

▲ *Watertight UV lamp.*

Thermometer

Absolutely essential. An alcohol thermometer, colored blue or red, is sufficiently precise, although variations of more than 1°C can be recorded between different thermometers. Although mercury thermometers are more precise, they are also a little more difficult to read. Whatever model is used, the thermometer is put into the water, away from the source of heating, to avoid being directly affected by its warmth. It can be attached to a weight, wedged into rocks, or stuck with a suction pad.
External thermometers with liquid crystals have failed to convince most aquarists, as their precision is not reliable.

Various models of thermometers are available, some in conjunction with a density meter. Not all have the same degree of precision. ▶

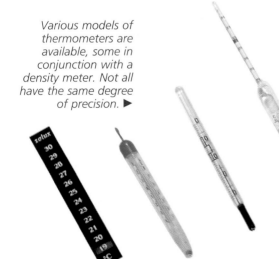

Hydrometer

We have already discussed this (page 25), but it must be stressed that it is a vital instrument for monitoring the density of sea water, i.e. the salt content.

Equipment for analyzing water

Several brands of simple tests, used to analyze water, are on the market. They generally work on the basis of a change in the color of the water, which must be compared with a scale printed on the packaging. They are sold separately or in complete kits, although it is possible to restock a basic product when it runs out, without having to buy the whole kit again. Four tests are more or less obligatory in fresh water: general hardness (GH), carbonate hardness (CH), nitrites, and pH. The last three are equally indispensable in sea water. There are other parameters that can also be monitored by small pieces of analysis equipment: nitrates, ammonia, oxygen, carbon dioxide, iron, and calcium (for marine invertebrate aquariums).

Landing nets

These are obviously absolutely essential for catching moving animals. The size of the latter dictates the size of the net, along with the space available for handling it. Choose a small net for small fish or aquariums with elaborate decor.
However, it is not easy to catch fish in a landing net. Aquarists will almost invariably tell you: as soon as you want to catch a particular fish, it seems to see you coming! Once the net is put the water, pandemonium breaks loose, with foreseeable consequences: wounded animals and the decor, both vegetable and inert, turn topsy-turvy.
One simple trick consists of putting the net into the tank at night, before switching off the lights. The fish will get used to its presence, and so it will be easier to catch the following morning, when you switch the lights back on.

The size of a landing net depends not only on that of the fish being caught but also on the space available in the aquarium for handling it. ▼

Magnets to clean the panes and vacuum cleaners connected to an air pump are commonplace instruments for tank maintenance. ▼ ►

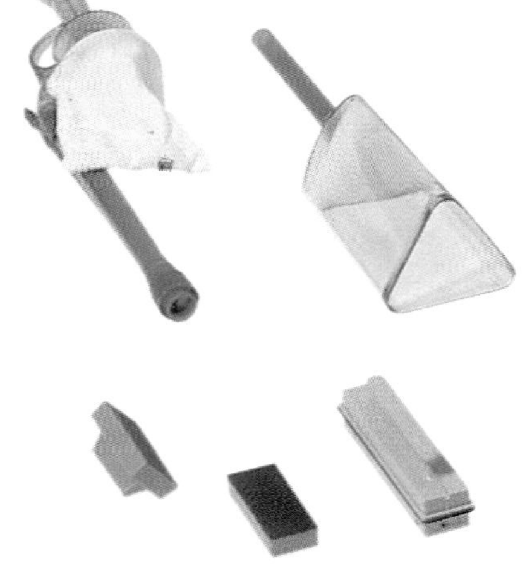

Another possibility is the use of two nets, with one remaining stationary to receive the fish being pushed forward by the second. Landing nets must be disinfected regularly with bleach (particularly after handling sick fish), and then rinsed several times.

Miscellaneous equipment

You can also stock up with some other pieces of equipment that often turn out to very practical:
– a long pipe for filling or draining the aquarium;
– plastic food containers to hold water;

► *Garden pincers are very practical in deeper tanks.*

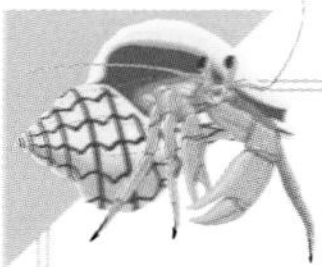

– pincers for planting, though many aquarists prefer using their hands;
– a scraper furnished with a razor blade or a small abrasive scouring pad, for cleaning the algae on the glass panes;
– a mini vacuum cleaner connected to the air pump, to siphon off waste products;
– suction pads, faucets, nozzles and connectors for air and water pipes, available from commercial aquarium stores;
– an electronic timer for programming the lighting;
– a notebook enabling you to keep track of certain tasks: purchase dates for fish, results of the analysis of water, maintenance schedule, etc.

The latter is particularly recommended for beginners, and also allows them to record their personal observations on reproduction, sickness and the general behavior of their fish.

Cables and pipes: labeling

A fully equipped aquarium quickly accumulates electric cables and pipes for air and water and these have an irritating tendency to get mixed up, meaning that it is sometimes difficult to find the right socket, or the pipe that needs to be disconnected. To find them more easily, just stick a self-adhesive label at each end of a cable or pipe and write on it the name of the corresponding element. In the case of aeration, for example, a first label near the pump indicates which diffusers it is feeding, while a second just before the point where the pipes enter the aquarium makes it easier to locate the diffusers in question.

▲ *Small plastic tanks sometimes prove useful for maintenance operations, or for providing a temporary home for plants and fish when an aquarium is being repaired.*

A BALANCED AQUARIUM

Although an aquarium constitutes a self-contained environment, it nevertheless evolves: fish get bigger and reproduce, while plants grow. Similarly, the water undergoes changes that may not always be visible – the nitrate concentration increases but the mineral salts depleate – which is why it is important to analyze it regularly. As for the bed, this is enriched by numerous organic substances (animal excreta, surplus food) that will normally be converted into mineral elements.

MAINTENANCE

The equilibrium of an aquarium is fragile and can rapidly be disrupted if a few simple rules are contravened. The first of these rules requires a daily inspection of the tank and its occupants, at feeding time, for example. In this way you can detect any sickness, worrying fish behavior, or an abnormal water color.

The second rule is to maintain the aquarium. When undertaken on a regular basis, the upkeep of an aquarium is not time-consuming, and only demands 1 or 2 hours a week. Some operations need to be performed every day, others less often.

Water analysis

Bad water can cause problems unnoticeable to even the most discerning eye, so it is important to monitor its quality regularly. In both fresh and sea water, three main parameters have to be monitored: the temperature, the pH, and the nitrites. Additionally, in sea water, the density must be checked, and, in fresh water, the hardness.

◄ The more regular the maintenance of an aquarium, the less time-consuming it becomes.

▲ Certain parameters of the water, such as the pH, must be monitored once or twice a week.

Checking the equipment

You must also keep a close watch on the systems for lighting, heating, aeration, and filtration.

As regards the lighting, make sure that the electrical contacts do not get rusty (especially with salt water). In the aeration system, the small lozenge which filters the air needs to be changed twice a year. The diffusers eventually get blocked by algae or calcium. It is best to change them, but they can also be unblocked. Clean the filtering medium regularly. Any malfunction in the heating will quickly be reflected in a decrease or increase in the temperature: in this case, it is necessary to change the equipment.

Cleaning the panes

The glass panes of the aquarium can accumulate green or brown algae (page 194), calcium, or biological deposits (bacteria and non-pathogenic micro-organ-

▲ *Scrapers allow access right to the bottom of the panes, to get rid of any unwanted algae.*

isms). These deposits vary from one aquarium to the next and do not in themselves represent any danger to fish – the damage sustained by an aquarium through a dirty front pane lies more on the aesthetic plane. So the panes must be scraped with a razor blade or one of the small devices found in specialist stores.
Domestic scouring pads can also be effective, but in the long term they scratch the glass of the aquarium. Do not forget to clean the glass lid, which gradually gets covered with algae and calcium (or salt, in a marine tank) on the inside and dust on the outside, restricting the passage of the light needed by plants.

Looking after the bed

An assortment of debris piles up on the bed: fish excreta, bits of plants, surplus food, and sometimes, in a quiet corner, even fish corpses. All this disrupts not only the visual harmony but also the balance of the tank as more oxygen is required to degrade this debris. These are two very good reasons for getting rid of it by siphoning (see box, page 255). Small specially designed vacuum cleaners are available in the aquarium trade, but you can also use a flexible pipe draining out into a plastic bowl, a sink, or a toilet.

Changing the water

Partial water changes, at regular intervals, are one of the keys to success in fishkeeping. The combination of this operation with siphoning eliminates both assorted detritus and some of the nitrates which eventually accumulate.
The clear water that is introduced supplies some mineral elements and provides a stimulus for the aquarium: the growth of fish, the triggering of egg-laying, and the growth of plants.
After 2 months or so you will see a striking contrast with aquariums in which the water has not been renewed. A change of 5–10% of the volume per week is therefore recommended. This obviously demands a stock of water with identical characteristics to that of the aquarium (especially pH, hardness, and salinity).

Parameters to be monitored

Parameters	Frequency of monitoring	Observations
Temperature	Every day	It must not vary by more than 1°C.
Nitrites	Once or twice a week	Ideally, they should be totally absent.
pH	Once or twice a week	The photosynthesis process and the respiration of animals cause variations from day to day.
Density	Once a week	Only in sea water. It must not vary by more than one or two units.
Total hardness	Once a week	In fresh water. Slight variations are not abnormal.
Carbon dioxide	Once a fortnight (sometimes less)	Mainly in quite densely planted aquariums.
Calcium	Once a week	In sea water, in aquariums containing corals.

In the event of any serious problem, you must immediately change one third of the water, then 10% per day for the following 5 days. The substitute water must always present the normal characteristics of the water to be replaced (particularly pH, hardness, and density).

A TRICK FOR SIPHONING OFF WASTE

People who live with aquarists dread siphoning time, as it often leads to floods! The pipes can be too flexible, with a tendency to slip out of the aquarium or the container for the siphoned water.
The trick is to get hold of a washing machine draining pipe or a snorkel, and slide the siphoning pipe inside it, making it possible to bend it over the side of the container or tank. A stiff bent pipe can also be used to siphon in the less accessible parts of an aquarium (grottoes, for example).

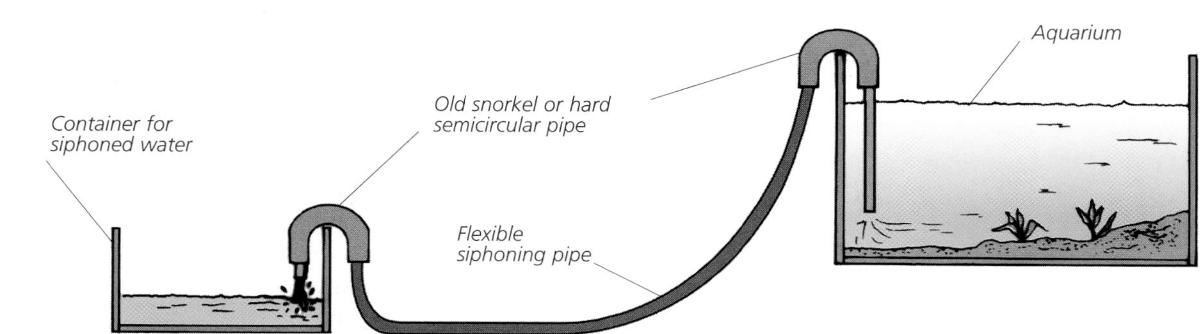

The ideal solution is daily renewal of a small amount, with the help of a drip (see page 256). This technique is becoming more common among experienced aquarists. It requires a special installation, and above all an overflow for the aquarium – equipment which is not readily available in every case.
However, many fishkeepers find this system the ideal solution:
– the maintenance is reduced, as the water changes are less frequent;
– there are no abrupt variations in the environment;
– various substances, such as nitrates, are regularly eliminated and therefore do not accumulate;
– it entails a regular, though limited, supply of the various substances contained in the water (mineral salts, trace elements);
– the pH is stabilized;
– this method seems to restrict the growth of certain somewhat unsightly algae.
A word of wisdom: the water siphoned off a freshwater aquarium is excellent for watering house plants as it contains dissolved organic matter!

Evaporation and the water level

The water in an aquarium evaporates. This has no ecological consequences, but it does mean that the surface of the water comes into view at the top of the panes, which is hardly attractive. This must therefore be adjusted on a regular basis, usually at the same time as you make a partial water change.
After a while a regular increase in the hardness of fresh water (or the salinity of sea water) is noticeable: the water that evaporates from the surface is fresh water containing no salts, even in sea water, and so there is a progressive concentration of salt or other mineral substances in the aquarium.
To avoid this problem, replace the evaporated water with very soft or demineralized water in order to readjust the hardness or density. This can be done when you change the water, by slightly diluting the new water with fresh water. Readjustment of the water level is not necessary if you are using a drip that functions automatically.

◀ When stemmed plants grow too big, you can consider taking cuttings.

A SIMPLE DRIP TECHNIQUE

Two points must be taken into account: the arrival of the new water and the overflow of the aquarium water.
Do-it-yourself experts may consider making a connection with the plumbing pipes in the home, but there is a more simple solution. Take a PVC container, such as a jerry can with a faucet, for use above the water level of the tank. For aesthetic reasons, this is hidden in a cupboard or other piece of furniture. A flexible PVC pipe can be used to connect the faucet with the aquarium.
Water from the aquarium can flow into another container, larger than the first, to avoid any risks of overflowing (diagram **1**).

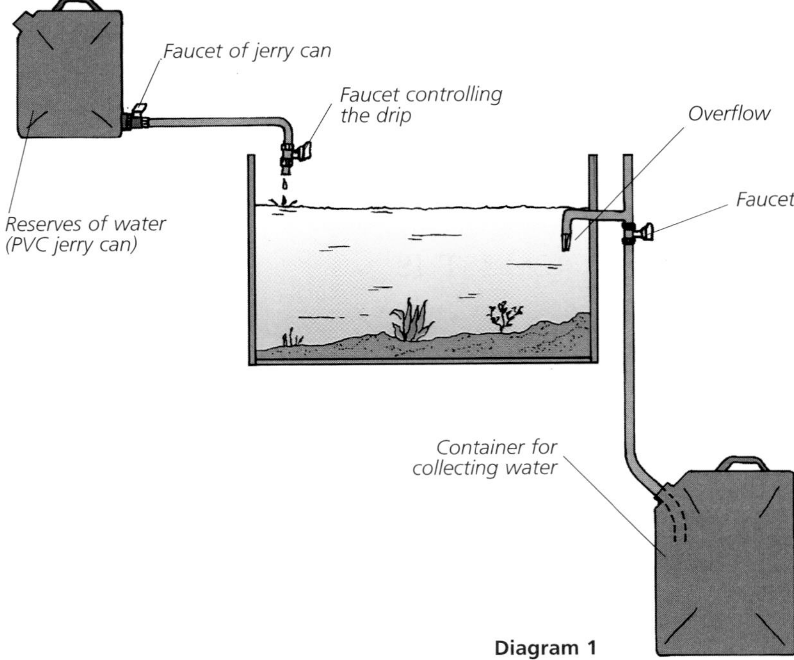

Diagram 1

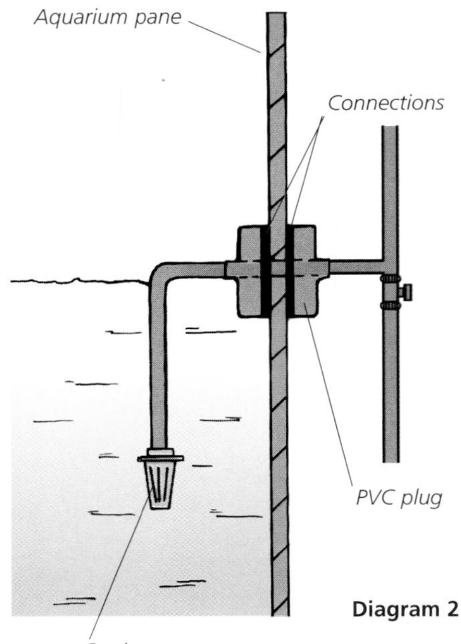

Diagram 2

There remains the problem of the aquarium overflow. You can get a glass store to make a hole in a side or rear pane when you are mounting or buying the tank. Insert a PVC plug with connections for the evacuation pipe; do not forget to also provide an escape for the water (diagram **2**).

There is another solution: use a siphon that functions continuously (diagram **3**). The water level can be regulated by raising or lowering loop A, and a small diameter (1 cm) ensures the continuity of the operation.
This device can easily be attached to the inside and outside of the aquarium with suction pads. It is best not to put a diffuser near the entry of the siphon, as there is a danger that bubbles may interfere with its functioning. Always put a strainer on the end to avoid any small fish or large pieces of debris from getting sucked up and causing a blockage. The system is set in motion by sucking on the pipe. You will have to adjust the drip by trial and error, after calculating the volume that needs to be renewed (around 1% of the volume of the aquarium per day).

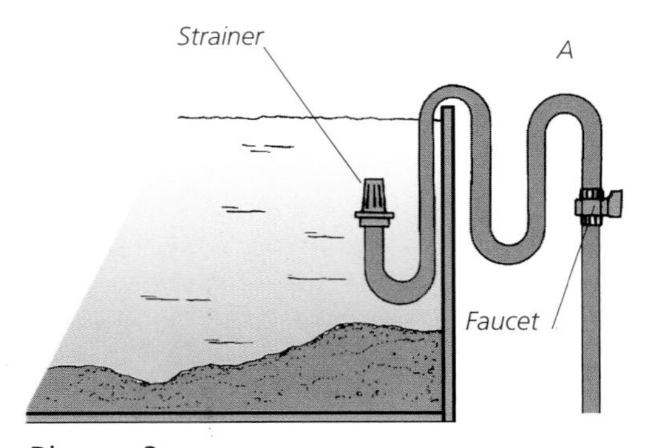

Diagram 3

Maintaining the vegetation

When you are siphoning on the bed, you must remove any dead leaves that may have fallen. Likewise, cut off, with a razor blade or scissors, any leaves that are starting to rot.

When the plants need a new lease of life, you can take cuttings or use another means of vegetative multiplication.

Liquid or solid fertilizer should be added regularly; the instructions on the pack will tell you how often and at what rate each product needs to be added.

When the aquarist is away

What do you do if you are away for more than a day? What will happen to the aquarium? This depends on the length of the absence, and certain precautions must be taken, especially for vacations.

Short absences do not represent a problem. Freshwater fish can go without food for two weeks, or even three in the most robust species, but marine fish, on the other hand, cannot endure fasting for more than a week. This only applies to adults, as the fry must always be fed on a regular basis.

A long absence

There are two options for a long absence:
– the first consists of using an automatic food distributor controlled by a timer, which can only be used with dry food;
– the second is finding a friend kind enough to feed your fish for you – preferably another aquarist who will monitor the feeding and the aquarium just as you would. If your friend is not a hobbyist, then you must prepare daily doses of dry food and leave him or her some instructions, in order to avoid any overfeeding. (However, this friend will not be obliged to drop by your home every day, one or two visits a week being generally sufficient). Plants can go without lighting for one week, but after any longer period they turn yellow and gradually wither. It is therefore advisable to install an automatic timer that will switch the aquarium lighting on and off at specific times. This means that there is no need to let the sunlight into your home and so you can close your shutters. This is particularly relevant in summer, as it avoids any excessive increase in the temperature, which will have repercussions on the aquarium.

◄ The use of batteries makes some food distributors automatic and very practical.

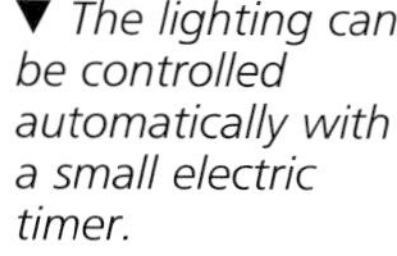

▼ The lighting can be controlled automatically with a small electric timer.

Vacations

• *Before leaving:*
– check the pH, nitrites, temperature, hardness, or density;
– check the equipment;
– clean the filtering media and panes; do the siphoning;
– increase the frequency (but not the quantity) of water changes;
– put the vegetation in order by trimming the plants and taking cuttings. You can also add plants with fine leaves for herbivorous fish, if they are not going to receive any other food;
– slightly overfeed the fish for a few days before your departure;
– switch on the automatic lighting system and, if you are using it, an automatic food distributor;
– make a final check the night or morning before you leave.

• *When you get back:*
– switch off the automatic devices and generally put the tank in order (siphoning, panes, filtering media, vegetation);
– change 5–10% of the water every day for a few days;
– give the fish smaller portions of food than normal – if possible including live prey or fresh food – and gradually increase these amounts until they reach the usual level.

▲ Automatic food distributor with a mains connection.

The water color, evidence of a good balance

The water in an aquarium should usually be clear and transparent. Coloring can appear gradually (yellowish or amber) or more quickly (turbid, milky, or green water).

Water color	Causes, problems	What to do
Turbid, milky.	Development of bacteria due to malfunctioning filter or overfeeding.	– Change 30% of the water immediately, then repeat the operation 48 hours later. – Check the filter and the filtering media. – Put a UV lamp into operation (in a marine aquarium). – Reduce the food for a few days.
Yellowish or amber (an amber color is normal when the water is acidified with peat, or when there are roots in the aquarium).	Accumulation of organic materials due to overpopulation, overfeeding, or a malfunctioning or undersized filter.	– Change 30% of the water immediately, then repeat the operation 48 hours later. – Check the filter, increase the strength of the filtration. – Reduce the numbers of fish, feed reasonably. – Put in an aerator or increase its strength if there already is one (in a marine aquarium). – Increase the oxygenation.
Green water (a rare phenomenon).	Proliferation of microscopic planktonic algae (maybe due to an excessive "richness" in the aquarium).	– Change 10–20% of the volume of the tank every day. – Do not illuminate the aquarium for a few days. – Increase the filtration rate, then thoroughly clean the filtering media a few days later. – Prevent any sunlight from reaching the tank.

POTENTIAL PROBLEMS – AND HOW TO SOLVE THEM

No matter how many precautions are taken, nobody is completely invulnerable to problems with the equipment or the equilibrium in an aquarium.

An electric power cut, for example, has no dramatic consequences over a short period, but it is worrying if it lasts a whole day (rarely the case, it is true). The aquarium cools, but the heat loss can be reduced by wrapping the tank in a blanket (also the solution to any malfunctioning of the heating system).

Generally speaking, in the event of a power cut there is a danger that the water stagnating in the filter will acquire substances that are toxic to the fish. It is therefore very important to empty it before turning the power back on and putting the filter back into operation.

An abnormal increase in the temperature can occur if the thermostat gets stuck in the heating position. The only real solution is to unplug it and adjust it, and allow the temperature to slowly drop to its initial level.

The temperature can also go up in summer, depending on the room where the aquarium is housed. The thermostat obviously turns the heating off, but the temperature can still sometimes exceed 25–26°C. There is no need to panic up to the 27–28°C level, but you must make provisions for cooling the room by darkening it, to avoid the penetration of sunlight. Note that substituting part of the water with domestic water or putting ice cubes in the aquarium have little effect.

The water color is a good indicator of the equilibrium of the aquarium: if it is clear and transparent, there are apparently no problems, but any coloring may be the sign of imbalance.

A drop in the pH is often the result of an excess of carbon dioxide dissolved in the water. This can be solved by increasing the rate of aeration.

Finally, you must be prepared for a rare accident, such as a leak, or a cracked pane. If this happens, you must act quickly, transferring the plants and fish to another tank, with their original water. The aquarium must then be completely emptied and dried, and you must locate and block the leak or change the cracked pane, using the gluing techniques described on pages 224–225.

▲ *A young hobbyist and aquarium club member remounting several tanks.*

Remounting an aquarium

A well-balanced aquarium can be self-sufficient for up to one year, or even more, if it is maintained on a regular basis.

If this is not the case, remounting must be considered. This can also be done when you want to change the decor, move the aquarium, or even move home. Plants and fish must be stored in another tank, with their original water. Then take out all the non-living elements, and clean and store them until they are used again.

Now comes the turn of the actual aquarium. Start to put it back into operation by reintroducing fresh water of the appropriate kind.

If the aquarium is to be remounted in a single day, it is advisable not to wash all the sand that serves as a bed, as it contains the good bacteria needed to undertake the nitrogen cycle. A rough rinse will get rid of the bigger pieces of debris, with only the top layer being cleaned several times, until the water is clear, for a good visual effect.

GOLDEN RULES FOR A GOOD BALANCE

Here are some important rules to follow as regards a well balanced aquarium:

1. Think big: the greater the volume of the tank, the easier it will be to maintain its balance, especially with sea water.
2. Make provisions for good filtration and aeration.
3. Consider planting the aquarium, even with sea water: many beginners do not put enough plants in their tanks.
4. Start with robust fish, easy to raise and recommended for novices: these are not unattractive, and are often found to be the least expensive.
5. Do not overpopulate.
6. Do not overfeed.
7. Regularly monitor the temperature, the pH, the nitrites, the hardness (in fresh water) or the density (in sea water).
8. Regularly siphon and change part of the water.

CHOOSING THE BED

The bed does not merely serve an aesthetic function – it must also contribute to the overall balance of the aquarium. It is a living environment in which various physical, chemical, and biological mechanisms unfold in accordance with its composition and granule size. It is therefore important to make the right choice of material at the aquarium's planning stage, in order to satisfy all these requirements.

The role of the bed

The main role of a good bed is mechanical: it supports the decor, made up of rocks and other elements. This is why, when an aquarium is being mounted, the bed is put in after the decor.
The bed also has a biological role that is no less important: it contains bacteria that contribute to the nitrogen cycle, and is therefore involved in the elimination of nitrogenous compounds. This is particularly valuable if you are using an undergravel filter.
Of course, the most obvious role for the bed is to enable plants to take root, particularly in fresh water.
For all these reasons, a bed must have the following characteristics:
– medium granule size;
– look both visually pleasing and natural;
– not too dense, although sufficiently so for plants to be well rooted.
Do not forget that a bed is heavy – 1.4–2 kg per liter volume – and so you must plan for an adequate support for the aquarium (around 30 kg of sediment for a

Granule size of different materials

Material	Granule size in mm
Pebbles	> 20
Thick gravel	8–20
Medium gravel	4–8
Fine gravel	2–4
Thick sand	0.5–2
Fine sand	0.05–0.5
Silt	< 0.05

What depth of sand?

Enough to enable the plants to take root, but not too deep, to avoid spoiling the appearance: 5–8 cm is a theoretical standard to be adapted to each particular case.
Only a hospital aquarium has no bed at all, for obvious hygienic reasons.
The table below gives the approximate weight of sediment for a surface of 1 m². Generally speaking, coarse sands never weigh less than 70 kg/m².

Sediments	Depth (in cm)	Volume (in liters)	Weight (in kg/m²)
Fine sands (Loire)	5	50	90
	8	80	144
Coarse sands (quartz)	5	50	75
	8	80	112

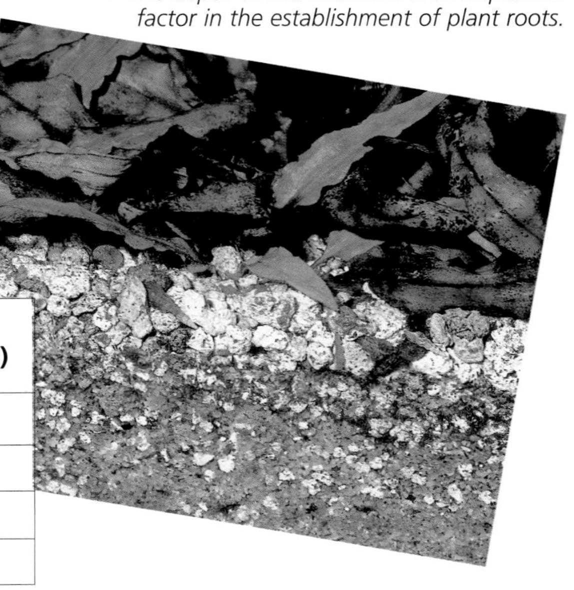
▼ *The depth of the sediment is an important factor in the establishment of plant roots.*

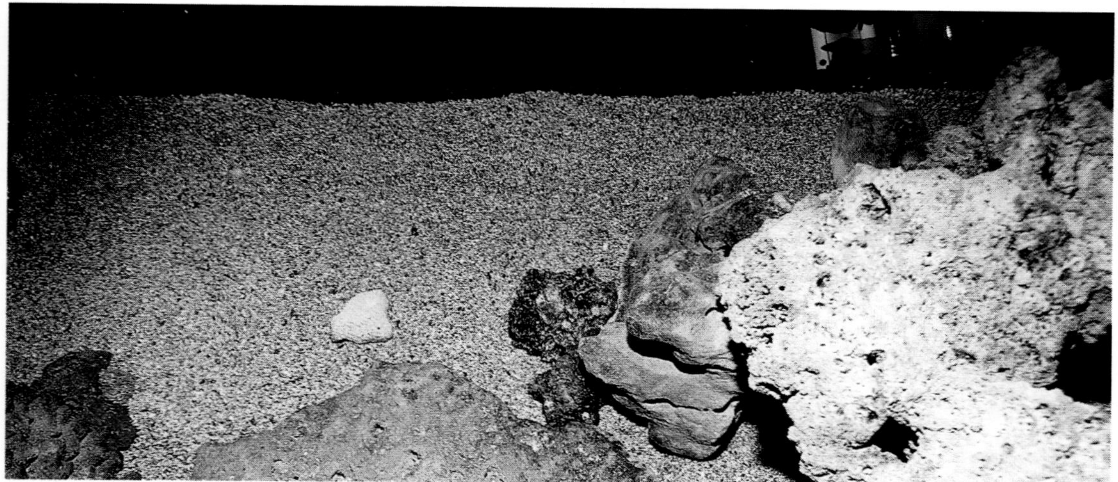

◄ *In this marine tank, seen from above, the bed serves as a wedge for the decorative elements.*

100 liter tank, with the whole aquarium amounting to some 150 kg).

Different types of bed

Natural beds in freshwater aquariums

• *Coarse sand and fine gravel*

These are the best sediments for aquariums. Quartz sand comes from crushed siliceous rocks (granite). Its grains, 1–3 mm long, have sharp splinters that can irritate burrowing fish, but it enables the water to circulate well. Its color varies according to its iron oxide content. Quartz sand is considered a sediment low in nutrients, and it is better suited to filtration.

Loire sand, as its name suggests, originally came from the bed of the river Loire in France. These days, identical sand is taken from other rivers or pits. The grains are more eroded, and therefore finer (0.5–1 mm), than those of quartz sand. When it has been taken from rivers, it contains residues of nutritive material that can be absorbed by plants.

• *Fine sand*

This pale-colored sand appeals to many hobbyists, but it has the disadvantage of not allowing the water to circulate freely. Moreover, unsightly deposits of plant debris, excreta, and leftover food show up very clearly, and, finally, the finest grains

There are various types of sand, with different sized particles and colors. ▼

Dark sediment can be used to set off pale fish. ▼

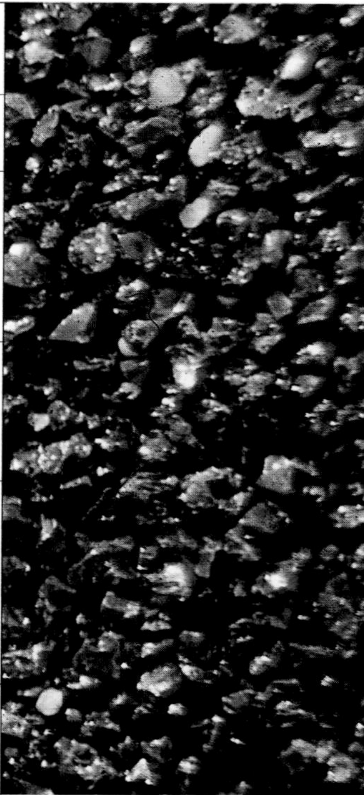

Different types of sediment

Sediment	Use
Dark or black sediment	Often volcanic, it is sometimes used to set off pale fish, while the traditional sands are better suited to dark or brightly colored fish.
Gravel	In sparsely planted aquariums, or those containing plants with sturdy roots, for big fish (Cichlids, for example, although it is not the most appropriate substrate).
Pozzolana and other volcanic rocks	These produce a very thick sediment when crushed, providing excellent water circulation. Some have a distinctive reddish-brown color. More widely used for their visual effect than for a natural look.
Peat	Support for the eggs of killies. (Egg-laying *Cyprinodontidae*, see page 95). See also page 16.

▲ *Some fish (here,* Sturisoma rostratum, *from South America) use fine sand to hide themselves, either wholly or partially.*

of sand may finish up suspended in the water. However, bottom-dwelling fish endowed with barbels seem to appreciate this type of sand. Other specific factors related to its use can be seen in the table on page 261.

• *Collecting sediment from a natural setting*

Some aquarists may be tempted to collect sediment themselves from a natural setting, although in theory this is forbidden. A clean and well-oxygenated watercourse must be chosen. The granule size gradually decreases as the water flows downstream. Sediment can often be found where it has collected in the inner part of a bend in a watercourse.

Enriching natural beds

Like a gardener, the aquarist can enrich these natural soils, as the most common sands, like quartz and Loire sand, are somewhat deficient in mineral elements, and so there is a danger of plants being affected by this when the aquarium is put into operation. Remember that it is possible to add both solid and liquid fertilizers to compensate for this deficiency. Once a good equilibrium has been achieved, the bed will gradually get richer and will start to be really beneficial to plants after about 4–6 months of operation.

Hobbyists who want their plants to grow more quickly can introduce an enriched substrate at the outset. This is available, already prepared, in the aquarium trade, but you can also make your own enriched bed on the basis of a recipe used and advocated by countless fishkeepers and specialist magazines (see box below). However, beginners are advised to start with a normal or commercially enriched bed, before moving on to create specific individual substrates.

The bed and oxygen

As a general rule, a bed must be considered as facilitating the movement of water. The water supplies oxygen to the microfauna living in it, enhancing the progress of the oxygen cycle. If the sand used is too fine, it becomes too compact to allow the water to circulate freely. This may give rise to black patches, a sign of oxygen deficiency and the presence of toxic substances.

Making an enriched bed

The classic recipe is:
– 10% clay: this enhances the use of mineral salts by the plants;
– 40% heath-mold without manure: beware of false heath-molds and various types of compost;
– 50% unprocessed Loire sand: if this is not washed, it contains mineral elements.

Mix the ingredients and put a 1 cm layer of quartz sand on the bottom, followed by 2–3 cm of the mixture and pack down thoroughly. Cover this with a few centimeters of quartz sand.

Obviously, you will not be able to dig around in this kind of substrate, so do not forget to put the decor in place beforehand. Do not use an under-gravel filter with this substrate. It might be argued that it is not oxygenated, as we have previously recommended, and this is true. However, it does produce other reactions, and accidents with it are very uncommon. Some aquarists have reported that this type of bed can remain effective for more than one year, sometimes more than two. Even if you are reluctant to apply this method directly in an aquarium, it can nevertheless be used in small aquatic *jardinières* containing plants. This certainly has practical advantages – they are easy to move – but you will have to camouflage the bed.

Natural beds in marine aquariums

In a marine tank the bed plays a different role, as the sparse vegetation found in this type of aquarium does not take root in the bed, and so the sediment does not need to be very dense and can be made up of coarser granules.

Two materials are used mainly, but they are often confused and grouped together under the term "coralline sand".

- *Maërl*

This is a coarse sediment, taken from certain sea beds and consisting of calcareous algae and the remains of mollusk shells and Anthozoan skeletons. It is very rich in calcium and reduces variations in pH.

- *Crushed coral*

The thickness of this sediment can vary, depending on the extent of the crushing. It consists entirely of pieces of the skeletons of corals and other similar animals. The fragments have been sufficiently eroded so that any injury to creatures that walk on the bed or burrow into it is unlikely.

It contains practically no calcium, but it does control any variations in the tank's water pH.

These two beds for marine tanks are available in the aquarium trade.

- *Live sand*

This is taken from the sea and sold moist by aquatic retailers. It contains a large number of micro-organisms, such as the bacteria in the nitrogen cycle. It is therefore, in theory, ready for action as soon as the aquarium is put into operation, which is not the case with other sediments. However, the results differ greatly from one tank to another, and many hobbyists are unconvinced about the beneficial effects of this sand.

There is a temptation to collect sand from the seashore, as it contains bacteria, but several precautions must be taken if you choose to do this.

Find an area free of pollution, with plenty of movement in the sea, and collect some coarse sediment. If this only comprises sand it will be deficient in calcium, but it can be topped off with crushed oyster shells. It is best to look for a shell sediment, mainly consisting of pieces of bivalve mollusk shells. Rinse the sediment thoroughly before introducing it into the aquarium, in order to eliminate the finest grains.

N.B.: dune sand is absolutely unsuited to marine tanks.

- *Crushed oyster shells*

These can be mixed with the above coarse sands to increase the levels of calcium. Wash them thoroughly, to get rid of any fine particles.

It must be pointed out that the last two types of sediments are not to be found in the regions inhabited by tropical fish. They cannot therefore be considered as really natural, but they can be used as a substitute for coralline sands as they are more accessible – and cheaper.

▲ *Two types of sediment are most common in marine tanks: maërl (above) and eroded and crushed coral, which is coarser, below.*

▼ *In principle, it is illegal to take large quantities of sand from a beach, but no aquarist has been known to encounter problems for extracting small amounts.*

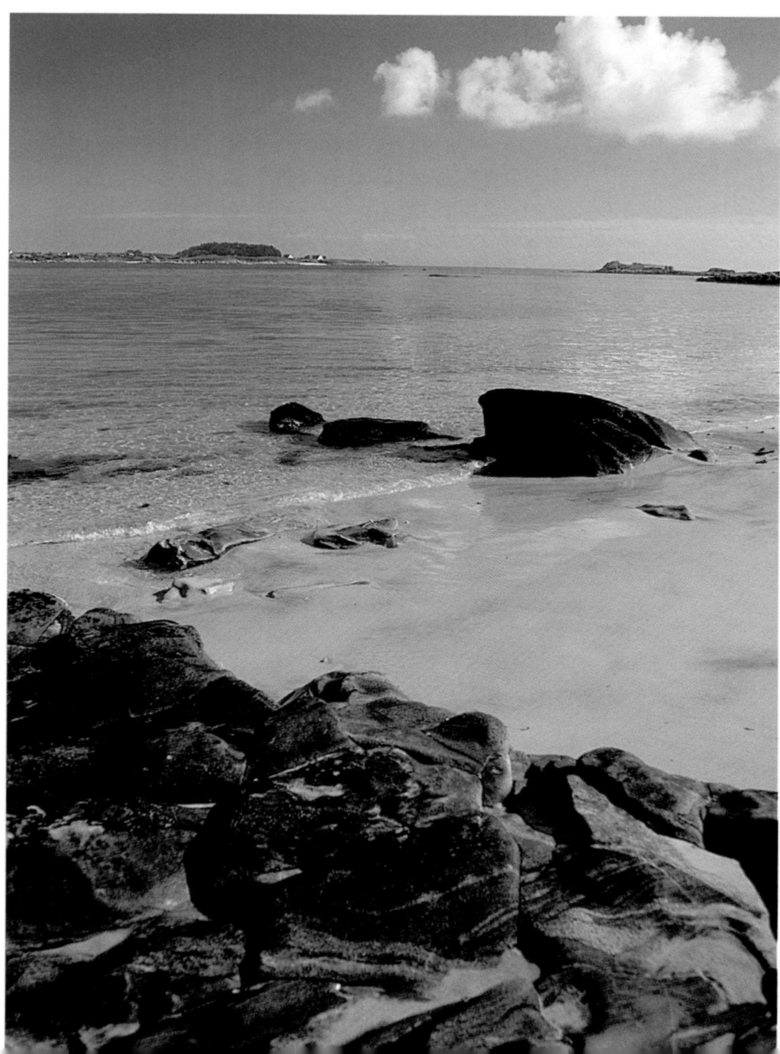

The decor is extremely important, as it exerts a decisive influence on the visual impact of the aquarium – and the pleasure derived from a beautiful scene is surely one of the main satisfactions of fishkeeping. However, do not get carried away, and make sure that the overall effect still has a natural look.

DECOR: A VITAL ELEMENT IN AN AQUARIUM

The role of decor

Decor is necessary for some animals and plants to feel at home. Shy fish look for permanent hideaways in it, while others find the refuge they need to reproduce, laying their eggs on vertical or horizontal rocks. Even if the residents do not make use of the shelter provided, the decor gives them physical reference points, which allow some species to mark out their territory.

These observations are equally applicable to invertebrates, some of which – Anthozoans, for example – live attached to elements in the decor. When an anemone is first introduced into an aquarium, it is not unusual to see it move around before establishing itself in the spot best suited to it. The decor also provides a support for certain types of vegetation: ferns and moss in fresh water, *Caulerpae*, and other algae in sea water.

In sea water, the decor can sometimes serve as a support for the invertebrates that live attached to it. ►

Finally, the decor allows you to hide equipment, mask the glass panes, and cut off the rear corners, thereby providing a backdrop and bringing harmony to the aquarium overall.

Main characteristics of decor

Apart from the search for a visual effect and a natural look, some rules must be respected when you are designing your decor. It must be functional, accessible, and easy to maintain. The material used, except in rare cases, must be neutral, i.e. it must not modify the characteristics of the water. It must also be solid enough to resist fish like Cichlids, which like to rearrange the furniture.

Of course, the decor increases the weight of the aquarium. Calculate for an average of 60 kg per square meter, although it will be a great deal less if you are using artificial materials, in freshwater tanks that are densely planted, Dutch aquarium style, and in marine tanks.

Once again, do not forget that the decor must be put in place before the bed is laid.

DECOR IN FRESH-WATER TANKS

Rocks

Rocks suitable for use as decorative elements in an aquarium can be found in natural settings or in specialist stores (see table page 265). Make sure they have no excessively sharp splinters: sand them down to ensure that the fish do not get injured when in contact with them.

How can you recognize a calcareous rock? By repeating a tried and tested experiment that some of us performed in school: pour a few drops of vinegar or acid onto the rock. If a slight effervescence does occur, which is caused by the release of carbon dioxide, this means that the rock contains calcium. The same method can also be used to test sand.

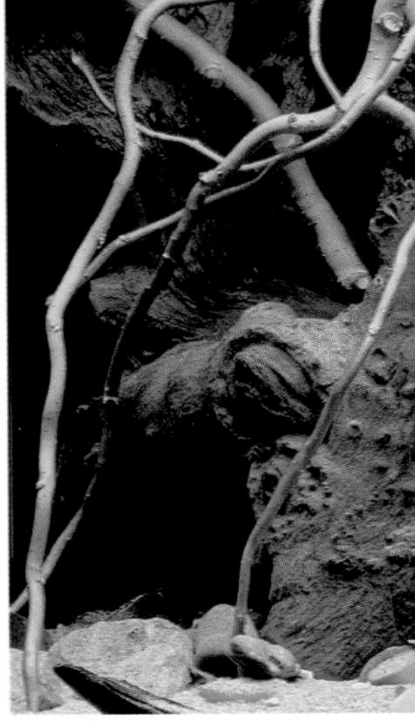

Decor based on plant material: peat-bog roots and willow branches. ►

Some rocks for freshwater aquariums	
Types	**Observations**
Calcareous	– only to be used to increase or maintain the hardness of the water (East African or brackish water aquariums).
Shale	– various colors: gray, greenish, or reddish; – it can be split into thin, light leaves, practical for hiding accessories.
Slate	– black sets off plants and fish well; – beware of slate with golden flecks, as it contains metals.
Lava	– light rocks broken off or thrown out in eruptions; – various colors: reddish, brown, black.
Basalt	– heavy lava with sharp splinters.
Shingle	– heavy but with smooth edges; – useful for building a small structure with shelters; – typical of flowing waters.
Petrified wood	– this is not a rock, but silica which has gradually replaced the living parts of the wood; the fibrous structure is still visible; – striking decorative effect, pale color.

▲ Rocks can be taken from natural settings, but they are also available in the aquarium trade.

Wooden materials

The natural environments of our fish often contain more vegetation than rocks: roots, branches that have fallen into the water, bark, and plants that become submerged in the rainy season.

When used alone or with a rock, wood creates a beautiful decorative effect, especially if it also plays host to moss or ferns.

It is therefore logical to use wood in an aquarium, but it must be treated first. Wooden materials have two major disadvantages. Firstly, they release acid substances that turn the water a yellowish amber color. Although this is no problem for Amazonian aquariums, this is not really the case in waters that have to be kept hard. Secondly, wood is light and must be wedged or weighed down.

• *Treating wood before putting it into the aquarium*

The treatment aims to:

– free the wood of all animate material, especially those found in a natural setting: bacteria, fungi, and other undesirable organisms;

– help water penetrate the piece to make it heavier;

– free it of most of its acid substances and colorings.

First brush down the wood carefully, then disinfect it by soaking it for 48 hours in:

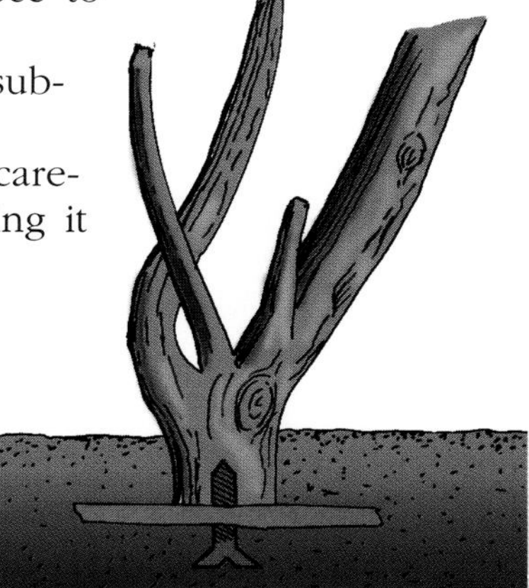

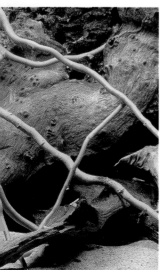

Wood can be held in place by screwing it to a small stone base. ▶

Wooden elements used in aquarium decor	
Branches, roots	Oak, beech, and vines are all possibilities, especially if they have already spent some time in water. Only use dead wood. Resinous wood is out of the question, as is wood washed up by the sea, which is saturated in salt.
Bark	Use cork oak to decorate the side and rear panes of the tank, putting it in place with silicone glue.
Peat-bog wood	Also known as peat-bog roots. As the branches and roots have been in this environment for a while, they rapidly release acid substances that color the water.
Bamboo	These are attractive in an Asian aquarium, combined with plants with ribbon-like leaves, such as *Vallisneria*.

– either bleach (1 ml/4 liters of water, using a concentrated sachet);
– or copper sulfate, at 1 g/liter.

Then boil the wood, replacing the water several times. If the latter is colored, this is proof that the acids are leaving the wood. Ideally, the treatment should be concluded by keeping the wood submerged for 1 or 2 weeks, so that it gradually fills up with water.

This is, however, often insufficient: the wood may still float and have to be wedged into the aquarium with a few rocks. You can otherwise also weigh it down with small stones attached by a nylon line that is all but invisible in the water, hiding this part of the wood in the sediment or else among other rocks on the bottom.

Natural or artificial? In reality, this marine decor is a mixture of the two, colonized by invertebrates. ▶

▲ *Coral skeletons are one of the classic elements of marine decor.*

Decor in seawater tanks

Tropical marine fish live in an environment lacking rocks but, on the other hand, abundant in corals and other elements that can be used to form the decor for an aquarium.

Corals

Calcified coral skeletons can be used for decor. They are often rough or sharp-edged and their stiffness depends on which species they belong to. They come in different shapes and sizes, and, with a few rare exceptions, are whitish in color. Bleaching them results in a perfect white. In aquariums, dead corals often gradually accumulate a covering of green algae. In this case, wash and brush them under running water and then soak them in bleach (1 sachet of bleach for 10 liters of water) for 1 week. This will not only whiten the skeleton but also destroy any organic particles that may have settled in it. Then rinse thoroughly and leave to dry in the open air for at least 8 days. Do not apply this treatment to corals from the *Tubipora* genus with a colored skeleton. These must be cleaned with a soft brush in hot water and dried as above.

Other elements of animal origin

Gorgons produce a dark skeleton that often gradually decays and even ends up crumbling. They must only be treated with hot water, never with bleach.

It is also possible to use the shells of mollusks (clams for example). Brush and wash them in hot water before putting them into the aquarium.

Some aquarists consider shells as potential traps for accumulated waste products, but they can also provide a refuge for small fish and, in the same way, crustaceans.

Live rocks can also play an important role in the decor of an aquarium.

ARTIFICIAL DECOR

Modern artificial products are rapidly growing in popularity, especially in large freshwater and marine aquariums. Their main advantage is the creative freedom they give to a fishkeeper, making it possible to choose decor that fits his or her exact requirements.

Two main types of material are used: polystyrene and polyurethane. They are both light and neutral.

Polystyrene

Available in blocks or sheets, it is usually used as a protection against bumps and heat (in some household electrical appliances, for example). You can recycle it or buy it in a store.

Small-grained polystyrene is preferable as it is stiffer. It is very light and floats on water, so it must therefore be fixed into the aquarium. Polystyrene can be prepared to meet your requirements before putting it into the tank.

• *Polystyrene decor*

Use a serrated knife or small saw to cut the cold blocks or sheets, or you can work with heated polystyrene, with a portable blowtorch or hot-air paint stripper. Be careful when handling polystyrene as it can melt, catch fire, and emit toxic vapors.

The diagram on the following page explains how to make this type of decor. Cut a block in the size and shape you need. If you are using sheets a few centimeters thick, you can heighten the relief by putting several sheets on top of each other. These are stuck together using resin mixed with sand. The design shown can be completed with other pieces of polystyrene, which can partially mask the side panes.

You can also combine sheets with large or small blocks. Then burn the parts that are visible to give them a natural look. At this point natural elements such as rocks or coral skeletons can be added, and resin and sand are applied to the structure (apart from the natural elements), before clearing up with a vacuum cleaner. This whole process is usually completed outside the aquarium, as it is more practical, and the decor is then stuck to the glass panes with silicone glue.

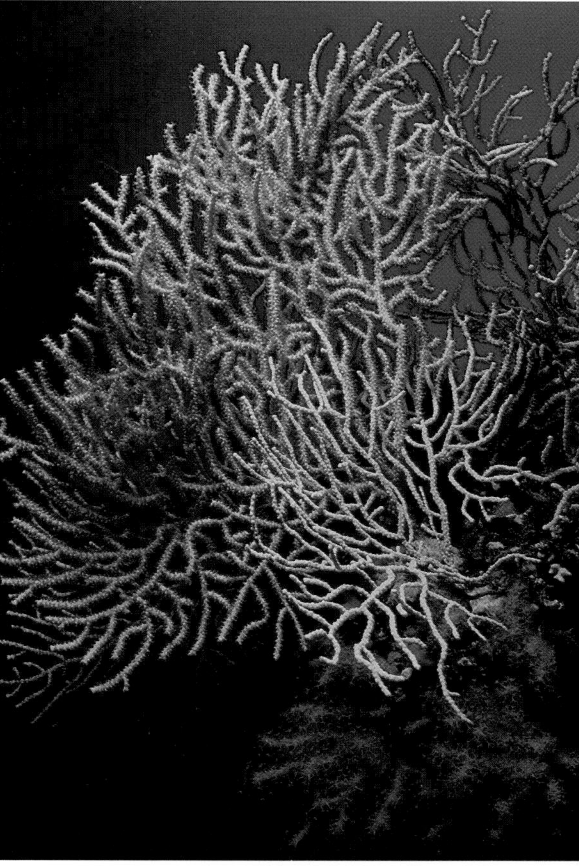

▲ *Gorgons have a dark skeleton that makes an attractive decorative element.*

Polyurethane

Polyurethane foam can be made from two components mixed together, but it is also available in aerosols that are more practical. The product released rapidly increases in volume and solidifies in a few minutes. It can then be sculpted with sharp instruments.

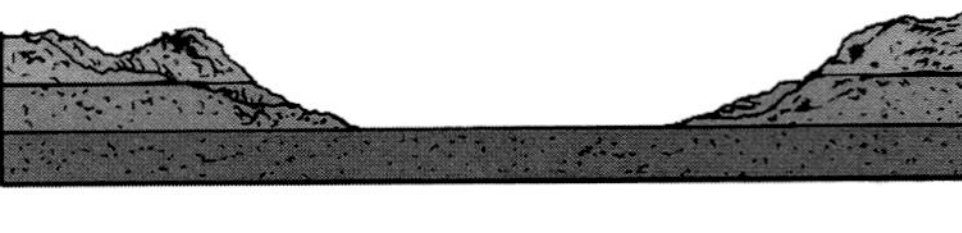

◀ *Decor made of polystyrene sheets: the entire sheet can be placed vertically against the back of the aquarium.*

• *Polyurethane decor*

Before taking the plunge into the construction of polyurethane decor, it is advisable to watch somebody else perform the same operation first, to avoid making mistakes.

In this case the decor must be created inside the aquarium. If you have made the tank yourself, it is also more practical to put the decor in place before adding the front glass pane, as this makes the process a lot easier.

The aquarium needs minor preparations beforehand to receive the polyurethane:

– stick small offcuts of glass, at intervals of a few centimeters, in the places that will hold the decor;

– another option is to make a mixture of sand and silicone glue and deposit this mixture at regular intervals in the areas to be decorated.

Polyurethane is increasingly used for decorating large tanks. Here it is combined with cork bark. ▼

Then pour on the polyurethane in small doses. You can work vertically to create a decor resembling a cliff; it is also possible to incorporate rocks, pieces of dead coral, or cavities for plants. In tanks equipped with a box filter, do not forget the passageways for the water coming in and going out; these can be molded on plastic pipes. The polyurethane dries very quickly and can be sculpted with a knife or small saw, to give it a finish that is more natural than its original smooth surface. Finally, use a vacuum cleaner to remove the offcuts.

Terracotta

Terracotta decors, made from clay to imitate the form of rocks, are commercially available from specialist suppliers.

Although some hobbyists make their own terracotta decor, polystyrene and polyurethane are more common, largely as a result of aquarium clubs and associations that offer guidance to beginners in these techniques.

• *Making a terracotta decor*

Contact a tile or flowerpot factory to obtain the raw material and to get it fired. Use clay, which is neutral and malleable. For a medium-sized decor, calculate around 100 g of clay per liter of volume, but only practice or the advice of more experienced aquarists will offer you more precise indications.

Model the clay in accordance with the decor you want:

– rocks of varying sizes;

– rocky cliff or slope;

– grottoes, arches.

The end results should have a natural look. All the elements must be dried in the open air and then fired in an oven at 800–900°C. This reduces their weight by 25–30% and endows them with a color resembling tiles.

A final option is the application of resin and sand on the surfaces of the decor.

Resin

This allows you to polish the decor. It is possible just to use artificial decor without treating it and wait until it acquires a patina after being in the tank for a few months. However, most hobbyists prefer to give it a natural appearance by incorporating a range of materials: sediments of varying textures, such as sand, gravel, coralline sand, or pieces of rock or coral. To make these adjustments, a so-called food resin, epoxy resin, is used, as it has no influence on the water. It is made up of two components which harden when they are mixed together, and it can be colored to look more natural.

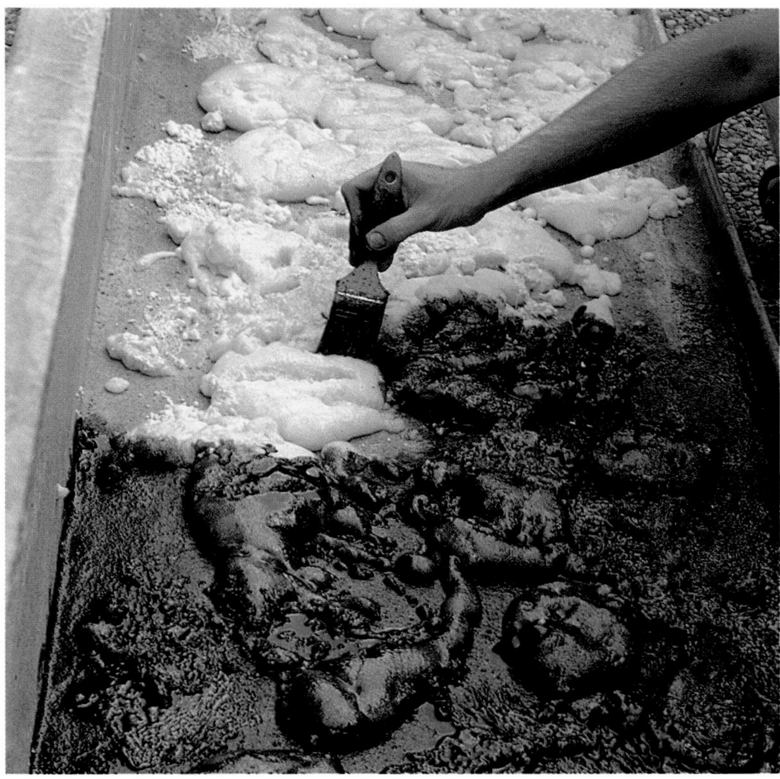

▲ *Resin applied to polyurethane can be dyed with food colorings, in this case a mixture of red and black.*

External decor

At first sight, it may seem surprising to talk of external decor. However, there is nothing more unsightly than the sight of the wall behind the aquarium covered with cables and pipes! The primary role of external decor therefore consists of masking these elements, but it can also serve to highlight the plants and fish.

Posters

Posters with various designs, representing freshwater vegetation or seabeds, can be found in aquarium stores, but many aquarists remain unimpressed by their visual effect. They are attached to the outer face of the rear pane.

Colored backgrounds

An alternative to posters is sheets in a single color, such as blue, green, gray, pale

Finishing artificial decor: resin and sand

Resin and sand completely insulate the decor from the water and give it a natural look. The sand used must be in keeping with the type of aquarium – freshwater or marine – and match the sediment. If you use fine sand, you will need to apply several layers.

• Polystyrene or terracotta decor

The resin and sand are added outside the aquarium. A coat of resin is applied with a paintbrush and sand is then sprinkled on top. Leave to dry (24 hours for the layer of resin) and repeat the operation 1–3 times, depending on the sand's grain size.

It is important to apply the resin carefully over all the decor, without neglecting any small reliefs, crevices, or grottoes. Only resin, without any sand, should be put on those parts of the decor that will be touching the glass panes of the aquarium.

Remove any leftover sand, firstly with a large paintbrush, and then with a vacuum cleaner. The finished decor is stuck to the aquarium with silicone glue, 48 hours after drying.

• Polyurethane decor

Follow the same process with the polyurethane set in the aquarium, and do not forget to apply resin and sand to the joins between the decor and the glass panes. Any leftover sand is removed with a vacuum cleaner.

brown, or black. Black highlights fish and plants particularly effectively. A few aquarists paint a color scale themselves, pale at the top of the aquarium and darker at the bottom, to simulate the penetration of the light. Another option is to paint directly onto the back of the rear pane.

Stimulating the imagination

The imagination is a capricious spirit that can sometimes desert you. You want to create your own decor, you have been dreaming about it ... but your mind goes blank! There are, however, several sources of inspiration:

- other aquariums, friends, clubs, public aquariums;
- books and specialist magazines;
- but also – and above all! – nature. Photos and sketches will help you to translate your ideas into reality, particularly as to how reliefs can be harmonized.

▲ *There are countless sources of inspiration if you want to create a decor but find that your imagination has failed you.*

▲ *The rear pane in this tank has been replaced by a mirror, to produce a striking effect.*

Mirrors

Always placed behind the rear pane, these give the impression that the tank is twice its initial size... but also that is has double the number of plants and fish!

Other possibilities

A polystyrene sheet with a coat of resin and sand can be placed against the outside of the rear pane.

Finally, you can consider putting natural decorative material, such as rocks, branches, and roots, behind the aquarium, in front of a black cardboard backdrop. These elements can be simply wedged together, glued, or held down with adhesive clay. The overall effect is to increase the depth of field, for when an aquarium is full it seems one third smaller, because of the refraction of light in the water. This type of decor can easily be changed, needs no prior treatment and very little maintenance, the only disadvantage being that it accumulates dust.

A FEW RULES FOR SUCCESSFUL DECOR		
Characteristics of the decor	**What to avoid**	**Recommendations**
Visually attractive and natural	– some accessories, found all too often, that do not look natural (although this is open to debate): deep-sea divers, amphorae, shipwrecks, chests that make bubbles; – extravagantly colored rocks; – too many different rocks.	– use a single type of rock, or two at most in bigger aquariums; – keep the decor in proportion to the volume of the aquarium: large rocks in large tanks, smaller ones in smaller aquariums.
Practicality, accessibility, easy maintenance	– overly intricate reliefs, in which it is difficult to intervene (to siphon or capture fish).	– build a modestly sized rockpile, create a grotto or a large and accessible overhang, make a large terrace; – use an artificial decor to imitate a cliff or rockpile.
Neutrality	– calcareous rocks in fresh water, apart from exceptional cases; – rocks containing metallic elements, sometimes difficult to detect if they do not gleam.	– use slate, basalt, lava, shale.
Solidity	– unstable rockpiles; – rocks placed on the sediment.	– insert the decor before the sediment; – possibly, stick the rocks together, or to the panes, with silicone glue.

ADVANTAGES AND DISADVANTAGES OF ARTIFICIAL DECOR		
	Traditional natural decor	**Artificial decor (polystyrene, polyurethane)**
Advantages	– easy installation; – modifiable; – neutral.	– light materials; – adaptable: sculpture, incorporation of natural elements; – wide range of creative possibilities; – neutral.
Disadvantages	– weight and size.	– immovable; – requires some experience.

FINAL PREPARATIONS

Installing an aquarium requires cool nerves and good organization. It is useless to rush, as you may end up spoiling the final results. Note that the aquarium will not be ready to receive fish as soon as it is put into operation, especially if you are using sea water. So, patience is called for!

HOW TO PROCEED

The steps to be taken when setting up an aquarium have a logical order, and this must be respected. These steps vary slightly according to whether fresh water or sea water is being used, but the underlying principle is the same: water is not poured into the aquarium until the decor, bed, and the necessary technical equipment are in place.

Installation, step by step

The order is as follows:

1. Cleaning the tank. Use a brand new sponge and warm water. It is best to avoid detergents.

2. Fitting the external decor (see page 264). Make sure that this is put firmly in place, otherwise it will be difficult to fix later on.

3. Mounting the aquarium on its support. Remember that the support must be absolutely horizontal and covered with a flexible material that will compensate for any possible unevenness. At this stage, make sure that you leave sufficient space behind the tank to allow you easily to open the gallery and the entrance that gives access to the pipes and cables. The aquarium will not be moved again after this point.

4. Fill the tank, to make sure it is watertight. Leaks are rare occurrences; a slight seepage is more common, although this can only be detected about 24 hours after putting in the water. When you are sure your aquarium is watertight, siphon out the water.

5. If you are using an under-gravel filter, position it so that the air-lift is in one of the tank's rear corners.

6. Installing the accessories. Place these directly into the tank or in the boxes of the box filter. The heating system must not come into direct contact with any plastic elements, and it must be near the diffuser. If you are using an external filter, do not forget the connecting pipes.

7. Putting the decor in place. Introduce the rocks or corals, taking into account both the visual and practical aspects and making sure to hide the accessories.

Take your time and experiment until you are happy with the overall aesthetic effect. Once you have filled the aquarium, you are unlikely to get another chance to make adjustments to the decor

8. Putting in the bed. Half the sediment is placed directly on the bottom of the tank, without any prior washing. The second half is rinsed in warm water until the latter is transparent. It is then put on top of the first layer. Make sure that the elements of the decor are firmly wedged into the bed. Some of them can be used to create raised sandy terraces at this point.

Putting the under-gravel filter in place, ready to receive the sediment. The water exit must be positioned in one of the aquarium's rear corners. ►

For aesthetic reasons, the sediment should slope downwards slightly from the back to the front of the aquarium: this gives the impression of a greater depth of field.

9. Filling the tank. Whatever method you use – a pipe connected to a faucet or buckets – break the fall of the water to avoid dislodging part of the sediment. The time-honored trick is to pour the water into a bowl or concave plate.

The aquarium must not be filled to its maximum height, as you may need to make corrections in the decor if, for example, a piece of wood starts to float. You can also put in your plants now.

The water will be slightly cloudy, with microparticles on the surface that can be eliminated with a very fine-meshed landing net, or through siphoning.

10. Switching on the equipment. First check that the heating element is totally submerged, then turn on the heating and regulate the temperature to 25°C. Plug the aeration and filtration systems into the mains. A quick glance will be enough to check that everything is working and after a few hours the water should have heated up and be clearer.

▲ *A tank must be filled with care, to avoid knocking over any decor.*

◄ *The sediment covers the undergravel filter, and the heating and aeration equipment must be camouflaged.*

11. Wait for another 24 hours, then recheck that the equipment is working. The water must now be clear, with a temperature around 25°C. It is sometimes necessary to make slight adjustments to the regulation of the thermostat to obtain the desired temperature. You can now add any other vegetation.

Operations specific to marine aquariums. The process is identical up to stage **6**. This is when you must install the aerator and the UV sterilization system.

Put the decor in place and then add the bed. The latter must all be washed beforehand and then placed on a thin layer of sediment. After that, fill the aquarium with the freshest water possible; only switch on the aeration. Now is the time to dissolve the salts. Weigh the amount you require, on the basis of the real volume of the water, before putting them into the aquarium. Leave the salts to dissolve for 48 hours, check the density, and make the necessary adjustments. Then move to stage **10**, without switching on the aerator or UV system, before continuing to stage **11**.

▼ *The vegetation can be planted by hand, or with specially designed pincers.*

Introducing plants

• *Source of plants and transportation*

Plants can be obtained from aquarium stores and clubs, or they can be a present from a friend. Wherever they come from, do not forget

ARRANGING YOUR PLANTS

When you plant your first aquarium, it is advisable to stick to a classical style and opt for an amphitheater layout. Distribute the plants that grow quickest along the sides and back of the tank; put those that grow at a moderate rate directly in front of them, with the smallest in the foreground.

This arrangement leaves space free in the center of the aquarium and gives a good impression of depth of field.

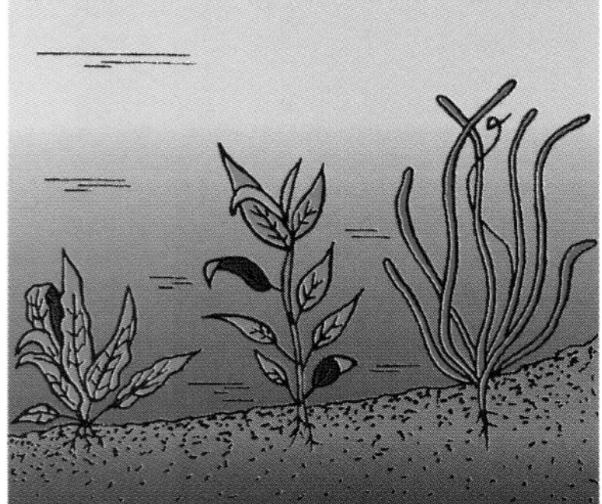

The arrangement of your plants must be visually pleasing, but also respect their ecology. ▶

that they are very fragile when handled outside water.

The best way of transporting them without any deterioration is to put them into an airtight plastic bag, like those used for fish, that has been inflated and sealed.

• *Planting*

Yet again, it is a question of satisfying both aesthetic and technical criteria. A small ground plan of the aquarium can be useful in achieving a successful layout, taking into account the species available.

Generally speaking, plants of the same type should be grouped together, setting off any isolated specimens.

Handling the plants with great care, start at the back of the aquarium and, above all, do not let your desire for a lush setting lead you to pack the plants too tightly together; it is best to space them out, even if the resulting vegetation looks sparse. There are three main reasons for this:

– the roots must have sufficient space in which to expand;

– you must also in bear in mind that the plants will grow and maybe spread out their leaves;

– finally, you must allow the light to penetrate to the base of the plants.

Do not cut the already existing roots, or bunch them together; on the contrary, spread them out as much as possible in the sediment. You should not bury clumps of plants very deep; only the roots and the lowest (often white) part of the stem should be covered by the sediment.

When planting cuttings, remove any damaged leaves at the base of the stem then bury them to a depth of 4 or 5 cm. This is easier if you dig a small hole first with your hand or an appropriate tool, and pile soil around the base of the plant at the end of the operation.

Plants like moss and ferns must be placed on the supports to which they are going to attach themselves. They will stay in place more easily if they are wedged or tied with a short length of nylon thread. Put floating plants on the surface of the water.

Do not be surprised if the plants look limp. They will quickly take on a normal appearance when the lighting is switched on, as the attraction of the light will make them straighten up. From this point on, the aquarium must be lit in accordance with the recommendations that are given on pages 226–233.

All that remains is to raise the water level to its final position and ... wait, before introducing the fish.

Preparing the welcome for your fish

The only thing your aquarium now lacks to be complete is the arrival of its residents ... Summon up your patience one last time, because the aquarium has yet to acquire a perfect equilibrium: the plants must take root and bacteria must develop for the nitrogen cycle.

• *A gradual introduction*

The minimum waiting period for a freshwater tank is 1 week, but 2 weeks is prefer-

Live rocks and the organisms they carry enhance the functioning of a marine aquarium. ▶

▲ *Patience is required to achieve results as beautiful as this in a marine aquarium.*

able. In the case of a seawater tank, the wait can sometimes be as long as 4 weeks. If you really cannot hold out that long, there are several ways of reducing this period. As we have already stated, the aim of this waiting period is to allow bacteria to develop and to avoid the presence of any toxic nitrogenous substances, so you can speed up this development artificially. The first short cut is good oxygenation – the bacteria need oxygen to respire and to transform the nitrogenous compounds – the second is the introduction of bacteria. This can be achieved by adding sediment or filtering material from another marine aquarium, sand, live rocks, or lyophilized bacteria, which can be bought in specialist stores. However, this last solution is not recommended, as it sometimes proves ineffective. Another alternative is to become a breeder of bacteria, feeding them on organic matter that they would not otherwise obtain in a tank that has been newly put into operation. The best menu comprises one or two cooked mussels, cut into small pieces and placed in the aquarium, with any leftovers being siphoned off a few days later.

Such measures can reduce the waiting period to 8–10 days. However, the nitrite levels must always be measured regularly, and no fish must be put into the tank until these levels have been stable at zero for

How many fish in an aquarium?						
Size of fish	**Density of population**					
	Fresh water			**Sea water**		
	General rule	100 liter tank	300 liter tank	General rule	300 liter tank	500 liter tank
Under 5 cm	1 fish per 5 liters	20	60	1 fish per 25 liters	12	20
5–8 cm	1 fish per 8 liters	12	37	1 fish per 40 liters	8	12
9–15 cm	1 fish per 15 liters	7	20	1 fish per 75 liters	4	7
Over 15 cm	1 fish per 30 liters	*	10	1 fish per 150 liters	*	3

* It is not advisable to keep fish of this size in such a small tank.

around 1 week. Only then can you switch on the aerator and UV sterilization (in marine tanks only).

• *Choice of fish*

The choice of residents depends on the type of tank (community, regional, or specialist), your tastes, and your budget. The number of species available on the market is more than sufficient for most fishkeepers, especially novices. A quick inspection of a few stores will give you a broad overview and enable you to make a well-judged selection.

There are some rules, however, that must be respected if you are to avoid results that are too often found: a "hold-all" aquarium, overpopulated with a motley collection of species. It is best to choose a few species and keep them in groups – this is possible for a great many species. Respect their natural behavior, as this increases the probability of eventual reproduction. However, aggressive species that usually live alone must obviously be kept as single specimens.

You can take advantage of all the different levels of the tank by combining free swimmers with bottom- and surface-dwellers that can live in harmony.

There remains the problem of living space. The general rule, for small species, is 1 cm of fish per liter of fresh water and 1 cm per 5 liters of sea water. The table above presents some more precise calculations, but you must bear in mind the maximum length that each species can attain in an aquarium.

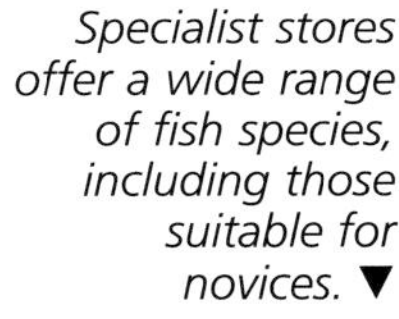

Specialist stores offer a wide range of fish species, including those suitable for novices. ▼

Acquisition and transport

Obviously, a fish must have a clean bill of health when it is introduced into an aquarium, and there are certain signs that indicate this. There is still a risk of an unpleasant surprise, however, as some fish are carriers of diseases that only come into the open once they are put into an aquarium.

Whether a fish comes from a store, a club, or a friend, it must always be scrutinized carefully before acquiring it. This is why you must not be in too much of a rush and should get to know a storekeeper or join a club, to look and learn. When you do finally introduce fish into the aquarium, you must adopt a particular strategy:

– It is best to populate the tank in one go, or at most in two, with a short interval between, rather than introduce the fish one by one. A newcomer, by definition, is perceived as an undesirable alien, which can give rise to conflicts that sometimes result in its death.

– If you are obliged to stagger the introduction of the fish over a period of time, it is best to start with smaller species and allow them to get accustomed to their environment; in this way, they will not be so alarmed by the subsequent arrival of bigger species.

Fish are quite easy to transport. Just put a small group into a closed plastic bag containing one third water and two thirds atmospheric air. In the case of species with spiny spokes, you can add a second plastic bag for protection. This system is effective for a short trip, of one or two hours, depending on the external temperature. After that, heat starts to be lost, although this effect can be reduced by surrounding the plastic bag with material or paper and putting it in a polystyrene bag.

◀ *Fish must be transported in airtight bags containing more air than water.*

◀ *The bags used for transport must be insulated for long trips to avoid any loss of heat.*

▲ *The bag used for transporting fish must be left to float for a while, to ensure that its temperature is the same as that of the tank.*

Transferring your fish into an aquarium

The fish will be stressed when it is introduced into its new home, on account of the transportation, the radical change of environment, and the difference in water quality. To alleviate this stress, you must never introduce a fish directly into a tank. Proceed in stages, allowing a minimum of 1–2 hours for the whole operation. For the first 30 minutes, just let the bag containing the fish float in the aquarium to make sure that the temperature is the same in both cases. Then open the bag and put a little water from the aquarium inside. Repeat this operation several times at regular intervals until the bag is full. You can then carefully transfer the fish into its new environment.

If there are already fish in the aquarium, you must take two extra precautions to increase the chances of the newcomers being accepted: distract the attention of the other occupants by giving them food, and introduce the new arrivals in the morning, before lighting up the tank.

In any case, the new fish is likely to hide for a while, and this is a completely normal attitude. When it reemerges will depend on its nature, but it sometimes reappears after barely an hour. Some may take longer to acclimatize, however.

It will soon grow accustomed to its new environment and the feeding schedule, and will become completely integrated into the aquarium. If the fish is healthy and you take all the necessary precautions, mishaps are very rare and the ecology of the aquarium will not be upset.

Central American Freshwater Tank

This type of aquarium, particularly suitable for beginners, reconstitutes a freshwater Central American environment. The fish living in it (the Poeciliid family) will soon reproduce if the conditions are right. It is advisable to provide yourself with a rearing tank, to help the fry develop. You can then move on to the true livebearers coming from the same geographical region: *Ameca splendens* and *Xenotoca eiseni*. The plants shown here grow fairly quickly and it is easy to take cuttings from them; they are therefore a good means for taking your first steps in plant decor, which is sometimes neglected by beginners at the expense of fish until they realise the importance of vegetation.

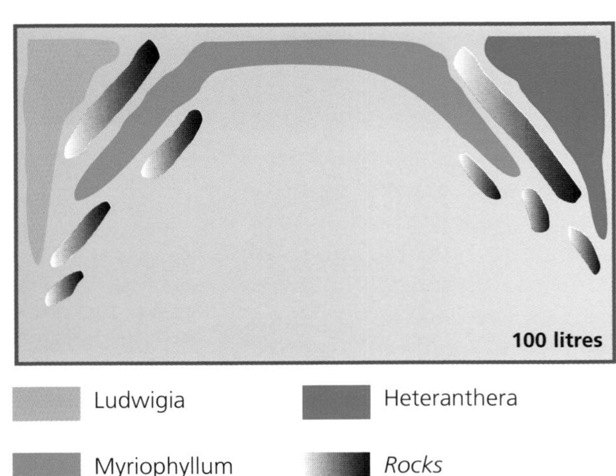

Dimensions (in cm)	Length x width x height: 80 x 35 x 35
Gross volume	100 liters
Region	Central America
Fish	Guppy, platy, xipho, mollies, around 15 specimens
Plants	*Ludwigia, Myriophyllum* (or *Cabomba*), *Heteranthera* (or *Bacopa*)
Bed	Fairly deep
Decor	Some rocks (shale or slate)
Temperature (°C)	23–28, preferably 25
pH	7–7.8
Hardness	Over 5.6°GH, preferably 8.4°GH
Filtration	Normal

▲ Xiphophorus helleri *(see p. 101).*

◄ Bacopa caroliniana *(see p. 202).*

South-East Asian tank

This tank must be well planted, but with enough room for the fish to move around. You can add a touch of originality by introducing some transparent species: the glass perch (*Chanda ranga*) or the glass Silurid (*Kryptopterus bicirrhis*). A small shrimp (*Atya* or *Macrobrachium*) and gastropods (*Ampullaria*) can complete the population: the visual effect of the plant decor will be highlighted by the addition of a single specimen of a spectacular specimen, such as *Barclaya longifolia* or a species from the *Nymphaea* genus available from specialist nurseries.

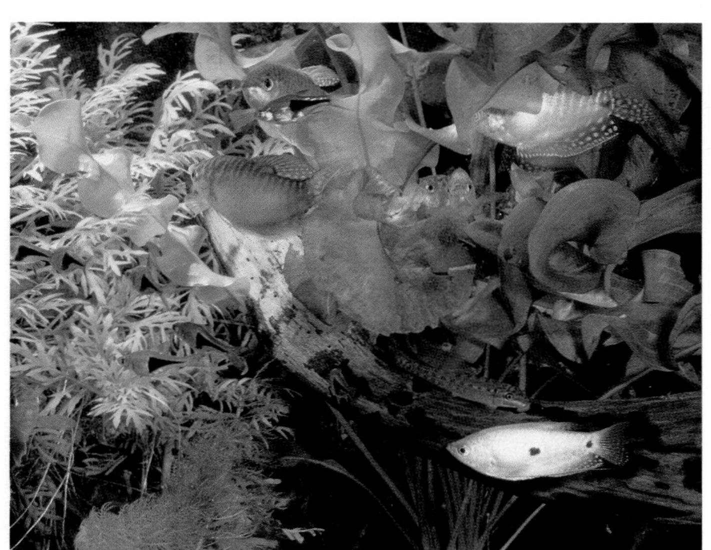

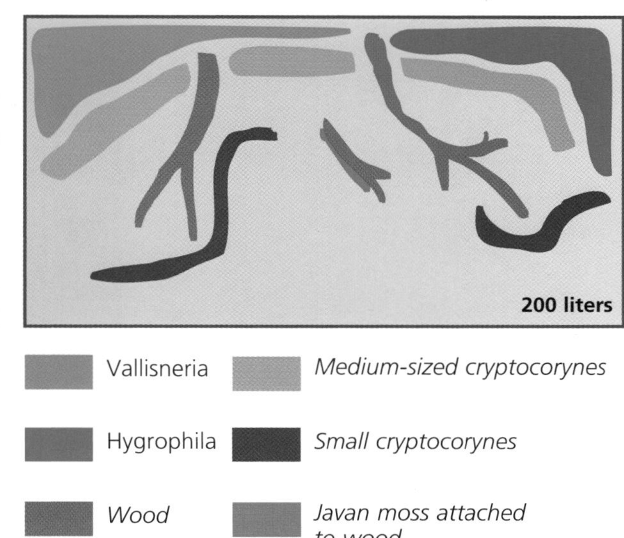

Dimensions (in cm)	Length x width x height: 100 x 40 x 50
Gross volume	200 liters
Region	South-East Asia
Fish	Barb, rasboras, danios, 1 kuhli, 1 labio, 1 botia (around 35 fish)
Plants	*Vallisneria, Hygrophila,* medium-sized cryptocorynes, small cryptocorynes, Javan moss attached to wood
Bed	Sand, quartz
Decor	Predominantly vegetal: branches, roots, bamboo
Temperature (°C)	24–28, preferably 26
pH	6.6–7
Hardness	Under 5.6°GH, preferably under 2.8°GH
Filtration	Normal

▲ Capoeta titteya *(see p. 83).*

▲ Cryptocoryne cordata *(see p. 208).*

African Cichlid tank

The absence of plants in an African Cichlid tank can be compensated by a rocky decor that provides the fish with shelters and hiding places; polyurethane and polystyrene can also prove very effective for fulfilling the same purpose.

For Lake Tanganyika, you can introduce the Cyprinodontid *Lamprichthys tanganicanus* or a species of *Lamprologus*, which takes refuge in a gastropod shell. For Lake Malawi, you can add species of the *Haplochromis* genus. These reproduce through mouth brooding, ensuring that the hobbyist can look forward to a fascinating spectacle once he or she has spotted a female with her mouth swollen by eggs.

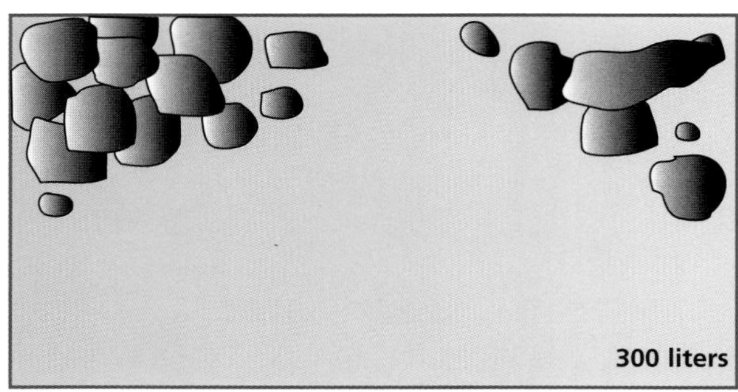

Dimensions (in cm)	Length x width x height: 120 x 50 x 50
Gross volume	300 liters
Region	East African lakes
Fish	*Neolamprologus, Julidochromis* for Lake Tanganyika (around 4 fish); *Pseudotropheus, Aulonocara, Melanochromis* for Lake Malawi (around 30 fish)
Plants	These are absent from the natural setting; possibly, a few *Anubias.*
Bed	Fairly coarse granule size
Decor	Rocks with shelters, grottoes, hiding places. Possibly artificial decor
Temperature (°C)	23–27, preferably 25
pH	Over 7.5
Hardness	Over 8.4°GH
Filtration	Fairly strong

▲ Julidochromis marlieri *(see p. 112).*

Pseudotropheus tropheops *(see p. 117).* ▼

Marine tank

This marine tank represents a basic model for a beginner in sea water. The species proposed are robust, and their behavior provides a fascinating show, particularly the clownfish in their anemone, which may be able to reproduce.

To diversify the animal population, you can add a shrimp or a hermit crab. It is also advisable to put in live rocks, which will contain small invertebrates. An artificial decor that includes coralline sand and even small pieces of coral is pleasing to the eye, and can be colonized by caulerpas. This type of aquarium requires impeccable water quality to guarantee its equilibrium.

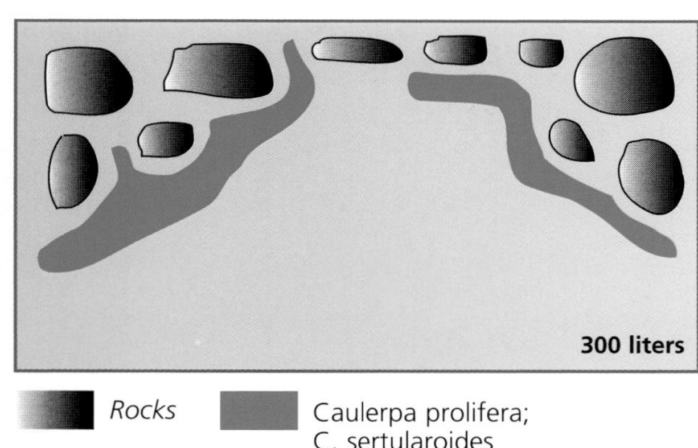

Rocks Caulerpa prolifera; C. sertularoides

Dimensions (in cm)	Length x width x height: 120 x 50 x 50
Gross volume	300 liters
Region	Coralline tropical region
Fish	A couple of clownfish (with 1 anemone), blue damsels, 1 *Chaetodon auriga,* blennies, or gobies (no more than 8 specimens)
Plants	Caulerpas (*C. prolifera* or *C. sertularoides*)
Bed	Maërl or thick coral sand
Decor	Dead corals, possibly artificial decor
Temperature (°C)	25–28
pH	Around 8.3
Specific gravity	1022–1023
Filtration	Strong (at least 3 times the volume of the tank)

Chaetodon auriga *(see p. 132).* ▶

▼ Caulerpa sertularoides *(see p. 215).*

BIBLIOGRAPHY

Dr. Axelrod's Atlas of Aquarium Fishes, Herbert R. Axelrod, Warren. E. Burgess, Neal Pronek, and Jerry G. Walls, T. F. H.
A Fishkeeper's Guide to Aquarium Plants, Barry James, Salamander Books.
A Fishkeeper's Guide to Fish Breeding, Chris Andrews, Salamander Books.
The Hobbyist's Guide to the Natural Aquarium, Chris Andrews, Tetra Press.
A Popular Guide to Tropical Aquarium Fishes, Dick Mills, Salamander Books.
The Practical Encyclopedia of the Marine Aquarium, Dick Mills, Salamander Books.
Reef Fish: Behaviour and Ecology on the Reef and in the Aquarium, Ronald E. Thresher, Bartholomew.
Our Native Fishes: The Aquarium Hobbyist's Guide to Observing, Collecting and Keeping Them. North American Freshwater and Marine Fishes, John R. Quinn, The Countryman Press.
The Optimum Aquarium, Kaspar Horst and Horst Kipper, Aqua Documenta.
The Book of the Marine Aquarium, Nick Dakin, Salamander Books.
A Guide to American Zoos and Aquariums, Darcy and Robert Folzenlogen, Willow Press.
A Practical Guide to Corals for the Reef Aquarium, Dean Puterbaugh and Eric Borneman, Crystal Graphics.
The Reef Aquarium, Volumes One and Two, Julian Sprung and J. Charles Delbeek, Ricordea Publishing.

USEFUL ADDRESSES

Resources

Catalog of Fish Species:
www.calacademy.org
Plants:
www.tropica.com
Invertebrates:
www.netvet.wustl.edu
General Information:
www.petswarehouse.com
www.actwin.com/fish/index.cgi
Aquarian Advisory Society, PO Box 67, Elland, West Yorkshire HX5 OSJ.

Public Aquariums

Steinhart Aquarium, San Francisco, California.
E-mail: aquarium@calacademy.org
Florida Aquarium, Tampa, Florida.
E-mail: srichardson@flaquarium.org
New England Aquarium, Boston, Massachussets.
E-mail: webmaster@neaq.org
Aksarben Aquarium and Nature Center, Louisville, Nebraska.
E-mail: akaq@ngpc.state.en.us
Deep-Sea World, Fife, Scotland
E-mail: deepsea@sol.co.uk
London Aquarium, London, England.
E-mail: info@londonaquarium.co.uk

Associations

American Zoo and Aquarium Association, 8403 Colesville Road, Suite 710, Silver Spring, MD, USA.
American Aquarist Society, 3901 Hatch Boulevard, Sheffield, Alabama, USA.
International Aquarium Society, PO Box 373, Maine, NY 13802-0373, USA.
Federation of American Aquarium Societies, 4816 E. 64th Street, Indianapolis, IN 46220-4728, USA.
North American Fish Breeders' Guild, 905 Alden, Lansing, Michigan 48910, USA.
North American Native Fishes Association, PO Box 2304, Kensington, MD 20891, USA.
Aquatic Gardeners' Association, 83 Cathcart Street, London, England.
International Marine Aquarist Association, PO Box 7, Ilminster, Somerset TA19 9BY, England.
Federation of British Aquatic Societies, 2 Cedar Avenue, Wickford, Essex SS12 9DT, England.
The Association of Aquarists, 2 Telephone Road, Portsmouth, Hampshire, England.

CONVERSIONS

Capacity:

1 l = 0.22 UK gal/0.26 US gal

Weight:

1mg = 0.04×10^{-3} oz
1 g = 0.04 oz
1 kg = 2.2 lb

Length:

1mm = 0.04 in
1cm = 0.39 in
1m = 3.3 ft or 1.1 yd
1km = 0.6 m

Temperature:

°C	°F
10	50.0
11	51.8
12	53.6
13	55.4
14	57.2
15	59.0
16	60.8
17	62.6
18	64.4
19	66.2
20	68.0
21	69.8
22	71.6
23	73.4
24	75.2
25	77.0
26	78.8
27	80.6
28	82.4
29	84.2
30	86.0

To convert Celsius into Fahrenheit: ($\frac{9}{5} \times$ °C) + 32

INDEX

PHOTO CREDITS

All the photographs are the property of Yves LANCEAU and Hervé CHAUMETON/agence Nature, with the exception of the following:

Aquapress: p. 167 – **Berthoule/Nature :** p. 12 ; p. 15; p. 25 (t); p. 30 (t); p. 51 (l); p. 52; p. 53 (t); p. 54 (b); p. 57 (t); p. 58 (l); p. 168 (t); p. 173 (t); p. 222; p. 223; p. 230; p. 234; p. 235 (t); p. 236; p. 236/237 ; p. 238; p. 240; p. 241; p. 242 (l); p. 247 (b) ; p. 248 (t); p. 250; p. 251; p. 252; p; 254; p. 257; p. 271; p. 272; p. 273; p. 277 – **Biehler/Aquapress:** p. 25 (b) – **Bretenstein:** p. 55 (b); p. 56 (b); p. 169 (b) – **Chambfort :** p. 24; p. 221 (t) – **Corel:** p. 43 (ml); p. 68; p. 128 (mr-bl); p. 129 (tr); p. 131; p. 132 (t) ; p. 134 (b) ; p. 135 (tl); p. 137 (t-b); p. 143 (tr) ; p. 145 (mr); p. 146 (ml); p. 148 (tr); p. 152 (tr); p. 153 (br); p. 154 (bl); p. 156 (bl); p. 161 (t); p. 163 (b) ; p. 164 (tr); p. 165 (tr); p. 171 (t); p. 176 (t-c); p. 182 (c); p. 231 ; p. 244 ; p. 258 – **Etcheverry:** p. 181 (c) – **Francour/Aquapress:** p. 28 – **Genetiaux/Aquapress:** p. 185 (mr) – **Guerrier/Nature:** p. 213 (ml) – **Heather Angel:** p. 81 (tr) – **Houtmann/Aquapress:** 182 (b) – **JM/ Bour/UW/Cameraman photographer:** p. 267 – **Lamaison/Nature:** p. 33 (t); p. 203 (br); p. 206 (ml); p. 210 (ml) – **La Tourette/Nature:** p. 133 (tl); p. 138 (mb-bl) – **Londiveau/Aquapress:** p. 35 (r) – **Louisy:** p. 61 (t) ; p. 76 (c); p. 87 (tr-b); p. 94 (br); p. 104 (c); p. 107 (tr); p. 108 (ml); p. 112 (b); p. 113 (c-br); p. 130 (bl); p. 130/131 (b); p. 135 (tr); p. 136 (tl); p. 137 (mr); p. 140 (br) ; p. 144; p. 145 (tr-bl); p. 146 (br); p. 150 (c) ; p. 164 (tl); p. 165 (tl-b); p. 177 (tl); p. 180 (t); p. 187 (tr); p. 208/209; p. 215 (tr) – **Maître-Allain :** p. 23 (b); p. 59 (t); p. 102 (t); p. 103 (bl); p. 109 (tr); p. 148 (b); p. 155 (tr); p. 164 (b); p. 174 (b); p. 175 ; p. 183 (c); 185 (ml); p. 190; p. 194 (t); p. 200; p. 220; p. 229; p. 248 (b); p. 249; p. 259; p. 261; p. 263 (t) ; p. 274; p. 278; p. 279; p. 280; p. 281 – **Pecolatto/Nature:** p. 94 (bl) – **Piednoir/Aquapress:** p.4; p. 5; p. 8; p. 9; p. 14; p. 20; p. 21; p. 29; p. 30; p. 31; p. 32; p. 33 (b); p. 34; p. 35 (l); p. 36; p. 37 ; p. 38; p. 39 (t) Aquarium de Tours; p. 39 (b); p. 40; p. 41; p. 42 (l); p. 43 (mr); p. 44 (b); p. 47; p. 48/49; p. 50 ; p. 51 (t – c); p. 52 (tl); p. 53 (b); p. 54 (t); p. 56/57; p. 58 (r); p. 59 (b); p. 60; p. 61 (b); p. 62; p. 63; p. 64; p. 65; p. 70; p. 71; p. 72 (b); p. 73; p. 74; p. 75 (b); p. 77 (tl); p. 77 (mr); p. 78 (mr); p. 80/81; p. 81 (ml); p. 82 (t); p. 87 (tl-c); p. 89 (tr-ml-bl); p. 91 (ml); p. 92 (tr); p. 93 (mbl); p. 96; p. 97; p. 98 (tr-ml-bl); p. 100 (mtr-b); p. 101 (c); p. 102 (ml-bl); p. 103 (t-c); p. 104 (b); p. 105 (tl-bm); p. 106 (t-bl); p. 106/107 (b); p. 107 (tl); p. 111 (mr); p. 112 (t-mt); p112/113 (t) ; p. 113 (tr-mbl); p. 114 (ml); p. 114/115; p. 115 (b); p. 116 (ml); p. 116/117; p. 117 (mtr-mbl-bl); p. 118 (bl); p. 118/119; p. 122/123; p. 133 (tr-bl); p. 139 (mbr); p. 138 (mtl); p. 142 (tr); p. 147 (b); p. 148 (ml); p. 149 (c); p. 150 (br); p. 151 (mr); p. 153 (bl); p. 154 (t); p. 157 (b); p. 158 (t); p 160 (t-bl); p. 161 (c-b); p. 162/163; p. 166 (l); p. 168 (b); p. 169 (t); p. 170; p. 173 (b); p. 174 (t); p. 176 (b); p. 177 (tr-b); p. 179; p. 180 (c-b); p. 181 (t-b); p. 182 (t); p. 183 (t-b); p. 184 (t-b); p. 185 (t-ml-br); p. 186 (t-b); p. 187 (tl-c-b); p. 188/189; p. 189 (t-b); p. 191 (bl); p. 192 (b); p. 193; p. 194 (b); p. 197; p. 198; p. 199 (t); p. 201 (b); p. 203 (bl); p. 204 (t) ; p. 204/205; p. 205; p. 207 (tr-b); p. 209 (tr-ml-br); p. 210 (br); p. 210/211; p. 211 (t-br); p. 213 (tl-mr-b) ; p. 214; p. 214/215; p. 215 (c) ; p. 216/217; p. 217 (t-b); p. 218; p. 219; p. 221 (b); p. 226/227; p. 228; p. 233 ; p. 235 (b); p. 242 (r); p. 243; p. 245; p. 246; p. 247 (t); p. 253; p. 255; p. 260; p. 262; p. 263 (b); p. 264; p. 264/265; p. 265 ; p. 266; p. 266/267; p. 268; p. 269; p. 270; p. 275; p. 276; p. 281 (t) – **Prévot/Nature:** p. 120 (ml) – **Quinn/Nature :** p. 172. – **Roulland/Aquapress:** p. 10/11; p. 23 (t) – **Sauer/Nature :** p. 56 (t) – **Tramasset & Etcheverry:** p. 166 (r).